The
Newbury & District
Motor Services Story

Written and published by Paul Lacey

Best Wishes
Paul

Typifying the Newbury & District fleet of the late 1930's is this 20-seater Thornycroft A2-type with bodywork by Wadhams of Waterlooville. No.31 (TP 7951) had been new in June 1929 to another rural independent, F.G. Tanner (Denmead Queen) of Hambledon in Hampshire, who had sold out to Southdown Motor Services in March 1935, the bus coming to N&D with two other similar vehicles from that same source in January 1937. It is seen parked in the wide High Street at Hungerford in the area used for many years by the country carriers and bus operators, before returning to Newbury on the service via the Inkpen road.

THE NEWBURY & DISTRICT MOTOR SERVICES STORY

Written, designed, typeset and published by
Paul Lacey, 17 Sparrow Close
Woosehill, Wokingham
Berkshire, RG41 3HT

ISBN 978-0-9567832-0-2

Printed by the MPG Books Group in the UK

Newbury Wharf is the centre of much of the Newbury & District story, and this view from the upper gallery of the Old Granaries shows the scene as it appeared in 1948. To the left is City of Oxford No.H301 (LWL 301), a 1946 AEC 'Regent' MkII with Park Royal body on the joint route to Oxford, whilst in the centre is Newbury & District No.99 (CRX 279), a Guy 'Arab' MkII 5LW with utility Park Royal body of 1944. To its right is a Wilts & Dorset 1940 Bristol K5G (CHR 49-) on the Andover route, with Thames Valley No.435 (DR 9636) behind, the latter being a Leyland 'Titan' TD2 with Mumford body new to Plymouth Corporation in 1932 and working as a relief on Route 10 to Reading with the 1946/7 Bristol K-type service bus parked in front of it at the Thames Valley shelter. Over on the extreme left, parked by the Kennet & Avon Canal, is one of the Bedford OWB utilities, along with the centre-entrance AEC 'Regent' No.117 (HG 1221), new to Burnley Corporation in 1932 and coming to N&D via Cheltenham District in 1946. Further variety was forthcoming with the vehicles of Venture of Basingstoke, Bert Austin of Cold Ash, Stout of Shalbourne, Tibble from St. Mary Bourne and Reliance of Brightwalton, along with regular express coaches and those stopping off whilst proceeding east/west along the A4 or north/south on the A34.

Thatcham in the mid-1930's with Newbury & District Thornycroft 20-seater bus. Note the pub, shop and road signs, period advertising, public notices and the general lack of traffic.

CONTENTS

Standard Body Codes - Throughout this work the standard codes are used to describe the types of bodywork, e.g. B32F is a single-deck bus seating 32 with a front entrance. See page 213 - Fleet List for full details.

OTHER TRANSPORT TITLES FROM PAUL LACEY

A History of the Thames Valley Traction Co. Ltd., 1920 –1930   **£15.00**
The detailed history of this vibrant period, including the 207 other operators sharing the roads with TV, published in 1995, 144 pages A4, perfect bound, 144 half-tones, route map, full fleet list, line drawings.

A History of the Thames Valley Traction Co. Ltd., 1931 – 1945   **£25.00**
Continuing the story of development through the expansion of the 1930's, railway shareholdings, and then through the difficult years of the wartime era, published in 2003, 208 pages A4 with laminated covers, 300 half-tone illustrations, maps and plans, full fleet lists and specialised appendices.

A History of the Thames Valley Traction Co. Ltd., 1946 - 1960   **£25.00**
This third volume covers the period of post-war reconstruction through the busy 1950's, including the addition of Newbury & District and South Midland operations, published in 2009, 224 pages A4 with laminated covers, 544 half-tone illustrations, route maps, full fleet list, allocations and service fleet.

Thackray's Way – A Family in Road Transport   **£10.00**
An in-depth study of this enterprising family, written with assistance from their descendants, published in 2001, 136 pages A5, perfect bound, 62 half-tones, plans of premises, route maps, full fleet list.

50 Years of South Midland, 1921 – 1970   **£11.00**
This comprehensive study of Oxford's premier coach operator and express service pioneer written by David Flitton, published in 2004, 192 A5 pages and laminated covers, 142 half-tone illustrations, full fleet list, details of premises and period adverts.

All titles in print are available direct from the author, post free, or through good book suppliers.

For further details see the website at www.paullaceytransportbooks.co.uk

ACKNOWLEDGEMENTS

This work is dedicated to all those who were involved in the daily operation of *Newbury & District* and other local operators, many of whom I have had the interesting task of interviewing over some 40 years of research. I also wish to say a big *Thank You* to everyone who has helped me in any way, no matter how small. Special mention goes out for the personal contributions of Tony Aldworth, Bill Allington, George Amor, Arthur Andrews, Lionel Barnes, Jane Billington, Charlie Bishop, Frank Burden, A.G. Brown, Edward and Michael Claridge, Walter Corneby, Bill Cripps, Jim Davies, Boss, Lionel and Trixie Denham, the Durnford family, Mary and Robin Gore, Gordon Hedges, Dot Hibberd, Reg Hibbert, Sue Hopson, various members of the Kent family, Jim Lawrence, Ron Meagrow, Olive and Stan Minchin, Derek Nobes, Bob Parkes, Dick Prothero, Miss L. Revell, Ralph Revell, Ken Rutterford, Dianne Scoles, John Taylor and Eddie Whitington. Also, I am indebted to the staff of Newbury Library, Reading Local Studies Section, Museum of English Rural Life, West Berkshire Museum and the Newbury Weekly News for access to their collections or by publicising my research, along with various local societies and parish clerks.

And from within enthusiast circles, my many contacts over the years from numerous geographical and specialised areas, all of whom have answered my queries or supplied photographs to aid this extensive research – George Behrend, Derek Bradfield, Geoff Bruce, Alan Cross, John Cummings, David Gray, John Gillham, Bill Haynes, Joe Higham, Peter Jaques, D.W.K. Jones, Pat Keane, Charles Klapper, Alan Lambert, Jim Lewington, Bob Mack, Roy Marshall, Ron Neale, John Nickels, Tony Norris, Alan Oxley, John Parke, David Pennells, Pete Pribik, Michael Plunkett, Martin Shaw, R.H.G. Simpson, Mike Sutcliffe, Chris Taylor, Dave Thomas, Andrew Waller, Reg Westgate, S.N.J. White, Dave Wilder, Peter Wilks, V.A.G. Willins and Jim Wingfield.

My thanks also go to the photographers, whose names are often unrecorded, who had the forethought to record the daily activities and vehicles of the erstwhile *'Newbury & District'* and other operators both local and further afield.

Chapter 1 – Setting the Scene

The west Berkshire market town of Newbury (1931 population of 13,336) was well connected by road transport links. On the one hand the famous Bath Road had for several centuries provided links westwards to Bristol (62.5 miles away) via Marlborough and Bath, along with eastwards to London (56 miles) via Reading and Maidenhead. Being practically half way between London and Bristol it had been an important staging post in the days of horse-drawn coaches, though such activities were actually focussed on the Speen end of town. With the motor age drivers still found Newbury a convenient break on longer journeys whether on the Bath Road or the A34 from the Midlands and southwards to Southampton and the coast.

In respect of localised links since the start of the 20th century, the services provided by the Country Carriers were still the main means of transport for villagers in the myriad of settlements whose focus was set on the market town. West Berkshire and beyond featured very few other significant towns, with Hungerford 9 miles away to the west, Wantage at 16 miles to the north, Basingstoke in Hampshire at 17.25 miles south, and the county town of Reading 17 miles to the east. Also, as most country carrier's services prior to the end of the Great War were operated using horse-drawn vans, only a few passengers were taken.

William Thomas of Leckhampstead Thicket had two carrier's vans like this, seen here with son Donovan at the reins and Harry Deacon as his assistant.

However, with the steady motorisation of such facilities, along with the advent of those operating as bus services, the links for the villagers both increased in frequency and also in terms of comfort. The motor vehicle also opened up new avenues for travel, with excursions, whilst also providing its owner with other opportunities such as haulage work. At 1932 there were some 40 carriers listed as serving Newbury from a radius of some 15 miles, along with a number of small bus operators, which left few villages without some regular transport.

On the other hand, the larger bus operators had not been much attracted to Newbury, which had resulted in something of a void. This was of course partly due to the pattern of traffic, with most journeys being shopping trips from outlying villages into the town and back. The *Thames Valley Traction Co. Ltd.* had made some attempts to establish a route between its base in Reading and Newbury, both along the main road and by way of Bradfield and Bucklebury, even having an outstation in the early '20's, but all of these activities met with only limited success, causing it to abandon the town altogether for a number of years.

Bill Kent of Baughurst motorised his daily carrier's service to Basingstoke (or Newbury on Thursdays) with this 30hp Daimler (BL 3536) in March 1914.

From the west the services of the *Bristol Tramways & Carriage Co. Ltd.* duly reached Hungerford, whilst from the north the buses of *City of Oxford Motor Services Ltd.* ran to Wantage, but neither pressed on to link those market towns with Newbury. Indeed the greatest period of expansion of bus services during the 1920's came from a perhaps surprising source - the Road Motors of the *Great Western Railway*!

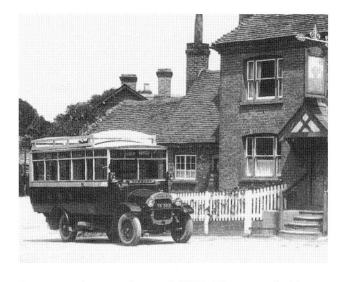

Brown-and-cream liveried GWR Thornycroft A1-type bus No.927 (YK 3821) with Vickers 19-seat body new in 1925 and is seen at The Wheatsheaf in Chieveley.

The latter had indeed tried to establish a network of bus routes in the area from June 1927, linking Newbury with Andover to the south and Hungerford to the west, whilst others were run to villages to feed the railway stations, and several were attempted without any discernable objectives. Such experimental ventures were soon reviewed, and the other routes were generally defeated by a combination of dogged determination by the local bus operators and the loyalty of their passengers to them. What remained of these operations by the passage of the Road Traffic Act (1930), duly passed to *Thames Valley* following a change in policy from railway direct operations to shareholdings in the territorial bus companies.

Taking a break from giving the GWR Road Motors a run for their money, 'Boss' Denham of Denham Bros. of Newbury stands in front of Andrews-bodied Talbot 14-seater bus KE 3196 on the Highclere route.

After *Thames Valley* had given up with the road from Reading, the gap was partially filled by the setting up of the Newbury branch of *Norton Motor Services* by a family already established in bus operation in the Lechlade area. Starting in December 1923 this was in the care of William Byrnes Norton, and their core operation was Newbury to Thatcham, with a frequent bus service, whilst other services were duly tried from Newbury to Lambourn and Newbury to Hungerford with varying success. They also attempted to extend to Reading in October 1927, despite a *Thames Valley* service having re-commenced in May 1926.

From the south there were several independents that connected their bases with Newbury, in particular *Edith Kent* from Kingsclere, her son *Bill Kent* from Baughurst, *Tibble* from St. Mary Bourne and *Lewis Horne* from Andover. However, Salisbury-based *Wilts & Dorset Motor Services Ltd.* commenced running between Andover and Newbury in June 1930, and also had a service from Andover to Hungerford which started in 1931. The Basingstoke-based independent *Venture Ltd.* developed links to Newbury from Basingstoke and Whitchurch from 1930 on.

Venture Ltd. was started by the Thornycroft family so it naturally used their products. This 1927 A2Long-type (OT 3117) was their No.4 and is seen at Newbury Wharf on a service to Whitway.

Double-deckers were indeed rare in the area, and almost all of them were former Thomas Tilling TTA1-types like LF 9916, shown here with boy conductor William Titcombe and driver Jim Lawrence in the Market Place at Newbury on the Thatcham service.

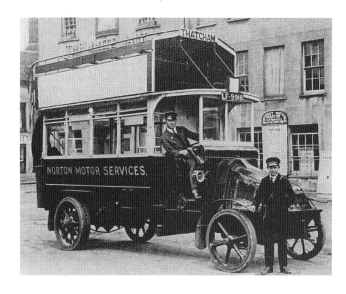

On the express coach front, developments had been steady since February 1925, when the Bristol-based *Greyhound Motors* had placed their Dennis coaches on its daily Bristol to London route which, in earlier days continued to use Newbury as the lunch-break stop, thus echoing the days of the fast mail coaches of an earlier era. At first the journey took 8 hours, though this was reduced by various later refinements.

In local terms the next most significant development on express services came after former London pirate bus and taxi operator Robert Thackray noticed that the coaches that passed his farm at Calcot, just west from Reading, were already rather full. He therefore set up his own express service to London from Reading, using a modern fleet of luxurious Gilford coaches.

Clearly demonstrating how the express coach grew from the fairly rudimentary Greyhound Motors 1925 Dennis (HU 1176) (seen above in Bath on the inaugural run), compared with the Thackray's Way Gilford (GF 6676) of 1929 at the Palace Theatre terminus in Reading. An identical coach eventually came to N&D as a source of spare parts.

These ran under the fleetname *Thackray's Way*, though the official title was the *Ledbury Transport Co. Ltd.* (so named after the original base at Ledbury Mews in Notting Hill). The Reading route started in September 1929, and a Newbury link service was added from that October, both taking the *Thames Valley* management totally by surprise!

Another development of local significance was when *South Midland* introduced a Summertime daily express route between its Oxford base and Southsea, which provided an alternative for Newburians who wanted to stay longer than for just a day trip. This started from 1929 and proved very popular indeed.

So, without the larger operators having settled on the town as a base, and it not being fully detailed in any territorial agreements in place between them, local bus services remained in the hands of small native concerns. Indeed, the passage of the 1930 Act had resulted in most operators continuing much as before. However, although the provisions of the legislation did offer smaller concerns respite from unscrupulous activities by operators with larger resources, it did bring with it several new issues.

The system of Road Service Licenses was presided over by the Traffic Commissioners, who also had to consider objections from other operators, including at times the railways. This involved time spent at the Traffic Hearings, which might be held many miles away, not something particularly convenient for small operators. Whilst the larger concerns could employ someone to prepare schedules and attend hearings, for many this was an additional burden, along with other administrative responsibilities relating to vehicles.

It was against this background that Theo Denham, who was the principle local bus operator, as well as the Chairman of the South Berkshire Bus Proprietors & Carriers Association, decided it was time to call a special meeting during March 1932. It was convened on a Thursday at the 'Old Waggon & Horses Inn' in Newbury's Market Place, the traditional watering-hole for the carriers and their road-dusted throats.

The purpose of this meeting was to pull the local operators together in order to keep the larger concerns from expanding in the area, particularly as there had been a notable increase in 'cheque-book' diplomacy since the Act came into effect on the first day of 1931, which in the case of *Thames Valley* was largely underwritten by the railway interests. Also a proper company structure for operating under the 1930 Act would mean the support of an administrative base, and take the burden from the individual owners.

Theo's proposal was both bold and straightforward and although the concept of co-operative bus operations was by no means unique, most other such ventures took place in urban or inter-urban conurbations and in more industrialised areas.

Theo, along with his brother Ambrose ('Boss'), operated a number of services based on Newbury and mainly to the south and west of the town. He had apparently already had some exploratory discussions with coach and haulage operator Charlie Durnford and Arthur Andrews, who ran coaches and hire cars, and these were indeed the three main players within the town.

From the outset the plan was to set up a single company and to better utilise the wide range of skills available between the operators. Whilst the proposal was indeed a timely one, there was a natural reticence amongst the other west Berkshire operators, so it was with only the three main Newbury-based firms that the initial company was formed, being registered on 26th April 1932 as *Newbury & District Motor Services Ltd.* Each of the three was allocated 2000 £1 shares, and the agreement between those parties came into effect from 2nd June 1932.

However, a number of others were evidently waiting in the sidelines to see how this developed and would join soon afterwards and, as the 1930's depression developed, the pace of amalgamations or acquisitions did indeed increase. To clarify the terms used in these sometimes complicated negotiations, when operators merged into the main company, that was termed an amalgamation, whilst those who sold out without any further involvement, were acquisitions. Indeed, it was the practice to include those who amalgamated on the letterhead and in timetable booklets, leading to the need for frequent updating of such details!

And there we have the background to the fascinating outfit that was *Newbury & District.* Known in the local parlance as 'Nubree District', or less kindly by the *Thames Valley* drivers as 'Newbury & Risk It', the often motley fleet nonetheless served the populace of west Berkshire well throughout the next two decades.

Firstly we will review the original three concerns that formed the embryonic company. Other operators will be fully reviewed as they come into the fold, with their previous history. For ease of reference these reviews commence on the page numbers shown below:

Date   Operator, type of business and page number

6/32   Arthur Andrews (Favourite Coaches), Newbury – page 9
Coaches, car hire, coachbuilding, motor garage and haulage – amalgamated.

6/32   Ambrose & Theophilus Denham (Denham Bros.), Newbury – page 15
Bus services, car hire and motor haulage – amalgamated.

6/32   Charles Durnford & Sons, Newbury – p.35
Coach operators, haulage and removal contractors – amalgamated.

9/32   George Hedges (Reliance Motor Service), Brightwalton – page 50
Bus services, excursions and haulage - amalgamated – later resumed independent operations as Reliance Motor Services.

9/32   John Prothero, (XLCR Motor Service) Beedon – page 52
Bus services, excursions and tours – amalgamated, but retained his garage business.

10/32   Thomas Holman, Ecchinswell – page 58
Carrier's bus and coal merchant – bus service acquired by N&D, but continued goods service and coal merchant's business.

10/32   Pocock Bros., Cold Ash – page 58
Bus services, excursions and tours – amalgamated, but retained taxi service.

1/33   Frederick Spanswick (Spanswick's Bus Service), Thatcham – page 61
Bus services, excursions and tours – amalgamated.

1/34   Durnford Bros., Newbury – page 66
Coach operation and haulage – amalgamated after a period of breakaway operation.

1/34   John Burt & Albert Greenwood, Inkpen – page 71
Carrier's, bus services, excursions and tours – amalgamated bus services and E&T's with N&D, employing Greenwood as booking agent and driver, but Burt retained goods carrying business in his own right.

1/34   Catherine Geary (Joy Coaches & Cars), Great Shefford – page 74
Bus service, excursions and tours, haulage and taxi service – N&D acquired bus service and E&T's, but other activities were retained.

1/34   George Brown (Wash Common Bus Service), Wash Common – page 75
Bus service sold to N&D.

2/34   George Howlett (Kennet Bus Service), Bucklebury – page 76
Bus services, excursions and tours – amalgamated.

3/34   W.J. White & Son (Tony Coaches), Hermitage – page 81
Bus services, excursions and tours – amalgamated.

1/35   Walter Cleeveley, Newbury – page 93
Sand and gravel merchant, general haulier and publican – sold sand and gravel and haulage business and lorries to N&D.

10/35   Charles Ballard (Southend Garage), Bradfield Southend – page 98
Coach operator, sold coach and E&T's to N&D, but continued with garage business.

3/36   Charles G. Colliver, Wickham – page 103
General haulage contractor who sold business and lorry to N&D.

4/37   E.G. Kent (Kingsclere Coaches), Baughurst – page 110
Bus services, excursions and tours – sold out to N&D and retired.

5/37   Pass & Co., Newbury – page 123
Ford Agents, haulage and coach operators – coaches and E&T's licenses only acquired by N&D, otherwise continued in business.

7/38   Ernest Nobes, Lambourn Woodlands – page 132
Bus services and excursions and tours – amalgamated and was employed as a driver.

Chapter 2 -
Arthur & Percy Andrews

Arthur Andrews was born in 1870 at Kennet Place, on the London Road in Speen, just to the north of Newbury. In fact Speen (or Speenhamland to be precise) had once been more prominent than the neighbouring town, as it was situated directly on the famous Bath Road, whilst also being the more ancient of those two settlements. Therefore the varied wheeled traffic using that busy thoroughfare would have been daily sightings for the growing boy.

By 1881 the family had moved a short distance to 35 Shaw Crescent, and it is worth noting that Arthur's 19-year old brother George was employed as a coach trimmer, whilst his 16-year old brother Francis was an apprentice coach maker, all of which must surely have influenced his future choice of employment.

At the age of 14 Arthur was apprenticed to Robert Lovell, who employed 20 hands at the Royal Albert Coach-building Works at 60 Northbrook Street, Newbury. Whilst there he would have learnt, over a period of seven years, the skills required to construct wheels, chassis frames and coachwork for the wide variety of wheeled vehicles then in use. After completing his apprenticeship he at first moved away to be employed as a wheelwright with Charles Dore of 5 Humbolt Road, in Fulham, where he was in 1891.

A later view of Arthur Andrews dressed for a trip on one of the family's charabancs to the seaside.

However, he soon returned to Newbury, where he set up his own wheelwright and coach-building shop in Northcroft Lane, and in 1894 he married Elsie Ann West, daughter of Mr. and Mrs. West of Yew Tree Farm at Burghclere.

He then set about building all manner of carts and vans for the local tradesmen, plus some more prestigious projects, such as the governess cart commissioned by Lord Porchester of Highclere Castle in the early 1900's. This particular gentleman duly succeeded his father as the 5th Earl of Carnarvon and is better known as the excavator of Tutankhamen's tomb in Egypt.

Percy Andrews at the wheel of the Fiat charabanc, with his fiancé Eileen in a 1920's cloche hat.

The wooden-wheeled vehicles of the period were indeed a real craftsman's job, having to withstand the rigours of the varied and often rough road surfaces, as only the turnpike roads were surfaced, everywhere else being crushed stones, or just as nature had provided – muddy or dusty according to the season! Indeed, the wheelwright's skills were therefore paramount in order to endure such usage, the wheels being constructed from shaped spokes, bent-wood rims, mounted on a good solid axle, and finished off with a metal rim (the tyre), which was heated before being allowed to shrink into place.

As all vehicles then were drawn either by hand or by animal power, the bodywork required a light but robust construction, whilst the finish was usually applied 'for life', which meant up to 16 coats of primer, paint and varnish, each hand-sanded for a glass-like finish, not forgetting that the main purpose of any such treatment was to keep the wooden construction watertight.

Arthur would undoubtedly have had assistants and probably an apprentice, whilst throughout the period 1901-1916 the coach-smith Aaron Cox, along with his son Walter, are also listed at the same premises as

Arthur. The coach-smith was similar to a blacksmith, in that he was responsible for making up the tyre rims, along with any brackets and other metal fittings used in coach building. Aaron lived nearby at 23 West Street, but is not mentioned after that date, by which time he would have been 68. It should also be noted that he had been preceded at Northcroft Lane by another of that trade, F.J. Cunningham.

The Northcroft Lane premises comprised a workshop frontage, with an opening to a yard alongside and behind that, where there would have been a timber store and the forge, these buildings occupying Nos.7/9, with the Kennet & Avon Canal running to the rear of the site. Arthur and Elsie, along with 5-year old daughter Elsie were, by 1901, living very close by at 6 Brighton Terrace. Son *Percy Arthur Andrews* followed during 1902, and the family had by 1911, relocated to 'Penshurst' in Carnarvon Street. A third and final move saw them duly move to 92 West Street.

The Newbury of the early 20th century provided the only sizeable town for many miles around, so there was much trade both out to the surrounding villages and the numerous large estate houses, all of which required wheeled vehicles suited to that particular trade. In the reverse direction came all types vehicles with produce brought to the market, along with some passengers on the country carrier's wagons. Even then, the Town Council was beset with the issues of congestion and parking, particularly on market day on Thursdays, when it seemed the whole countryside descended upon the town!

All of these trades required vehicles, originally horse-drawn, though the motorised variety featured in the coach-building tasks to an increasing extent prior to the Great War. Unfortunately, no detailed records have survived of the output from Northcroft Lane, though it is known that the 'bicycle craze' of the Edwardian period was also catered for, the skills of the wheelwright applying equally to the repair of cycle wheels, whilst that type of wheel also found its way onto lightweight carts as a cheaper alternative to the conventional wooden wheel, with the advantage of inflatable tyres.

Following the end of the Great War Percy was right up with the modern era, training as a motor mechanic at Nias of 73 Northbrook Street, who it should be noted were also Talbot agents. He also looked after the cycle repairs, using No.7 Northcroft Lane, with father Arthur (now termed motor coach-builder) at No.9. The advent of cheap chassis, such as the Model T Ford and the imported Italian Fiat, soon formed the basis of lighter-weight projects, whilst other ex-War Department chassis flooded the market, both in the lightweight class and for 3 tons and over. Percy also soon developed a skill at refurbishing Talbot 25-50hp

chassis, some former private cars, which were then re-bodied by Arthur as vans, buses or charabancs.

With such availability of cheap chassis, and in view of their combined skills, father and son then embarked on a further joint venture of charabanc operation. Indeed, they had already produced a van on a Ford T chassis (MO 218) in July 1922, and this could be fitted with detachable seats for 14 passengers, ideal for outings, sports teams and social events. This van was sold on to the Newbury Sanitary Steam Laundry in January 1925, who used it for local deliveries.

For the Summer of 1923 an ex-WD Fiat 15TER chassis was fitted out with a 14-seater charabanc body, painted in 'heliotrope'. This was registered MO 1714 and ran under the name *The Favourite*. In view of the livery then chosen, the term *Favourite Mauve Charabancs* was used from the following Summer, though much later on the livery changed to one of cream with green relief.

Both the Fiat and the 14-seater Lancia had similar bodies, the above being the latter of the two.

Apart from the bodies produced on rebuilt Talbot chassis for *Denham Bros.* and *George Hedges* (the carrier at Brightwalton), a number of Ford T and AA-types passed through the coach-building shop for use as vans, charabancs and buses with local operators. A Ford T one-tonner was also re-bodied for *John Prothero* as a 14-seater bus. Whereas these projects were small vans or vehicles seating up to 14 passengers, other larger bodies were constructed for *Charlie Durnford* (de-mountable for use on ex-WD chassis, and later a large Luton-type van on a Maudslay ML2 former coach) for his removals business, and there was also a large van on a Reo chassis for the Moulding & Joinery Works of Elliott's of Newbury, based in Albert Road, in December 1930 (RX 7787), along with vans of various sizes for both the Newbury Sanitary Steam Laundry and the Woodlands Laundry of 86 Bartholomew Street (the latter including a neat little three-wheeler).

Whilst it would be true to say that some of the earlier bus bodies were rather squarely-built and basic, this may have reflected the purchaser's budget, as certainly later products were much more lightly-built and curvaceous. Several of *Andrews'* own vehicles, along with one of *Denham's* Talbots, were duly re-bodied with updated bodies.

Percy married Eileen James in 1929, and by 1932 they were living at No.5 Northcroft Lane, a house property on the other side of the entrance to the yard of Nos.7/9. However, by 1936 they had relocated to 46 Northcroft Lane. It should be noted that his elder sister Elsie had also married back in 1916 to Stanley Giddings, but as a soldier in the Royal Berkshire Regiment she had lost him to the Great War in April 1918, at which point he was a Sergeant in the Tank Corps of the Army Service Corps serving in France. This was such a common theme, with so many war widows left after the conflict, but happily Elsie re-married Percy Taylor in 1927.

A certain amount of haulage work had also featured in the business since Percy had joined, and much of this fitted in with the seasonal nature of charabanc work. However, unlike nearby *Durnfords,* who regularly used the same chassis for both passenger and goods work, *Andrews* retained a lorry specifically for haulage, though the same pool of drivers was used, some of whom also worked on coach-building or painting tasks when not driving. Regular tasks undertaken were the collection of wheat from surrounding farms for use by Hovis Ltd. at their Town Mills on the River Kennet or Dolton & Son at Shaw Mill on the River Lambourn, as well as barley for the South Berks Brewery in Bartholomew Street. A variety of feedstuffs were also brought in for Chas. Midwinter & Son based at Cheap Street.

By July 1922 1-ton covered vans were available for hire, whilst in May 1923 Percy was disposing of an unknown make of 15cwt open truck, which he was replacing with a Ford 'tonner'. Precise dates for the haulage vehicles are not known, but those known later are a Leyland, then a Thornycroft J-type, both of which were fitted with drop-side lorry bodies and canvas covers.

To return to developments with the passenger fleet, the intake for 1925 consisted of one of Percy's rebuilt Talbot 25-50hp chassis and a former War Department 40hp Dennis 3-tonner. The Talbot had been registered as BL 6490 in April 1920 as a private car, and that registration was retained when it re-emerged in the Spring of 1925 bearing a 14-seater charabanc body. In contrast to this lightweight, pneumatic-tyred vehicle, the Dennis was on solid tyres and had been re-registered as XK 7225 by the previous owner in April 1922, who used it as a lorry, though with *Andrews* it ran as a 28-seater charabanc. Whereas the Talbot would see many more years of service, the big Dennis was re-declared as 'goods' in August 1926, though the records do not state if this was still with them.

A private hire car was also available from at least July 1923, with a Studebaker landaulette in use to October 1925. By 1926 a Daimler saloon car was available for hire, and this remained in use for a number of years.

The Talbot 14-seater BL 6490 as it appeared with its first body and in the mauve livery.

The original charabanc driving had been carried out by Percy, as in the early days such drivers also needed to be their own mechanics, but as that work expanded hired drivers were added. The first of these was Stan Minchin in 1925 (who much later married *Charlie Durnford's* daughter Olive), and in due course George Amor (who had driven previously for *Freddie Spanswick*), his brother Arthur (who had driven for *Bill Norton*), and *Bert Greenwood* (who originally handled cycle repairs and later went into partnership with *Jack Burt* at Inkpen). The Andrews's also made use of the services of Alfie Smith of Marsh Road as coach-painter and sign-writer, (and who was also later a conductor on *N&D*). *Bert Greenwood's* daughter also recalled that *Arthur Andrews* was referred to as 'Pop', presumably to distinguish him from the son.

George Amor also worked on the coachwork side as well as driving duties. The *Favourite* drivers had hat badges with soldered brass letters of the type common then, but one young driver arranged his over another badge with the lettering 'driver', thus displaying 'favourite driver'!

On the garage side, Percy continued to overhaul cars etc. for re-sale, also having the advantage of the coach painting facilities, and much of this work took place out of the charabanc season. A 1919 Hobart-Villiers motorcycle combination was offered in March 1924, whilst October 1925 saw a Ford van for sale. During 1927 a 1921 Ford van and a 1923 Ford 'tonner' truck were sold, and some of these may have seen service on the haulage side. Other examples of cars sold were a Ford sedan and a Rover 12hp 5-seater tourer, both for sale in February 1928.

The excursions side was further developed, though there was still a notable concentration of advertised trips on Sundays and Wednesdays. Examples were those on Sundays to Bournemouth and Southsea, whilst on Wednesday there were full-day trips to

Bournemouth and Southsea again, plus a day trip to London (6s) and an afternoon run to Oxford (3s 6d).

Stan Minchin was the driver on this Inkpen Methodist outing to Bournemouth on 7th September 1929.

The first of a number of Lancias operated by Andrews came into the fleet for the 1926 season but, apart from bearing a Z-type chassis with an operator-built seating 14, little else is known of it. A second Lancia, of the 35hp 'Tetraiota' type with an Andrews' 18-seater body was added, but its identity is also unknown, and there was also a circa 1925 Guy, which had been bodied with a 20-seater all-weather body by Andrews and came into the fleet about 1927.

The 18-seater Lancia 'Tetraiota' charabanc at the coast, with Arthur Andrews standing in the centre.

Similarly, a Reo, seating 26, was also added in 1929, though this is believed to have been secondhand. Also, about 1930/1, the Talbot BL 6490 was fitted with a new coach body, with a dual-doorway 14-seater body which extended its working life through to 1935! It is also possible that several other vehicles were given saloon coach bodies to extend their stay.

Although bus work had not been included in the Andrews activities, they found themselves in possession of a partly-completed 20-seater bus body on a Ford AA chassis, which had apparently been the subject of a cancelled order. George Amor had been working on this particular project, and he recalled how this was finished off with a canvas 'sunshine roof', with fixed front and rear sections of roof, in order to make it more readily useful for excursions. Apart from that, *Andrews* found a daily worker's transport contract to and from Colthrop Mill on which it could earn its keep, the vehicle becoming RX 8261 in March 1931. It is also worth noting that the original license application included another service over the Newbury – Speen – Wickham route, though this was withdrawn before the application was determined, and so avoided a clash with the established *Denham Bros.* service.

The Ford AA RX 8261, which Andrews inherited due to a cancelled order, is seen with George Amor.

Around the same time another Lancia was obtained, in the shape of VA 3156, a 'Tetraiota' with a 20-seater saloon bus body which had been new in December 1924 to *Rankin* of Glasgow. Whilst on the subject of Lancias, the following advert appeared in the Newbury Weekly News on January 28th 1932 under a box number but no name: *Lancia 26-seater front-entrance saloon bus 1928, upholstered in leather throughout and in excellent condition, has been in service up to Christmas, ideal for local service, luggage rail on roof, £250 or near offer.* This vehicle is currently unknown in respect of local operators, but may have featured in the *Andrews* fleet?

The 20-seater Guy is seen on an outing to Southsea in 1930/1. This was something of a family event, as there is Arthur Andrews standing at the front, with driver George Amor at the wheel, then grandson John Taylor in the light-coloured jacket, with his mother behind him. To the left of John is his half-sister Dorothy Giddings, with Eileen Andrews behind her, whilst on the right is grandmother Elsie Andrews. The dual-doorway all-weather coach has typical Andrews bodywork of the later 1920's.

A steady turnover continued on overhauls at the garage and saw a pair of 1925 Morris cars for sale in April 1930, these being an 'Oxford' 4-seater for £45 and a 'Cowley' for £30. Later that year a Buick cabriolet could be had for just a tenner.

Photographs reveal that the Andrews fleet was a well-kept one, with vehicles being regularly repaired and repainted before each season, all such facilities being available on-site for both bodies and chassis.

For May 1931 Andrews had the opportunity to buy 3 coaches that had been acquired with businesses taken over by the *Ledbury Transport Co. Ltd.,* which was better known as *Thackray's Way.* The owner of the firm, *Robert Thackray,* had been consolidating his hold in the Reading area by buying up operators whose finances had been weakened by the recession of the early 1930's, though his real intention was to increase the number of licensed vehicles he could put on his express services between Newbury, Reading and London. Indeed, the Newbury – Reading section was licensed as a stage-carriage service between those towns, and therefore competed with the *Thames Valley* route. However, he did not attempt to expand his services in the Newbury area.

The oldest vehicle acquired from *Thackray's* was a 20-seater Lancia of 1925 vintage, registered in the DP series and bodied by Vincents of Reading had come from *Edward Molesworth. Hope,* who was also based in Reading.

The others were both Gilfords previously with *Charlie Tanton* of Reading, though each was quite different. RD 1886 was another Vincent-bodied vehicle, with a 30-seater dual-doorway coach body with all but the front and rear domes fitted with a canvas sunshine roof, this being mounted on a 168OT chassis new to him in June 1930. The other was a normal-control 166SD-type of April 1929, registered VM 8638, with a Lewis & Crabtree 26-seater body which had been supplied by them as dealers to an operator in the Manchester area. The latter is also recalled as having a habit of 'boiling like a kettle' unless regularly allowed to cool down!

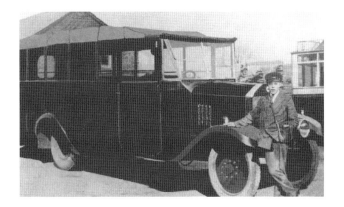

Lancias were certainly popular in the Andrews fleet, and this example (known only by the registration mark DP) was duly used by Newbury & District on service routes on busy days, noted here with boy conductor Bill Eggleton, who later became a driver.

The Talbot BL 6490 was given a new body circa 1930/1 and repainted cream with green trim. It is seen here with George Amor. This type of chassis was well suited to the work, being fitted with a powerful engine but light to handle. Note also the bulb-horn projecting through the front offside and the leaf-springs attached to the chassis.

George Amor is also seen with the Gilford 166SD-type coach VM 8638, which featured a full-width sun-visor for the driver. The large side-lights, mounted on the front mudguards must have given a good spread of light along with the headlamps, which was welcome as few roads were well lit at that time.

Car hire with driver continued to be featured through to the formation of *Newbury & District*, latterly using a Daimler saloon car. The haulage side was also kept up, the final lorry in use being a Thornycroft J-type of Great War origins.

As already noted, there were numerous bodies built for local concerns, often on refurbished chassis from *Percy Andrews* or new chassis supplied by Pass & Co. No records of the bodies built have survived, but where known these are noted in Appendix 2, which reviews the known fleets of the operators absorbed into *Newbury & District*, whilst other bodies are referred to in the text throughout this volume.

Adverts with this wording were placed in the Newbury Weekly News on 13th May 1926, announcing the charabanc trips and the facilities for motorists.

Chapter 3 – Denham Bros.

Theophilus Albert Denham was born in August 1888 at Taunton, Somerset, the son of Great Western Railway Engine Driver Edward Denham and his wife Emma. The family moved around the country with their father's job, initially to The Mumbles near Swansea then, by 1901, to Stourbridge in Worcestershire. On the 1911 census Theo was still living with his parents in the Stourbridge area, and had a shop where he was as a cycle-maker.

Shortly after commencing with the garage, Theo acquired a trio of secondhand vehicles which, after overhaul, would form the basis of his passenger-carrying fleet. These were indeed a mixed bag, with AF 1344, a Star 20-25hp, new in June 1914 as a charabanc of *W. Randell* of Penryn, Cornwall, though it came to *Denham* via several other owners, during which time it had acquired a 12-seater front-entrance bus body.

Theo Denham during the Great War.

With the outbreak of the First World War he enlisted in the French Army and later the Army Service Corps as a Private, driving and maintaining motor vehicles in often appalling conditions of mud and under enemy attack. Like his brother Boss, who we shall hear more of shortly, he was lucky enough to survive the conflict, though their brother Lionel was not so fortunate. Towards the close of the war he was in the Royal Berkshire Hospital at Reading, where he met his bride-to-be, who was a hospital visitor to the troops there and lived in Newbury, where her parents had a business in Bartholomew Street.

In December 1921 he announced to the public that he had set up a motor repairs garage at No.1 Kings Road in Newbury. Apparently he was not a particularly good mechanic, but liked tinkering with things mechanical and re-building vehicles, which would be a recurring theme in the years to come.

The Star AF 1344 in service with Theo Denham.

The second was a Buick, with left-hand drive acquired from the Military Disposal Sales. The identity of this is not known, but what was originally a body intended for field ambulance work was adapted as a wagonette with face-to-face seating for 10 and still with a centre rear entrance. It seems very likely that Theo had been familiar with this type during his war service, and perhaps chose it because of that.

The left-hand drive Buick wagonette ready for service.

The third vehicle was a Delauney-Belleville 28-32hp which had been a large private car new in 1918, but it was re-registered BL 9861 in April 1922, and fitted with a 14-seater charabanc body possibly built by Arthur Andrews. This was in a fawn livery and christened *The Pride of Newbury*, and was advertised as being the 'next best thing to a Rolls Royce', having a large smooth engine and pneumatic tyres.

The Delauney-Belleville chara BL 9861, with its circular radiator, is shown with its later owner Charlie Holland of Lane End, near High Wycombe.

Although Theo was evidently joined by this brother *Ambrose (Boss)* during the Spring of 1922, at that time his involvement seems limited to assisting in preparing the above vehicles, as he took employment elsewhere, before later returning to Newbury, both of which we shall hear more of in due course.

During early March 1922 quite a variety of vehicles were offered for sale by Theo, these being a 14-20hp Argyll landaulette, a 12-14hp Hupmobile 2-seater, a Ford Model T open tourer and a Clyno 6hp motor-cycle combination. At the same time two English-built van bodies, suitable for Ford chassis, were on offer, together with spare parts from Ford and Panhard cars being broken up. Hire cars were also available from that date.

The initial bus route was from Newbury to Woolton Hill, some 5.7 miles south of Newbury. Evidently the charabanc proved popular, particularly suited as it was to smaller parties, and a second one was added from August. This was known as *The Newbury Rover*, and this was a 14-seater GMC K16-type with 19.6hp engine and light enough for pneumatics tyres, though the exact identity is not known. There were also plenty of more local opportunities for special journeys, such as the Police Sports, or the Littlecote Fete on 7th July 1922, when HRH Princess Beatrice opened the event, as a fundraiser for the Savernake Hospital.

By May 1922 a number of other bus routes were in operation, though it must be appreciated from the outset that timetables were often inter-worked, so a bus out to one village would return to work out to another, and so on through the day, most services only providing a few journeys per day, and some only operated on a Tuesday, Thursday and Saturday basis. The routes now ran from Newbury to Thatcham and Cold Ash, and from Newbury to Chieveley and Beedon, the latter extended from that month through to East Ilsley on Thursdays and Saturdays only, the full timings being as follows in this (re-set) advert.

DENHAM'S MOTOR SERVICE

TUESDAYS, THURSDAYS and SATURDAYS between
NEWBURY, THATCHAM and COLD ASH.

SUMMER TIME TABLE –

NEWBURY	9.15	12.0	1.45	4.15
THATCHAM	9.30	12.15	2.0	4.30
COLD ASH	9.37	12.23	----	4.38
COLD ASH	9.38	12.24	----	4.39
THATCHAM	9.47	12.32	2.1	4.47
NEWBURY	10.0	12.47	2.15	5.5

SATURDAYS ONLY –

Newbury: 5.5; 8.20.   Thatcham; 5.15; 8.35
Thatcham: 5.16; 8.36   Newbury: 5.30; 8.50

Extension of Motor Service to East Ilsley
Commencing SATURDAY, 19th May –
and Revised Times to Chieveley and Beedon.

THURSDAYS & SATURDAYS only –

Leave-

NEWBURY	12 noon and 4p.m.	
CHIEVELEY	12.18	„ 4.18
BEEDON	12.27	„ 4.27
EAST ILSLEY	12.45	„ 4.45

Return –

EAST ILSLEY	1.0	„ 4.45
BEEDON	1.18	„ 5.3
CHIEVELEY	1.27	„ 5.12
NEWBURY	1.45	„ 5.30

The Cars are available for Private Hire other days.

Apply T. A. DENHAM, King's Road Garage, NEWBURY

An increasing number of excursions during 1922 saw the charabancs travelling to Brighton on Saturday 5th August, Weston-super-Mare on Monday 7th August and Weymouth on Saturday 12th August. A circular tour, taking in Glastonbury Monastic Abbey, Cheddar Caves and Gorge, Wells Cathedral and Bath ran on Wednesdays 2nd and 9th August, with a fare of 17 shillings and 6 pence, departing from the Market Place at 7.30am. It was also announced that a trip would shortly be arranged to Stratford-upon-Avon.

The 14-seater chara could also be hired on a private basis, either at 1shilling 2pence per mile or 1d per mile per person on distances over 50 miles. With so little private transport, these rates were favourable.

The GMC chara had a central gangway and just a front door. It was snapped during a rest stop on an excursion to the coast.

In order to cover the additional mileages a further variety of vehicles were placed in service, but this time two of them were purchased new. One was a Ford Model T ordered through local Ford Agents Pass & Co., which was fitted with a varnished wooden 14-seater bus body and registered MO 1797 in July 1923, also having a grey-painted lorry body. Also ordered new was a 20/30hp Fiat 15TER-type, which was fitted with a rear-entrance 20-seater bus body and registered in December as MO 2406. The third vehicle acquired that year is believed to have preceded both of the above, and was a Talbot 25-50hp, which had been re-registered in Middlesex during July 1921 as MD 8213, when it was declared as a 12-seater. In view of the make of this vehicle, it seems quite likely that it had been prepared for its new role as a bus by Percy Andrews and re-bodied by his father Arthur.

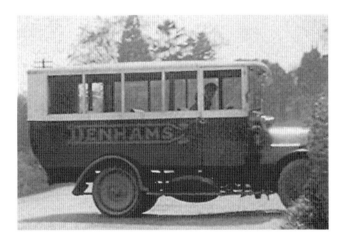

The 1923 Fiat 14-seater bus MO 2406.

Although disposal dates for the initial buses used are not recorded, the Delauney-Belleville charabanc was let go in July 1923, when it saw further use with *Charlie Holland (Pioneer Bus Service)* of Lane End, Bucks.

For the June 1923 Royal Ascot Race Meeting Denham's ran buses on Tuesday-Friday 19th-22nd at 6 shillings each and departing from the Market Place at 10am. At that point the total available seating of the fleet was stated to be 80.

The motor garage continued to produce overhauled vehicles for sale, with a Trumbull car in July 1922, whilst Theo was seeking a Ford van. September saw a Belgian-built Minerva 20hp chassis for sale, which he said would make a good 15cwt van, whilst October saw a further Hupmobile, this time a 6-seater, offered at £80 inclusive of road tax.

By 1923 Theo was living at 151 Bartholomew Street, Newbury, above Whitington's Florist, Fruiterers & Corn Stores, with his fiancé and her family. In 1925 he married Margaret (Mags) Whitington and the couple remained at that address. Although Theo played no part in the family business, he did apparently help them out financially when things became difficult during the recession of the 1930's. The shop was, however, used as the booking point for *Denham's* excursions, being situated centrally in the town and at the end of a short shopping arcade leading from the Market Place. By 1933 he and Mags had relocated to 40 Howard Road, where they would remain, and she is recalled as 'a strong-willed lady who kept Theo's nose to the grindstone'.

Expansion of the bus operations led to the establishment of a garage in Wharf Road from the Summer of 1922, whilst another garage at No.7 Craven Road was added by May 1925. The Kings Road premises are not mentioned after February 1923, though those at Wharf Road were extended in due course, especially as Craven Road was vacated sometime between 1928 and 1930. After *Denhams* left Craven Road, the premises were used by a builder A.N. Hughes, who in turn is believed to be related to them through the Whitington side, and was also undertaking haulage work by 1932. Another relative, Mrs. Elizabeth Whitington, actually ran the Florist & Fruiterer's shop known as Hughes & Co. in Market Street. Her son *Eddie*, who was cousin to Mags, came into the N&D fold in due course and remained there until he went in with *Sid Taylor* to form *Enterprise Coaches* in 1950.

Further notable vehicles offered for sale were a 1914 Ford 7-cwt truck in February 1923, followed by a 2-seater Trumbull of 1916 for £78 in March 1923. Hire cars were also available throughout the 1920's, though these cannot generally be distinguished from the throughput of vehicles acquired for re-sale.

A further 14-seater front-entrance bus was purchased new in July 1924, this being a Chevrolet B-type registered OR 4295, having been obtained through a dealer in Basingstoke.

Evidently a rumour had started that Theo was selling his Woolton Hill route, so he was obliged to place a notice in the Newbury Weekly News on 10th April 1924 pointing out that this was totally without foundation!

Denham acquired his first and only double-decker, when he re-registered former Thomas Tilling LF 9044 locally as MO 3875 in September 1924. This was a 1913 Tilling-Stevens TTA1 petrol-electric bus fitted with the standard Tilling-built 34-seater open-top body for London use. This was operated, still painted in red and black livery, on the Woolton Hill route in that form, but the numerous roadside trees in that area made this somewhat perilous, so the body was soon cut down and re-declared as a 20-seater single-decker from 1st January 1925! Indeed, a second and similar bus had also been acquired, and this re-emerged in March 1925, when it re-registered MO 4984, though its old identity was not recorded, being one of a large number of Tilling-Stevens TTA1's built in 1912-3 for *Thomas Tilling* of Peckham, South London, at that time London's largest single operator of motorbuses. In view of previous experience, this took to the road as a cut-down 20-seater, and in each case the original rear platform area was modified to form an entrance to the saloon.

Tilling-Stevens MO 3875 had been rebuilt with a front-mounted radiator, as the TTA1-type usually had the radiator at the rear of the bonnet in 'coal scuttle' style. This vehicle had several body alterations, and this sketch of the final version with the ex-BT&CC body is based on a very poor photograph.

An unusual purchase during 1924 was a Bristol C50-type (AE 3792) with a 26-seater *Bristol Tramways* bus body, which had been first licensed for their own fleet in July 1914. However, this had been acquired cheaply for some fairly rough lorry work on manure haulage and was not used as a passenger vehicle. The body would, however, see further use, as it was placed on the rebuilt Tilling-Stevens MO 3875 in May 1925.

1925 was when *Boss Denham* came back to Newbury to join in with *Theo* as *Denham Bros.*, after which expansion, and in particular opposition to competition was stepped up.

Ambrose Henry (Boss) Denham was born at The Mumbles, near Swansea in South Wales on 21st October 1897, but by 1901 the family had relocated to 37 Upper Hill Street, Stourbridge in Worcestershire. However, he 'fell out' with his family aged 15 and left to seek employment in Birmingham, where he added a few years to his age. Family legend has it that he 'was driving taxis around Birmingham at 15', and indeed his first license as a hackney carriage motor driver was issued on 28th November 1913, just one month after he turned 16! At that time his address was 14 Greenfield Road, Harborne, Birmingham, and a letter from Thomas Whitehouse of Linden House, 95 Greenfield Road, Harborne shows that he was with him as a motor car driver/mechanic.

With the outbreak of the First World War he sought a posting through the British Ambulance Committee, which had been set up to aid facilities for rescuing the injured from the developing nightmare of the Western Front. Boss obtained one reference dated 15th September 1914 from Mr. R.J. Curtis, The Cottage, St. Marys Road, Harborne, which stated he had been employed by him as a chauffeur for 6 months. A second reference letter dated 14th July 1915, and from his then current employer, came from the Harborne Garage & Suburban Taxi Co., High Street, Harborne, which complimented him on his skills both as a driver and mechanic.

In July he was successful in joining the French Red Cross, though it was by no means an easy option. His duties involved driving ambulances to and from the front, through the maze of trenches and shell holes of the Alsace region. Apart from the physical risks and the terrible sights he must have seen, even these vehicles marked with the insignia of the red cross were often fired upon, as it was the habit of the Officers to hitch a ride, something known to the Germans, resulting in them being targeted. Added to that, the appalling conditions, especially in the wetter months, made vehicle maintenance very difficult indeed, and so many practical skills were learnt out of sheer necessity.

In 1916 he returned on leave to England but, as conscription had been introduced in January of that year, he was stopped at Southampton Docks. This meant that he could not return to his former duties, so he joined the Royal Marine Artillery at Portsmouth, later returning to the front in France.

Luckily Boss was one of those who survived the great conflict, and he returned in the early months of 1919. Later that year he was living at 282 Mary Street, Balsall Heath, Birmingham, and in September an advert for a chauffeur's position came to his attention. The Countess of Aylesford of Packington Hall (at Meriden, some 13 miles east of where he was living) was seeking a chauffeur/mechanic for her Panhard & Levassor car. This had the refinements of a 3398cc 4-cylinder engine which incorporated the patent sleeve valve cylinders designed by the American Charles Yale Kinght. It was an X7-type rated at 20hp as built in France (25hp in Britain), and it was one of 151 built for export between February 1910 and October 1911, in this case through the company's showrooms at Great Portland Street in London's West End. Such a car was at the forefront of mechanical design then, though the body perpetuated many features from the earlier horse carriage era, with the driver sitting in an open-sided cab, complete with an ornate 'communication tube' for the occupants of the rear enclosed saloon whose doors bore the armorial crest. As the chassis manufacturer did not construct its own bodies, it would have arranged for one of the many coachbuilders in London to build it.

Boss Denham as driver of the Panhard et Levassor.

This was indeed a good position, and no doubt his excellent references previously supplied, along with his war service stood Boss in good stead for gaining the post, paid at £2-10-0 per week, with board and lodging provided free. He stayed with the Aylesfords for several years, but a letter dated May 1922 seeking payment for the lock to a toolbox he had damaged, puts him as c/o his brother Theo, *Denham's Motor Garage*, Kings Road, Newbury. As already noted this is when his brother Theo entered bus operation, and he had come to assist him with preparing vehicles for the enterprise, though he did not stay for long despite entreaties by his bother to join him.

Instead, he went to work at the Humber Car Works in Coventry, and was there from about 1923-5, before returning once again to Newbury to finally join Theo's expanding bus operation, which was now re-titled as *Denham Bros*. Initially he lodged at 68

Craven Road, handy for the main bus garage also in that road. He had evidently already met Grace Warmingham, as they married at Meriden in 1926, after which they took up residence at 'Glenhurst', 1 Albert Road, off Northbrook Street in Newbury.

Daimler charabanc TB 2522 seen at Cheddar Gorge.

Returning to the development of Denham Bros., two Daimlers were also acquired during 1925, each of them originating from War Department lorries. One was BL 7936, a 30hp CC-type new in December 1912 and which had been used by *Charlie Durnford* as a charabanc and lorry from its re-registration in 1920. This did not come to *Denham* direct, and with them it became a bus, but other details are not known. The other was a 22hp CK-type, which had been re-registered in Lancashire as TB 2522 for use as a 28-seater charabanc in 1920. It was used in this form, and also went on to haulage work through to April 1932.

In late December 1925 Theo advertised for sale a 4hp Douglas motorcycle combination with a sidecar featuring a Sandum screen and hood, along with 3 Lucas acetelyne lamps, taxed and insured, all for £25. As he used his home address for this item, it must be assumed this was a private sale. Just two months later he had for sale at Wharf Road an Overland tourer with electric lights and starter for £25.

By May 1926 another Talbot 25-50hp was acquired through Percy Andrews and fitted with a maroon and white liveried front-entrance bus body which had longitudinal seating for 10 passengers. This vehicle had originated in 1922, probably as a large private car, and it retained the original registration PM 581. This bus was one of the longest lived with the *Denhams*, being re-bodied after a few years with a more spacious 14-seater bus body, also built by Andrews and then wore a white livery relieved by blue mudguards and roof.

From May 1926 routes were further expanded to cover Newbury to West Woodhay (8.8 miles), Newbury to Ball Hill (4.9 miles), Newbury to Stockcross (3.3 miles) and Newbury to Hungerford via the Bath Road (9.6 miles). By May 1927 the Woolton Hill route had been extended through to Highclere (now at 7.1 miles), and another route been developed from Newbury to Inkpen by way of Hamstead Marshall (9.1 miles). Another of those popular local fetes was held on Whit Monday 1926 at Wash Common (1.8 miles south of Newbury), so *Denhams* ran buses from St. John's Church in Newbury to the site 'every few minutes'.

The little Talbot PM 581 with its original body and seen with Walter Ravenning at the Wickham lay-over.

It is difficult perhaps in these days of widespread personal transport, to fully appreciate how the provision of these early bus services altered the otherwise limited horizons of the villagers they served. Services were mainly geared for shopping trips, often only on the market days and other peak day of Tuesday, as also no one had refrigerators in those days. Fresh food was therefore bought more often, which is why services were often to a Tuesday, Thursday and Saturday pattern. Apart from shopping, the buses also gave opportunities to visit the cinema, often followed by the treat of a fish-'n'-chip supper, something which the driver usually joined in with too before setting off!

It is also worth noting that, apart from the various villages directly served, other passengers lived in tiny hamlets or isolated cottages, many thinking little of walking a mile or three to the nearest point served, as at least in those days there was little prospect of being mown down whilst walking the country back-roads!

The vehicle intake for 1927 saw two further Andrews-bodied 14-seaters added to the fleet, though each was quite different. One was a charabanc based on a former WD Fiat 15TER, which Andrews had put on the road for their own use in July 1923 as MO 1714. The other was a another Percy Andrews refurbished Talbot 25-50hp, which had started out probably as a private car in February 1921, retaining its original registration KE 3196, but now carrying a front-entrance bus body. As a result of these arrivals, the Ford T bus/lorry (MO 1797) was sold in January 1927 and the GMC charabanc departed by June.

On the lorry front, another scarce make was represented by the arrival of a Palladium YE-type 3/4-tonner in April 1927. This had been new in March 1920 as BL 0301, but re-registered by its original owner under the 1920 Road Traffic Act in 1921 as BL 8474, and it is not known how long this lorry stayed with *Denhams*.

A Palladium lorry of the type used by Denhams, this example also having originated in the Reading area.

Also, at some point after Boss had returned to the area, *Denhams* kept a car available for hire with a driver, as again few people owned cars and there was a steady stream of visitors to the surrounding large houses. Due to the high losses in the First World War many of these now found it very difficult to find or retain good chauffeurs, but of course Boss had already proven his credentials in that aspect and may well have traded on that.

Although full details are lacking of the cars used as hire cars by *Denham Bros.*, it is known that both a Ford landaulette and a 6-seater Daimler landaulette were disposed of in August/September 1926, the latter being quoted as 'late property of a titled lady'.

Of course, there were times when *Denham's* bus services came under serious threat, in turn from *The Thames Valley Traction Co. Ltd.*, *Norton Motor Services* and the Road Motors Department of the *Great Western Railway*. Each of these was different in its origins and complexity and, in the interest of clarity each will now be reviewed in turn.

The Thames Valley Traction Co. Ltd.

Even prior to the formation of the *Thames Valley* company, the parent *British Automobile Traction Co. Ltd.* had identified Newbury as an objective, and a route from Reading reached there in October 1919. However, due to fuel economies the route was suspended in December 1919, and then reinstated from the following 1st July only to be discontinued once again from 31st December 1920.

On 20th April 1922 the Company advertised in the Newbury Weekly News that services had commenced between Newbury – Speen – Stockcross – Kintbury – Hungerford and Newbury – Thatcham – Cold Ash, these routes duly being given numbers 18 and 19 in the May timetable booklet. The notice was dated 7th April, and the pair of routes was inter-worked by one single deck Thornycroft J type saloon, which was outstationed somewhere in Newbury and crewed by Driver Hillier and his conductor, both of whom were local men. Indeed, Hillier had previously tried his hand at haulage and charabanc work back in 1919, which we shall hear more of shortly. The crew worked all week on the two routes, though the hours of 8am to 8pm were not that unusual in those days. On Thursdays and Saturdays the Cold Ash route had an additional journey for market shopping. It is therefore interesting to note that *Theo Denham* opted to run over the Newbury – Thatcham – Cold Ash – Westrop road from May 1922.

Thames Valley Car 40 (DX 2174) is seen with driver Bert Sawyer and conductor Archie Lock outside the Bladebone Inn at Bucklebury. Note that the vehicle has canvas tied in place of the central section of the roof, and it is painted in the green and white livery then still in use.

During June and July *Thames Valley* advertised a number of charabanc excursions from Newbury, though that to Ascot Races even started at Lambourn, some 13.7 miles north-west of the town. Whatever the take up was for these is not recorded, but they were not repeated the following year. It is believed that the charas used were those based at the Reading garage.

On the services side June 1922 saw the existing Route 11 (Reading – Bradfield – Bucklebury Common) extended onto Cold Ash – Thatcham – Newbury once a day in each direction, this extended route being placed in the care of a second Thornycroft J-type saloon based at Newbury. Another locally-recruited crew, consisting of Driver Bert Sawyer and Conductor Archie Lock were used for this operation. At this point Routes 18/19 were reduced to operate on Tuesdays, Thursdays, Saturdays and Sundays, which duplicated the *Denham* service (except that the latter did not run Sundays).

The route map in the timetable booklet for July 1922 also shows a link from Newbury to Lambourn, though no evidence for such an operation has been found, but it must be assumed that such a route was considered.

By August 1922 Route 19 (Newbury   Thatcham Cold Ash) disappeared as a separate entity and was incorporated into Route 11. A new Route 19 was opened up at the same time as Newbury – Falkland Memorial – Ball Hill – East End – Woolton Hill – Highclere, and *Theo Denham* was not happy! This service also ran as Tuesdays, Thursdays, Saturdays and Sundays, and this along with the Route 11 and 18 workings were still covered by the pair of outstationed Thornycroft saloons. That Summer saw certainly saw some antics along the Newbury Woolton Hill road, with *Denham's* and *TV's* buses vying for passengers!

Robert Hillier

Quite how the Newbury services were fairing financially by October is unclear, though all still appeared in the timetable booklet for that month. However, *Robert Hillier*, who lived at 8 Madeira Place, announced in the Newbury Weekly News on 12th October that he intended 'to start his own operations to the same local destinations, using a 14-seater bus', which he obviously thought he could do a better job of! It might be that Hillier had already gauged that *Thames Valley* might withdraw the services. Whatever TV's considerations at that time, they were so dismayed that they withdrew completely from the area, even deleting the entire Newbury portion from the timetable route map!

In respect of Hillier's background, there were two recurring themes, firstly his increasing involvement with mechanised transport, and secondly those events in his life connected with the Newbury area. Indeed, he was not a local man, having been born in 1873 at Burbage, near Pewsey in Wiltshire. After working initially as an agricultural labour, he moved to Swindon and was lodging with his brother who worked on the *Great Western Railway* 1891.

However, in 1895 he married a Kingsclere girl, and by 1901 he and wife Elizabeth were living at Speen

Waterworks, where he tended the stationary steam engine. Sometime after 1903 his wife died leaving him with two young daughters, though happily he re-married in 1907 to another Elizabeth, who came from Newbury, the family relocated to 2 West Villas, West Street, Newbury, at which point he was the driver of a traction engine.

By the time of his enlistment in February 1915 the family had again moved, now being at 148 Landguard Road, Eastney, Portsmouth, by which time Robert had progressed to a motor driver. In view of that he was selected for the Army Service Corps (Mechanical Transport) and initially sent to the large marshalling centre at Grove Park in Lee, South London. After that he saw service with 132 Company in France throughout the conflict, during which time his wife and children went to live with her mother, Mrs. Benham of Stanley Road, Newbury, where the family ran a greengrocer's shop.

He was discharged at Chiseldon in January 1919 and initially worked in Reading, but on 21st August 1919 he advertised that he would undertake haulage work and was living at 8 Madeira Place in Newbury. One week later he advertised 'pleasure trips' using a lorry-chara, though the identity of the vehicle is not known. He continued with the haulage work, though no more attempts at passenger carrying were noted through to March 1920, no doubt due to an increase in local competition offering more suitable vehicles.

It seems likely that he was attracted to the vacancy with *Thames Valley* because it offered a steadier means of employment, though as already noted, he duly had to reconsider his position.

His 12/14-seater wagonette (of unknown make) ran from the Market Place 'at the usual times', though a subsequent notice stated that there would be no Sunday service during the Winter months. Probably due to the limited comforts of this vehicle, it was replaced by the middle of December by an unknown Garner. The next to be heard of him was when he offered the 20-seater 1920 Garner bus for sale on 5th May 1923. As this advert was placed in the Portsmouth Evening News, though still using his Newbury address, it would seem to indicate that he was perhaps relocating to that area once again. No actual date for the cessation of his service is known.

****

Thames Valley returns once again

The Company finally returned to Newbury from 22nd May 1926, this time with a feel of determination to set up a base in the town. The service along the Bath Road between Reading and Newbury (now as Route 19) was re-commenced, putting their Thornycroft J-type double-deckers into competition with *Norton's* Tilling-Stevens buses between Thatcham and Newbury. However, of more significance to *Denham's,* they also reinstated the Highclere route from June, together with short-workings between Wash Common and Newbury. The single-decker for that route (which had no route number allocated), together with the 2 double-deckers working from the Newbury end on Route 19 were outstationed in Newbury, and in due course plans were drawn up for a Dormy Shed in Mill Lane, which opened in the Summer of 1927.

From 1st October 1927 the Reading route was re-numbered as 10, which is was to remain for many more years. An improved service was put on the Highclere route from 23rd October, along with a cut in fares, as competition for that road with *Denhams* intensified, though no route number was allocated (this not being unusual for 'experimental' services). The Reading route had included short-workings between Newbury and Thatcham, originally aimed at competition with *Nortons,* and from January 1928 these were combined with the Wash Common to Newbury shorts to form a cross-town local service, with the section south of Wash Common being withdrawn. This combined route was now covered by 2 saloons and was known as Route 10a. However, in June of that year that facility was withdrawn, leaving only the 2 double-deckers for the Reading service based at Newbury, and the buses of the *'Valley* were once again absent on the other local roads for a further few years.

Norton Motor Services

The Norton family had already established bus operations in the Fairford and Lechlade area of Gloucestershire, when *William Byrnes Norton* came to Newbury to set up another branch in that town, initially living at The Ferns in Kings Road. In line with vehicles already being used at the other branch, he acquired two former *Thomas Tilling* double-deckers in order to inaugurate a regular daily service between Newbury (Market Place) and Thatcham (Broadway). The service commenced on Tuesday 18th December 1923, and the red and white-liveried buses were Tilling-Stevens TTA1-type petrol-electrics, carrying the standard open-top, open-staircase 34-seater body built in Tilling's own Peckham coachworks. These were LF 9826 and LF 9916, and a boy conductor was employed to collect the fares. Young William Titcombe recalled that as such an employee, when relief buses were operated on Saturdays, no additional conductor was provided, and he was expected to switch between buses to collect the fares! He stayed on there for about 9 months prior to entering the Royal Navy at age 15, cycling in from Upper Colthrop for a 7am start, and generally working through to 10pm daily.

The return fare between Newbury and Thatcham was 8 pence and, apart from providing journeys mainly aimed at shoppers and for the cinema, other journeys were timed to suit those travelling to Thatcham Works. The main competition in respect of this Thatcham route was *Freddie Spanswick*, who retaliated by getting his smaller buses to overtake the slower Tilling-Stevens at popular stops in order to cream off traffic, whilst he also engaged in a fares war and invested in better buses. *George Howlett* similarly reminded his patrons to support the local operator and only travel on *The Kennet* buses between Thatcham and Bucklebury.

However, as *Bill Norton* was not local, he remained something of an unknown quantity, so other operators must surely have wondered what was going on when they advertised several excursions for Easter 1924! In reality this was because of a temporary surplus of vehicles, so they ran an excursion from Newbury to Reading on Saturday 19th April, then another to High Wycombe on Monday 21st, both excursions being bookable in advance.

However, the next development did directly put them in conflict with the *Denhams* area of operation, when from 26th July 1924 a new Newbury – Kintbury – Hungerford service commenced. At Hungerford passengers could access the *Bristol Tramway's* bus service to Swindon whilst, co-incidentally, the buses of the *Great Western Railway* had reached Hungerford (though from the west) only two days before! Of course it should be appreciated that none of the large territorial operators had established a base at Newbury, leaving the town in a no-man's-land, which would be a significant factor in future developments.

The competition on the Hungerford road saw the *Denhams* emerge victorious, and in January 1925 *Nortons* ceased their operation. However, they switched resources to further enhancing the Newbury – Thatcham service from 22nd January 1925, including the addition of a Sunday service. The latter had 6 return trips between 2.30pm and 9.35pm, whilst there were 7 return trips on Mondays, Tuesdays and Fridays, 11 on Thursdays, 12 on Saturdays, but only 4 on Wednesdays (due to early-closing day).

By that date *Denhams* were not particularly interested in expanding to the east, concentrating more on developing services to the south and west of Newbury. However, *Nortons* next move was again regarded as an incursion, with the introduction of a Newbury – Boxford – Great Shefford – Lambourn service during October 1926. This was worked by a single-decker bus on a Whiting chassis (AD 7426) due to restricted headroom en route, The route ran on Tuesdays, Thursdays, Saturdays and Sundays only, and the bus was outstationed at Lambourn. However, this route was also abandoned in March 1927, whilst

competition from *Spanswick* and the return of *Thames Valley* to the Reading – Thatcham – Newbury road from 22nd May 1926 were both affecting the viability of the Newbury – Thatcham service. With the opening of its Dormy Shed in Mill Lane, Newbury in Summer 1927, TV's Route 10 was re-equipped with the more powerful Thornycroft JB's, which put further pressure on *Nortons*. In response the latter applied to Reading Borough Council in October 1927 to license 2 buses to run through from Newbury to Reading, but this was refused. The Newbury – Thatcham route continued through to June 1928, when it ceased, though *Nortons* other operations in Gloucestershire continued in family hands until 1959. It seems that the Newbury based fleet was laid up at this point, as all were scrapped together in November 1929.

The buses used by *Norton Motor Services* in the Newbury area were as follows:

<u>LF 9826</u> Tilling-Stevens TTA1 petrol-electric with Tilling O34ROS body new in 1913, acquired by 12/23, scrapped 11/29 - was B20- from 3/27*

<u>LF 9916</u> Tilling-Stevens TTA1 petrol-electric with Tilling O34ROS body new in 1913, acquired by 12/23, scrapped 11/29

<u>MO 4421</u> Tilling-Stevens TTA1 petrol-electric with B26- body, chassis new in 1913, acquired 1/25 and scrapped 5/26

<u>LF 9920</u> Tilling-Stevens TTA1 petrol-electric with Tilling O34ROS body new in 1913, acquired 7/26 and scrapped 11/29

<u>AD 7426</u> Whiting 25hp with B--- body re-registered 6/20, acquired 10/26 and scrapped 11/29. Ex-WD lorry in 1920

<u>LF 9893</u> Tilling-Stevens TTA1 petrol-electric with Tilling O34ROS body new 1913, acquired 1/27 and scrapped 11/29

<u>Notes:</u>
LF 9826, 9893, 9916 and 9920 were formerly *Thomas Tilling* Nos. 318, 350, 361 and 365. MO 4421 was formerly *Thomas Tilling* No. 321 and had originally been registered LF 9445. It was rebuilt and/or re-bodied as shown prior to use at Newbury. The double-deckers received front windscreens, which were not permitted for London use.
* LF 9826 was either cut-down from the original double-decker or possibly re-bodied (see below).
Nortons also purchased a former *Newcastle Corporation Tramways* Tilling-Stevens petrol-electric with B20- body (BB 1073), which is believed to have been used for spare parts, whilst the body may have been mounted on LF 9826.

The vehicles used were similar to those in the Gloucestershire area, whilst the Whiting had been registered in that County, so it may have been used there before transfer to Newbury.

Bill Norton moved to Oak Cottage, 147 Andover Road, Newbury by January 1925, but the buses were kept at the Pelican Garage in London Road, and by May 1926 at Boulton's Yard, 13 West Mills, whilst the outstation at Lambourn was the yard of one of the inns. Bill Norton drove the buses, along with Arthur Amor, Jim Lawrence and several others.

Great Western Railway

Although chronologically the last of the three major competitors to *Denhams* to appear on the scene, this one would nonetheless result in the most intense period of all the trials and tribulations sent to test their determination.

The Road Motor Department of the *Great Western Railway* had been responsible for many pioneering bus routes since 1903, the original intention being to operate buses where the construction of a railway line could not be justified or was geographically difficult. Later on there was more provision of feeder routes to extend the catchment to railheads, but the phase of increased development in the late 1920's had other purposes, in that the powers to operate buses were being reviewed under what would become the Road Traffic Act 1930. The thinking had therefore turned to establishing routes which, in due course of time, could be traded off to the larger territorial bus operators in exchange for share-holdings in those companies.

Indeed, the *GWR* had obviously noticed that Newbury was not particularly well-served by any of those territorial operators. It also seems possible that it had noted *Thames Valley's* interest in the area, and so it was in June 1927 that it commenced services between Newbury and Andover (via Highclere) and from Newbury to Hungerford, the latter town already being connected by a route from Marlborough. Indeed, by August of that year, the Newbury – Hungerford and Hungerford – Marlborough routes had been combined, with a further extension west to Calne, and also eastwards to either Kingsclere or Reading (via Mortimer).

For May 1928 the services were recast as Newbury – Kingsclere – Basingstoke, Newbury – Didcot, Newbury – Newtown, Newbury – Cold Ash and Newbury – Lambourn, though the latter was as a Sundays-only supplement to the Lambourn Valley Railway. In June a Newbury – Stockcross route was put on (again in direct conflict with *Denhams*). Also from that month the rather over-long route from Calne to Reading was divided at Newbury, though buses only ran between Newbury and Reading on Mondays and Saturdays. The Newbury – Highclere – Andover service continued, which was the main battleground for *Denhams,* whereas the road between Kingsclere and Basingstoke was equally fiercely contested by *Edith Kent* and her son *Bill.*

It was during this period that *Denham's* little Talbot bus came into its own, and a caption on the reverse of a photo of KE 3196 states quite clearly 'this if the famous Talbot bus which had a lot to do with the finishing up of the *GWR* on two routes, another one to go and that will do it'. Readers may also recall that the *Denham Bros.* father had been an engine driver on the *GWR* and, in view of his experiences of the hard working life there, the issue was also 'personal' to the sons. Despite the relatively infinitive resources of the *GWR*, these would prove no match for such dogged determination from the natives!

Talbot KE 3196 is seen here with Boss Denham as the driver and Douglas Warmingham, his relative by marriage, who was a conductor after formation of Newbury & District, and also drove in due course.

Apart from the effort put in by the above families and their crews, local loyalties also helped, and fares were reduced in order to favour the shorter journeys most passengers realistically took, something which the railway company found difficult to respond effectively to. Quite how the *GWR* recruited the crews for these services is not known, though in over 40 years of research the author has not come across anyone in the Newbury area who worked on them, which suggests that these were not local men?

By September 1928 the tide had definitely turned, and the *GWR* withdrew the Newbury – Hungerford section. That same month the Newbury – Didcot route was cut back to run as far as East Ilsley only, whilst the Cold Ash route ended completely, there also being effective competition in those areas from *John Prothero* of Beedon, *Bert Austin* of Cold Ash and *George Howlett* of Bucklebury in particular.

At the end of January 1929 the Newbury – Basingstoke route was cut back to Kingsclere, whilst the Newbury – Andover route was curtailed at Highclere from the following month. July of that year saw the end of the Newbury – Kingsclere section and that to East Ilsley, whilst even the Lambourn route was abandoned later that year.

This left only the three local routes out of Newbury, to Highclere, to Newtown and to Stockcross still in operation, and this meagre residue remained active when the *GWR* passed a number of bus services to *Thames Valley* in September 1931. These three routes were inter-worked by one outstationed bus, and the threat to *Denham Bros.* was effectively overcome. Despite some initial optimism regarding this expansion of its Newbury operations, it was not long before *Thames Valley* found these routes were not economical, and after a number of attempts to reduce costs, they also disappeared.

****

Before returning to the chronological sequence for *Denham Bros.,* it is also worth noting a couple of other operators who had early bus operations to the south of Newbury over roads also served by them.

Ralph George Iles

Ralph Iles of Malt House Farm, West Woodhay had commenced a bus service from there to Newbury via Ball Hill – Wash Water – Wash Common from June 1921, operating on Thursdays and Saturdays only. This seems to have been in response to the withdrawal of the *Newbury & Andover Motor Co.* buses which had operated between June 1920 and June 1921, which left the locals without buses once again. Ralph had been born in 1885 at Quenington, near Fairford in Gloucestershire, the son of a blacksmith who trained as the same but in the forge of his cousin Hungerford Barrett at nearby Ashton Keynes, just over the border in Wiltshire. Enlistment for war service in August 1914 saw him initially in the Royal Wiltshire Yeomanry before transferring to the Army Service Corps, where he learnt to drive and maintain motor vehicles, coming home again in March 1919. Ralph's vehicle is unknown, though quite likely a war-surplus purchase, whilst he spent the rest of the week offering repairs to agricultural machinery and motor vehicles, in which he could also use his blacksmith's skills.

Norman Edward Phillips

However, from March 1925 advertised a very similar service was advertised by *Norman Phillips*, who was also a farmer based at Bricklayers Farm, West Woodhay. As he also owned Malt House Farm by 1928, there would seem to be some connection between these two ventures, perhaps with Phillips providing some capital, as certainly he bought a new Chevrolet 1-tonner with a varnished 14-seater bus body (MO 4344), which had been licensed on the last day of 1924. With this new vehicle a number of additional short-workings were added, plus a later Saturday-evening journey at 8pm. However, as this was still only used on Thursdays and Saturdays, it is likely that it also had an alternative goods body for

farm use. Nothing of note occurred through to the close of 1930, when the Chevrolet ceased to be licensed, presumably Phillips having decided not to apply under the 1930 Act, after which *Denham Bros.* continued to serve those points, though he was still farming at Bricklayers Farm until at least 1933.

****

The only known disposals of passenger vehicles in 1927-9 concerned the departure of Ford T 14-seater MO 1797 and the Buick (latterly used as a van) in January 1927, followed by Tilling-Stevens MO 4984 in May 1927 and Daimler CC BL 7936 in December 1928, the emphasis at that time being on smaller faster buses due to the competition outlined above. In August 1929 a Ford T 14-seater charabanc (BL 8006) was acquired from *Joseph Baldwin* of Peasemore, though this was not licensed by *Denhams.*

Vehicles were still being overhauled for sale on a regular basis, and in October 1927 an Austin 7 could be viewed at the Craven Road Depot. In May 1928 a small bus body was offered for sale and noted as 'would make a good garden shed', and this was probably part of a clearout of Craven Road for the move to Wharf Road. A Ford 'tonner' lorry followed in June 1928, whilst during May 1929 two further bus bodies were disposed of. August 1929 saw a Ford touring car for sale, though again from Theo's home address, whilst in October there was another Ford tourer car and a Ford 'tonner' chassis being disposed of 'due to space needed at the Wharf Road Garage', after which all such sales cease in favour of concentrating on the bus and taxi operations.

In June 1930 the Chevrolet bus OR 4295 was taken off the road, as was the Fiat chara MO 1714. Also the Fiat bus MO 2406 was sold for further service during that year, all 3 having served *Denham Bros.* well. Fleet replacements came in the shape of a Star 'Flyer' VB4 with Strachans (of Acton) 26-seater dual-doorway coach body (HX 1059), which had been new in July 1930 to *Spartan* of London W3 and came to *Denhams* later that year.

The other acquisition was the first of many little Thornycroft 20-seaters that would make their way to the Newbury area over the next few years, this being TR 8198, an A2-type with 20-seater front-entrance bus body by Wadham of Waterlooville. This bus had been new in February 1930 to *Ellen Easson* of Spring Road Garage, Sholing, Southampton, but after a short time it had been found to have a cracked chassis. The local Thornycroft Agent obliged with a replacement frame, but the *Easson's* decided it was best to get shot of it towards the close of 1930. However, this was quite unknown to *Denhams,* and as the bus ran through to at least 1940 maybe they had the last laugh?

In June 1930 the buses of Salisbury-based *Wilts & Dorset Motor Services Ltd.* first appeared in Newbury with its lengthy route to Romsey via Andover and Stockbridge. This used brand new Leyland 'Lion' buses, though it only ran three times per day, departing Newbury at 11am, 3pm and 7.30pm, with an additional Newbury – Andover journey at 9.30pm on Saturdays, along with a reduced Sunday operation. This did not really affect the *Denham Bros.* buses, but no doubt it did serve to show how interest from the larger firms could alter the balance if they applied the resources. On the other hand, *Lewis Horne* of Andover did find this new service abstracting from his established service, so a fares-and-frequency war did break out as time passed.

| Please note: The wider story of developments on the Andover road will be found at the end of this chapter. |

A happy bunch of Denham's crews standing in front of Talbot PM 581 with its original body. Left to right are Mr. Bally, not known, Albert Miles and Walter Ravenning, the bus being used on the Stockcross run.

That same Talbot was rebodied by Andrews with this 14-seater body, painted white and blue. It is seen at the Red House terminus at Highclere.

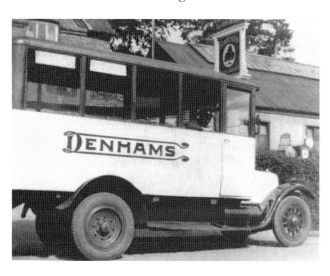

With the successive waves of competition now behind them, *Denhams* set about consolidating their services and getting set for the next challenge, that of the Road

Traffic Act 1930. To be fair, good operators with established routes were generally treated fairly by the Traffic Commissioners, and in some respects the Act afforded some protection to independents in that it made many of the dubious 'competitive practices' illegal. However, it did involve a lot of work, including time away from the daily operations in order to attend the Traffic Hearings (which could be many miles away), whereas the large territorial companies could easily afford to appoint someone solely to handle those tasks.

The Act took effect from 1st April 1931, though the actual Hearings were not all heard until later that year, so in the meantime existing operations could continue. *Denhams* were successful in respect of all the routes they were currently operating, and these were as follows:

Newbury – Inkpen, Tuesdays and Thursdays, extended to Hungerford on Saturdays;
Newbury – Ball Hill – Heath End – East End – East Woodhay, daily except Sundays;
Newbury – Speen – Stockcross – Marsh Benham – Clapton Crossroads – Avington – Denford – Hungerford, daily;
Newbury – Wash Common – Wash Water – Woolton Hill – Highclere, daily, extended onto Broad Laying – Griffins Corner and The Mount on Thursdays and Saturdays;
Newbury – Speen – Stockcross – Wickham Heath – Wickham, daily;
Newbury – Stockcross, extra short-workings on Thursdays, plus journey extended to Hoe Benham;
Newbury – Enborne Street – North End, Thursdays and Saturdays only;
Newbury – Enborne – Hamstead Marshall – Kintbury – Inkpen, Thursdays and Saturdays only;
Newbury – Enborne – Hamstead Marshall – Inkpen Common – Upper Green, Thursdays and Saturdays only.

Thornycroft MW 825 when new to Charlie Haines.

In order to cover these routes, and especially the peak demands on Thursdays and Saturdays (without too much recourse to relief buses), the fleet took in a number of larger types during 1931, along with other smaller examples. A further Thornycroft A2, with a

20-seater front-entrance bus body by Challands Ross of Nottingham arrived in the shape of MW 825 in April 1931. This had been new to *Charlie Haines* of Durrington in Wiltshire in November 1927, but he had sold out to *Wilts & Dorset* in March 1931. It should of course be noted that many bodies built at that time on Thornycroft chassis were to standard designs prepared by the chassis supplier.

A more medium-sized vehicle was TR 1231, a Leyland E-type of November 1925 which carried a 26-seater front-entrance body constructed by its former owner *Southampton Corporation*, which was ideal in several ways for *Denhams*. Firstly, it had been built specifically for one-man-operation on sparser routes, useful as only the larger buses carried conductors with *Denhams*, but also quite handy as it was already in a royal blue livery, which was close to what had become the fleet standard!

When the Leyland TR 1231 arrived it was the largest vehicle in the fleet, and is seen parked in front of the Travis Arnold wood-yard at The Wharf.

A further couple of Tilling-Stevens buses, though of more modern types with conventional gearboxes and petrol engines were also added for their front-entrance 32-seater capacity. One was VT 184, a B10A-type of July 1927 carrying a Strachan & Brown body and was added in May 1931, having originated with the *Norton Bus Co.* of Norton-in-the-Moors in the Potteries area (but no connection to *Norton Motor Services*!).

Tilling-Stevens bus VT 184, which served through to 1940, when taken by the War Department.

The other acquired at about the same time was a newer B10A2-type (BU 5690), with a Northern Counties of Wigan 32-seater front-entrance bus body, new in November 1928 to *T.H. Lockett* of Aston-under-Lyne, both of these Tillings being ultimately acquired through the same dealer. The same may also be true of the other front-entrance 32-seater acquired in 1931, this being a Gilford 166OT with Strachan & Brown body (TO 9554), which had been new to *Reynold's Bulwell Bus Service* of Bulwell, Nottingham in March 1929. The latter was a well-liked vehicle and it was not unusual to find it used on larger excursions as well as peak-day bus operations.

Gilford bus TO 9554 as delivered to Reynolds Bros., which was also often selected for coach duties.

Another vehicle was also evidently acquired in the 1930/1 period, though only incomplete details are known, this being a further Gilford, but a 28-seater service bus.

Also as a result of the 1930 Act, the established carrier *A.J. Mercer*, who had used his Ford T 1-ton 14-seater (HO 7468), ceased to take passengers. His service to Ball Hill, Enborne, East End, Penwood, Burghclere, Newtown and his base at East Woodhay continue in the family for many years, but for goods traffic only. Because of this his passengers now switched to the *Denham's* buses.

The only vehicle recorded as being acquired during 1932 arrived in January in the guise of a Belgian-built Minerva (WU 9870), which carried a 20-seater bus body by Metcalfe of Romford and had been new to *Booth* of Otley, Yorkshire in February 1927. Minerva were well known for their high-quality cars, often compared to Rolls Royce, but made very little impression on the British PSV market. With so many larger vehicles, further garage space was rented from 1932 in the shape of the former GPO Motor Depot in Mill Lane and next to *Durnfords* garage.

Boss was still at Albert Road when he gained his first PSV Driver's Badge under the 1930 Road Traffic Act, which was issued on 17th October 1931, but by the renewal a year later they had moved again to 'Dalkeith', 93 Greenham Road, Newbury, which was certainly more convenient to the new garage location in Mill Lane.

Another view of Talbot PM 581 with conductor Walter Ravenning at The Wharf. Note the long-wheelbase bus on Ford Model T 1-ton chassis parked behind.

Boss and Grace had daughter Joyce in 1928 and son Lionel in 1936 (so named in commemoration of his uncle who perished in the Great War), after which a further move took them to 28 Paddick Road, one of a number of local 'semis' built by George Durnford, the brother of coach and haulage operator Charlie.

Boss Denham in his later role as a taxi driver outside the Queens Hotel in Newbury Market Place, and still wearing his Newbury & District driver's cap!

The *Denham's* experiences in opposing, and indeed defeating, the local attempts by the *GWR* to establish local bus services (along with the efforts of *Edith and Bill Kent)* had certainly highlighted the need for the smaller operators to work together, and that point was duly focussed on further by the progress of the 1930 Road Traffic Act. Indeed, there was already a South Berks Bus Proprietors & Carriers Association in existence, and *Theo Denham* was an active participant in efforts to defend local operators. It was a natural progression for this to become the springboard for a co-operative approach in order to address what were seen as the inherent disadvantages that the Act imposed on smaller concerns and the resulting cheque-book spree that invariably followed as many gave up the fight and sold out to the territorial firms.

ANDOVER ROAD PERSPECTIVE

Although *Denham Bros.* provided many of the services to the south-west of Newbury, they were not alone. Indeed, the history of route developments on the Newbury to Andover road is fairly complex, and much of the story is an interwoven one of cause-and-effect, which this perspective now seeks to provide an appreciation of.

Victor John White

The first motorised carrier's service to ply the road between Newbury and Andover was that of *Victor White* of 'Penarth' in Hurstbourne Tarrant, though the route was initially split at his base at Church Street, where he lived with his widowed mother and two unmarried sisters. He operated in different directions on specific days, the whole run of some 15 miles being out of the question with a horse-drawn cart and the condition of the roads at that time. Items collected from Newbury were taken onto Andover on the next working day, which limited the types of goods to non-perishable.

Victor White had been born at West Grimstead, some 13 miles south-west of Andover and over the border into Wiltshire in 1875. In 1901 he was at Emmetts Farm in that village, working as a wood dealer. White had evidently succeeded the carrier *West*, who was running on Tuesdays, Thursdays and Saturdays from his home in the same village to The Globe in Bartholomew Street, Newbury and back. West is shown in the carrier's lists for 1904 and 1906, but in 1911 White is shown. There is reason to suspect that he inherited the same horse-drawn van as, when in 1912, he decided to purchase a motor chassis, he cut the cost by having the old body re-mounted on the Salisbury-built Scout 3.5-ton chassis, and the completed vehicle was registered AA 2394.

Now equipped with a motor vehicle, Vic White could operate as a through link, which he continued to do on Tuesdays, Thursdays and Saturdays. Some of the points he served were indeed remote, and a contemporary account of 1918 refers to the area as being *'the back of beyond, with great lonely stretches, lofty hills, and roads of abominable looseness about the district of Highclere'*. His service was therefore much welcomed, and at one point he experienced some problems with the Scout, having to buy a smaller tradesman's-type van, but that could not cope with the capacious loads and passengers handled by the large van. Indeed, as a sideline, he also used the Scout for household removals and general haulage.

Victor White's green-painted Scout van AA 2394.

At some time between 1914 and 1917 he changed his Newbury lay-over point to 'near the church', which was just around the corner from The Globe and still in Bartholomew Street, whilst his layover in Andover was at The George, from where he departed at 3.30pm on Mondays and Fridays. Later developments of *Vic White* will be covered further on in this section, in view of how these were shaped by the actions of the other players.

H. Tibble & Son

Another pioneering service also ran between Andover and Newbury, though it did not form part of the main road scene, being primarily concerned with serving the St. Mary Bourne area. However, in view of the long duration of this service, it is reviewed as part of the links to the two towns.

Henry Tibble was born in Alresford, Hampshire in 1877, but by 1901 he and his wife Rosa and son *Oliver Reginald* were living at Pemberton Road, Lyndhurst in the New Forest, where he was working as a domestic gardener.

Oliver had been born at Longstock in 1896, and from 1914 went to work at the Imperial Motor Works in Lyndhurst as a trainee mechanic, and during the Great War he had enlisted in February 1917 and served with the Army Service Corps in France, returning home in June 1919. Whilst he was away the family relocated to take over the grocery and baker's shop in St. Mary Bourne, in north Hampshire.

When Oliver returned he naturally wanted to use the skills he had learnt in driving and maintaining heavy vehicles, so he and his father purchased a circa 1914 Dennis 'Subsidy' lorry from the war surplus sales during August 1919, which Oliver then thoroughly overhauled. Once work on the chassis was completed the vehicle (LP 8746) was taken to Rowden & Son in Lyndhurst, who built a large van body with windows and seating for 20 for the new venture.

They put this vehicle onto a carrier's service from their home village, which was situated some 6 miles from Andover, and 15 miles from both Newbury and Basingstoke. From the outset the service ran on specific days to Newbury, Andover, and Basingstoke and was known as the *St. Mary Bourne Motor Service*. However, on the original of the photo of the Dennis van the legend *Pioneer* can be seen on the headboard of the cab, and in due course *Pioneer Motor Service* came to be used for the venture.

Originally Newbury was only served on Thursdays, with the van leaving the Market Place at 3.30pm. Andover was served on Fridays, and on Wednesdays the van went to the market day in Basingstoke. Facilities were also in place to forward goods onto Winchester, though not by their own vehicle.

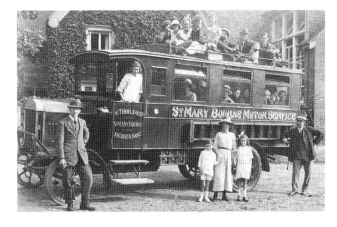

The original Pioneer vehicle Dennis Subsidy LP 8746.

The Dennis also saw some use on Sundays and Bank Holidays for pleasure trips, notably to Bournemouth and Southampton, whilst it also probably undertook some localised excursions to fetes and other public events, such vehicles greatly extending the horizons for those in such rural locations. It should also be appreciated that apart from performing the role of the country carrier, it was also useful for stocking the shop and supplies for the bakery from wholesalers.

Indeed, such was the popularity of the motorised trips that a purpose-built charabanc was added from August 1921 in the shape of a 14-seater Ford T 1-tonner (HO 7561). This was painted dark green, but the colour of the original Dennis is not recorded. This Ford proved a worthwhile investment, though it was replaced on passenger duties from May 1924 by a French-built Berliet with a 20-seater charabanc body (OR 4242).

The Ford was then re-classified as goods and used on the carrier's service at times. The original Dennis remained in use until 1926. Whether any other buses were purchased before 1929 is not known.

Basingstoke continued to be served, with Saturdays also being added by April 1929, when there were two full journeys between St. Mary Bourne and that town on Wednesdays and Saturdays. On Wednesdays there were two short-workings over Whitchurch – Overton – Basingstoke, and one more on Saturdays. However, this route was not continued after the 1930 Act, as the *Venture* services in that area had been developed.

During 1930 a new Chevrolet U-type 14-seater bus (OU 5737) was purchased, and this was followed by the purchase of two Thurgood-bodied Chevrolet LM-type 14-seater front-entrance buses. RO 6641 came from *Knowles* of Little Berkhampstead in December and was new in April 1927. The second of these arrived in early 1931 (RO 8162) and had been new in May 1927 to the Thurgood family's *Peoples Motor Service* of Ware. These were duly joined by another Chevrolet, a LQ-type 14-seater coach (VF 6943), new in September 1929 and supplied by Thurgoods in their other capacity as a dealer in January 1935. This little quartet then formed the fleet through to 1938.

The increase in fleet size allowed the service to be expanded, with three return journeys all the way between Newbury and Andover on Thursdays and Saturdays, whilst it also ran on Tuesdays but only twice. On all three days there were departures from Newbury Wharf at 10.30am and 3.20pm, whilst on Thursdays only there was an additional run from there at 7.30pm and on Saturdays one hour later instead. The route took in Crux Easton, Woodcott, Binley and Stoke, all places not served by any other operator.

The service was duly licensed under the 1930 Act, and by March 1932 the operations show that a bus left St. Mary Bourne at 9am on Tuesdays, Thursdays and Saturdays and reached Newbury at 9.50am, where it formed the 10.20 departure to Andover, which it

reached at 11.30am, again by the back-roads route via Wyke, Finkley and Smannell, all settlements not otherwise served. The section between St. Mary Bourne and Andover also ran on Mondays but started from the base in the village and omitted the earlier journey into Newbury. On Tuesdays, Thursdays and Saturdays the bus then returned from Andover at 12.45pm, arriving at Newbury at 1.50pm. On Tuesdays and Thursday it left for St. Mary Bourne at 3.15pm, but on Saturdays that journey ran through to reach Andover at 4.25pm, where it turned and reached Newbury again at 5.50pm, with another layover until forming the 7.10pm departure on Tuesdays and Thursdays. On Saturday an additional bus left Andover at 6.15pm, returning from Newbury at 8.45 to reach Andover at 9.45pm, from where it returned as dead mileage.

By September 1936 a weekdays service from St. Mary Bourne to Andover, but running by way of Stoke – Hurstbourne Tarrant – Enham was also in operation.

The little Chevrolets continued in use through to 1938, when they were replaced by a pair of secondhand Bedford WLB-types, JG 4856 and HB 4788, new in 1934 and 1935 to operators in Canterbury, Kent and near Methyr Tydfil in Wales.

The active partnership between father and son continued through to 1941, when *Henry* retired, passing away in 1951 at the age of 84. *Oliver* ran the business, which continued in similar fashion and even saw additional journeys added postwar, particularly between St. Mary Bourne and Andover earlier in the mornings. By November 1946 there was also a service between Hurstbourne Tarrant and Whitchurch by way of Stoke and St. Mary Bourne, though the service to Andover via Hurstbourne Tarrant had ceased by then. They were also contracted to carry schoolchildren to secondary school from the villages on behalf of the Education Committee of Hampshire County Council.

The fairly long layovers at Newbury continued to feature for many years, so it was a common sight to see the *Pioneer* Bedford, of which there were a succession of OWB, OB and SB-types, parked over by the side of The Wharf bus station. *Oliver* continued with the bus operation through to April 1969, when he retired, the service having run for practically 50 years! He duly moved to the New Forest and died in June 1986 at the age of 90.

Newbury & Andover Motor Co. Ltd.

The first provision of an actual bus service was by the *Newbury & Andover Motor Co. Ltd.,* which was set up by a number of non-local business men and had a registered office at 277 Regent Street in London. Their local base was quoted as Hillview Works in Hurstbourne Tarrant, the 'long overdue' service commencing on Wednesday 30th June 1920. The buses ran every 2 hours, setting out from both the Andover and Newbury ends at 8am, and continued running through until 8pm each evening. The service ran through Wash Common – Highclere – Three Legged Cross – Hurstbourne Tarrant – Enham Alamein, whilst it also ran 'nearby' the communities of Ashmansworth, Stoke, Vernham Dean, Faccombe and Woodhay, and the Company was keen to point out that the fare of 2 shillings and 6 pence compared very favourably with the third-class rail fare of 3 shillings. The bus also took only half the time that the journey would do if undertaken by rail. However, it soon became the subject of letters in the Newbury Weekly News that the 1 shilling and 6 pence charged between Newbury and Wash Common was regarded as too expensive by residents. To be fair to the operator, seating was quite limited and the priority was for through passengers, though it responded to these comments by intimating that a local service might be developed in due course.

Indeed, in contrast to the initial publicity that had referred to 'Daimler saloon buses', the actual vehicles used were all rather small in size. The initial vehicles were a pair of Siddeley-Deasey car chassis, fitted with Daimler sleeve-valve Silent Knight engines, and re-bodied as 12-seater buses (DP 3099/3100). That they were registered in Reading may suggest that these were supplied and bodied by William Vincent of that town, as the bodies are similar to others by that firm. The type of chassis had been used during WW1 as the basis for ambulances, possibly the origins of these?

Newbury & Andover Siddeley-Deasey bus DP 3100.

Additional vehicles were an Albion (HO 2951) fitted with a 17-seater bus body and an ex-WD Austin 20hp fitted with a 12-seater bus body (HO 2978), both of which came into use in February 1921. There was also a Ford 1-tonner with a 12-seater bus added in April 1921 (HO 6949), which was transferred to the associated *Newbury & Hants Motor Omnibuses*, but this was a matter of re-distribution of shareholdings rather than an operating entity. These three vehicles carried a blue livery, which may have also been the case with the initial pair used, but Reading BC motor tax records are incomplete for that period.

The Company also sold vehicles from its base at the Hillview Works, and during September 1920 it was offering 2 and 4-seater open cars, landaulettes, as well as lorries, all 'at bargain prices'.

Although the *Newbury & Andover Motor Co. Ltd.* was still operating, by May 1921 it is evident that *Vic White* had acquired a double-deck bus seating 32. The identity of this vehicle is not known, but he advertised an excursion on Tuesday 31st May from The Broadway in Newbury to the West & Southern Counties Agricultural Show at Bristol, the vehicle leaving at 8am at a return fare of 15 shillings, and tickets could be obtained from the agent Tufnail.

A further advert appeared on 26th May offering the same vehicle for outings for 'a good view of the countryside', though with double-deck vehicles a rarity in the area, routes would need to be carefully chosen to avoid low trees and other obstacles such as railway bridges!

Nonetheless, he also advertised a further excursion for Wednesday 8th June, this time to Bournemouth for the Royal Agricultural Show. On this occasion the vehicle left from Newbury Market Place at 6.30am and for a return fare of 18 shillings. These charges were higher than the comparable charabanc trips that were starting to run locally, so take up may not have come up to his expectations, and no more adverts were forthcoming.

That *White* had acquired such a vehicle begs the question as to whether he had an inkling that the *Newbury & Andover* service might not continue, as certainly there were those who found their fares too high, and he would also have heard any relevant comments from his many local contacts.

Quite how the *N&A* buses fared is difficult to gauge, as the Company did state that numbers of users were high, whilst also pointing out that 'the inclement weather had made joy-riding less popular'. As Andrew Waller pointed out in an article delving further into this operator, it is not clear quite why these investors should see this venture as potentially worthwhile, and of course the vehicles used could never have generated much in fares. What is evident is that the ending of the *Newbury & Andover* service, stated at the time to be a 'temporary suspension', from a notice issued in the Newbury Weekly News on 23rd June 1921, was the springboard for *White* (and indeed others) to fill the void.

Ralph George Iles

Ralph Iles responded to both the needs of the residents of West Woodhay and those in the Wash Common area by providing a service, which is fully detailed under the *Denham Bros.* chapter. The appetite of the latter for a motor service had been alerted by the *N&A*

venture, although most had not used it due to the high cost and limited seating capacity.

White, on the other hand, was already experienced over the full route, though it should be appreciated that the carrier's service actually continued separately to the development of the bus service. The latter commenced on Saturday 2nd July 1921, presumably using the double-decker mentioned above. This daily service was entitled the *Hurstbourne Tarrant Motor Service*, with buses leaving Andover at 10am and 2pm, returning from Newbury at 12noon and 4pm. On Thursdays, Fridays and Saturdays there was an additional bus from Newbury at 8am and also from Andover at 6pm which ran short to Hurstbourne Tarrant, where the bus was kept.

Some changes to the service were made from Monday 25th July 1921, with the service reduced to run on Monday, Tuesdays, Thursdays and Saturdays only, at slightly different timings but still the same number of journeys. White also pointed out that his bus called at the railway stations at both Newbury and Andover Junction.

Lewis Austin Horne

Interest in a bus service had also been forthcoming from within Andover, and on Thursday 21st July 1921 the buses of *Lewis Austin Horne* of 103 High Street, Andover commenced operation. His service also ran Mondays, Tuesdays, Thursdays and Saturdays only, with 3 return journeys over the whole route, leaving Andover at 9am, 1.30pm and 6.15pm and returning from Newbury at 11am, 4.15pm and 8.15pm, using the Market Place as the terminus in Newbury. This *Andover & Newbury Bus Service* was amended slightly from Monday 3rd October, though Horne made the point that his 7.30pm departure from Newbury ran through to Andover, whereas *Vic White's* only went as far as Hurstbourne Tarrant.

Below and opposite – two views of Lewis Horne's Thornycroft all-weather coach OT 7731, known as The Pride of Andover. Note the rear end arrangement and canvas roof which could be un-buttoned in good weather, along with the spare wheel on stored under the near side of this 'Don' type body.

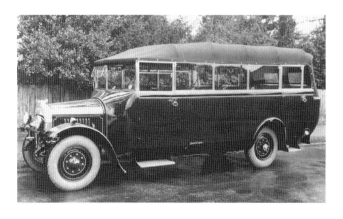

Horne had been born at Wherwell in 1889, this hamlet being some 3 miles south of Andover. By 1901 the family was only a short way east of there at Newton Stacey. They had relocated again by 1911, to the estate at Bransbury (near Barton Stacey), Lewis's father being the water bailiff on the River Dever, his brother Alfred as a groom and, rather more significantly, himself now as a 'motor car driver domestic' (i.e. chauffeur).

Horne's Thornycroft A2Long-type saloon bus OU 3610, fitted with an 'Emerald' type 20-seater body in blue and cream livery.

Lewis Horne used a smaller, but no doubt faster, 14-seater bus, which was a Ford 1-tonner, painted green and registered as HO 7295 for commencement of the service. A Fiat bus registered HO 8804 joined this in April 1922, and these sustained the operation through to 1926, when they were replaced by OT 595, a Chevrolet new in March, along with an A1-type Thornycroft 20-seater (OT 943) in April. The latter was the first of a succession of that make, used for both bus and coach duties up to April 1932, these being an A1Long-type new in March 1927 with a 20-seater bus body (OT 4036), an A2Long-type 20-seater coach new in March 1928 (OT 7731), an A6 with coach body (OU 943) in February 1929, along with another A2Long bus (OU 3610) in October 1929. There was also another Chevrolet, a U-type 14-seater new in May 1930 (OU 5679). The livery duly became blue and cream and a fleetname of *Pride of Andover* was also adopted.

Victor White's original Scout van had served him well, and it was still in daily use in February 1921. On the bus service, the double-decker proved rather slow and expensive to operate and was in need of replacement, so he put a new Ford Model T on the road in January 1922. This was BL 9512 and had a 14-seater bus body which was painted grey. After this arrived the operation was referred to as the *Grey Bus Service*, and operations continued as before and until the next major events on the Andover road.

Lewis Horne decided to refine his workings from Monday 7th May 1923, in order to provide different levels of service on different days. He also added a bus from Andover to Hurstbourne Tarrant, Upton and Vernham Dean, which ran on Fridays only. A Sunday service was also added, with 2 return journeys each way between Andover and Newbury, though this ran only throughout the Summer until 16th September.

Frank Holt

The driver for *White* for some time had been *Frank Holt*, who also lived at Hurstbourne Tarrant and married about this time. He had decided to set up an alternative bus service between Andover and Newbury from the third week of May 1923. Details of his vehicle have not come to light, but by 1931 he was also advertising a coach for hire.

Victor White placed an announcement in the Newbury Weekly News on 31st May pointing out that there was no connection between his service and that of his former driver! He also brought the 9.15am journey from Hurstbourne Tarrant to Newbury forward to run at 9am, whilst reducing his fares as well. However, *Frank Holt* was not that easily defeated, so the services on the Andover road settled down to those of *Holt, Horne and White*, though the latter pair did not really compete with each other as their clientele had allegiance to their respective local areas.

Great Western Railway

September 1929 timetable for Newbury – Highclere service on weekdays (Saturdays only):*

Stopping place	a.m.	a.m.	p.m.	p.m.	p.m.	p.m.
Newbury (Station)	7.25	10.15	1.45	4.10	7.05	9.00*
Wash Common	7.33	10.23	1.53	4.18	7.13	9.08*
Derby Arms Inn	7.38	10.28	1.58	4.23	7.18	9.13*
Woodhay (S'tion)	7.41	10.31	2.01	4.26	7.21	9.16*
Woolton Hill Sch.	7.46	10.36	2.06	4.31	7.26	9.21*
Highclere	7.54	10.44	2.14	4.39	7.34	9.29*
Highclere	8.00	10.50	2.15	4.40	7.36	9.30*
Woolton Hill Sch.	8.08	10.58	2.23	4.48	7.44	9.38*
Woodhay (S'tion)	8.13	11.03	2.28	4.53	7.49	9.43*
Derby Arms Inn	8.16	11.06	2.31	4.56	7.52	9.40*
Wash Common	8.21	11.11	2.36	5.01	7.57	9.51*
Newbury (Station)	8.29	11.19	2.44	5.09	8.05	9.59*

Buses also depart from Newbury on Sundays at 11.05a.m., 3.00p.m., 6.20p.m. and 8.30p.m.

Former Great Western Railway No. 1468 (YX 5680), a 1928 Thornycroft A1-type with 18-seater body, seen on collection by Thames Valley at Highclere.

Also appearing on the Newbury to Andover road from 20th June 1927 were the Road Motors of the *Great Western Railway*. The intense competition with *Denham Bros.* over local passengers on the Newbury – Wash Common - Highclere section is dealt with elsewhere, though of course the rest of the route lay outside the area served by *Denhams. Lewis Horne* also put up a good fight by varying his journeys to suit the locals, whereas the *GWR* was inclined to suit themselves in respect of timetables.

From 28th February 1929 the route was cut back to just Newbury – Highclere, which was worked by one Thornycroft A-type single-decker that also covered the Newbury – Newtown and Newbury – Stockcross services in a dove-tailed timetable. That was still the case when the railway company handed the surviving services in the area over to *Thames Valley* in September 1931.

No doubt in view of a rumour of a new bus service to cover the route, *Lewis Horne* found it necessary to announce in the Newbury Weekly News on 15th May 1930 that his service was to continue. He also added that the revised timetable being prepared would include journeys on Wednesdays and Sundays.

Wilts & Dorset Motor Services Ltd.

Indeed, his concerns were soon realised, when on 5th June 1930 the Salisbury-based territorial operator *Wilts & Dorset Motor Services Ltd.* announced that it was commencing a bus service over the 35 miles between Newbury and Romsey by way of Andover and Stockbridge, with connections possible to Salisbury and Southampton. Leyland 'Lion' LT1 saloons were used for this route, with buses departing Romsey at 9am (not on Sundays), 1pm and 5pm, and from Newbury at 11am (except Sundays), 3pm and 7.30pm, as well as a bus from Andover to Newbury at 9.30pm on Saturdays only.

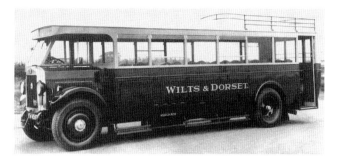

Leyland 'Lion' LT1-type No.69 (MW 4597) of the type used on the Andover to Newbury service. Note the large roof-mounted luggage carrier reached by the conductor using a ladder at the rear. The bus was new in 1929 and the livery was deep red and white.

Lewis Horne reacted to this new intruder with an enhanced service from Monday 16th June 1930, and his approach was to offer different levels of service based on key days of the week. Buses left Andover on Mondays, Tuesdays, Thursdays and Saturdays at 9am, 9.45am, 12.30pm, 1.45pm, 5pm and 6pm (and 7pm on Saturdays), with buses from Newbury at 8.30am, 10.45am, 12noon, 2.45pm, 3.30pm, 6.15pm and 7.30pm (and 8pm on Saturdays). On Fridays the buses left Andover at 9am, 9.45am, 1.45pm, 3.30pm and 5.45pm, returning from Newbury at 10.45am, 12noon, 2.45pm, 6pm and 7.20pm. Wednesdays saw less activity, with buses from Andover at 9.45am, 1.45pm and 5.45pm, returning from Newbury at 10.45am, 2.45pm and 7.20pm. The Sunday service consisted of journeys from Andover at 9.45am and 1.45pm, returning from Newbury at 10.45am and 2.45pm. With this improved service, *Lewis Horne* was able to hold his own against that level of competition.

There is no record of any initiatives by *Victor White* during this period of competition from *Wilts & Dorset*, but it might be that he managed to retain the loyalty of his customers, based largely as they were in his home village of Hurstbourne Tarrant.

On the other hand *Frank Holt*, had less resources at his disposal and seems to have felt the pinch. He was now running as Vernham Dean – Hurstbourne Tarrant – Andover, and was largely sustained by a schools contract he ran on behalf of Hampshire County Council, along with some private hire work. However, *Wilts & Dorset* felt it worth eliminating him from the equation, so it offered him £50 for the goodwill of his service and the school contract, along with a job as driver at £3 per week, which he accepted with effect from 1st January 1931.

With the passage of the 1930 Road Traffic Act *Wilts & Dorset* was also granted a license for the Andover – Newbury route, along with *Lewis Horne* after the initial license hearings of 1931, when he was granted licenses for both the route between Andover and Newbury via the main road, along with journeys deviating via Ashmansworth (as *Vic White* had also done), along with some journeys between Andover and Vernham Dean.

On the other hand *Victor White*, who was now living at 'Rosemore', Northfield Road in Thatcham and was around 56 years old, initially applied for a Road Service License, but subsequently withdrew the application before it was determined. Although his service did appear in the March 1932 local transport guide this was in error, as no license was in place. Vic died in 1946 aged 71, one of the pioneer motorised carriers of the Newbury area, but more often recalled for the sight of his little grey Ford speeding down the local hills, along with his habit of driving with one arm horizontally across the steering wheel! Also worthy of note is that his daughter Eleanor married in the year of his death, to Tony Aldworth, one of the *Newbury & District* drivers.

After the 1930 Act had come into force, territorial concerns such as *Wilts & Dorset* could no longer use some of the dubious tactics of earlier days to remove competition, so they reached for the cheque book instead, supported as they were by railway money.

Lewis Horne had noted the increase in journeys of the *Wilts & Dorset* service, along with additional journeys on peak days, and was now feeling it was time to sell up. So, on 13th April 1932 he sold his bus operations to that operator, though he continued as a local coach operator for many more years. He lived to age 78 and died in 1968.

And so the Andover to Newbury road now became the sole province of the *Wilts & Dorset* buses on Route 12 and, although various other operators ranged out from Newbury to serve specific villages, along with passing through the growing area of Wash Common, no others chose to operate a service linking those two towns on a daily basis. Even so, it found after experience that a different level of service was advisable on different days of the week, something the local operators had known all along.

The Wilts & Dorset Newbury to Andover timetable at March 1932 (a – Thursdays, Fridays and Saturdays, b – not on Sundays, k – Saturdays and Sundays only):

Departures from Andover –
8.00a.m., 9.30a.m (b), 11.30a.m., 1.30p.m., 2.30p.m. (a), 3.30p.m. (a), 4.30p.m. 5.30p.m. (a), 6.30p.m. and 8.30p.m. (k)

Departures from Newbury Wharf –
9.00a.m., 10.30a.m. (b), 2.30p.m. (a), 3.30p.pm., 4.50p.m. (a), 5.30p.m., 6.30p.m. (a), 8.30p.m. and 9.30p.m. (k)

The journey time Newbury – Andover was 55 minutes

Chapter 4 –
J. C. Durnford & Sons

John Charles Durnford was born on 20th October 1884 at Bottlesford, a hamlet near Woodborough, between Pewsey and Devizes in rural Wiltshire. By the age of 16 was he employed as a Milker on a local farm, living at The Sands, Woodborough with his parents. His father was a Carpenter, and his brother Leonard George ('George') Durnford followed that trade, and we shall hear more of him in due course.

There is little doubt that 'Charlie's' life in the milking barns was a hard one, so seeing the passing trains of the nearby Great Western Railway must have surely tempted him to extend his horizons. Added to that, the Edwardian era saw motor vehicles appearing more widely, though they were still very much the preserve of the rich.

The hiring of cowmen and shepherds still followed the age-old pattern of the annual fairs, meaning that the family moved on to another tied cottage most years. Certainly, with a growing family, a change of career beckoned him to forsake such rural drudgery and he duly made his way to Reading, where trained at the pioneering Motor Engineers *William Vincent* in Castle Street. That firm had originally been Coachbuilders, and this continued throughout the developing motor age. They were also Jobmasters, hiring out everything from hackney taxis to 32-seater charabancs, all of which they were in the forefront of replacing with the motorised variety, which no doubt also planted seeds in Charlie's mind.

His training there would certainly be the bedrock of future enterprises, as it should be noted that the operation of early motor vehicles was not for the faint-hearted and a sound mechanical knowledge was an essential pre-requisite to success!

In the meantime he married Inkpen-born Annie Maria May in the Summer of 1905. The couple had 5 children (Leonard Charles 1906, William George 1907, Henry Albert 1908, Ernest Anthony 1912 and Olive Kate 1915), which would all be important building blocks for future business developments. In 1911 the family were living at Haremoor Farm, just east of Faringdon, which was then still in Berkshire, though the first three sons were born in Shaw, Tidmarsh and Reading respectively. He was then still a cowman, whilst the fourth son was born at Cookham, where he had relocated to work at Spencers Farm, part of the estate of local MP Ernest Gardner, by February 1912. Their daughter Olive was born at The Pit in Sonning in August 1915, where the staff of the Holmes Park Estate of local JP John Martin Sutton resided. There he was employed as chauffeur, indicating that his training with motor vehicles had

taken place between 1912 and 1915. This was, however, the time when this large estate, which also took in large areas of Woodley, was being sold off.

Whatever the precise order of events, Charlie had certainly learnt to drive in the process (in 1909 according to his later testament), and he moved on to become chauffeur to Dr. Little of Midgham Cottage, situated just north of Woolhampton on the Bath Road between Reading and Newbury. The first evidence of Charlie living at Midgham Green (where Hunts Cottages now stand) comes in March 1917, though he may have gone to his new post prior to then. At Midgham Cottage there were in fact two 'Dr. Littles', with Colonel Charles Colhoun Little, retired from a lifetime's service in the Madras Medical Service and was resident at Midgham by 1911, along with his son Major George Charles Colhoun Little, who had followed a similar career. The latter entered the service in 1908 but was invalided out in 1920, and pre-deceased his father in May 1921. The elder one died in April 1924, though by then he was in a nursing home in Hove, Sussex. Charlie sold a Studebaker 12-14hp 2-seater on behalf of his employer in June 1920.

In the meantime, by 1907, Charlie's brother 'George' had moved up to Newbury, and by the outbreak of the First World War he was employed as a Joiner at Elliott's of Newbury. These skills were transferred to the Royal Aircraft Factory, and he even saw some service in France maintaining the wood-and-wire aeroplanes of that era. Later he become a local builder and, with the assistance of his wife and son opened a Greengrocer's shop at 9 Cheap Street. By 1911 his residence was 29 Railway Road, whilst at No.31 there were other Durnford relatives from the same Wiltshire family, so all of this would no doubt influence the focus for future events relating to Charlie.

Charlie's younger brother Percy had also left Wiltshire and become a Boilermaker at the works of the South East & Chatham Railway in Ashford, Kent. Although this brother served throughout the whole of the Great War as a Sapper in the Royal Engineers, there are no traces of military service in respect of Charlie. Family sources have mentioned that one of Charlie's brothers later came to Newbury and worked with him, which was possibly Percy.

We also hear of Charlie in March 1917, when he offered a refurbished Swift gent's cycle in the For Sale columns of the Newbury Weekly News, followed by a motor cycle in August of that year. A quartet of cycles followed during 1918, plus a further trio in 1919. In December of that year he offered his 'Ideal Anthracite Stove, patent applied for'. An Imperial JAP 2.75hp motorcycle, complete with 2-speed counter-shaft gears and TT handlebars, was offered for sale in January 1920, along with a similar capacity Royal Ruby motorcycle. A further step up in scale occurred with the offer of an overhauled Ford Model T delivery van in February. The latter vehicle may also assist in resolving the claim sometimes made by Charlie that his haulage business had commenced earlier than other evidence has substantiated, assuming that his comment that 'the owner has no further use for it' actually refers to him?

Whether the above projects constituted his full-time occupation, or were merely a sideline to working as a chauffeur, it was nonetheless part of Charlie's plan to save up to buy his first motor lorry in order to establish a haulage business. Despite the availability of large numbers of ex-War Department vehicles for sale at that time, he opted to purchase a new Commer WP3 in June 1920. This was a 22hp model fitted with a drop-side lorry body, painted grey and registered in the Berkshire CC Heavy Motor Car Series as BL 0336. It is quite possible that he was attracted by a tempting hire-purchase deal, as many manufacturers used this to counter falling sales caused by the flood of ex-Great War chassis.

The Newbury area offered quite wide scope for haulage work, though much of it was seasonal and followed the harvest cycle. However, Charlie had already noted that the area was rich in gravel beds from the valley of the River Kennet, and also there were a number of brick and tile producers in the area. The latter work was very hard labour, all loaded and unloaded by hand, some being transported locally and more transferring to rail at Newbury Station. The products of the Curridge Brick & Tile Works regularly took that route, whilst backloads from the London Brick Company were sometimes carried when such bricks were specified locally.

It seems that Charlie also soon realised the possibilities for passenger transport, and during June, July and August 1920 he advertised that his 25-seater lorry-charabanc would undertake a number of excursions, the vehicle being fitted with bench seats and a canvas top for this purpose. Whilst such lack of comfort might seem to us now to be severe, it should be appreciated that no one else in the Newbury area was offering anything better of that capacity, so these relatively infrequent opportunities to undertake such excursions were seized upon by a public hungry to shake off the wartime years! At that point only *Walter Stoneham* had a full-size lorry-chara available in Newbury, in the shape of his ex-WD Thornycroft J-type, whilst *Doug Houghton* of Donnington also undertook a few trips using his 30-seater, including picking up passengers in Newbury.

Prior to the coastal excursions, he had already received requests to transport local football teams etc., so the progression to excursions was a logical (though nonetheless brave) step to take. The first of those Summer months saw the Commer travel to Southsea, which was developing as a particular attraction for charabanc day-trippers, with its large fun fair and convenient seaside parking area. Such a journey started out from The Broadway in Newbury at 7.30am, and there were real issues of whether the trip would be accomplished successfully, the excitement (together with some apprehension) being shared by passengers and driver alike!

In these days of high-speed motorway travel it is not easy to contemplate setting off for the 60-mile trip to Southsea, on a solid-tyred 3-ton lorry chassis, and with a legal speed limit of 12 miles per hour! These trips included a 'comfort stop', which also gave the engine a chance to cool down. Such stops duly developed into road houses or breathed new life into old halts, the popular ones often situated before the vehicle tackled a substantial hill climb, such as Petersfield and the South Downs. For trips to Southsea and Bournemouth the first hazard was quite near to home, with 'White Shute' over the Hampshire Downs south of Whitway. At that time the road surface was not metalled, so the chalk surface became rutted, resulting in unwary drivers getting stuck. In Charlie's case, the skill was to pick a line which would not endanger the chain-drive of the Commer, and he is credited with being the first Newbury operator to put a full-size 'chara' over that obstacle.

Trips to Bournemouth (at 66 miles) and Brighton (85 miles each way) followed, and these left at 7am, the former sharing the same hazard as the Southsea run, whereas the trip to the Sussex coast meant crossing the South Downs at some point. Most of these trips gave 5-6 hours in the resort, the charas usually leaving at 5pm, so hopefully everyone was home by dark! Bookings for these trips could be made at Mr. Wheeler's Cycle Shop in The Broadway, Newbury, which is where the vehicle left from, the Southsea excursion costing 8 shillings and 6 pence.

Other excursions in that first season were to more local destinations, such as London's Hyde Park or Regent's Park (for the Zoo), or to specific annual events such as Ascot Races and Henley Regatta, plus a couple of full-day or afternoon tours to the New Forest or Berkshire Downs. The significance of half-day tours (often with a tea stop) was that most shop workers then enjoyed an early-closing day, Wednesday in the case of Newbury, which gave a rare opportunity to get out of the area on a weekday.

It should also be noted that, with so little annual holiday for those in work, many people channelled their leisure activities into clubs or groups of one kind or another. Therefore, the annual outings organised by such bodies, from the Women's Institute and Sunday Schools through to local pubs and Social Clubs, were very popular and provided a steady stream of private hire work. Some of these outings were sedate and sober affairs, whereas others were accompanied by crates of beer, resulting in the need for additional road-side 'comfort stops' which did nothing to endear charabanc parties to the Authorities!

Charlie also advertised that from 27th August 1920 he would run the lorry-chara from Woolhampton to Newbury on Thursdays, this excursion being intended for market-day shoppers. He also offered to carry parcels etc., but how long this continued for is unknown. The other aspect of work which Charlie sought was that of house removals, with only Stoneham, Camp Hopson and Windsor & Neate already active in Newbury. Camp Hopson were of course the proprietors of the large department store in Northbrook Street, who used their large box-van lorry for household removals, whilst they were also local undertakers. Windsor & Neate were furniture dealers who also dealt with removals, especially those requiring onward shipment, though still hauled by steam wagons until an ex-WD Austin arrived.

Walter Ronald Stoneham

Walter Stoneham was, on the other hand, more typical of the new entrants to the transport world, being an ex-serviceman and initially using former Great War lorries. He had been born at Lee in Kent in 1895, and was driving his father Edward's removals lorry before the war started. He frequently travelled through Newbury, lodging with the Kimbers at West Street, which led to him marrying Bertha Kimber on Christmas Day 1915. In April 1916 he enlisted in the Army Service Corps and was sent to Wilton in Wiltshire, spending the war allocated to 650 Mechanical Transport Company, being demobbed in May 1919, by which time he was Acting Sergeant.

His transport venture is first noted 17th June 1919, initially with an ex-WD Karrier 3-tonner, which he kept at The Pelican Garage in London Road, his private address being at 10 Waterloo Terrace in West Street. Further large vehicles were Thornycroft J-types, the first originally laid down under war production and direct from the Thornycroft factory in early 1920 and bearing a lorry-bus conversion of the standard military body. It carried a registration in the HO series allocated by the maker's, whereas that was followed by another ex-WD J-type (BL 8658) in July 1921, which had a canvas-covered goods body and the standard WD pattern canopy over the cab.

By November 1922 he was offering 1 to 4-ton box van lorries for hire, the old lorry-bus body now having been replaced or modified. The 1-tonner was evidently a Buick van that he advertised for disposal in July 1923, the identity of which is not known, though no doubt another former military vehicle. He continued his passenger business with a 14-seater pneumatic-tyred charabanc of unknown specifications

Stoneham's Thornycroft J-type lorry-bus in 1920.

for the 1922 season, whilst also being the local booking agent for *Thames Valley* excursions! However, passenger carrying ceased after 1923, until a brief return in the 1930 season with a 20-seater Berliet coach named *The Broadway*. It would seem that the passing of the 1930 Act persuaded him to stick to the goods side, along with his secondhand furniture business, continued from The Broadway, until 1954, and he died at Newbury in 1960 aged 65.

****

In respect of road developments, it should be appreciated that a significant boost to the standard of trunk roads, such as the Bath Road and the Oxford to Southampton route, came in the early 1920's when the War Office allowed reparation claims from Highway Authorities to redress the damage done by heavy wartime convoys. As a result of this many roads were metalled over for the first time, which had an important part to play in the rapid development of road passenger transport during that decade. Time spent at seaside coach parks also provided the opportunity to see other types of vehicle and discuss their pro and cons with drivers. This was an important, and often overlooked, network which boosted sales of some makes more than any advertising campaign might have done!

The first of the Daimler charas BL 7936 at Southsea, with Charlie at the wheel and one of the sons in front.

Having established that passenger excursions would be a good direction for expansion, Charlie set about eclipsing the limited local opposition for the 1921 season by obtaining a pair of ex-WD 30hp Daimler chassis, each of which was fitted with proper charabanc bodies, albeit secondhand. The first to be registered was BL 7936, a CC-type built in 1912, which initially took to the road in December 1920 with a grey-liveried van body and could also be fitted with a 28-seater charabanc body when required. This was followed by BL 8804, a slightly shorter-wheelbase B-type of 1914 vintage, which had alternative grey-painted lorry and 25-seater charabanc bodies, which was ready in May 1921. On the removals front, *Durnfords* were able to advise clients that, as they were insured for passengers, they could ride with their property and save the rail fare! He also included a few 'digs' at *Stoneham*, stating that he was using luxury Daimler charas, whereas *Stoneham* fielded his Thornycroft J-type lorry-bus once again. Although the latter did later purchase a 14-seater during 1922, he did expand in that direction.

The second Daimler chara BL 8804 on an outing to Bournemouth, with Charlie Durnford standing just behind the windscreen.

Such expansion did not, however, suit the other residents of Midgham Green, leading to a visit from PC Gallop. Someone had alerted the constable to the fact that Charlie was storing petrol in his house, and sure enough the policeman found 26 2-gallon cans of petrol in his larder! This was something for which a license, along with more appropriate storage, was required, but Charlie stated that 10 of the cans were being stored for his employer Dr. Little, which would indicate that he still also driving for him. However, the court thought little of that and fined Charlie £1, though one suspects that the true target of the complaint was his lorries being parked on the green.

From January 1921 the title *Midgham Haulage Charabanc Co.* was in use, but for the 1921 season the charabanc starting point was moved to the Black Boys Inn at 62 Bartholomew Street. An advert for April was also the first to state *'Durnford & Sons'*, as each of the 4 sons joined the business as soon as they were old enough, taking up driving from when they reached the appropriate age. It must be appreciated that Charlie is recalled as a 'tough little character', and there is no doubt from interviews with the sons that he worked them harder than he could reasonably have expected

from any hired staff! When one reviews his numerous adverts listing recent removals jobs, along with the excursion work, long driving hours and day after day of hard work that was put in by the sons is readily apparent. However, as some consolation they probably had less to worry about unemployment that many of their fellow countrymen as the depression years wore on. Charlie did, however, also have a softer side, and would sometimes let his poorer clients bring their youngsters along on seaside trips without charge, as long as they sat on laps. He also later introduced a 'tourist club', whereby clients could pay in money when they could and then use the funds to book seats.

With expansion now in progress, the issue of a more appropriate base was brought to the fore. On the last day of June 1921 a notice appeared in the NWN advising that *'C. Durnford & Sons*, Removal & Pleasure Outing Contractors, and *Maynard Bros.*, Woolhampton, Motor & General Engineers, beg to announce that they have formed a Company. A garage will shortly be opened on the Bath Road, Thatcham, where turning, overhauling, and work of every description will be carried out under guarantee of satisfaction, both at Woolhampton and Thatcham. We also expect delivery of a first class charabanc at an early date'. However, exactly 3 months later, *Maynards* placed a notice in the NWN, informing enquirers that the proposed merger with *Durnfords* had not gone ahead. *Maynards* did continue with their garage business in Woolhampton and even added charabanc operation from the Summer of 1924, which they continued to offer through to 1930. Despite the abortive merger, good relations must have endured, as in due course *Durnfords* would regularly hire-in *Maynards* vehicle when more capacity was required. Charlie always preferred to hire-in from them, and also *Arthur Bason* of Woolhampton or *Eddie Keep* of Burghfield Common rather than turn away a job.

Cyril Maynard's dark red-painted Garford MO 6228 was often hired in to help out at busy times.

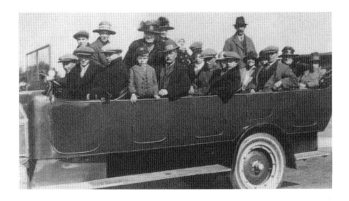

The search for new premises did, however, continue with a postscript to the excursions advert in July 1921 seeking a cottage in Thatcham or Newbury. The Midgham Green address remained in use, but by September 1921 Charlie was using the term Benham

Hill Garage for his base, along with the *Newbury Haulage Charabanc Co. & Gravel Merchants*. For the latter he was supplying gravel from that location at 1 shilling a cubic yard, inclusive of delivery anywhere in the Newbury district. For December 1921 an address of 'Thatcham Road, Newbury' was in use, though such a location does not exist, this being the stretch of the Bath Road between Thatcham and Newbury also known as Benham Hill. His base was south of the main road and on a backlands plot reached by a track, and beyond a cottage and garage was his gravel deposit which stretched down towards Lower Way. By then the charge for gravel had been slashed in half to just 6 pence per cubic yard!

The year 1921 had been a good one for both the haulage and passenger aspects of the business, making the resolution of the premises issue even more pressing. No doubt with some assistance from his Newbury-based relatives, a suitable premises was identified in early 1922 at 16/17 Market Street, with a open parking ground behind, this being adjacent to the Cattle Market. The on-street premises comprised a shop frontage on the lower floor used as offices, whilst a separate doorway led up to the living accommodation above. Charlie's wife Annie took the bookings whilst Olive was at school, and the latter joined her in due course, both looking after the office side, making it a real family affair. Olive duly married Stan Minchin in 1940, a former *Andrew's* coach driver who continued with *N&D*.

Hallford charabanc CR 4021 arriving at Southsea.

With a base in Newbury at last, further developments took place in 1922, with the acquisition of 2 further charabancs towards the end of May. One was a 1912 chain-driven Hallford EA-type, which after War Service had been re-registered as CR 4021 in 1919 by *Robert Leach* of Shirley, Southampton. He had run it with a light blue-liveried 30-seater charabanc body. The other vehicle was also a former WD chassis, which Charlie had purchased from the Slough Disposal Sales, this being a 1915 Dennis 3-tonner re-registered as MO 53 and fitted with a 20-seater charabanc body painted yellow whilst the chassis had red-painted wheels. From the Spring of this year the excursion advert referred to the *Newbury Charabanc Co.* Although it was not specifically mentioned in

contemporary adverts, the move to Market Street resulted in the excursions leaving from that point instead, perhaps with some additional local stops. It was also possible for passengers to leave their cycles safely at the office, whilst in July 1922 Charlie ran a trip to Savernake Forest, donating the day's proceeds to the Newbury Hospital Fund.

It should be noted that the *Durnford* fleet never achieved a standard livery as, although some new purchases were to a specific livery, other vehicles acquired were not routinely repainted. The grey originally used for the lorries and vans gave way to green by the mid-1920's. It is also evident that bodies from goods vehicles were often transferred onto replacement chassis where practical.

For the 1922 season the Daimlers came off passenger duties, with BL 7936 being sold at the end of April, whilst, BL 8804 went over to haulage duties. Of course, when not required for charabanc duties, the other chassis could also be found on haulage work. The supply of sand and gravel was further expanded by the offer to construct roads and paths by *Durnfords*, whilst Charlie had a personal sideline as a water-dowser and well-digger. He is also recalled for his neatly trimmed and waxed moustache!

However, Charlie would no doubt have noticed that the *Thames Valley Traction Co. Ltd.* also offered some charabanc excursions from Newbury during June and July, even running the Ascot Races trips from the famous racehorse village of Lambourn, some 13.7 miles north-west of Newbury. For these they even used *Stoneham* as the booking agent, but the venture met with little success, and they did not return the following season!

It is perhaps worth noting the relative merits of the early chassis selected by Charlie. As already noted, the Commer saw only a short career on passenger work, and that was a chain-driven type. The Hallford was also chain-driven, though evidently regarded as reliable. The Daimlers had the characteristic smooth-running engines, but they were only 30hp compared with the Hallford at 32hp. However, the Dennis 3-ton chassis had 40hp engines, making them the favoured choice for charabanc work.

As 1922 wore on it became apparent that there was quite a lot of trade that only warranted a 14-seater, so from August such a vehicle was on offer. This is believed to have been the Dennis, of a smaller model than previous examples, which had been re-registered in 1919 as MC 3937, this also being the first vehicle in the fleet on pneumatic tyres. The original motor tax details for this vehicle have not survived, but the chassis number indicates it was new c.1915 and probably a 30-cwt model, whilst the later registration would indicate that it had been used by the military.

Douglas Wilfred Houghton

As already noted, *Doug Houghton* had been operating as a haulage and charabanc contractor from his base at The Yews in Donnington, a short way north of Newbury, using American–built ex-WD FWD lorry (BL 0335) acquired by him in September 1920.

He had been born at Sutton Coldfield in 1882, and the family moved to Knapps Farm, Westbrook, near Boxford in 1885. In 1903 he emigrated to Canada with his grandparents, but he returned in 1905 and married his cousin Caroline Augusta ('Gussie') Houghton. They, with daughter Stella, his brother Frank and sister Delcie went back to Canada after 1906 to homestead in Saskatchewan returning yet again in 1913-4. After this he is believed to have seen military service, as his choice of vehicles would indicate prior experience of such types.

During 1921-2 he continued to advertise enclosed lorries for 3-5 tons, but by October 1922 *Charlie Durnford* had acquired the business. The FWD lorry had apparently already been disposed of, but this acquisition is believed to have been the origins of the ex-WD Maudslay 40hp A-type 30-seater charabanc which appeared about this time. The identity of this vehicle has not come to light, but this was a much heavier-built vehicle than the Dennis and Hallford, being capable of 5-ton loads when fitted with a box-van body, 'the heaviest lorry capacity in the District' as Charlie advertised it.

Houghton relocated to Thatcham by December 1922, from where he was disposing of another American-built wartime lorry, in this case a 3.5-ton Kelly-Springfield fitted with a large furniture van body for £180. After that he worked as an engineer and died at Hermitage in 1966.

****

The Dennis and Maudslay were used as lorries/vans on a regular basis, but the Hallford is not recorded with an alternative body or class of registration. Also, the disposal of the original Commer does not appear to have been recorded, though it did not feature on passenger work after that first pioneering season. Another regular feature of *Durnford's* extensive adverts in the Newbury Weekly News was the seeking of back-loads on certain dates, which offer another insight into how far the lorries travelled, with mentions of Basingstoke, Bournemouth, Bristol, London, Oxford and Portsmouth. Indeed, during the relatively quiet months of January and February, the following house removals were undertaken between the stated dates: January 29th 2 vans from Newbury - Basingstoke; 30th Bedwyn - Newbury; 31st Clapham - Newbury; February 1st Thame – Compton; 2nd Newbury – Highclere; 3rd Reading – Newbury; 5th

West Street (Newbury) – Speen and 6th Chieveley – Portsmouth, whilst amongst the printed testimonials were a Vicar and a Police Inspector (retired). *Stoneham* responded to these detailed ads with his own lists of removals jobs, and added a 'dig' that his lorries were 'only used for household goods, not brick-hauling as well'!

The 30-seater Maudslay on a Southsea excursion.

During September 1922 Charlie advertised the supply of bicycles fitted with Sturmey-Archer 3-speed gears, though there are no further mentions of this business. In November he advertised for sale a 1-ton van of unknown make, though whether this featured in the fleet or was just a re-sale project is not known.

For the 1923 season a further 2 Dennis 3-tonners were added. MO 1763 was another former WD example from the disposal sales, re-registered in June and fitted with a red-liveried 25-seater charabanc body, along with being taxed for goods use. The other was a 1919 civilian delivery, with the slightly lower bonnet line than specified by the military, which was registered EL 3769 and new to *T.R. Brooke* of Bournemouth, passing to *C. Pounds*, also of Bournemouth. As the latter had the fleetname *'Charlie's Cars'*, I wonder if *Charlie Durnford* was tempted just to change the address and phone number only on the rear? The livery of this vehicle was not recorded, but it was probably the scheme used by the previous owner, as it was not Charlie's usual practice to repaint vehicles. In early June 1923 an advert announced their 20-seat charabanc as the *Pride of Newbury,* a title used in the previous season by *Denham Bros.*

Dennis 3-tonner MO 3343 in its passenger guise.

During the Summer of 1923 *Durnford's* charabancs took 97 parties to the seaside, the advert adding that all such journeys had been accomplished successfully, whilst records show that up to 5 removals took place on one day alone. A twice-weekly Newbury to London carrier's service was also introduced during that year, along with two of *Durnford's* catch-phrases, those being 'we are moving every day' and 'we go to the seaside every day'. He also added that all drivers were strict abstainers on the road, a dig at some other charabanc drivers who laid the road-dust with a pint or two on the homeward run!

For 1924 the passenger fleet saw the addition of a 28-seater Leyland charabanc, acquired by May, but other details are not known. Then in June a further ex-WD sales 1915 3-ton Dennis was put on the road as MO 3343, carrying a cream-liveried 25-seater charabanc body, and also available for use as a removals van.

The Star 14-seater chara at the Esplanade, Southsea.

The worth of smaller vehicles was also acknowledged by the addition by July of a Star 50-cwt carrying a 14-seater body. This body was rather crudely constructed out of sections, rather than like a proper charabanc or coach, being fitted with only a front door and a canvas, demountable hood, this layout being termed a 'gangway charabanc'. The identity of this vehicle has not come to light, whilst the chassis type had featured

amongst those used during the Great War, which is where its origins may have lain? Despite its unattractive body, it remains the most photographed of the *Durnford* charas, so it was evidently kept busy, being transferred to goods work after a couple of seasons.

The Thornycroft J-type charabanc leaving Newbury.

For the 1925 season similar capacity charabancs were on offer, though there was no mention of the Leyland during this Summer, though it re-appears during the next year. However, from June a Thornycroft seating 28 is advertised, though this is not heard of in subsequent years, and was most likely a former WD lorry, perhaps transferred to haulage work as lighter 6-cylinder models came into the fleet?

The 1925 season was certainly a busy time for the fleet, so it is interesting to note the work undertaken by the charas, both for advertised excursions from Newbury and private hires from other locations between 1st July and 4th August:

Wednesday 1st July – Headley to Hayling Island – 3 charabancs;
Thursday 2nd July – Kintbury to Wembley – 1 charabanc, and Ramsdell to Donnington – 1 chara;
Friday 3rd July – Kintbury to Southsea – 6 charabancs;
Saturday 4th July – Shefford to Southsea, tour from Bucklebury via Basingstoke, Salisbury and Andover, Newbury to Southsea and Newbury to Crystal Palace – 1 charabanc on each;
Sunday 5th July – Newbury to Southsea and Bournemouth – 3 charabancs;
Monday 6th July – Kintbury to Southsea – 2 charas;
Tuesday 7th July – Stockcross to Wembley – 1 chara;
Wednesday 8th July – Chieveley to Southsea – 1 charabanc, and Newbury to Beacon Hill – 2 charabancs;
Friday 10th July – Brightwalton to Southsea – 2 charabancs;
Saturday 11th July – Winterbourne to Bournemouth – 1 chara, and Newbury to Southsea – 2 charabancs;
Sunday 12th July – Newbury to Bournemouth, Newbury to Southsea and Newbury to Pangbourne – 1 charabanc each;
Monday 13th July – Peasemore to Wembley – 1 chara;
Tuesday 14th July – Inkpen to Salisbury – 1 chara;

Wednesday 15th July – Newbury to Southsea, Headley to Southsea, Bucklebury to Southsea and Newbury to Woodhay – 1 charabanc on each;
Thursday 16th July – Curridge to Southsea – 1 chara;
Friday 17th July – Woolhampton to Southsea – 1 charabanc;
Saturday 18th July – Hermitage to Wembley – 2 charabancs, and Greenham to Bournemouth – 1 chara;
Sunday 19th July – Newbury to Bournemouth and Newbury to Southsea – 2 charabancs on each;
Monday 20th July – Newbury to Bournemouth – 2 charabancs;
Tuesday 21st July – Newbury to Calne – 1 charabanc;
Wednesday 22nd July – Headley to Bournemouth, Chilton Foliat to Bournemouth and Ecchinswell to Southsea – 1 charabanc on each;
Thursday 23rd July – Stockcross to Holyport – 1 chara;
Friday 24th July – Inkpen to London Zoo – 3 charas;
Saturday 25th July – Ecchinswell to Bournemouth – 2 charas, and Beenham and Newbury to Bournemouth – 1 charabanc;
Sunday 26th July – Hungerford to Southsea – 4 charas;
Monday 27th July – Elcot to Wembey and Stockcross to Savernake – 1 charabanc on each;
Tuesday 28th July – Kintbury to Bournemouth – 3 charabancs;
Wednesday 29th July – Woolhampton to Banbury – 1 charabanc;
Thursday 30th July – Kintbury to Savernake – 3 charas and Chieveley to Newbury – 1 charabanc;
Friday 31st July – Newbury to Godalming – 1 chara;
Saturday 1st August – Hungerford to Bournemouth, Thatcham to Bournemouth, Wickham to Southsea and Tidworth Tattoo (evening) – 1 charabanc to each;
Sunday 2nd August – Hungerford to Southsea and Newbury to Southsea – 2 charabancs on each;
Monday 3rd August – Newbury to Southsea – 4 charabancs;
Tuesday 4th August – Stockcross to Southsea and Newbury to Tidworth (evening) – 1 charabanc each.

The only other change recorded for the fleet during 1925 was sale of MC 3937 at the close of the season in September. However, the emphasis that year was on consolidation and providing a covered garage for the growing fleet, and over the Winter a brick-built garage was built behind the Market Street offices. This was some 40ft wide and about 45ft deep, with a frontage onto the access road in Mayors Lane, and reached on foot by a covered walkway from the rear of the offices. Also installed was a 500-gallon fuel tank, whist the rear of the garage was equipped with the usual workshop apparatus. Despite this accommodation, it was also necessary to find further parking on a plot of land in Mill Lane, where a wooden shed was erected, and the contents guarded by a rather fierce dog!

For 1926 consideration was given to updating the passenger fleet, so a 14-seater was ordered from

Arthur & Percy Andrews, this being one of Percy's famous refurbished Talbots fitted with an gangway chara body. This was originally built in 1918 for the WD and probably served as an ambulance, the finished article arriving in May, being registered MO 7924 and carrying a buff livery. Over the Winter the Leyland charabanc was fitted with pneumatic tyres, though further details still remain a mystery.

14-seater Talbot MO 7924 seen with a party dressed for a pageant at Reading Abbey after sale to Harold Cordery of Spencers Wood, who repainted it red.

Charlie was fortunate in obtaining a neat Lancia with pneumatic tyres and a 20-seater saloon coach body. This was CC 5083, a Z-type chassis imported from Italy and fitted with a body by Spicers Motors of Southport and new to *Caernarvon Motors* in December 1924. It came to Newbury in June 1926 in a grey and white livery, being repainted in July 1928 as (in what was then the favoured scheme) of plum and yellow. This vehicle, with its fixed roof and drop windows was a very popular vehicle and definitely a sound purchase, leading to others of that make.

PLEASURE OUTINGS.

IT IS A "LANCIA."

TRAVEL IN COMFORT, FREE FROM DUST and RAIN. We supply 14, 20 and 25 Seaters, on PNEUMATIC Tyres, with Careful Drivers only. Our reputation, your Guarantee, I have stood the test for seven years. Every Party gets THERE and BACK. You know your Driver; we know the Roads and our Cars from A to Z, thus adding to YOUR COMFORT and SAFETY. If you want a Charabanc Outing, DURNFORDS' every time. Bookings now taken for Southsea, Bournemouth, Brighton, Bognor, Weymouth, Worthing.
ENQUIRE AT OFFICE FOR DAILY TRIPS.

DURNFORDS' CHARABANCS, NEWBURY
'Phone—43.

Apart from the obvious comfort advantages of pneumatic tyres, there was also the ability to undertake longer trips, with Weston-super-Mare and Weymouth being added to the list of coastal destinations. However, there were two drawbacks with such tyres, firstly that they could be punctured (many roads still not having metalled surfaces) and, secondly, that vehicles could only too easily be driven in excess of the still official 12mph speed limit for the larger types! Indeed, some Police Forces were quite aggressive in catching speeding charabancs, leading to discussion in the trade press regarding the need for an increase in the limit for PSV's on pneumatics, this eventually being raised to 20mph from 1st October 1928.

Sketch of the Mayors Lane garage with one of the later Maudslay all-weather coaches CW 8602 and Dennis 3-tonner MO 3343 as a removals van.

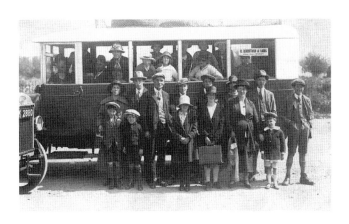

Lancia CC 5083 at Southsea on an outing from the Chalkers Arms, Woodlands St. Mary in 1927. Inside, and under the customary paper sticker proclaiming ownership, is young Derek Nobes with his mother Winnie to his left in the straw hat, his father being the local carrier and bus operator based at Lambourn Woodlands. The pregnant lady is Mrs. Wareham, who acted as the local midwife and also laid-out the dead!

It is also worthwhile considering how the, 'motor coach' developed rapidly during the 1920's. Indeed, the terms 'coach' and 'charabanc' are widely misused, and originally a coach was any type of fully enclosed body, so the idea that the crude charabanc developed into the coach is in some ways a misnomer. From pre-Great War days, larger motor vehicles were fitted with (usually) detachable bodies which had rows of seats accessed by a door to each row (if indeed it had doors at all), hence the adoption of the French term *char-a-bancs*, or 'carriage with benches'.

These might have a fixed roof or a folding canvas hood, which in time was also supplied with removable side screens. This latter arrangement was cumbersome and took up limited storage space, where the beer crates, luggage or picnic hampers might be better accommodated, so the next development was to have fixed side windows and a folding hood roof, which was referred to as the 'all-weather' coach. Some small charas had only had one or two doors, with a zig-zag gangway to reach the rear seats, properly known as the 'gangway-charabanc'.

The addition of fixed front and rear domes to the body also provided opportunities for better designs for the opening roof section, a number of which were subject to patents. This also saw the reduction in doorways, with a dual-doorway arrangement being commonplace as these fitted in structurally with the fixed domes of this 'sun-saloon' type, and there was a central gangway throughout. Fixed roof sides also developed during this process, and it was commonplace to fit a roof-mounted luggage rack, accessed by a ladder or built-in steps.

With the advent of the Construction and Use Regulations in 1931, all aspects of body design and layout were covered, which included the provision of an emergency exit on another side of the body other than the normal service entrance in order to give a means of escape if the vehicle was on its side. This basically did away with the dual-entrance arrangement on coaches, and a number of those with that layout had one of the doors relocated to the offside to form the emergency exit. However, many older types would not meet the new requirements and had to be phased out or re-bodied. Coaches could still contain an opening roof section, but otherwise the enclosure process had now been completed.

Thus the rather crude lorry-based vehicles of the early post-Great War era had developed rapidly during the 1920's, as new low-frame chassis were developed, particularly in response to foreign imports, and then in annual increments through the above process of body design until by the late '20's coaches of a high standard of comfort and reliability plied the roads of Britain. These developments were also paramount for the local operators, though vehicles in use might, like hat designs in rural Newbury, be a year or two out of mode. In the case of the *Durnford* fleet there was the added advantage that outmoded types could still see further use on haulage duties, particularly the lower – built types of chassis in respect of removal vans.

Indeed, ex-WD Dennis 3-tonners MO 53 and MO 1763 had latterly run as lorries, and were disposed of in December and September 1926 respectively.

Similarly, Daimler BL 8804 and the Maudslay A-type departed after being used in the goods fleet, whilst the Hallford CR 4021 was duly disposed of, all at unrecorded dates.

The smaller Dennis's DL 2122 and RX 1992 at the Mill Lane yard with Lancia CC 5083 to the right.

For Easter 1928 the excursion adverts noted that a brand new Dennis all-weather coach was awaited, and this was registered as RX 1992 on the last day of March. This was a 30-cwt G-type, which had been fitted with an 18-seater body finished in plum and a yellow line, and this useful vehicle was also later used with a Luton-type body on smaller removals jobs. The earlier Dennis vehicles had evidently suitably impressed Charlie, plus of course the works were relatively nearby at Guildford should spares be required. To supplement the fleet, he acquired a 1921 Dennis 2-tonner from an Isle of Wight operator by May 1928. This was DL 2122, new to *F. Plater (Isle of Wight Tourist)* of Ryde, and it carried an all-weather 20-seater body built on the Island by Margham at Newport.

Reo 'Major' all-weather coach (registration not known) in 1929 on a Sunday outing. Winnie Nobes is 4th from the right with son Derek in front. The couple next to her are Eva & Percy Bew, who kept the local bakery and general stores at Woodlands St. Mary.

Also acquired for the 1928 season was a secondhand 25.6hp GMC K41-type 20-seater, which was several years old but has otherwise only been identified from photographs. Similarly, other coaches known to have been acquired during the 1928-30 period, but for which full identities are not known, were a London

Lorries all-weather 25-seater on Lancia 'Pentaiota' chassis, a Reo 'Major' 20-seater and a Guy, the latter pair also duly becoming lorries. During February 1929, another Lancia 'Pentaiota' was acquired, this being new in September 1926 to *F. & J. Webb* of Street in Somerset, registered YB 7442 and carrying a 20-seater front-entrance saloon coach body by Wray of Waltham Green, London SW6. It must be assumed that the first Lancia had also suitably impressed.

Again in 1928 Charlie found himself in court, this time for switching the tax disk from a charabanc not in use to one of the lorries, no doubt in response to his policy of never turning a job down. There were two occasions reported, one where Charlie and son Len were involved, for which they were fined 40 shillings and 10 shillings respectively, whilst the other count was against son Bill, who was transporting a piano to Speen when spotted and was fined 20 shillings. On another occasion Charlie was stopped on the Bath Road for a defective light, though he said it was working shortly before, so he subsequently brought the lorry to the hearing to show it was now repaired!

The Wray-bodied Lancia YB 7442 as new.

On the plus side, the retiring vicar of Midgham, the Reverend Boyd Johnstone, did favour Charlie with his removal to Eastbourne during 1928. The removal vans also regularly took loads of furniture to London for Elliotts joinery, returning with animal feedstuffs for Midwinters. *The following advert is from 1929.*

Lancia CC 5083 departed in June 1929 for further use by Portsmouth-based coach operator *John Horner*, whilst September saw the end of the line for Dennis 3-tonner EL 3769, latterly engaged on haulage work. Also outgoing that Spring was Talbot MO 7924, which spent one season with *Harold Cordery (Pride of the Valley)*, at Spencers Wood, south of Reading. It is interesting to note that *Durnfords* continued to specify the availability of a 14-seater for the 1930 season, presumably meaning that there was either another (as yet unknown) coach of that capacity?

Maudslay all-weather coach YE 8768 is seen in later years with N&D and driver Bert Greenwood.

Also offering quality low-loading chassis was Maudslay, and Charlie was able to purchase a 1927 ML4A-type from North London coach operator *George Ewer* in November 1929. This was YE 8768, which carried a London Lorries all-weather 28-seater body built in Kentish Town, North London. He also obtained a slightly earlier 1926 ML2-type (CW 8602) from *Allison (Prudence Motor Coaches)* of London W6 in January 1930, which carried a 28-seater all-weather body. The unknown make of body was of quite a wide construction which, under the Construction & Use Regulations of the 1930 Road Traffic Act, could not be suitably modified to come within the maximum permitted width. However, all was not lost, as the chassis was sent to Andrews in late 1931, re-appearing in January 1932 with a pantechnicon body for the removals business! Please note that this corrects previous information that it was Maudslay 'YE' that was so treated, as that remained in use as a coach until sold in 1934. The latter is also notable for having a sphinx figure on the radiator cap, which was not a standard Maudslay feature or seen on other *Ewer* coaches, though the significance of this item is not known.

1930 saw further updating of the passenger fleet, resulting in some cascading of chassis to goods work. As already noted, Dennis G-type RX 1992 ran as a removals van until it departed in February 1931, whilst the last of the ex-WD Dennis 3-tonners (MO 3343) continued in a similar role through to March

1931 carrying an Andrews-built large van body. A further feature of operations was the 'extended service', whereby a car would be sent on request to outlying districts to collect passengers who had pre-booked for excursions, though that advert appeared only the once.

Buckingham-bodied Garner all-weather YT 9565, which although a rare model was to last through to August 1936 and was popular with N&D drivers.

The other incoming secondhand vehicles for 1930 were a 1927 Garner 55hp with Buckingham 26-seater dual-entrance coach body (YT 9565) acquired from *Banks* of Southampton, and later in the year a pair of 1929 Gilford CP6-types were obtained. These were VX 43, which was new to *Essex County Coaches* of London E10 in May 1929 and carried a 20-seater dual-doorway coach body by Thurgood of Ware, whilst the other was UV 9116 and came from *Blue Belle Motors* of London SW9, being new in July 1929 with a front-entrance 20-seater coach body by the Gilford-associated Wycombe Motor Bodies of High Wycombe. The latter was acquired in December, but the date for 'VX' is not known.

Sketch of Thurgood-bodied Gilford CP6-type VX 43 based on a contemporary Gilford advert. It passed to N&D but was sold in June 1933.

Readers of the previous volume on Newbury & District may also recall a 32-seater Gilford RX 7578, which was attributed to *Durnfords*. However, although shown working for them on a large party outing to the Police Sports, it is now known that this vehicle actually belonged to *Eddie Keep* of Burghfield Common! However, a further new purchase for March 1930 was a Reo 'Pullman', which was registered RX 6264 and carried a Wray 25-seater all-weather coach body finished in maroon and yellow.

Maudslay CW 8602 as re-bodied by Andrews for use as a removals van. The original windscreen has been retained and a Luton-type body extends over the cab area, providing a useful low-loading vehicle.

Whilst earlier secondhand vehicle purchases had relied largely on adverts in Commercial Motor or the ex-WD Disposal Sales at Slough, as the '20's wore on Charlie developed good relations with several dealers in both London and Southampton, and this was to stand him in good stead over the years in obtaining sound purchases. He also got on well with *Theo Denham*, which would have some future relevance.

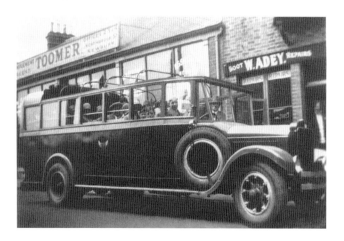

Reo 'Pullman' coach RX 6264 was another speedy and reliable addition to the Durnford fleet, and was retained by Newbury & District until September 1938. It had an all-weather style of body with a fixed rear dome. Note also the position of the spare wheel.

Charlie was also attracted to the 6-cylinder engined American chassis types then being imported, so he must surely have seen the repeated adverts in Commercial Motor for a Diamond T coach by Blue Belle Motors (in their capacity as dealers) throughout

January and February 1931. This was described as a 'one only' and fitted with a 20-seater sun-saloon coach body by Newns (of Thames Ditton in Surrey, who specialised in all-metal bodies). The description went on to say it was 'America's most reputed chassis, with Lockheed hydraulic brakes on all 4 wheels and a 4-speed gearbox, the cheapest new job ever offered at £625'. The vehicle was finished in a livery of yellow with a grey band, and so it was that Charlie bought it and registered in as RX 8210 on 20th March 1931. Whether the vehicle lived up to all the claims, or if some other factor intervened is not known, but it was delicensed during April 1932 and nothing more is heard of it! Indeed, this is the only coach of this make the author has come across in England, so perhaps spare parts were also an issue?

The only other known vehicle was acquired in January 1932, with the arrival of 26-seater Wilton-bodied GMC (UU 7594), which had been new to *Kings Service Coaches* of London SW12 in June 1929. It is worth noting that the GMC featured a 6-cylinder Buick engine, and these American imports were selling well in Britain at that time, and they would in turn influence chassis manufacturers during a period of rapid technical advances in PSV designs.

The GMC chassis offered low-loading and powerful models ideal for coach work, as seen in a 1929 advert.

Chapter 5 – 1932

The three original partners in *Newbury & District* brought with them a wide range of facilities which would cover all the needs of the new enterprise.

Arthur Andrews contributed the coachbuilding shop in Northcroft Lane, where for some years major painting and bodywork attention took place, whilst his son *Percy* was next door with a motor garage for general work and for the coaches kept there. Despite fairly limited resources the vehicles were turned out to a high standard. Under *N&D* all those facilities continued to be advertised for the general motorist as well, including re-painting and the repair of hoods.

Denham Bros. had their main garage in Wharf Road, but from early 1932 they had also rented the former GPO Motor Department garage in Mill Lane.

Charlie Durnford had his main garage in Mayors Lane, where a quite large brick-built garage housed most of the fleet, and this was joined to the rear of the Market Street offices by a covered walkway. However, for some years it had been necessary to use an additional garage in Mill Lane, which was situated between what became the site for the *Thames Valley* dormy shed and the GPO garage latterly used by the *Denham Bros.*

At the incorporation of the Company, the registered office was declared as 16 Market Street, which was of course *Durnford's* business address. Also, the name of the latter continued to be included in adverts in respect of the removals side of the business, whilst enquiries regarding coachbuilding and motor repairs were to be directed to the Northcroft Lane premises.

As can be seen, Mill Lane had been something of a focus for local operators, being situated in a relatively undeveloped area just a short drive from The Wharf. It will be noted that when *Thames Valley* finally decided to return to Newbury, it had invested in a large brick-built dormy shed intended to house some 8 vehicles. That allocation was never achieved, though in the earlier years it was also used for the winter storage of charabancs. From 1931 a small increase in allocation came in order to cover the former *Great Western* bus services, plus some further storage of acquired buses. However, by the Summer of 1932 the allocation had once again reduced to the pair of Leyland 'Titan' TD1 double-deckers outstationed for Route 10 to Reading.

It must be assumed that any optimism that *Thames Valley* had back in 1927 had now completely faded, as they agreed on 3rd June 1932 to accept an approach by *Newbury & District* to rent the shed! It was agreed that *N&D* would pay £104 per annum rental for a period of 3 years, conditional on *Thames Valley* being able to keep its pair of buses there. Whilst this was undoubtably a sensible use of the 'white elephant' of a shed, it does however seem strange that the larger firm could be so accommodating to the independent concern when the *GWR* shareholding is considered.

Above -The Thames Valley dormy shed was situated on the western side of Mill Lane, and is seen from the front in later days. *Below* – The rear elevation shows the doors through to the spacious rear plot. To the right can be seen the Durnford motor sheds, whilst the white spot between the two buildings is the glass globe of their petrol pump, which along with the old wooden picket fence can also be seen to the left of the front view.

Apart from the actual garage space, there was a large rear yard, which could be reached through the rear doors, something *TV* had earmarked for expansion! So, apart from a couple of coaches still kept at the Northcroft Lane premises, the rest of the passenger fleet was now centred on Mill Lane, albeit in the three adjacent buildings. The Mayors Lane garage continued in use, but was the base for the removals and other haulage activities. *Durnford's* Mill Lane sheds were apparently not included in the original merger, though these and the land were purchased from him for £250 in November 1932, including the construction of an additional shed.

The Wharf Road garage continued in use as a workshop, handy for any problems that developed with buses during the day, and this was retained until circa 1936. Many years later, when the area was being pile-driven for the Newbury by-pass, a large deposit of oil was discovered. However, this was not a 'black gold' strike in Newbury, but a discarded sump tank apparently from the old garage!

Theo Denham was the Company Secretary and looked after the passenger side, whilst the first Chairman was Charlie Durnford. In reality there was little initial difference in the daily operations, as Charlie took charge of vehicle maintenance, and the coachwork and painting was under the care of Arthur Andrews.

From the perspective of the bus operations, the focus remained The Wharf, just a short walk from the town centre and the Market Place, the area having originally been a basin on the Kennet & Avon Canal that had been filled in by the Corporation to provide a parking ground for carrier's carts and the increasing number of bus operators from 1921.

Opposite this area stood The Old Granaries, where once the barges had unloaded their goods, a long line of timber-framed buildings with an upstairs gallery. From the end of September 1932 N&D took a rental on No.7 for use as an Enquiries & Traffic Office, but the Registered Office remained at Market Street.

Sketch of the Old Granaries buildings as restored with bow window fronts and gallery walkway above, the latter providing a very convenient place for bus crews to leave their bicycles!

It should also be noted that initially the three operators continued to use their respective starting points for excursions, as stipulated in the individual licenses, but clearly this needed sorting out as soon as practical. In fact each of the three actually held licenses for varied periods of operation, with Andrews using 15th May to 16th October as his season, whilst Denhams used 1st June to 30th September, and Durnford kept his options open by just specifying May to October!

In September 1932 an application was made to the Traffic Commissioner for *Newbury & District* to take over all the licenses, together with the addition of an excursion to Burnham Beeches and requesting an authorised pick up point in Hungerford at the Corn Exchange. Unfortunately, the latter was rejected, though the licenses were approved. However, whereas the three operators had been authorised to run a total of 12 coaches (5 for Andrews, 6 for Durnfords and just 1 for Denhams), the consent limited *N&D* to just 5! This was a great disappointment, but both of these matters would indeed be further pursued in due course.

With the bus services, all the licenses held by *Denham Bros.* were transferred to *Newbury & District* without modification during November 1932.

Some taxi work had been undertaken by both *Denham* and *Andrews*, though *Durnford* had not been involved in such work. The new company continued to offer this for some years, though few details of the vehicles have survived. Available information shows that there were 4 cars in use from 1932, but by 1935 this had reduced to just 2, usually looked after by Boss Denham and Percy Andrews.

As noted, each of the three operators had also undertaken some haulage work, with the *Durnford* business doing more of that than passenger carrying. Andrews had used a couple of lorries, whilst *Denhams* always featured some regular haulage work, all of which was now brought under Charlie Durnford's supervision.

As all three concerns had originated as family outfits, the following were active in the new firm, though not as shareholders at that time: Percy Andrews (son of Arthur); Boss Denham; Edwin Whitington (cousin by marriage to Theo Denham); Charlie Durnford's sons Len, Bill, 'Nin' (Henry) and Ernie, along with his daughter Olive.

The fleet at formation

The *Newbury & District* fleet at formation was a very mixed bag indeed. Even the haulage fleet of 6 known vehicles comprised the same number of makes, with examples of Daimler, GMC. Guy, Maudslay, Star and Thornycroft chassis all present.

Whilst with the passenger fleet it would be true to say that certain makes had found favour in each of the three constituent fleets, a considerable variety nonetheless existed. Of the 26 known vehicles, there were 15 makes of chassis, covering Dennis (1), Ford (1), Garner (1), Gilford (6), GMC (1), Guy (1), Lancia (3), Leyland (1), Maudslay (1), Minerva (1), Reo (2), Star (1), Talbot (2), Thornycroft (2) and Tilling-Stevens (2).

Vincent-bodied Gilford 22 (RD 1886) from Andrews.

The bodywork carried by these was similarly varied, with 14 as coaches and 12 as service buses, though not all were strictly used solely for one or other role. The coachbuilders totalled at least 15, not including the 3 vehicles whose provenance has not been found. These bodies were built by Andrews (Newbury 4), Buckingham (Birmingham 1), Challands Ross (Nottingham 1), Lewis & Crabtree (Manchester 1), London Lorries (Kentish Town, London NW5 1), Metcalfe (Romford 1), Northern Counties (Wigan 1), Southampton Corporation (1), Strachan or Strachan & Brown (Acton, London W3 4), Thurgood (Ware 1), Vincent (Reading 2), Wadham (Waterlooville 1), Wilton (Croydon 1), Wray (Waltham Green, London SW6 2) and Wycombe (High Wycombe 1). *Full details of the fleet will be found in Appendix 1.*

Denhams had settled on a livery of blue and white, though some vehicles with sound paintwork may not have been repainted. The earlier *Andrews* livery had been mauve, giving way to maroon, then latterly to a cream and green scheme. As they were local coachbuilders and painting specialists, their vehicles were certainly the best turned out of all three fleets. *Durnfords* gave a greater priority to mechanical reliability and did not usually repaint acquired vehicles. However, in respect of new vehicles purchased, a plum and yellow scheme had generally been the chosen livery.

Former Andrews Ford RX 8261 became N&D No.6 and is seen on an outing to Southsea in 1932. Winnie Nobes features once again, holding daughter Beryl, with son Derek in the white shoes.

So, certainly for the first couple of years, all of these variously coloured vehicles were still in evidence. In fact the ongoing expansion of the early years led to even more variety, though of course most passengers were only really concerned with the business of getting from A to B. Destinations were usually catered for by printed paper stickers or painted route boards displayed at the front, unless suitable blinds were available.

The *Newbury & District* fleetname replaced the previous inscriptions on buses, whilst coaches carried it, plus the phone number, on the rear panel. The style was a script with flourishes, whilst some vehicles also carried an *N&D* monogram on the front dash. Good use was also made of such features as headboards, luggage carriers and even roof panels to promote the fleetname and associated slogans. These were the work of freelance sign-writer Alfie Smith, who later worked on *N&D* as a conductor.

The original style of lettering for the fleetname was quite ornate, applied to the sides of service buses and across the rear of the coaches. 1925 Dennis 2.5-tonner PE 2077 came into the fleet just as the Company was formed from Aldershot & District.

Although no decision is recorded in respect of a policy on a livery prior to January 1934, it is evident that a number of vehicles were repainted as maroon and cream in the interim. Those known to have treated were former *Prothero* Fords RX 7256, RX 7772 and RX 9005 (ex blue and cream) and *Spanswick's* Ford RX 6662 (ex blue and white), though the latter's older Ford MO 6744 was evidently earmarked for early disposal and was not repainted. Similarly, the Morris-Commercial bus (RX 3553) acquired from *George Brown* during January 1934 received some cream to its existing maroon livery.

None of the constituent operators had used fleet numbers and, until about January 1933, the fleet was referred to by registrations only. Due to the various changes in the fleet during that initial period, when the make up of the active fleet was continually changing, a full reconciliation of the original fleet numbering scheme has not proved possible. It is, however, clear that initially the plan was to number the service buses between 1 and 20, starting from 21 for the coaches. This was also because the coaches travelled further afield, thereby giving the impression that the fleet was larger than it in fact was! This aspect continued for some years, with the next available new number being allocated to coaches, whilst buses tended to take vacant numbers in the lower series. However, it should also be appreciated that whilst an old coach-bodied vehicle might be purchased for bus duties, a few of the better buses were regularly used for excursions, so there was no hard and fast rule. Indeed, a number of the latter were even given 'coach' livery in recognition of their dual-purpose status.

One vehicle from the *Durnford* fleet that does not seem to have seen use by *N&D* was Wycombe-bodied Gilford CP6-type 20-seater coach (UV 9116) which, although a mere 3 years old, was sold in July 1932 – though it was no 'dud', remaining in use until 1948, long after most of that make had disappeared from the road!

It is also believed that former *Andrews* 1924 Lancia 'Tetraiota' VA 3156 had only a short period of use or was disposed of without service by the close of 1932.

During August 1932 it was decided to see if *George Hedges* of Brightwalton and *John Prothero* of Beedon were still interested in becoming part of the Company. Both were indeed agreeable to the proposal and came into the fold from September 1932.

George Edmund Hedges

George Hedges was born in August 1892 at Peasemore, and by 1901 the family had moved a short distance to Lilley in the adjacent parish of Brightwalton. His father *James Edmund Hedges* was a self-employed woodman and haulier, whilst his grandfather George was also a woodman over at Peasemore. James made hurdles, an essential item in an area of sheep farming, and also sold faggots, taking these to the local markets and sheep fairs. His son When George left school in 1905 at 13 years old he joined his father working as his assistant. By 1911 George had obtained a position as a servant, living at The Stables, Marydown Park, Wootton St. Lawrence in north Hampshire.

The established carrier for the Brightwalton area at that time was *William Thomas*, who lived at Thicket Villas and forms an integral part of the origins of the Hedges family as carriers. He had been born in 1857 at Leckhampstead Thicket, starting his carrier's service in the late 1870's. By the start of the 20th century he had two large vans covering the route to Newbury from Leckhampstead, Leckhampstead Thicket, Catmore, Lilley, Brightwalton, Chaddleworth, North Heath, Winterbourne, Boxford

and Bagnor, though it is known that they actually shared out these points between the two vans. A service to Wantage also ran from Leckhampstead, via Thicket, Chaddleworth, Brightwalton, Lilley, Catmore and Farnborough on Wednesdays. The Newbury base was The Chequers in Oxford Street, and the service departed at 3.45pm Mondays to Saturdays.

Mr. Thomas had already become something of a legend locally through his endurance in all weathers on his routes across some very exposed roads over the Berkshire Downs. In due course he employed 2 men and 2 boys who worked in pairs, whilst he also hired out horse-drawn broughams to meet trains and for use on special occasions, and he still found time to run his farm!

In the years prior to the Great War he had been aided by his son *Donovan* on the carrier's service, whilst his brothers Laurence and William assisted on the farm. Donovan recalled vividly the rigours of the 'great blizzard' of 25th April 1908, which also gives an interesting insight into the lives of the carriers –

'On that particular Saturday one of the men fell sick, and my father said I'd have to fill the gap with my brother-in-law Percy Ford. I was then just 15 years of age.

We started off the usual journey, one van to Chaddleworth and the other to Brightwalton. At 8am it started to snow and did so all day until 4pm. My father, who had been caught in the snow storm of 1881, sensed we would be in difficulties and walked to Boxford Station (some 5 miles) and came into Newbury by train to help us home, ordering a man to bring two horses to Boxford. Thinking we wouldn't make it there, the man turned back, but John Uzzell, the other Chaddleworth carrier helped us out with his horses. We arrived at (Leckhampstead) Thicket at 8.30pm. My father promptly got three fresh horses and returned to collect the van that had got to Bagnor, but due to the conditions had put the horses in the stables at The Blackbird pub. They eventually returned about 3am on the Sunday morning. We went out on the Sunday morning on horseback and delivered meat parcels to Chaddleworth, then a great thaw set in which caused flooding in places.'

With the outbreak of the First World War, brothers Donovan and Laurence both joined the Royal Horse Artillery, the latter being invalided out after being awarded the DCM in the Gallipoli campaign against the Turks. Older brother William stayed to assist on the farm, whilst at some point the youngest son Charlie had run off to join a circus!

Apart from the loss of the services of the two sons, William also found the military requisitioning offers taking many of his horses, as was the case with many thousands of working horses from the countryside. He therefore had to operate the carrier's service with a single van, and this is where the established haulier *James Hedges* comes into the frame. However, it is not known if there was any arrangement between the two men, though it is inconceivable that they would not have known each other in such a small community of the local settlements.

Whatever the resulting accommodation, it is clear that *Thomas* had found the wide-ranging and quite long route had warranted two vans on a daily basis. So, by 1917 *James Hedges* was covering a carrier's service on Mondays, Thursdays and Saturdays, the return journey departing from the Queens Hotel in the Market Place at 3.30pm. He ran the some 15 miles from Brightwalton to Newbury, by way of Catmore, Lilley, North Heath, Winterbourne, Boxford and Bagnor. Presumably on the other days he continued his other activities, though on Wednesdays he went to Wantage, and had already been going to both market towns previously with his own goods.

James would have also understood how it was to have a son fighting abroad, as *George* had joined the 9th Lancers as a Private on 1st June 1915 and served in France. During the time of his war service he became engaged to Eliza Glanville, an assistant teacher at Brightwalton School from Harwell, who lodged with the Hedges family during the week. They married in early 1918, and when he returned safely in 1919, it was natural that he would take up the reins of the carrier's service, after which his father reverted to his previous activities. On the other hand, although William's sons did also safely return, the carrier's business remained covered by one van only from that point on. It must have also been then that Hedges adopted a more direct route and no longer took in Boxford and Bagnor, which *Thomas* continued to serve. His son William later looked after the carrier's business, whilst the founder passed away aged 80 in 1937, a much respected local character of many parts.

In April 1922 the George Hedges' service become motorised with the arrival of a new Ford Model T carriers van (BL 9886) fitted with bench seating for up to 14 passengers. This allowed the route to be extended to take in other local points including Farnborough.

As with most of the carrier's services, the advent of a motor van led to an increase in passenger carrying, both on the route and at other times. From the outset the 14-seater Model T was used to carry the usual range of sports teams and social parties, and no doubt some haulage tasks from time to time. The success of the passenger route is borne out by the purchase of a larger Ford 'Tonbus' in August 1924, which unlike the earlier example featured 14 forward-facing seats. This was probably when the service attained a daily

frequency, though no service ran on Sundays in line with *George's* active participation in local church life.

With a most purpose-built bus in use, the older Ford was then put to work on coal deliveries, with supplies being collected from Great Shefford station on the old *Lambourn Valley Railway*.

To cover increased demand for private hire work, along with the start of advertised excursions, a 14-seater charabanc was put on the road around 1925. The precise date has not been confirmed, nor has the identity of this vehicle, though it had an Andrews body mounted on one Percy's rebuilt Talbot 25/50hp chassis. As a similar chassis with a carrier's van body had been supplied by the Andrews's, it seems likely that it was the same vehicle with alternative bodies.

No record exists of the colour scheme of the Ford vehicles, though it is most likely the wooden bodies were finished in a brown stain and varnished, both having been obtained through Pass & Co. the Ford Agents in Newbury. The Model T was down-seated to 8 from January 1929, and then re-declared as 'goods' only between then and its final withdrawal at the end of December that year. The coal deliveries carried on until about 1930.

As already noted, a steady amount of private hire had been forthcoming, but from 1929 the emphasis was on providing better quality vehicles and more advertised excursions. To match all these aims, a new Ford AA-type with 14-seater 'all-weather' type coach body was purchased and this was registered RX 4556. This was new on the last day of May 1929 and bore a livery of maroon and white, though the bodybuilder has not been confirmed. In June 1930 this was joined by a further AA-type, but with a 14-seater 'sun-saloon' coach type body. This was registered RX 6888 and the body on this was built by Duple Motors of Hendon and finished in a brown and cream livery.

The second AA-type RX 6888 followed a common trend with country bus operators, in being equipped with a sunshine roof section, making it suitable for use on pleasure trips as well as covering bus duties. In this shot it is actually parked on the beach!

With the advent of newer stock which, much to the delight of passengers also saw use on the bus service, the Ford 'Tonbus' was sold in October 1930. The title *Reliance Motor Service* first made its appearance in an advert of October 1931 and, along with the livery carried by RX 6888, was applied as the fleet standard from then on.

It should be noted that *George Hedges* was well entwined in the fabric of local life, both through the church and other social activities, none of which did him any harm when party organisers were looking for coach hire. He was a churchwarden at Brighwalton, as well as a keen bell-ringer, the latter activity taking him and the party all other the South of England (by his coach of course!), whilst he also served as a Parish and Rural District Councillor. He was also a founder member and the first chairman of the Leckhampstead & District Billiards League, and held a similar position with the Brightwalton & Leckhampstead Branch of the British Legion, so all these organisations would have naturally turned to him when requiring transport. When he and his wife Lizzie duly went to live in Chaddleworth, he occupied similar roles there as churchwarden and Parish Councillor, whilst also finding time for his keen interest in gardening and active membership of the Freemason's Lodges in Newbury, Wantage and Hungerford.

The pattern of service had remained much the same throughout the late 1920's, via Chaddleworth and Leckhampstead rather than the original Boxford road (which was further west), and he had been granted the necessary Road Service License under the Road Traffic Act 1930. At the amalgamation with *N&D* on 1st September 1932 these were from Brightwalton to Newbury via Chaddlleworth, Leckhampstead Thicket, Lechampstead, North Heath and Winterbourne, which ran daily other than Sundays. Extensions to this provided a link northwards to Wantage, via Lilley and Farnborough on Tuesdays, Wednesdays, Thursdays and Saturdays, a total route mileage of 18.7 miles from Newbury. It should of course also be appreciated that there were no other links between those two important market towns of west Berkshire apart from the *Reliance* service. Indeed, after *N&D* took over, the only loss was the Tuesday journey, whilst Wednesdays remained the same with a single return journey, the Thursday journeys increased by one to three, those on Saturdays by another to make four, whilst there were also three journeys over the whole route on Sundays for the first time.

On the excursions front, at the time of the merger the residents of Brightwalton had on offer excursions to the following destinations (with return fares shown in brackets): Southsea (6 shillings); Bournemouth (7 shillings); Weymouth (8 shillings and 6 pence); Weston-super-Mare (8s. 6d.); Bognor (7s.); Brighton

(8s. 6d.); London (7s.); Newbury (1s. 6d. or 2s.); Swindon (3s. 6d.); Oxford (3s.); Faringdon (2s. 6d.); Wallingford (3s.); Abingdon (2s. 6d.); Reading (3s. 6d.); Windsor (5s.), Basingstoke (3s.); Hungerford (1s. 6d or 2s.); Marlborough (3s.) and Tidworth Tattoo (4s.). It should be noted that the excursions to Newbury and Hungerford were in respect of special events, and therefore the fare depended on the duration of the stay.

Whereas *Hedges* had managed to fill his 14-seaters on excursions from his nearby locality, *N&D* were keen to build on this excursion traffic and sought in November 1932 additional pick up points at Farnborough, Lilley, Peasemore, Leckhampstead, Chaddleworth, Boxford, Winterbourne and Fawley. They also requested an increase in the maximum permitted number of vehicles in use by one more to three, and all these were granted in January 1933.

Ford AA-type RX 6888 after transfer, with an N&D fleetname but still retaining brown and cream livery and seen with driver George Amor.

N&D acquired the Talbot chara, the pair of Ford AA-types and a lorry of unknown make. *Hedge's* Brightwalton garage continued to be used as the base for *N&D's* operation, with four vehicles kept there, though the actual allocation varied. The Ford AA coaches were transferred to Newbury, where their small capacity was put to good use on private hire work in particular, whilst the Talbot may not have even seen further service. *George Hedges* was paid in 2000 £1 shares, which was identical to the arrangements made with *John Prothero* on the same date.

****

John Prothero & Robert Revell

In January 1921 *John Prothero* of Beedon Hill and *Robert Revell* of West Ilsley started up a carrier's service between West Ilsley, East Ilsley, Beedon and Chieveley to Newbury, and they used a new Ford Model T van (BL 8278), which also had seating for 12 passengers. At that time the population of West Ilsley was 313, East Ilsley was 429 and Chieveley was at 1041, whilst the distance from West Ilsley to Newbury was 12.6 miles.

Robert Revell

Robert Valentine Revell had been born on 14th February 1884, hence his middle name, and was then at Chillenden in Kent. In 1901 he was working as a groom at Acrise Place at Eltham, Kent, but in 1911 he was in a similar position at Bowden Hill Gardens, a large property near Lacock, Wiltshire. In 1913 he married at Wincanton in Somerset, and by October 1914 they had moved again to the Billericay area of Essex, then one year later he enlisted in the Army Veterinary Corps. He worked at stables with polo ponies shortly after the war years, which is how he found himself moving to the Berkshire Downs.

John Prothero had been born in 1885 in Dymock, Gloucestershire, and his initial employment was as a farm labourer with his uncle and aunt over the border in Herefordshire at Much Marcle by 1901. However, like many young men in that dawning age of motor vehicles, he was duly attracted away from the farm life to train as a driver/mechanic at the Hereford Motor Co., City Garage, Eign Street, Hereford, who considered him very good at both and a careful driver. He married Flora Revell (Robert's sister) in April 1911, after which he held two posts as chauffeur/mechanic, one for an industrialist in Swansea and other for the Bishop of Llanduff, taking him through to 1915, when he enlisted in the Army.

With his background, along with the three excellent references, he was assigned to the Army Service Corps (Motor Transport), serving in France, then Egypt, followed by a return to France, during which time he was variously a driver of cars, petrol lorries and an instructor. He was discharged in June 1919, but had some initial difficulty obtaining new employment, making several moves between then and when he and his brother-in-law *Robert Revell* came together on the transport enterprise.

However, in December of that year the partnership was dissolved for some reason, with *Revell* continuing as the carrier using the Ford van, and in order to attract the attention of this service a card marked 'R' was placed in a window, gate or hedge. In the Spring of 1922 Robert also purchased a 14-seater charabanc on a Talbot 25/50hp chassis. This was of course one of the Percy Andrews 'specials', with a body built by his father. The registration of this vehicle is not known, though it most likely retained the original mark from its previous life, as many of the others that passed through the Northcroft Lane workshops. This was painted medium blue and had the legend *The Bluebell* across the rear in gold lettering. Apart from the seasonal charabanc work and the carrier's service, there was also a contract to collect refuse for the local council prior to them having their own transport, suggesting that the Talbot had an alternative lorry body for that purpose.

Both Robert Revell and John Prothero had Talbot charas with bodywork by Arthur Andrews. This example is the latter's, with John at the wheel.

Unfortunately, *Robert Revell* was taken ill in 1928 as a result of the malaria he had contracted whilst serving during the Gallipoli Campaign and died later that year, aged only 44. Due to this, the chara was sold in June, but his widow *Ellen* carried on with the carrier's service, using the Ford T in that role until it was replaced by a newer Ford lorry at the end of September 1931. She used hired help and the service continued through to the early years of the Second World War, effectively ending with petrol rationing. On the other hand, their son Ralph (who had been born in Billericay, Essex in October 1914) did enter passenger transport when he joined *Newbury & District* as a driver, later promoted to Inspector at Newbury, and retiring from there in 1979.

Prothero purchased another Ford T (BL 9316) in November 1921, which was painted green and also seated 14 passengers, which suggests it had the extended wheelbase option then available for that type. He concentrated on developing a passenger service between Beedon, Chieveley and Newbury, initially on the popular days of Thursday and Saturday only, and using the title *Prothero's Bus Service*. This was a distance of 8 miles, and the initial bus was parked on the site of an old cottage at the rear of 33/4 Beedon Hill. At other times the bus, which John also called *The Dixie,* was available for private parties, there being quite a steady trade in those days taking sports, darts and cribbage teams to matches, along with dance parties and other nearby events such as fetes, regattas and village shows.

John Prothero as chauffeur to the Bishop of Llanduff.

Early in 1923 *John Prothero* asked young Charlie Bishop over to the garage and offered him a job on the single hand-cranked petrol pump, and he joined him on his 17th birthday on 17th March. One day John asked him if he would like to drive a bus, then he taught him to drive the Ford and helped him obtain his driver's license. There was actually no driving test requirement then of course, and his driving instruction had consisted of an explanation of the controls, followed by a careful drive to Newbury, dodging the

drovers and their cows or sheep, all done without incident, so that was good enough!

At about that time there was also a 14-seater bus on an Austin chassis. This was a 20hp type which had a 3510cc engine and earned a good reputation as a reliable vehicle that required minimal attention. This had probably started life as a private car, though the identity is not known. The body on this had a frame built by a retired master carpenter, whilst John and his staff panelled it before it was fitted out internally by Arthur Andrews.

Initially the Ford, along with a lorry of unrecorded type (thought to be another open-fronted, canvas-topped Ford), were kept in a shed near his house, first on the left along the Stanmore road, though a larger garage to take 3 buses and with 4 petrol pumps, was built in the mid-1920's and known as the Beedon Garage. The petrol sales were good, as the old A34 was still the main route to the South Coast. Also, as the Prothero's had one of the few telephones locally, they were very much a focal point for such events such as the need to call for a doctor.

Charlie stayed for 3 years, and he even managed to teach *Flora Prothero* to drive the Ford, something which John had never managed to achieve, after which she drove one of the buses. On her regular bus she fixed a small vase on the dash and passengers would bring her flowers to put in it to keep the bus smelling nice. She was also popular on private hires, and on one occasion around Christmas 1928 she took a party of carol singers around the villages, complete with a piano wedged in the rear, opening the rear door to let the sound out at stops!

Flora Prothero is seen with Ford AA-type RX 4272, which John bought for her in due course. Flora is the only lady bus driver recorded in the area at that time.

A revised timetable came into effect from 26th January 1925, marking the start of a new partnership with a *Mr. Wild*, who lived just south of Beedon Hill at Worlds End. The revised service saw journeys between Beedon – Chieveley – Newbury on Mondays,

Tuesdays, Thursdays, Fridays and Saturdays. On Wednesdays a link was provided between Westons and Newbury, by way of Chieveley. The service was now publicised variously as the *Chieveley & Beedon Bus Service* or the *Beedon & Chieveley* Bus *Service,* perhaps depending on the direction of travel? However, this was certainly more convenient than the alternative railway service as the nearest station was at Compton, some 2.5 miles away on the *Didcot, Newbury & Southampton* line.

With the input from *Wild* a new site came into use, with the establishment of the Beedon Garage, with a petrol-filling station, situated at the junction of the old main road (A34) and the Peasemore turn. The buses were kept there, whilst *Mr. Wild* also undertook haulage work from that base. *John Prothero* was based at the garage and they employed as a mechanic one Antonio ('Toni') Riccotti. As his names suggests, he was a native of Italy, who had come to the Newbury area during the First World War. He duly went to lodge with friends at East Ilsley, and from around 1928 also drove for *Prothero* and onwards into *N&D,* and he is recalled for his particularly hair-raising driving at speeds not usually seen on the local roads! However, as he never sought naturalisation, he had to report to the Police weekly throughout WW2, though he was allowed to continue as a bus driver. He was most generally an amiable character, but if upset would rage on in Italian, and although it was not known exactly what he was saying, the sentiment did certainly got through!

Toni was for some years later the conductor on the East Ilsley – Reading route in *Thames Valley* days, with regular driver Charlie Bishop, who also originated with *Prothero*. In the early 1960's he was working with another driver, and they regularly took a girl and her mother into Reading. The mother was known as 'the Baroness', as indeed she was, being Eva von Sasher-Mosach, the Vienese Baroness Erisso, a Hapsburg aristocrat and former ballerina. After a time she felt she could trust Toni to see her daughter into her boarding school at St. Joseph's Convent – this was Marianne Faithfull, later better known as Mick Jagger's girlfriend and a singer/songwriter and actress in her own right. Toni passed away in 1974 aged 88.

Later in 1925 the route was extended onto East Ilsley, a further 2.6 miles northwards, *Denham's* having now withdrawn their service. Ford BL 9316 was operated until the end of September 1925, by which time a larger Ford 'Tonner' had been acquired. Registered XH 8592, it had been a van in the large contract-hire fleet of McNamaras, who had used it on Post Office mail contracts. The van body was stripped off and offered for sale in May 1925, and a new, though rather square, bus body with 14 forward-facing seats was constructed by John in similar fashion to the earlier Austin and finished internally by Arthur Andrews of Newbury. 'Dixie' Ford BL 9316 was advertised for disposal in February 1926.

In April 1926 charabanc work was added with the arrival of a Percy Andrews' rebuilt Talbot with 14-seater blue-liveried body by his father (registration number not known). The name *XCLR* (a play on the word excelsior) was included in the advert for the chara, and the *XLCR Motor Service* name was also adopted for the buses. During the late 1920's a 14-seater Chevrolet bus was purchased as a replacement for the Ford XH 8592, though fuller details are lacking other than it being a secondhand purchase. The latter did, however, see further service with *Ramsbury Motor Services*, a dozen or so miles further west, and is illustrated in that operator's section.

Charlie Bishop recalled that *Prothero* was very friendly with *George Hedges*, and that the pair would go to the vehicle auctions at Charing Cross Road in London to buy secondhand vehicles, which is no doubt where the above Ford came from. However, John and Charlie fell out in the Spring of 1926, when his employer accused him of being rude to his wife, so Charlie went to look for another job.

As the General Strike of May 1926 was getting underway, the local Labour Office sent Charlie to drive a milk lorry from Wantage, so he went to lodge with his parents who were now at Farnborough. Once that job had ended he got another at Marlborough, refurbishing ex-WD lorries for haulage operator Rawlings, who he then also drove for, cycling there and back each day for the first few weeks until lodgings could be found. After a while he left that job and went to work on the Lockinge Estate on farm work and later sheep-shearing, his father having been a shepherd. However, on his way back from the 1926 Royal Agricultural Society Show held at Caversham during early July, he stopped in a pub at Hermitage, where he met *Bill Silvey*. More on his time with that operator will be found in the section dealing with *W. J. White & Son,* but in 1928 *John Prothero* saw him in Newbury one day and tempted him back once again. With this move he returned to Beedon and lodged with his sister, keeping his bus in the lane next to 41 Beedon Hill or at the nearby pond.

One of the reasons *Prothero* was looking for drivers was the new threat posed by the Road Motors of the *Great Western Railway*. The original plan was to forestall the attentions of the *Thames Valley Traction Co. Ltd.,* so the *GWR* opened up a base in Newbury during 1927. However, when the routes were re-organised from 24th May 1928, a new link was formed between Newbury and Didcot. Thornycroft A-type buses were used on this route, though from 25th September of that year, it was cut back to run from Newbury as far as East Ilsley only.

John also experienced some more localised competition, when *Frank Holliday* of Peasemore tried his hand at bus operation during 1928. No details of his bus are known, other than it was covered in adverts both inside and out, and it is also not known how long he operated for, though certainly not into the next year.

As had occurred elsewhere in the Newbury area, the locals preferred to support their own operator, who could also pitch his timings and fares to suit them better, so in about July 1929 the *GWR* gave up on that road. Research has also shown that at the time the railway company was not too highly thought of locally, having provided some pretty ancient rolling stock on the local branch lines, whilst bus fares were invariably much cheaper than those of the train.

With the *GWR* threat out of the way, expansion took place with the purchase of a new Ford AA-type in April 1929. This was registered RX4272 and it carried a green and yellow-liveried 14-seater bus body. This was followed by a similar bus in July 1930 as RX 7256, then by a long-wheelbase AA-type with seating for 20 in December 1930 as RX 7772. Yet another example, similar to the previous one, arrived in July 1931 as RX 9005. The latter three were finished in a livery of blue and cream, and the emphasis was now on providing higher quality buses with features making them suitable for private hire and excursions, and the body on RX 7772 is recorded as of the 'sunsaloon' type with an opening roof section. Most of the bodies prior to that are believed to have been constructed by Andrews.

Driver Charlie Bishop is seen in a later view of Ford RX 4272 after the XLCR headboard had been added.

The influx of new vehicles displaced the Chevrolet bus, though no disposal date is known. In order to cater for the increased fleet a further garage was established at Chieveley and known as the Langley Garage. At some point during 1930 the partnership with *Wild* ended, the latter evidently taking the haulage interests with him.

Another outing with Charlie Bishop at the wheel, this time with Ford AA-type RX 7256 arriving at Southsea.

By 1930 the service had been fully extended to East Ilsley, other than on Wednesdays and Sundays, the new vehicles allowing both an increase in frequency and adding some Sunday journeys. Also, from December 1930, a new service commenced from East Ilsley to Reading (a distance of 18.8 miles), by way of Compton – Aldworth – Upper Basildon – Pangbourne. As *Prothero* did not have the benefit of a license with Reading Borough Council, his bus used a stand on private land by the Palace Theatre, for which he paid a weekly rental Indeed, he had applied to the Council for such a license, but at that time that authority had become quite restrictive with issuing licenses. However, with the new bus in stock, he still went ahead without being able to 'ply for hire' in the street. It is worthwhile noting that once the matter of service licensing came under the Traffic Commissioner, and at the sitting held in Reading in March 1931, *Prothero* was actually granted the Road Service License! Harry Dore joined as a driver at this time, and would become another long-service local bus driver, others being Eric Bond and Ernie Moreby, the latter usually driving the lorry on the carrier's run (aided as a young boy by John and Flora's son Francis when off school).

Indeed, his services were not adversely affected by the 1930 Road Traffic Act, and an interesting feature of the Reading service was the late-evening journeys on Tuesdays, Thursdays and Saturdays. This was timed at 9.15, but the timetable noted that it 'will await the conclusion of racing at the Greyhound Stadium', conveniently situated virtually on the route at Tilehurst, making that a popular form of entertainment. This service otherwise ran daily except on Wednesdays, which was early-closing day.

However, it should be noted that a restriction was put on carrying no passengers wholly between Reading and Pangbourne, in response to objections by *Reading*

& *District* and *Thames Valley*. Individual drivers did of course ignore this at times, especially if they knew the passenger, but Charlie Bishop did so to his cost, being fined £2 for that contravention.

By March 1932 the services were arranged as follows:
East Ilsley – Beedon – Chieveley – Newbury;
East Ilsley – Compton – Aldworth – Upper Basildon – Pangbourne – Reading;
Peasemore – Chieveley – Newbury;
Connecting journeys between West Ilsley and East Ilsley to meet the Newbury and Reading services.

The carrier's origins were not forgotten with the expansion of the bus operations, and the 4pm journey from The Wharf was designated as the 'parcel's service', whilst a similar facility existed on various journeys of the service to Peasemore. Similarly, although a full carrier's service was no longer practical with the scheduled bus route, special requests could be arranged, such as a side of bacon or sack of sugar, which the shopkeeper would request from the Reading wholesaler to be delivered to the bus at its layover. However, on one occasion Charlie Bishop was driving home from Reading when he thought he could hear a mooing sound from inside the bus. He went back to find Mr. Walters of Bowers Farm at Aldworth with a small calf standing in a sack! Everyone had a good laugh, then off they went again.

The bus service to Newbury commenced service at 7.40am from the Beedon Garage, working towards East Ilsley, where it formed the 7.55 departure into Newbury, arriving there at 8.35am. Journeys then ran back and forth until 7.50pm, finishing with a short-working back to the garage from East Ilsley. Extra services were operated on Thursdays and Saturdays, though less ran on the early-closing day of Wednesday. Saturday evenings saw a late bus leaving East Ilsley at 9pm to form the 10.15 run back from Newbury, the cinemas etc. then finishing at 10pm. On Sundays a service was operated during the afternoon and evening only, as was commonplace in those days.

Prothero had shown some interest in the concept of *N&D* when it had been formed, but so far had not acted to join with them. However, during August 1932 N&D decided to see if he was still interested, resulting in him coming into the fold in September on receipt of 2000 £1 shares. He did, however, retain the garage business and continued to trade. *N&D* applied for transfer of the Road Service Licenses in November 1932, and that went through during the following month. The new operator made some detail changes in order to fit in with revised operating arrangements, and 3 buses were kept outstationed at the Swan Inn at East Ilsley, initially being some of *Prothero's* Fords. All the quartet of Ford AA's passed to *N&D*, along with the Gilford coach. The Fords all saw further use

until 1934-6. The identity of the Gilford is not known, though the type was standard to *Newbury & District.*

On the services front, *N&D* altered the East Ilsley route to start from that point at 8am as its Route 1, with an extension on that journey to Newbury High School. A corresponding journey was provided for the benefit of school children at 3.50.pm. The East Ilsley to Newbury run took 35 minutes with a return adult fare of 1 shilling. West Ilsley fared less well under the changes, losing the 9.55am trip. This left it with no bus until 12.50pm, and even that now only ran on Thursdays and Saturdays.

The Reading service had been operating daily other than Wednesdays. This became Route 2, and *N&D* re-timed this to a basic daily pattern of four return journeys, but on Tuesdays, Thursdays and Saturdays some journeys were extended the additional 2 miles onto West Ilsley from December 1932, which provided some compensation for residents there. On Fridays and Saturdays later evening journeys were provided for patrons of the cinema etc., whilst on Sundays the service covered the afternoon and evening only. The journey time to Reading was one hour, with an adult fare of 2 shillings and 6 pence.

The Peasemore service covered 8.5 miles and ran daily other than Wednesdays, though the long layovers at Newbury were a reflection of the old carrier's service. *N&D* put on a basic two return journeys, with additional runs on Thursdays and Saturdays only. The 5.15pm departure from Peasemore only ran as far as Chieveley, were passengers would transfer to the service from East Ilsley for onward travel to Newbury, this allowing the bus to return to the outstation.

N&D applied for *Prothero's* excursions and tours licenses during November 1932, and these were all authorised from January 1933. The start point was amended from the Langley Garage at Chieveley to The Square at East Ilsley, and *N&D* was permitted to run up to three vehicles per day from there. No changes to the destinations were requested, and these were Bognor, Bournemouth, Bath – Wells – Cheddar, Southsea, Brighton, Tidworth and Aldershot Tattoos, Reading, Henley, Pangbourne, Wallingford, Didcot, Thame, Oxford, Abingdon, Wantage, Swindon, Marlborough, Andover, Newbury, Highclere, Winchester, Kingsclere, Basingstoke, Thatcham, Cold Ash, Marlston, Hermitage, Hampstead Norris, Compton, Streatley, Winterbourne, Curridge and London. The long list of Thameside destinations reflects the popularity of this 'inland resort' and the added attraction of boat trips, whilst a number of the other local destinations echo the importance of the half-day tour on early-closing days for the shops.

****

At the Board Meeting of October 1932, and under the new Chairmanship of George Hedges, it was resolved to increase the capital of the Company to £15,000 in order to take in the bus and coach activities of *Tom Holman* of Ecchinswell and *Pocock Bros.* of Cold Ash.

Thomas Holman

William Trigg was the established carrier between Ecchinswell, Sydmonton and Newbury by 18887. His son of the same name was born in Newbury and had married an Ecchinswell girl, initially working at Chapel Farm as a miller's labourer. However, by 1901, he had succeeded his father on the carrier's service and now resided at Brock Green, just north of Ecchinswell, whilst other relatives also had the post office in the village. His service ran once a day on Mondays, Wednesdays, Thursdays and Saturdays, the horse-drawn van leaving the Kings Charles Tavern in Cheap Street, Newbury at 3.30pm, though at 1pm on Wednesdays, due to early-closing of shops. He enlisted in the Hampshire Regiment in May 1918, at which point he had ceased as carrier and was an agricultural labourer, though he was certainly still listed in the 1914-6 local directories.

Tom Holman first appears in the local Cosburn's directory as the carrier for the above points from the 1917 edition, operating on the same days, except that he substituted Tuesday for Wednesday and from the same point in Newbury as Trigg had done. Whether he continued as a horse-powered service, or had a motor vehicle from the outset is not confirmed.

Indeed, he was not a local man, having been born in the hamlet of Beachamwell, near Swaffham in rural Norfolk in 1882. By 1901 he was employed as a footman at 'Roselands', Portsmouth Road, Sholing in Hampshire. He married Isabella Lamb (who originated from Lauder in Berwickshire, Scotland and was known as 'Bella') in Kensington, London in early 1909, and the 1911 census shows them living at 47 Kenway Road, Earls Court, London and that he was now a butler. How he came to Ecchinswell is not recorded, though it is likely that he took a post in the area, after which he became aware of the opportunity to take on the role as carrier and become his own master, the couple living at Elderfield Cottage.

In September 1923 he purchased a Ford Model T carrier's van, which had removable seats for 14 passengers and was registered OR 2576. The advent of this vehicle enabled him to also serve Burghclere and Whitway, as *Soper* who had previously served these points had evidently ceased operation.
He was also the local coal merchant, removing the bench seating from the van when engaged on such work, and collected his supplies from Highclere

Station on the *Didcot, Newbury & Southampton Railway.*

The carrier's business over the 8-mile route to Newbury only occupied him on Tuesdays, Thursdays and Saturdays, now with two return journeys provided between Ecchinswell and Sydmonton on Tuesdays, whilst three operated on Thursdays and Saturdays. Also on Tuesdays and Thursdays only he ran a return journey from Whitway and Burghclere to Newbury. Although no evidence has come to light to support the theory, it is quite possibly that he ran to Basingstoke on Wednesdays, probably ceasing once other bus services had been established?

The Ford T was sold in June 1929, though details of the replacement vehicle are lacking. Under the Road Traffic Act 1930 Tom was granted the Road Service License between Ecchinswell, Sydmonton and Newbury, and he also added Mondays to the service days. However, he did not apply for the Whitway and Burghclere section, again no doubt because *Venture* had established their bus service.

Tom only sold the goodwill and the licensed service to *N&D*, as he retained the coal business and his vehicle. *N&D* paid him £30 in cash and issued 50 £1 shares. The new owners quickly re-arranged the timings in order to cover the route with a Newbury-based vehicle, this being their Route 15. He continued as the carrier of goods until at least 1941, although from 16th May 1935 he reduced his service to just Thursdays and Saturdays, passing away in March 1951 at the age of 69, and Bella died in 1964.

****

W. C. Pocock & Sons, later as Pocock Bros.

The origins of this business lay with the activities of William Charles Pocock, who was born at Ashmore Green in 1868. By 1901 he was at the nearby Cold Ash Post Office on Cold Ash Hill, where he was Postmaster, Grocer, Baker and Market Gardener.

In order to be able to take produce into Newbury and to bring shop supplies back he had originally used horse-power, though he acquired a car sometime around the Great War, which he would also undertake some taxi work with. Although he did not function as a carrier's service, he did see the potential for passenger transport, so when he purchased a Ford T van in June 1923 he also had seating for 14 fitted, This was registered MO 1573 and was in the then common varnished wood finish. Passengers were taken the 5.4 miles into Newbury on Thursdays (for market day) and Saturdays (for shopping and cinema visits), whilst at other times local sports teams and dance parties were regular bookings. This vehicle served him well, remaining in use until September

1932, though latterly only on goods work, and it was about then that the shop and post office was also sold.

The elder of his two sons, Percival Brice Pocock (Percy) was born in 1898, joining his father on leaving school, being joined by his younger brother, Norman William Pocock (born 1906) in due course. The latter was responsible for developing the garage and taxi business in particular, with a Renault landaulette on offer in February 1924 (possibly BL 8180, which was owned by the family from March 1921). By that Summer both a taxi and a landaulette were available, and by 1926 several landaulettes were apparently available, whereas by the Summer of 1927 there were open and closed cars available. A purpose-built 14-seater bus based on a Chevrolet X-type chassis was purchased new in order to improve passenger comfort. This was registered as MO 8231 in July 1926 and bore a green-painted body, and after its arrival the original Ford was relegated to goods work.

A later view of the garage and stores at Cold Ash Hill, the original wooden garage having been replaced by a brick-built one with accommodation above. Note the petrol pump for ROP (Russian Oil Products).

The passenger-carrying activities had certainly become more frequent as the 1920's went on, particular in relation to private hire to the South Coast and other popular spots and, for the 1926 season, a 14-seater charabanc christened *The Scout* was placed on the road. By the following July adverts mention charabancs for hire, but fuller details of other vehicles are lacking. At this point in time the business was known as *W.C. Pocock & Sons*. However, during the 1928 season only *The Scout* chara is referred to,

whereas for 1929 this was updated to *The Scout Motor Coaches,* '14-seater open or closed coaches always available'. It is also worth noting that Pococks would use vehicles as lorries in connection with the market garden, either on demand, or after their passenger days were past, so the known fleet is currently incomplete. Certainly there was an unidentified 14-seater Chevrolet coach, as that passed to *N&D* in due course. Sid Coxhead was for many years one of their drivers and also went onto *Newbury & District*.

Another acquisition took place in October/November 1926, when 3 former *London General* double-decker bus bodies were purchased from *Thames Valley,* but these were for use at the market garden as greenhouses. Such bodies were reduced to single-deck appearance and stripped of seats etc. before being deposited by Thornycroft chassis earmarked for re-building to forward-control and new bodies. They could be purchased for a few £'s and were useful in their new role, being joined in May 1927 by the 20-seater bus body taken from *Lovegrove Bros.* Fiat bus (DP 4919), which *Thames Valley* had acquired. It is not known if this body saw any passenger use or was intended for the market garden.

A 1925 Chevrolet 14-seater (MO 6416) was purchased secondhand (from *W.J. White & Son* of Hermitage) in July 1929, the service having expanded to operate on a Monday to Saturday basis. That same month further expansion was considered, when an application was made to Reading Borough Council for Hackney Carriage licenses for 2 buses to be used on service between Newbury and Reading, though the actual route was not specified. The application was rejected on the grounds that adequate services were already in operation, and this Chevrolet was sold in December 1930.

The pattern of operations by the coming of the 1930 Act had become: 2 return journeys at 9.45am and 2pm from Cold Ash (Downe House, a private girl's school) to Newbury on Mondays, Tuesdays and Fridays; 1 return journey on Wednesdays (the afternoon run being omitted due to early-closing in Newbury); a more intensive pattern of journeys throughout the day on Thursdays (up to 6.36pm from Newbury) and on Saturdays (until 10.35pm), the latter two days seeing the buses in almost constant use. Excursion & Tours Licenses were also secured for the following destinations: Southsea, Southampton, Bournemouth, Aldershot and Tidworth Military Tattoos, Wallingford and Pangbourne Tour, Savernake Forest, a number of local annual events including Hungerford Carnival, as well as Reading and Oxford, the latter mainly in connection with football fixtures for those home teams.

The last vehicle to be added came in March 1932, in the shape of a 20-seater front-entrance bus on a

Bedford WLB chassis (very much the 'English Chevrolet'), which was registered as RX 9971. By this time the business was known as *Pocock Bros.*, though their father was still active in other ways, and his name was also included on the Agreement to sell. However, when the business was offered to *N&D* with effect from 1st October 1932 it did not include the taxi operation, which *Norman* would continue in his own right. A total of £800 was paid, with £600 covering the almost new Bedford and the not-so-young Chevrolets. *Percy* and *Norman* were allocated 500 £1 shares, as the nominees of the vendors, the rest being paid in cash. Neither of the brothers passed into the employ of *N&D*, whilst the latter was able to reclaim some of the purchase cost, when it re-sold the Chevrolet X-type (MO 8231) back to *Pococks* for £50, the latter continuing to use it as a lorry through to June 1935. The market garden continued to at least 1947, but had ceased by 1950.

The Cold Ash Garage continued to operate for many years, the facilities being updated as time went by, and was still under *Norman's* control in 1954, finally closing in 1976. *William Pocock* died in September 1942, followed by *Percy* in September 1967 and finally *Norman* in 1982.

****

N&D numbered *Pocock's* route as 13, despite not using that 'unlucky' number for a fleet number, and initially a bus was kept at the Cold Ash garage for its operation. The service continued in similar fashion until revisions brought in under the general review of December 1933, of which we shall see fuller details in due course.

However, the general expansion of the Company during 1932 had resulted in a shortage of office accommodation, not even fully overcome by the addition of the use of 7 The Wharf. In response, Charlie Durnford made the suggestion that his property at 17 Market Street could be converted into accommodation for the Secretary's and General Office Departments, and this work was duly approved and carried out, whilst the Enquiry and Traffic Offices remained at The Wharf. In order to facilitate better organisation in the expanding Company, the Board made (or renewed as appropriate) the following appointments in November 1932: Theo Denham (Company Secretary); Charlie Durnford (Traffic Manager); George Hedges (assisting with Traffic & Returns); Arthur Andrews (Coach-building and Painting); and John Prothero (Engineer at Garage). The latter looked after the passenger fleet, though the haulage fleet continued to be based at Mayors Lane and was cared for by the Durnfords.

In respect of the haulage fleet, Charlie managed to obtain a further trio of Dennis vehicles formerly in the *Aldershot & District* fleet, though in this instance,

they were intended for use as lorries. These were all Dennis G-types, new in December 1927 (OT 6861/2) and March 1928 (OT 7923). The first pair had carried 20-seater saloon bus bodies by Hoyal of Weybridge, whilst the third had a Strachan & Brown coach body seating 18. These were acquired in September 1932 and are believed to have replaced the lorries on GMC, Guy and Star chassis originating with *Durnfords*, all of which had departed by the following April. In October another non-standard type was eliminated, with the sale of former *Denham's* Minerva WU 9870.

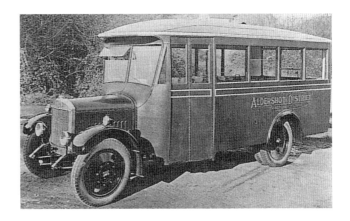

One of Dennis pair OT 6861/2 (above) and OT 7923 (below) as they were when new to Aldershot & District.

During December 1932 the Company once again sought excursions and tours licenses originating from Hungerford, applying for 9 destinations - Aldershot Tattoo, Bognor Regis, Bournemouth, Brighton, Pangbourne, Southsea, Tidworth Tattoo, Weston-super-Mare and Weymouth. All of these were to operate between May and October, other than those for the specific dates of the military tattoos. A maximum of 5 vehicles authorised for any one day was requested, but the application was objected to by *Lampard's Garage* of Pewsey, who already provided excursions from Hungerford, whilst the *Great Western Railway* and the County Surveyor of Hampshire (in respect of increased coach traffic wearing out the roads) both weighed in for good measure. As a result *N&D* were once again refused the use of Hungerford for E&T's.

However, when it is considered that the Company had only been in existence for a mere 6 months, the expansion to the end of 1932 was indeed remarkable.

Chapter 6 - 1933

The year 1933, though not a great period of expansion, was nonetheless an important time for taking stock and adjusting both the services and fleet.

However, the year did start with the proposal for yet another local operator to join ranks with *N&D*. At a Special Meeting on 21st January the offer by *Freddie Spanswick* to amalgamate his business was discussed. This provided a useful and busy service between Newbury and Thatcham, along with his established link between Newbury and Lambourn.

Frederick George Spanswick

Freddie Spanswick was born in 1877 at Aldbourne in Wiltshire, and his father Charles was both the Blacksmith and the Postmaster at the Lower End Post Office in Chaddleworth, aided by his Postmistress daughter Jane. The latter had also become the Telegraphist by 1901, by which time Freddie was a Blacksmith in his own right at nearby Nodmoor Pond, Chaddleworth. He had married Emily in 1899 and in 1900 they had daughter Gwendolyn.

Unfortunately Emily died in 1909, and by 1911 he was living back with his parents, though now he had become a Cycle Agent, the 'cycle craze' being very popular at that time, as developments in bicycles were allowing many people to explore a countryside as yet almost devoid of motor vehicles. However, in respect of the latter, the village forge was of course the origins of many a country garage, so as motors became more common he came to have more involvement with them and Freddie re-married in late 1913 to Nellie Callis.

In the meantime the role of the Thatcham carrier fell largely to *Fred Maslin*, who was evident by 1899 and used horse-power on his very regular service to Newbury. Maslin was based in Broad Street (later known as The Broadway), just off the Bath Road in Thatcham, an address shared with his brother George, who was a coachbuilder employing others. Also notable was the fact that the neighbouring property had Frank Pinnock and his son Edmund, both of whom were coachbuilders, whilst the same road housed wheelwright William Child and his apprentice Arthur Baker.

Maslin left the Waggon & Horses in Market Place, Newbury (3.9 miles away) on Mondays, Tuesdays and Fridays at 12noon and 5pm, whilst on Wednesday this was reduced to just the midday journey. For Thursdays he also ran at 3pm, whereas Saturdays saw three journeys at 12noon, 5pm and 7pm. For this he used a large van drawn by two horses, but on 25th April 1914 he became one of the first in the district to go over to motorised transport, though details of his

vehicle are not known. He also employed a 16-year old Carrier's Servant James Morris, who lodged with his family and would run the numerous errands around Newbury town, whilst he attended to the market area and caught up on the latest news from the other carriers. Indeed, the latter were a good source of news, hearing more than most folk. They also brought the news to the villages in the form of the Newbury Weekly News, which in those pre-radio and television days, also included some news from the wider world.

Also having some significance to the pre-Great War carrier's scene at Thatcham was *Johnson*, who hailed from Theale and came through only on Thursdays. He also went motorised, using an Argyll, but both he and *Maslin* went into the Forces for the war.

It is believed that there were indeed some family ties between the Spanswicks and Maslins, the latter having married a lady from Aldbourne and having a daughter born in Chaddleworth. It therefore appears that *Freddie Spanswick* was invited to operate the Thatcham carrier's service from 1915 'for the duration', though evidently *Maslin* did not return to take up the reins again. Indeed, Freddie continued to be listed as the cycle agent and petroleum spirit dealer at Chaddleworth in 1917, again indicating that he saw the Thatcham situation as only a temporary one.

Freddie generally wore breeches and gaiters, which were of course very practical considering that many roads could be very dusty or muddy according to season. If customers wanted to attract him they only had to place a white card with a large letter 'S' on it where it could be seen from the roadside. He too had a boy assistant, George Amor, who would go on to drive for him in due course. The latter recalls some regular unusual loads for the Thatcham traders, such as a full 'hand' of bananas for the grocer's shop and barrels of beer for The White Hart!

Freddie Spanswick and Ford BL 884 outside his home and base at 21 The Broadway in Thatcham.

The first vehicle recorded with Spanswick was an Argyll 45hp, which had originated as a private car in August 1906. This was registered BL 946 and passed to Freddie in July 1912 and was classed as a hackney carriage, which suggests he may have tried his hand at taxi work. However, exactly one year later the class was changed to 'goods', and it is assumed he used this in connection with his trade activities.

Surviving records for the next vehicle to be registered with him are incomplete. However, the original vehicle bearing the registration BL 884 was a Covre car new in May 1906 and transferred to Freddie in September 1911. In January 1921 a vehicle bearing this mark was re-declared under the 1920 Road Traffic Act as a 1919 Ford Model T, with a grey-painted 14-seater carrier's van body, which was the extended-wheelbase Ford he had purchased as the replacement for the vehicle he had inherited from *Fred Maslin*. Details of the latter's vehicle have not so far come to light.

The advent of the motor van meant that the service ran daily from Mondays to Saturdays, with up to 3 journeys on the busier days, and continued to use the stand at the Waggon & Horses in the Market Place. As with other carriers, the use of motor power invariably led to increased taking of passengers. The *Thames Valley Traction Co. Ltd.* had made various attempts at serving Thatcham, but these were not really a threat to *Spanswick*, and fuller details of these routes can be found in the *Denham Bros.* section.

However, a much more serious threat to *Spanswick's* livelihood came in December 1923, with the appearance of the *Norton Motor Services* with a route specifically between Newbury and Thatcham. Again, the full details are reviewed in the *Denham Bros.* section, but these events made Freddie invest in some better rolling stock as his carrier's service developed into a more frequent bus service. In January 1926 he put a pair of Andrews-bodied 14-seaters on the road, both painted in a livery of blue and white. One was another Ford T of the 1-ton variety which was registered MO 6744, whilst the other was a Morris-Commercial 25-cwt which became MO 7043. Both featured forward-facing seats, rather than the longitudinal bench seating of the old Ford, which now was generally used as a lorry without the canvas roof and celluloid side-screens. The parcels traffic still proved to be an important aspect, with regular loads between Thatcham and Newbury, and such items could be left at his home and business premises at 21 The Broadway. Given the frequency of the bus service, this often meant that virtually anything (including live animals such as chickens and baskets of laundry) could be at their destination within a short space of time.

The new buses were much speedier than the lumbering old Tilling-Stevens of *Nortons*, so they would race ahead of the latter to cream off passengers at stops, a practice generally referred to as 'chasing' (or 'sandwiching' when two vehicles were employed against the other operator). However, on one occasion

George Amor was driving one of the little 'tonners when Bill Norton deliberately let his heavy double-decker roll back towards him!

With *Thames Valley* reappearing in June 1926, followed by developments with the Road Motor Services of the *Great Western Railway* one year later, the little *Spanswick* buses were kept busy! However, 1928 would see both *Nortons* and the *GWR* out of the frame, after which the little buses were not unduly threatened by *Thames Valley's* service from Reading to Newbury.

The original Ford BL 884 was re-painted blue by October 1927 and was still in use the following May. However, it then passed to William Pinnock, his near neighbour in The Broadway, who was then operating a Coal Merchants and used it as a lorry through to the last day of 1930.

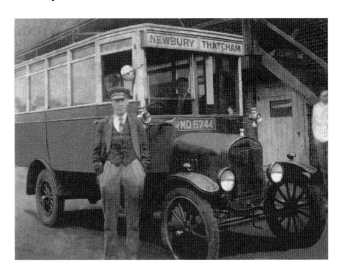

The second Ford T (MO 6744) had a proper bus body with forward-facing seats for 14, seen outside the Old Granaries at The Wharf with driver George Amor.

During the very competitive mid-1920's Freddie had also started to undertake some private hire. Initially the off-duty buses sufficed, as most requests were for local sports teams or for excursions on a Sunday. However, in common with a number of other local independents, he soon realised that offering a higher degree of comfort was necessary for the long trips. One answer for the local bus operator was to invest in a 'sunsaloon' type of vehicle, which in Freddie's case was a Ford AA-type 20-seater new in April 1930 as RX 6662. This carried a blue and white painted Andrew's body with a front entrance and all the roof except the front and rear domes was fitted with a canvas cover which could be folded back in good weather.

With a trio of PSV's now at his disposal, one of the 14-seaters was assigned to a new service between Newbury and Lambourn (which *Nortons* had also shown an interest in a few years before), and this was initially a Mondays to Saturdays operation. However, by March 1932 this had been reduced to run three journeys on Tuesdays, Thursdays and Saturdays, though it had gained two afternoon journeys on Sundays. At that point in time the Thatcham – Newbury service had settled down to the following pattern: six return journeys on Tuesdays and Fridays; none on Mondays; three on Wednesdays, nine on Thursdays and twelve on Saturdays.

Under the 1930 Road Traffic Act, *Freddie Spanswick* was granted the Road Service Licenses for his bus service and activities then settled down, resulting in the sale of the Morris-Commercial MO 7043 to *Bert Austin* of Cold Ash in August 1932.

The Ford AA-type (RX 6662) is seen resting by the war memorial in The Broadway at Thatcham.

Spanswick was one of a number of local operators who were not initially attracted to the idea of joining with N&D, but at an Emergency Meeting of the Company on 21st January 1933 it was agreed that George Hedges, Theo Denham and John Prothero should approach him. The resulting agreement was signed two days later, with Spanswick accepting £100 in cash, 1500 £1 shares, and *N&D* agreeing to pay off £200 in liabilities. The Ford T tonner MO 6744 and the Ford AA RX 6662 then both entered the *N&D* fleet.

N&D applied for transfer of the Road Service Licenses in February, and the grant was made in May. On the Thatcham route they increased both the level of service and the days of operation, with the route becoming their number 12. A service was also provided on Mondays and Sundays, whilst in general there were more evening journeys. To cover this route two buses were out-stationed at Thatcham, though Spanswick's original stock was soon replaced in that role. Also, due to some enforced co-operation by the Traffic Commissioner over the timing of services

between Thatcham and Newbury, the threat of cut-throat competition had now come to a close.

Another view of the war memorial, with Ford Model T MO 6744 awaiting departure to Newbury, and the car to the right is the only one included in the full photo!

The Lambourn service had latterly been in the hands of the little Ford 1-tonner MO 6744, though this was replaced by June 1933. That route was numbered 6 and remained substantially as before, though it was altered slightly to allow for a more direct approach by way of Bagnor Turn rather than travelling via Donnington.

Spanswick's private hire and excursion trade had grown steadily since the advent of the Ford AA sunsaloon, so *N&D* took over the licenses to Burnham Beeches, Cold Ash, Lambourn, Marlborough, a Newbury Commons tour, Oxford, Pangbourne (circular tour), Salisbury, Stockcross, Swindon, Thame and Weymouth. However, due to objections from other local operators, they were refused transfer of the licenses in respect of Henley and Windsor, though they did manage to gain additional pick ups at Midgham, Woolhampton and Crookham.

Freddie Spanswick died on 25th May 1952 at 21 The Broadway, which had been both his home and business address throughout his years at Thatcham.

****

However, to return to *N&D's* efforts to gain licenses for excursions and tours from points on the western flank, a further application was placed before the Traffic Commissioner in January 1933. This sought approval for 24 destinations to start from Kintbury, which it was hoped would overcome some of the loss felt from the refusal to gain licenses from Hungerford, but again this was turned down.

At that time the most popular South Coast destination was Southsea, which it would be true to say had seen development specifically to cater for the charabanc trippers, with its large coach park, fun fair and close proximity to Portsmouth. *Newbury & District* coaches ran there on numerous occasions during the Summer months, both on advertised excursions and for private parties, so it was only natural that it should consider seeking a license for a daily express service. The plan was to run from 1st June to 30th September, which also would provide a more convenient transport for those wishing to stay for longer periods or use the route as a stepping stone to the Isle of Wight. It should of course be noted that *South Midland* of Oxford already ran such a daily service, though *N&D* contended that its service would also benefit passengers at pick up points en route not covered by that service. Under the circumstances, the refusal to grant the licenses does seem unfair, not to mention being a disappointing outcome for the Company.

The opportunity was also taken during January 1933 to sort out the idiosyncrasies in respect of the E&T's inherited at formation. As a result, all excursions from Newbury were arranged to start at The Wharf. *N&D* also succeeded in having the 5-coach limit raised to 9 on any one day from Newbury, whilst also requesting additional picking up points at Donnington, Speen, Thatcham, Highclere, Woodhay, Enborne, Burghclere and Ecchinswell.

All the above might have proceeded smoothly, had the application not also included a request to add a further 29 destinations! This soon brought objections from the operators in certain quarters, notably those in the Cold Ash and Thatcham areas, along with *Edith Kent* to the south. In reality, this once again demonstrated a lack of expertise in dealing with Road Service License applications. *Newbury & District* had sought to add the destinations of Abingdon, Andover, Basingstoke, California-in-England, Cold Ash, Compton, Didcot, Eastbourne, Faringdon, Hampstead Norris, Henley, Hermitage, Kingsclere, Lambourn, London, Marlborough, Reading, Salisbury, Southampton, Stratford-upon-Avon, Thame, Thatcham, Wantage, Winchester, Windsor, Worthing and Yattendon, along with a circular tour of the Wye Valley.

Due to the complexity of the application, together with the range of objectors it evoked, no conclusion had been reached by May 1933, with the 'season' imminent, so it was decided to put forward a less ambitious alternative. This reduced the additional pick up points to Burghclere, Ecchinswell, Highclere and Woodhay, whilst the destinations sought were pruned down to just Eastbourne, Henley, London, Reading, Stratford-upon-Avon, Windsor and Worthing! This was finally approved in July, though the licenses in respect of Reading and London were both refused after objections from *Thackray's Way* and *Thames Valley,* as these already had established and frequent services between those towns and Newbury.

There was another instance of forced co-operation in January 1933, as this was something which a good Traffic Commissioner could insist of in the interest of the travelling public. This concerned the transfer of the Stage Carriage License from *Pocock Bros.,* where the Commissioner insisted that *N&D* and *Bert Austin* of Cold Ash produced a mutually-agreed timetable for approval. In other respects, the Traffic Commissioner had the power to insist of fares and inter-availability of return tickets where more than one operator covered the same route, something often sadly lacking in modern times and to the detriment of travellers.

The Ford AA's inherited from Spanswick and Hedges were a popular choice for smaller private parties, and RX 6888 is seen at a stop en route.

In respect of the E&T destinations, readers may not be familiar with 'California-in-England'. This was a fairly large area of pine woodland and heath around Longmoor Lake, off the Nine Mile Ride, south of Wokingham and in an undeveloped area between Arborfield and Finchampstead. *Mr. A.E. Cartlidge* had purchased the former brick-working from the large Walter Estate during the 1920's, following his war years at the Royal Aircraft Factory, some 10 miles south at Farnborough in Hampshire. At first he ran 'mystery tour' trips from London to the site, where the scent of the pine trees and lakeside setting was appreciated by city dwellers, whilst also highly recommended for TB sufferers.

He initially used ex-WD Daimler chara LX 8521, adding a new Maudslay MT 8204 in 1928. By 1931 the site had been further developed, with bathing pool, boat hire, amusement park and cafeteria, and he set up the *Crimson Rambler Coaching Service*, with a license to operate between his Teddington base and what had now been named as Califonia-in-England. Further developments saw the erection of chalets, in what was a forerunner of the post-WW2 holiday camps, whilst the popularity grew with the addition of a Speedway track and large ballroom, complete with the glass floor recovered from when London's Crystal Palace burnt down in 1936. Visiting coaches were also welcome, with free parking, so this became a regular venue for *N&D* coaches for day, half-day excursions and evening dance parties.

Some detailed re-arrangements took place to the workings from East Ilsley from March 1933, though it would remain a base for *N&D* buses throughout the Company's history.

In addition to various other minor adjustments to times effective from March, a new route commenced from that date between Hungerford and Shefford Woodlands, running via Hungerford Newtown on Wednesdays, Thursdays and Saturdays only. This was covered by the bus that had worked out to Hungerford for Newbury, with two journeys leaving Hungerford at 10.10am and 3.10pm, and this provided a replacement for much of the former *Ramsbury Motor Services* Aldbourne – Shefford Woodlands – Hungerford bus which had run on Wednesdays only.

With the adjustments to services, a number of the inherited vehicles could be disposed of. The former *Andrews'* Thornycroft J-type lorry went by April 1933, along with their Lancia 'Tetraiota' coach (DP ????). From the *Denham's* fleet Talbot 14-seater bus KE 3196 and the former *Southampton Corporation* Leyland E-type 26-seater (TR 1231) also departed at sometime during 1933. Also by April *Denham's* Daimler lorry (TB 2522) was disposed of or scrapped, along with the GMC, Guy and Star lorries originating from *Durnford's*.

Although the Registered Office remained at 16 Market Street, bookings for excursions and private hire could also be made at the Northcroft Road premises and The Wharf Enquiry Office.

However, during April Charlie Durnford gave notice that he intended to withdraw from active participation in the Company with effect from 1st July that year, this apparently resulting from a difference of opinion with other Directors. In fact, with so many strong-willed, self-made characters drawn together, such situations would inevitably arise from time to time!

Arrangements were therefore made during May 1933 for the Registered Office to be transferred to 7 The Wharf and, by October of that year, the lease of No.6 had also been taken over to be the Enquiries Office.

June 1933 saw a further clear-out of surplus vehicles, with the demise of the former *Andrews's* 20-seater Guy coach and *Denham's* 28-seater Gilford bus, a 14-seater Chevrolet coach ex-*Pocock Bros.* (all with identities unknown), along with former *Durnford's* 20-seater Gilford CP6 coach VX 43. The latter found a new owner on the Isle of Man, where it was re-registered as MN 8844. Also sold that same month was former *Spanswick's* Ford Model T 14-seater MO 6744, along with Dennis 2.5-ton 20-seater bus PE

2077, acquired the year before. Indeed, all of these, except the Ford T, had been advertised for sale in the columns of Commercial Motor, with a note stating this was due to fleet standardisation.

One replacement vehicle was obtained locally in July 1933, when *John Spratley & Son (Blue Star)* over at Mortimer offered a 1929 Thornycroft A2-type 20-seat bus (OU 3317) for sale. This was a good opportunity to purchase a type favoured by the Company and in very good condition, the vehicle becoming No.10.

Also acquired in July was a Dennis GL-type with a 20-seater body by Wray, which had been new in July 1929 to *Usher,* London E3, and this became No.53 (UV 6002).

Wadham-bodied Thornycroft A2-type OU 3317 is seen when on delivery to John Spratley & Son in August 1929. This type was ideal for one-man-operation. The use of the offside spare wheel carrier was not uncommon at the time, though as time went by these were generally panelled over by N&D.

Another vehicle acquired in mid-1933 was a Star 'Flyer' VB4-type with Robson 20-seater bus body. It had been new to *Rutherford* of Craster, way up on the Northumberland coast in June 1929, but he sold out to *United Automobile Services* in March 1933, then it came south via a dealer to *N&D* as No.3 (TY 6174).

The departure of Durnford was indeed a blow for the expanding Company, particular as he had been largely responsible for the haulage and private hire aspects, along with the maintenance of vehicles. As his sons had long been the backbone of his business, he made arrangements during June 1933 for them to be set up as *Durnford Bros.*, operating from the Market Street base as haulage and coach operators!

Although the brothers took the Maudslay furniture van (CW 6802) with them (as it was apparently still owned by Charlie, who transferred it to his son Bill), much of their coaching work was initially in association with others.

Durnford Bros.

This situation saw all of Charlie's sons back working with him, as it was he who bankrolled the enterprise. Indeed, Bill and his father handled the removals and haulage aspect, trading as *C. Durnford & Son* from 16 Market Street, whist Len, Ernie and Henry ('Nin') traded as *Durnford Bros.* from No.17 as motor coach proprietors.

The Maudslay furniture van CW 6802 was generally driven by Bill during this episode, and this was duly joined by a 1929 Ford AA lorry (RX 4356), which Charlie purchased from *Arthur Bason* of the Angel Hotel in Woolhampton. The coach side was provided with two 26-seater 1929 coaches, one being a Star Flyer VB4 with Thurgood body (GU 7545) and the other a Gilford 166SD-type with unknown make of body (HJ 8718). The Star had been new to *H.E. Lang* of Lambeth, London, whilst the Gilford had been with *E. Brazier* of Southend-on-Sea, Essex.

Star GU 7545 is shown later in use by N&D on the service to Curridge.

Despite the relatively small fleet, adverts quoted that coaches of 14, 20, 26 and 28 seats were available, this being achieved by the use of 'associated' operators from the ranks of those who had at that time not yet come into the fold. These were *George Howlett* of the Oak Tree Garage, Bucklebury and *Arthur Bason* of Woolhampton, as noted above. In addition to these, there was also a booking agency with William Thomas, licensee of The Plough Inn in Thatcham.

Howlett's activities will be fully reviewed later, as his operations would indeed become part of an expanded *N&D* in due course. However, in respect of his association with *Durnford Bros.,* the trade was evidently a two-way affair, as bookings for his *Spartan* coach could also be made at Market Street, though reference to this ceased from August 1933, suggesting that maybe the arrangements had not worked out as originally envisaged?

The latter is also likely due to the acquisition by *Durnford Bros.* of the Road Service License for the Excursions & Tours held by *Bason*, as approved by the Traffic Commissioner in August 1933. This at last gave them the ability to run advertised excursions, though the transfer was conditional in that no passengers could be picked up at Newbury. The approved destinations for *Bason* had been Bognor, Brighton, Weston-super-Mare and Weymouth, but at the time of the transfer application, California-in-England, Oxford, Pangbourne, Pewsey, Salisbury, Swindon, Theale Fete and Winchester were all successfully added.

Arthur Bason had in fact for some years hired his coach to *Charlie Durnford*. He had moved to Woolhampton in 1925 to take over the Angel Inn, at that time still a busy roadside stop on the Bath Road, having previously traded as a corn chandler in London. His main line in transport had been his carrier's service from Midgham Station, which dealt with the onward delivery of *Great Western Railway* parcels, whilst also catering for the boys at the nearby Douai Abbey School, who arrived by train with their travel trunks and boarded there.

Arthur had purchased a new Austro-Fiat in May 1925 (MO 5203), which was used both as a lorry and as a 14-seater charabanc with a maroon-painted body. In July 1926 a 20-seater Gotfredson 22hp was purchased new, and that was built in Canada and registered as MO 8141, also with an alternative lorry body. In due course the Austro-Fiat ceased to be used for passenger work, continuing on haulage duties until replaced by a new Ford AA-type lorry (RX 4356) in April 1929. When *Maynard Bros.* decided to give up charabanc work in 1930, in order to concentrate on their Thatcham-based garage business, *Bason* took over their 1925 Garford 20-seater (MO 6228), which he repainted red and green. As it was, *Maynards* had also often hired to *Charlie Durnford*, whilst Arthur's own vehicles were driven by his son Percy, Teddy Wheeler and Dennis Adams.

It is not clear whether the sale of the Ford AA lorry coincided with the transfer of the E&T's licenses, but it seems that the Gotfredson remained in *Bason's* ownership, being hired to *Durnford Bros.* when required. His vehicles were known as the *Scarlet Runners,* a title also adopted by *Durnford Bros.*

This contemporary Gotfredson advert emphasised the model's climbing abilities, and certainly Arthur Bason was impressed by his example.

Arthur was himself well connected, being Chairman of the British Legion for Aldermaston, Midgham & Woolhampton, as well as a Parish Councillor, so little escaped his notice locally. The Gotfredson chara continued in use until the era of *Durnford Bros.* came to a close, but after that Arthur retained it for goods use only through to the end of October 1935. It is probable that this marked the end of his transport activities, as he relocated in 1936 to the Heroes of Waterloo in Waterloooville, Hampshire.

However, the expansion of *Durnford Bros.* did not quite end with the acquisition of *Bason's* licenses as, in October 1933, they pioneered a new 'express' service between Newbury and the Berkshire Mental Hospital by the River Thames at Moulsford. This was for the benefit of visitors to the patients there, as no direct link existed, and it ran a single return journey on the 1st and 3rd Thursdays of the month, departing Newbury at 1.30pm and leaving Moulsford at 4.30pm. One of the license conditions was that only return tickets could be issued (at 3 shillings), perhaps to ensure no one used the bus as a means of unofficially leaving the hospital? The service picked up at Market Street in Newbury, then operated direct, other than an approved pick up at Thatcham, and it should be noted that *Thames Valley* had also already operated a similar link from Reading for many years.

****

In response to the above period of competition, *N&D* reacted by reducing the cost of mid-week coach hire, and did at least gain some comfort from the refusal by the Traffic Commissioner on Newbury pick-ups.

To return to matters concerning the Officers of the Company, during June 1933 Mr. Hobbs (who had assisted with the accounts) was appointed as Assistant Secretary to work under Theo Denham. The latter also proposed Freddie Spanswick should be appointed as Director, but no seconder was forthcoming.

A further 20-seater Thornycroft was purchased during September 1933, though unusually for a bus this had a rear-entrance body. The new arrival was RA 1794 (fleet no. unknown), which was an A2Long-type new in February 1927 to *Henshaw & Brooks (The Newell)* of Ilkeston in Derbyshire. After that it passed through *J. Williamson & Sons* in 1929, before they were acquired by *Midland General* in due course. The body was built by Challands Ross, who also acted as the local agents for Thornycrofts in Nottingham, and due to the rear-entrance layout this vehicle was more often used for coaching duties.

Thornycroft RA 1794 had several unusual features for a bus of its size, with a recessed rear doorway and a nearside spare wheel carrier. It is shown above when new to its original owner, whilst the sketch below shows the nearside layout.

Also purchased about that time was a pair of Leyland 'Lion' PLSC1-type 31-seaters through one of the London dealers. However, these had started their lives much further north during July/August 1928 in the service of *W. Baxter* of Blantyre in Scotland. Both had Leyland-built bodies, and they subsequently passed to *Torrence* of Hamilton, before again moving to *Central Scottish Motor Traction* in 1932, after which they were to become *N&D* Nos.39/40 (VA 7942/3).

Throughout the period since the departure of Charlie Durnford, he had of course remained a shareholder in the Company, and in October 1933 both he and Freddie Spanswick put their names forward for election to the Board. An extraordinary meeting was convened the following month in order to review the matter, during which Durnford gave the necessary assurances that he would curtail his 'outside interests' in due course if elected. Both he and Spanswick were successful and became Directors, which also effectively meant that any competition from *Durnford Bros.* would soon be brought to a close.

The pair of Leyland 'Lions' acquired as Nos.39/40 (VA 7942/3) proved to be a sound purchase and led to more of the same type. These were unusual in not having cab doors, whilst No.39 has also had its destination screens rebuilt in typical SMT fashion. The advert boards were commonplace on the service buses, and Newbury Laundry a prominent advertiser.

Another investor joined in September 1933, when Mr. F. McNairmie of Tilehurst, who was an accountant by profession, bought an unrecorded shareholding, though evidently enough to see him appointed as a Director from November 1933. It is also clear from other research that the full extent of loans, inter-loans and other sources of financial backing for the Company is actually much more complex than the official account might suggest!

A review had taken place of the local links provided, resulting in the development of new Local Services. The licenses for the three new routes were granted and operation commenced on Thursday 9th November. As will be seen on page 69, careful timings meant that a single bus could work all the routes in rotation throughout the day, starting at 8.48am and continuing until ending its day at 10.32pm. Special arrangements were made in respect of race days at Newbury Race Course, whereby the service to Hambridge Road was augmented to a 15-minute headway for an hour before and after the race meeting. On such days, the Police had conditions on traffic movements, so the town centre stop moved to The Wharf in order to comply.

Another full-size bus was acquired in November 1933 in the shape of a Dennis E-type with 32-seater dual-entrance bodywork by Strachan & Brown. This was one of a batch new to *National* in May 1927, passing to the *Southern National* company when the division of January 1929 took place. It was registered PR 9053 and became No.41, being used mainly for school runs and at peak times.

During October 1933 a number of detailed changes were proposed to the services inherited, which allowed the number of vehicles required for the schedules to be reduced. General permission was also sought from the Traffic Commissioner to allow the running of later journeys in respect of dances, whist drives etc., which had been a regular feature before the 1930 Act. Such permission was indeed forthcoming, but on condition that the journeys were not operated until at least 30 minutes after the cessation of authorised services.

The more significant changes introduced to services effective from 10th December were as follows:

Route 2 - East Ilsley – Reading – the early-morning 7.45am journey to Reading was deleted. Later evening journeys were added on Thursdays and Saturdays, whilst some workings on Route 1 - (Newbury – East Ilsley) were re-timed to become through journeys to Reading on Mondays, Tuesdays and Fridays.
Route 3 - Newbury – Peasemore – in order to remove the long layovers at Newbury, the service was recast to provide three return journeys on Tuesdays, Thursdays and Saturdays, with a later evening service on Saturdays. This allowed the service to be covered by a Newbury-based bus, thus reducing the East Ilsley allocation to just two.
Route 4 - Newbury – Wantage – a generally enhanced timetable was provided, operating on Wednesdays, Thursdays, Saturdays and Sundays. The latter day had not featured on *George Hedges'* timetable, though it was popular with those visitors to The Ridgeway, the ancient trackway over the Berkshire Downs.
Route 5 - Newbury – Brightwalton – most days saw an improved timetable, though Wednesday and Sunday workings were reduced. Some later evening journeys were run on Tuesdays, Thursdays and Saturdays by using a Newbury-based vehicle.
Route 13 - Newbury – Westrop – a third journey from Newbury at 6.10pm was added on Tuesdays, whilst an 11.20pm was provided between Newbury and Cold

Ash on Saturdays only. In respect of the changes on this service, this again had to be co-ordinated with those provided by *Albert Austin.*

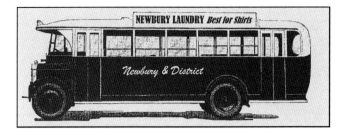

Dennis E-type No.41 (PR 9053) was another sound buy and reduced the need for duplicates on busy days.

The services inherited from *Denham Bros.* had also been reviewed, and from the same date the following changes were implemented:

Route 7 - Newbury – Hungerford – a generally improved service was provided, including an earlier morning service, along with later evening journeys on Saturdays.

Route 8 - Newbury – Shefford Woodlands – wheras it had originally operated as Newbury – Wickham, with a Thursdays-only projection to Hoe Benham, the new schedule saw further projections to reach Wickham Heath and Shefford Woodlands on Thursdays and Saturdays, which also went some way to covering the erstwhile *Ramsbury Motor Services* route between Aldbourne and Newbury.

Route 14 - Newbury – Lower Green (Inkpen) – a generally enhanced service was provided.

Route 16 - Newbury – Highclere – whereas the journeys to Broadlaying, Griffins Corner and The Mount had previously only operated on Thursdays and Saturdays, these were now served throughout the week. Also an additional journey from Newbury at 7.25am provided an effective replacement for the one previously provided by *Thames Valley* before it gave up on that route. A later bus was also provided for Thursday and Saturday evenings, leaving Newbury at 10.35pm.

In respect of the East Ilsley operations, during early December Messrs. Andrews, Durnford and Prothero went to see some land there for the siting of a shed for the 2 buses, but in January 1934 it was resolved that the sheds behind the Swan Inn at East Ilsley would be rented instead.

There were many other detailed changes to timings or days of operation, all in the light of findings during the first year of operation. All routes were also now allocated numbers, though they never appeared on the buses at this time, these becoming:

Route 1   Newbury – Chieveley – Beedon – East Ilsley
Route 2   East Ilsley – Compton – Reading
Route 3   Newbury – Chieveley – Peasemore

Route 4   Newbury – Brightwalton Holt – Wantage
Route 5   Newbury – Leckhampstead – Brightwalton
Route 6   Newbury – Boxford – Eastbury – Lambourn
Route 7   Newbury – Speen – Avington – Hungerford
Route 8   Newbury – Wickham – Shefford Woodlands
Route 9   Newbury – Inkpen – Kintbury – Hungerford
Route 10 Newbury – Ball Hill – West Woodhay
Route 11 Newbury – Ball Hill – East Woodhay
Route 12 Newbury – Thatcham – Colthrop Mills
Route 13 Newbury – Thatcham - Cold Ash – Westrop
Route 14 Newbury – Kintbury – Lower Green
Route 15 Newbury – Ecchinswell – Sydmonton
Route 16 Newbury – Woolton Hill - Highclere
Route 17 Newbury – Ball Hill – North End
Route 18 Newbury Local Service
Route 19 Newbury Local Service
Route 20 Newbury Local Service

DAILY LOCAL SERVICES.
ROUTES 18, 20 & 19.

CAMP CLOSE NEWBURY & DONNINGTON.
via Broadway, Cheap St., Station Rd. & Howard Rd.

	a.m.	NS	NS	NS	p.m.	p.m.	p.m.	p.m.
Broadway	...	8 52	10 52	12 52	2 52	...	6 52	8 52
Donnington	...	9 0	11 0	1 0	3 0	...	7 0	9 0
Broadway	...	9 8	11 8	1 8	3 8	...	7 8	9 8
Station Road	...	9 12	11 12	1 12	3 12	...	7 12	9 12
Camp Close	...	9 20	11 20	1 20	3 20	...	7 20	9 20
Station Road	8 48	9 28	11 28	1 28	3 28	5 28	7 28	9 28
Broadway	8 52	9 32	11 32	1 32	3 32	5 32	7 32	9 32

SHAW, NEWBURY & KINGSBRIDGE ROAD.
via Broadway, Bartholomew St. & Craven Rd.
returning to Shaw, via Cheap St.

	NS	NS	NS	p.m.	p.m.	p.m.	p.m.
Broadway	...	9 32	11 32	1 32	3 32	*5 32	7 32	9 32
Shaw	...	9 40	11 40	1 40	3 40	5 40	7 40	9 40
Broadway	...	9 48	11 48	1 48	3 48	5 48	7 48	9 48
Craven Road	...	9 51	11 51	1 51	3 51	5 51	7 51	9 51
Kingsbridge Road	...	10 0	12 0	2 0	4 0	6 0	8 0	10 0
Craven Road	...	10 8	12 8	2 8	4 8	6 8	8 8	10 8
Broadway	...	10 12	12 12	2 12	...	6 12	8 12	10 12

HAMBRIDGE ROAD, NEWBURY & SPEEN.
via Broadway, Cheap St., Station Rd. & Queen's Rd.
and to Speen, via Bartholomew St.

	NS	NS	p.m.	p.m.	p.m.	p.m.
Broadway	...	10 12	12 12	2 12	...	6 12	8 12	10 12
Speen	...	10 20	12 20	2 20	...	6 20	8 20	10 20
Broadway	...	10 28	12 28	2 28	...	6 28	8 28	10 28
Station Road	...	10 32	12 32	2 32	...	6 32	8 32	10 32
Hambridge Road	...	10 40	12 40	2 40	...	6 40	8 40	...
Station Road	...	10 48	12 48	2 48	...	6 48	8 48	...
Broadway	...	10 52	12 52	2 52	...	6 52	8 52	...

NS—Not Sundays.   *—Depart Station Road at 5.28 p.m.
On Race Days a Special Service of Buses will be run from The Wharf to Hambridge Road, via Cheap Street and Winchombe Road, before and after the Races.

The dove-tailed timetable for Routes 18, 19 and 20, shown above was usually worked by one of the 20-seater Thornycroft buses.

As previously noted, Charles Durnford had agreed to end the competition taking place through his support of his sons and, although that process had not been completed, it is should be noted that the 'Mouslford Special' actually appeared in the *N&D* timetable book issued with the changes in December 1933. Rather cryptically is advises enquiries to call 'Newbury 43' (Durnford's at Market Street) or 'Woolhampton 7' (which was *Arthur Bason* at The Angel Hotel). This would, however, illustrate that the transfer was indeed well under way, though in view of previous events, the necessary documents would need to be finalised.

Indeed, further negotiations with Charlie Durnford also produced a resolution over the outstanding amount on the Mill Lane land, whereby at his suggestion the Company allocated 50 shares to Percy Andrews, along with 25 each to Boss Denham and Olive Durnford to cover the value.

Fares charged on the Local Service Routes18, 19 and 20, ranging between 1 and 4 old pence.

FARES.

1d.	2d.
Kingsbridge Road—Rockingham Road	Queen's Road—Broadway
Hambridge Rd.—Station Rd.	Kingsbridge Rd.—Parish Church
Craven Rd.—Broadway	Camp Close—Station Rd.
Chesterfield Rd.—Station Rd.	Chesterfield Rd.—Broadway
Shaw Rd.—Newbury Parish (Greyhound Inn) Church	Donnington—Newbury
	Speen P.O.—Broadway
1½d.	Cheap St.—Hambridge Rd. *(Race Day Specials)*
Parish Church—Grammar School	
Station Rd.—Broadway	**2½d.**
Rockingham Rd.—Broadway	Shaw—Craven Rd.
Shaw (Brickfields)—Broadway	Kingsbridge Rd.—Broadway
Kingsbridge Rd.—Craven Rd	Hambridge Rd.—Broadway
3d.	**4d.**
Donnington—Station Rd.	Donnington Camp Close
Camp Close—Broadway	Speen P.O.—Hambridge Rd.
Speen P.O.—Station Rd.	Shaw—Kingsbridge Rd.
Shaw—Station Rd.	

The 20-seater Thornycroft A-series proved to be a good choice for the 20-seater saloon requirement, and N&D had 17 examples including No.10 (OU 3317).

Despite being an odd-man-out, the Garner coach No.29 (YT 9565) continued in service, and is seen here at Southsea after re-painting and a new hood.

The entrance to The Wharf parking ground from the Market Place was reached by way of Wharf Street, and was constricted by the position of the Old Cloth Hall. The Old Granaries were beyond that, whilst to its right was the entrance to the yard of the White Hart Hotel, a popular base for several carriers.

However, despite serious attempts at standardisation, the fleet still offered a considerable variety at the close of 1933, with 31 known passenger vehicles with chassis by Bedford (1), Dennis (2), Ford (8), Garner (1), Gilford (3), GMC (1), Lancia (1), Leyland (2), Maudslay (1), Reo (2), Star (2), Talbot (1), Thornycroft (4) and Tilling-Stevens (2), whilst the 3 known lorries were all on Dennis chassis. Therefore, Newbury Wharf presented an interesting sight on peak days, when the coaches and lesser-used service buses would be pressed into service in order to meet the demand for transport from the surrounding area.

Chapter 7 – 1934

This was a year when further operations were added in all four geographical directions from Newbury, and a greater degree of organisation was also put in place. However, it also had some setbacks, with further instances of partners falling out, as we shall see in due course.

However, the year started with positive moves over the situation with the breakaway Durnford operations, and at the Board Meeting of 1st January it was agreed to purchase the business of *Durnford Bros.*, which also included the haulage aspects covered by Charlie and his son Bill.

In respect of the vehicles purchased from *Durnford Bros.*, the Company paid £245 for the Gilford 166SD coach, with 26-seater body of unknown make (HJ 8718) and this became *N&D* No.51. It also purchased the Ford AA lorry (RX 4356) for £47, plus £10 insurances and £98 in respect of the E&T's Road Service License. In addition, Len, Bill, Ernie and Henry were allocated £100 shares each, and were guaranteed full time employment as drivers or mechanics for 3 years minimum at £2 per week, subject to acceptance of the clauses relating to non-participation in any competing business.

The Maudslay furniture van (CW 6802) had gone out of the fleet with Bill at the time of the split, as it was actually still owned by his father. Charlie had also bought a 26-seater Thurgood-bodied Star 'Flyer' VB4 coach (GU 7545), and these were subject to a separate purchase. The Star duly took the fleet number 28, which was about to be vacated, whilst the lorry is recorded on the log book as 'L4'. However, it carried the fleet number 4 on the dash when photographed at the time of conversion from coach to removals van, i.e. before *N&D* was formed. It also seems likely that the number was not allocated by *Durnfords*, but was already in place from its previous ownership, so it appears that this continued to be the case. All four of the vehicles were to see further use.

Arthur Bason, through his association with *Durnford Bros.*, then became the *N&D* booking agent for the Woolhampton and Midgham area. Indeed, the latter also took the opportunity when seeking transfer of the E&T's license to add further destinations to run to Aldershot Tattoo, Ascot Races, Bognor Regis, Brighton, California-in-England, Marlborough, Oxford, Pangbourne, Pewsey, Salisbury, Swindon and Tidworth Tattoo, all of which were approved.

Ever since the formation of the Company, there had been no apparent policy on a fleet livery, but in January 1934 the Board resolved that service buses would be painted green with cream relief, whilst the coaches would wear the reverse scheme. However, as

has already been noted earlier, the definition of what was a bus or coach was not always clear cut.

Although virtually all coachwork and painting was undertaken at the Northcroft Lane premises, it is known that occasionally such work was sent out, one such example being a Gilford coach urgently painted by a firm in Basingstoke during the mid-1930's and taken there and back by Driver George Amor.

However, to return to the other events of this busy January, on the 15th of that month the passenger aspect of the business of *John Burt & Albert Greenwood* based in Inkpen was added.

John Burt & Albert Greenwood

John Francis ('Jack') Burt took over the existing carrier's service from *'Wilfred' Davis* of Inkpen during 1930. He continued to run between Inkpen and Newbury (a distance of 10.6 miles) on Thursdays and Saturdays, along with journeys to Hungerford on Wednesdays and Fridays, starting from Lower Green and running by way of Upper Green – Inkpen Common – Hamstead Marshall – Enborne, some 5 miles in all.

Burt also took over the existing 1926 Ford 'Tonbus' (MO 7517), which had seats for 14 passengers. In addition to the carrier-cum-bus services, a certain amount of haulage was also undertaken, but expansion got underway once *Bert Greenwood* had joined him.

Albert Victor Greenwood came from Brighouse in West Yorkshire, but soon after he returned from army service in the Great War he tragically lost both parents to the terrible Spanish 'flu epidemic of 1918. This caused him to move south, where he found a job with Mr. Edwards, an Engineer based in Inkpen. After a while he went to work for *Arthur Andrews* and his son *Percy,* mainly undertaking bicycle repairs, though as the charabanc side of the business developed Bert also took to driving duties, and he married Mabel Bowsher in 1926. He was living in Kintbury and sometime in 1930 he ran into his old army pal Jack Burt of 'Ambleside', Inkpen, so he joined him in expanding his carriers and bus operations. Bert took over driving the bus journeys, whilst Jack concentrated on managing the business and the haulage side.

A further Model T had been purchased in late 1929 as a charabanc, seeing use in that form and as a lorry during its stay until December 1930. This was MO 2059, which had been new in August 1923 to *Archie Arlott* of Beenham.

With the new partnership a larger coach was purchased in the shape of a 1930 Federal, a quite rare import from the USA. The registration of this vehicle is quoted as GJ 9733 in *N&D* documents, whilst the alternative of GJ 7973 has also been quoted, though neither checks out on what has survived of the motor tax records for that mark. One operator, *Beattie Coaches* of Acton, W5 is known to have had 3 Federal A6B-types 28-seaters, 2 of which were GJ 5370 and 5825, though both were retained for some years. However, the exact identity of the third one has not been confirmed, making it a possible candidate for the above.

The Hungerford journeys still ran on Wednesdays (market day) and Fridays, whilst the Newbury service had two return journeys on Thursdays, with a third journey departing on Saturdays at 5.45pm and returning from Newbury at 10.15, ideal for patrons of the cinema etc.

A later photo of Bert Greenwood with Bedford No.70.

Under the 1930 Road Traffic Act, the bus services continued to be licensed, whilst the coaching side had been increased to cover excursions and tours to Aldershot Tattoo, Bournemouth, Hungerford Sports, Pangbourne, Savernake Forest, Southsea and Tidworth Tattoo. At the same hearing, which was finally heard in May 1932, they were also successful in adding Bognor Regis, Brighton, Hayling Island, Highcliffe, London, Whipsnade Zoo and Weston-super-Mare.

However, *N&D* had also been busy in that area, being granted licenses for excursions to 24 destinations from

nearby Kintbury, which must have concerned Jack and Bert. Indeed, it is evident that they gained approval for an increase of permitted vehicles to two on any one day, even though they still only had the one coach, as they would hire in from *Durnford Bros*.

The bus service, along with the Federal coach, was sold to *N&D* with effect from 15th January 1934, though the carrier's and coal business was retained by *Jack Burt*. Arrangements were made to take over the Federal coach, but Burt disposed of the Ford MO 7517, with *N&D* selling him former-*Prothero* Ford AA-type RX 4272 for use as a lorry.

Whereas Burt continued to trade in his own right, subject to the usual restrictions as outlined in the agreement, *Bert Greenwood* became an employee of *N&D*. Jack Burt received £200 cash and 440 £1 shares, along with 10 shillings per week for the use of his premises as an outstation. Bert Greenwood on the other hand, received £20 cash and 200 £1 shares, after which he was paid £2 and 5 shillings per week as a driver, with an additional 5 shillings per week for his wife to maintain a Booking Agency from their home at 1 Newbury Street in Kintbury, to which *N&D* also paid for a telephone connection.

> Before we leave this area, there are two further small operators who provided services to Newbury from the 'south-west frontier', both of whom were based just over the border in Wiltshire.

Walter Humphries

Walter Humphries was based in the small settlement of Fosbury, some 8 miles south of Hungerford. He had been born 5 miles north of there at Great Bedwyn in 1868. By 1881 the family were resident a short way north of Fosbury in the hamlet of Oxenwood, where his father James was the blacksmith. At that point 13 year-old Walter was a farmer's boy, though he duly became an assistant to his father at the forge. After he had trained and married, by 1896 he was working in that trade in Orts Road, Reading, a street which housed a number of large stable blocks at that time, and they were still in Reading in 1907.

However, by 1911, they returned to Wiltshire and he is noted as being established as a carrier by 1915, though the exact date of commencement is not recorded. His route to Hungerford ran from Fosbury via Oxenwood and Shalbourne on a Wednesday (market day) and on Saturday. At first the service was a horse-powered one, *Walter* being very familiar with handling horses of course.

Motorisation came in much the same fashion as with many other carriers in the area, in the shape of a Ford Model T 1-tonner (MO 4726), purchased through Pass & Co. of Newbury and fitted with a blue-painted body with seats for 14 in March 1925. This is likely to have been when his son *Leonard George Percival ('Percy') Humphries,* born in late 1906, became involved. The advent of this vehicle allowed the service to expand, with a market-day journey to Newbury on Thursdays, which took the main road from Hungerford to Newbury, avoiding any conflict with *Stout's* service from Shalbourne to that town, which went by way of Ham and Inkpen. The bus also travelled to Andover on Fridays only for market day by way of Vernham Dean – Upton – Hurstbourne Tarrant, meaning that in the course of the working week his little bus could be found in 3 counties!

As was often the case with operators serving such a rural district, few changes took place over the years. In Newbury he used The Bear, leaving there at 4pm, though around 1932 he relocated to The Wharf. Under the 1930 Act he was granted licenses for the route to Hungerford, along with the Newbury extension on Thursdays, though the latter had the restriction that he could not carry passengers solely between Newbury and Hungerford, in order to protect the established service of *Denham Bros.* The Andover service also continued, though still only on Fridays.

When the original Ford departed is not known, though it had been in use elsewhere before 1934, nor have any details come to light of its replacement. *Walter Humphries* passed away in 1944 at the age of 76, and on 21st March 1946 *Percy Humphries* sold the goodwill of the Fosbury – Andover and Hungerford routes to *Wilts & Dorset* for £150. Although the latter had been in touch with *Newbury & District* regarding the run to Newbury on Thursdays, it had subsequently decided not to continue with that part of the operation, being only interested in consolidating its position on its established Andover – Hungerford route.

Stout Family

The Stout family of the village of Shalbourne, some 4 miles south-west of Hungerford, had a long pedigree in the business as country carriers. As early as 1871 we find *Jason Stout* operating a carrier's service to Hungerford and onwards to Newbury on Thursdays. He had been born in the village in 1829, though he was still a labourer in 1861. His service continued until at least 1891, and he died in 1895, after which the service passed out of Stout family hands to *Thomas Levy* of Bars Lane, who did in fact have distant family connections through local marriages.

One of Jason's sons, *Charles,* who had been born in 1855 was an agricultural labourer in 1871, but is absent from the area in the censuses of 1881-1901, though he married Ellen Wicks in 1886, she having been born in Andover in 1866. They had their son, *Charles Henry Valentine Stout* in 1892, who will re-appear in due course.

It is evident that there was a real need for men from the area to seek work elsewhere, which affected several generations of the Stout family. Firstly, Charles senior went to work as a maltster's assistant, no doubt expanding on what he had learnt as a young farm labourer. He was working away in 1891, 1901 and 1911, though he returned home to see his wife and growing family regularly. Indeed, Ellen was one of three adjacent households in the village whose husbands were away on the same trade. Charles was at the Morland Brewery in Abingdon, Berkshire for a time, though by 1911 he was at The Malt House in the High Street, Goring-on-Thames in Oxfordshire.

The younger Charles also moved away to work, and he is found in 1911 lodging with his married sister Edith Ellen Rolfe in York Road, St. Pancras in North London, both he and his brother-in-law Fred working as railway porters at the station. The Rolfe family also had connections to the Levy family, along with some involvement with the Kings Arms in Shalbourne, all threads that helped to shape relevant events.

Under Charles senior the carrier's service returned to family hands by 1917, though *Thomas Levy* was still listed in the 1915 local directory, and the layover in Newbury was changed from The Globe to The Dolphin in Bartholomew Street, where the horse-drawn van departed at 3pm, travelling via Enborne – Hamstead Marshall – Lower Inkpen – Ham, on Thursdays only. On Tuesdays, Wednesdays, Fridays and Saturdays the van ran into Hungerford, also taking in the village of Ham on the way.

Charles junior served in the Wiltshire Regiment during the Great War, marrying Dorothy Watts in the Spring of 1916, and duly returning home.

No changes were evident by 1923, but in June 1925 a Ford T 1-tonner was placed in service as MO 5051, the money for this having reputedly been saved in a jar. It carried a stained and varnished bus body with seats for 14, and at that point *Ellen Stout* was running the service, though no doubt son *Charles* was now involved. This particular vehicle was changed to the latter's ownership in January 1930 and after that all were registered in his name. Whereas his mother lived at Ropewind, Shalbourne, by 1927 he was at the Kings Arms also as a beer retailer, whilst earlier generations had been at The Barracks in that village.

Charles Stout senior died in 1928, after which his son took the lead in the family business, which was also notable for the long working lives of their vehicles, and the original Ford continued in use until 1933. In April 1929 they added a Ford AA-type (RX 4367), which carried a blue-painted 14-seater bus body, and that remained in service until October 1944! No doubt there was also some private hire and excursion work when the buses were not occupied, with the usual whist drives, darts teams and dances to cater for, along with trips to various local gatherings or to the coast.

The two services to Hungerford and Newbury were duly licensed under the 1930 Act, leading to an increase of service on the Newbury route, with two journeys on a Saturday added to the established run on Thursdays. Whereas the latter continued to operate a single run which returned at 3.30pm, on Saturdays the two journeys left at 12noon and at 3pm, all still using The Dolphin. However, by 1934 the Newbury base had moved to The Wharf.

A coach-bodied Bedford WLB was added during the early 1940's to cover a wartime contract run. This had a 20-seater 'sunsaloon' body in a brown and buff livery, registered RX 9323 and had been new to *Thomas Clare (Eagle Coaches)* of Faringdon in October 1931, passing to *C.J. Bodman* of Devizes by May 1940, and thence to Shalbourne. It continued in use until June 1947, by which time it was blue and grey, and *Charles Stout* was still at the Kings Arms.

Bedford WLB-type coach RX 9323 in wartime.

A further generation was represented by *Richard Henry Stout,* who was born in 1922, and he assumed control of the business in July 1960. The name of the firm was changed to *St. Valentine Coach Co. Ltd.* from December 1965, with an address at Valentine House in Shalbourne. From the post-WW2 era only Bedford vehicles were purchased and a livery of dark and light blue was used. In July 1966 the firm finally passed out of family hands, when it was sold to the established local operators *H.R., R.C. & J. Elgar (Swansdown Coaches)* in Inkpen. *Charles Henry Valentine Stout* died in 1973, and the remainder of developments are outside the scope of this history.

****

During January at least one of the former *Prothero* Ford AA-type buses was sold. This was RX 4272 which, as noted above was disposed of to *Jack Burt.* Another similar Ford (RX 7256) from the same source

was also sold around that time, whilst the fleet numbers for both remain unknown.

The end of January saw a further two small businesses being taken over, one very rural and limited in nature, whilst the other was more local and intensive. Firstly we will review the activities of *Mrs. Geary* of Great Shefford.

Catherine Geary

Catherine Mizen had married Edward Geary in 1919 locally and she was the proprietor of the *Joy Coaches & Cars,* based at Church Road in the Lambourn valley village of Great Shefford. She also undertook some haulage and removals work, with her first vehicle being a Ford AA truck-cum-bus, registered RX 3981 in March 1929. The vehicle had 14 detachable seats, had a varnished wood finish and was supplied by Pass & Co. of Newbury, and from the same dealer she added a second Ford AA, registered RX 5432 in October 1929, and that was fitted with a 14-seat coach body which bore a red livery.

Exactly when she added the bus service is unclear, but certainly with the second vehicle it was established as a Saturdays-only service from Fawley (sometimes referred to as North Fawley) to Newbury, a distance of some 13 miles, which ran by way of South Fawley – Whatcombe – Great Shefford – Shefford Woodlands – Welford – Boxford – Woodspeen – Speen. It should be noted that the area she served on the Lambourn Downs was in fact one of the most sparsely populated, with the entire scattered population only numbering 192 at the 1921 census, whilst Great Shefford had 382 residents then.

As her base was some half-way between Wantage to the north and Hungerford to the south, it is possible that she also ran to those towns on their respective market days, though her service was not listed in the local directories as a carrier's link. Apart from the bus service, regular private hire and excursions work was found for the coach, whilst cars were available to meet trains on the Lambourn Valley Railway, there being a number of large private estates along the valley environs.

Under the 1930 Act, Mrs. Geary was granted the Road Service License for continuation of the bus service to Newbury, though it remained a Saturday-only run. On the excursions and tours front she was granted licenses to operate from Church Road, Great Shefford to Aldershot Tattoo, Ascot Races, Bournemeouth and Tidworth Tattoo, though being in a prime area of race horse training there were a number of private hires to other race meetings within a day's drive, along with those held at Newbury Racecourse. By 1931 her husband Edward was listed in Kelly's Directory as a petroleum merchant at Great Shefford (or rather West

Shefford, as it was generally known at that time), though not as a motor garage, of which there were already two in the village.

The exact reason for her offering to sell the licenses to *N&D* is not recorded, but these were offered for £150. The Company was not interested in acquiring her Ford coach due to its poor condition, but arrangements were made whereby Pass & Co. agreed to pay £90 for it as soon as *N&D* took it off Mrs. Geary. The Ford truck, which was by then used solely for goods, was retained by her, remaining in use in that capacity until the end of January 1937. In 1935 she was also listed as the local coal and coke merchant, by which time the earlier petroleum business had developed into a filling station.

Mrs. Geary's service and E&T's licenses were acquired in January 1934, taking *N&D's* buses further up the Lambourn valley and beyond. The journeys were increased to two return journeys over the full route, preceded by a positioning journey from Newbury which ran the more direct route and called at Great Shefford only. Despite being a limited service, residents could nonetheless enjoy the facility of leaving Newbury at 10.15pm. On arrival at Fawley at 11.15pm, the bus ran back 'dead' to Newbury. At first the service appeared without a route number, though this would be catered for in due course.

Mrs. Geary also took on the role of local booking agent for *N&D*, remaining as such for several years.

****

George Brown

George Brown of Bourne Terrace, Wash Common was a relative newcomer to the local bus scene, though the origins of his Wash Common route preceded him by some years.

Richard Augustine Pestell

The catalyst for this was *Richard Pestell,* who had served as an Officer in the Great War, and from February 1920 was offering himself as the driver of 'a comfortable Wolseley touring car, any distance any time'. During August 1920 he purchased The Stores in Essex Street at Wash Common from Mr. Wheaton and his wife ran the shop and post office. *Pestell* had been born at Gibraltar, though this was the Buckinghamshire village of that name just west of Aylesbury, not the colony on the Iberian peninsular, during November 1876. Initially he worked with his father in High Wycombe as a bead-worker, but by 1901 he was in Chesham and a baker. A further move, now doubt in connection with his marriage in June 1905 at Poplar, London saw him relocated to Cheam in Surrey as confectioner and baker.

The *Wash Common Bus Service* originated on 2nd March 1925, when Pestell decided to provide a regular service between there and Newbury. Although the route was only a couple of miles, the housing had increased after the First World War, whilst many found the long steady climb back up Wash Hill a bind with shopping to carry. Indeed, one maiden lady made a point of saving the outward fare by cycling into town, and then rode back on the bus with her machine tied to the rear!

For this venture he had registered a Ford 'Ton-bus' on 28th February as MO 6416, this having been supplied by Pass & Co. with varnished wooden bodywork for 14 passengers. Although the service already had been referred to as above, the fleetname carried was *The Doris*, in honour of Mrs. Pestell! The bus left the Falkland Monument at 7.40am, 8.55am, 10.45am, 4.45pm and 7.45pm on weekdays, returning from Newbury Market Place at 7.55am, 9.30am, 11.30am, 5.15pm and 8.15pm, and it also called into the railway station, making it useful for those travelling onward by rail. On Saturdays there were additional journeys from the Monument at 5.45pm and 9.15pm, and those returned at 6.15pm and 10.15pm.

The service was undoubtedly popular, and from 25th March 1925 some extra journeys filled in the timetable more evenly throughout the day. Carrying was not included in the strict sense, though parcels could be left at the shop for onward transport into the town. Also, although excursions were not advertised, a certain amount of local private hire was undertaken when the bus was not required for service.

The Ford bus continued in use until January 1929, when it was replaced by a more spacious 14-seater bus on a Morris-Commercial 25cwt chassis, which was registered as RX 3553 on 4th January. However, unlike its predecessor it did not carry Mrs. Pestell's name. The Morris-Commercial was being promoted locally by Stradling's Garage as a rival to the products of the Ford Motor Company, and this example carried a maroon painted body built by Morris.

Sketch of a typical Morris-Commercial 25-cwt bus.

The outgoing Ford was, however, to see further service with *Ernie Nobes* of Lambourn Woodlands, of whom we shall hear more in due course.

At some point soon after the Morris-Commercial arrived Pestell decided to add some journeys to serve the Kingsbridge Road area, where housing developments were taking place between the Andover and Enborne roads. This new local service linking Newbury town centre also passed the railway station, and it is clear that the bus inter-worked the services, which then occupied it from 8.30am through to 8.30pm on weekdays. On Saturdays services continued until 10.30pm, whilst there was a reduced operation on a Wednesday in reflection of the early-closing day.

Both services were duly licensed under the 1930 Act, but in October 1933 *Richard Pestell* sold his operation to *George Brown* of Wash Common. The Pestells kept the stores, and Richard died in 1940 aged 63.

Brown ran the service in similar fashion, using the 14-seater Morris-Commercial. As there was some duplication with the *N&D* routes along those roads, the Company was happy to consider his offer to sell out, though his offer of £400 was reduced to £350. The services and the bus were acquired in January 1934, and the 14-seater remained in use until about September 1935, by which time the livery had been altered to maroon and cream.

****

During February another 20-seater Thornycroft bus was purchased, in the shape of Strachan & Brown-bodied front-entrance A2-type KM 3028. This had originated in February 1929 with *Weald of Kent* based in Tenterden, passing to *Maidstone & District,* though it came to Newbury via a London dealer, becoming No.11. A Strachan-bodied Gilford 166OT coach was also acquired around February, possibly TM 5639.

Thornycroft No.11 (KM 3028) as new at the Strachan & Brown coachworks in Acton, this firm becoming just Strachans from October 1929.

Meanwhile, attention was also given to the excursions side, with activity well in advance of the season, and in January a number of applications were made.

In respect of excursions from Brightwalton, a further pick up point at Newbury (The Wharf) was added in order to combine capacities when appropriate. On the other hand the excursion to London from East Ilsley was surrendered, along with the Bath, Cheddar and Wells tour, though additional destinations added were Ascot Races, Weston-super-Mare and Weymouth.

The destinations served from Thatcham were reduced to cover those to Aldershot Tattoo, Ascot Races, Bournemouth, Hungerford, Oxford, the Newbury Commons evening tour, Pangbourne, Southsea, Swindon and Tidworth Tattoo. Further destinations from The Wharf were added, these being an Andover, Basingstoke and Winchester circular tour, East Woodhay, Epsom Races, Pewsey, Whipsnade Zoo and the Wye Valley, and all of the above applications were granted as requested.

It should of course be appreciated that the inclusion of a number of relatively local destinations in the license applications was to take account of popular annual events, such as carnivals, sports days, donkey derby's, fetes, agricultural shows and point-to-point meetings. Indeed, the Company was always quick to respond to requests for supplementary bus services whenever a local event warranted it, and such an example during February 1934 was when the Newbury & District Amateur Dramatic Society (no connection to the bus company!) put on performances of Gilbert & Sullivan's 'The Mikado' at the Town Hall, extra buses being run before and after the shows.

A further significant addition to operations came on 22nd February 1934, with the *Kennet Bus Service* of *George Howlett* of Bucklebury.

George Perry Howlett

George Howlett was born in Thame, Oxfordshire in 1875, marrying Sarah from Thatcham in 1898. At 1901 they were living in Chapel Street, Thatcham, and he was working as a Japanner of Brushwares (meaning that he applied the lacquer finish to brush handles), which was a prominent local industry that tied in with the practice of coppicing in the woods.

They relocated to 'The Hawthorns' in Cold Ash and commenced a horse-drawn carrier's service between Cold Ash, Ashmore Green and Newbury in 1908 (a distance of some 5.5 miles), running each way on Tuesdays, Thursdays and Saturdays, using the Waggon & Horses in the Market Place as his standing point as had *Hamblin* before him. By 1911 he had moved again, this time to Bucklebury Alley, just a short way east of Cold Ash. His service was one of the first in the area to go over to motorised transport, using initially a Wolseley-Siddeley 18-24hp, which was placed on the road as BL 3415 in January 1914, though it did not prove to be particularly reliable! This was replaced by a CPT 18-20hp registered as BL 027 in March 1914, which was an American make constructed by the Consolidated Pneumatic Tool Company and featured an 'overtype' layout (or forward-control in England), which gave a lot more space for goods and passengers, the latter being provided with bench seats running down the two sides of the grey-painted body. This vehicle was re-registered as BL 3850 under the 1920 Road Traffic Act, and it must have been a good purchase, as it lasted until 1927. With the coming of the CPT he transferred his stand in Newbury to by the Monument near the Town Hall.

The CPT carrier's van BL 027 photographed in 1918. Note the baskets on the roof, some for livestock or for the Newbury Sanitary Laundry, along with the rear tail-board for heavy items. The forward-control layout was virtually unknown in Britain then, but provided ample carrying space.

Commer bus referred to in the following paragraph.

A somewhat curious event took place, evidently in 1913, which resulted in *George Howlett* being in a photograph taken outside his cottage on the occasion of an apparent excursion in a large Commer WP-type bus registered AH 0132. Although this has come down to modern times just as that, the record of one of his excursions, there are reasons why this is, at least, not strictly true! The bus was in fact new to *United Automobile Services* and, despite the Norfolk plate, it actually served in the Bishop Auckland area of County Durham. It had a body built by Liversidge of Old Kent Road, London SE1, and careful examination of the photo by *United* historians confirms that this is in brand new condition and before certain changes in appearance took place. The only options seem that either it was on an official demonstration on behalf of Commer Cars, or that someone who knew George had called by with it whilst on delivery? We may never know, but it certainly did not belong to *Howlett*!

Having now motorised, *Howlett* found he could also run to Reading on Fridays from 1917, as well as developing a steady business in haulage and house removals. However, in July 1919 he took the unusual step of selling his Cold Ash to Newbury carrier's service to the recently de-mobbed *Albert Austin*. It would seem that he considered that the Reading operation, along with haulage and private hire would be enough for him. Indeed, he even secured a Hackney Carriage License with Reading Borough Council, an unnecessary move for a carrier's service using the private yard of the Sun Inn in Castle Street as its terminus.

He acquired a second vehicle in June 1921, which was again an unusual type, being a Garner Model 15, also known as the 'Busvan' and aimed specifically at the Country Carrier market. This was registered BL 8684, had seating for 20 and could handle loads up to 35cwt, but it was also equipped with 4-wheel brakes and the makers claimed a top speed of 40mph! Passengers entered through a nearside entrance, whereas goods could be loaded through double doors at the rear, along with the familiar roof rack. This vehicle came as a complete entity from the Garner Motors Birmingham factory, and the grey-liveried body also featured removable side windows for when the weather was obliging. This vehicle was the only example of the type purchased in the Newbury area, despite the high number of carriers, and it was christened *The Kennet*, this description also becoming synonymous with the overall operation. Up until this point all the driving had been undertaken by George himself, but he now took on a hired driver in the shape of A.G. Brown, who was to remain 'on the buses' until retirement from *Thames Valley* in 1962.

Private hire work consisted mainly of local journeys for sports team, whist drives, cinema and dance outings, but the Busvan even ventured further afield on some private hires to the South Coast as the public appetite for such excursions grew in the early post-war years. The haulage and removals side remained significant, and the CPT was used mainly for these tasks after the Garner arrived, though it was always good to have a spare vehicle in case the need arose. Once he had another driver, some Sunday excursions were added, as George himself was a lay preacher and did not work on the Sabbath. In fact it had been his intention to sell the CPT, which his adverts noted was 'already familiar locally as the *Cold Ash Motor Bus*', though he apparently got no response.

☞ FOR HIRE ☜

"THE KENNET" Motor 'Bus : 20-Seater.

Well Ventilated : Electric Light. New : Comfortable : Removable Windows :
Protection from Cold, Wind, Rain and Dust.

FOOTBALL PARTIES TAKEN AT PER MILE OR PER HEAD.
DAY OR HALF-DAY TRIPS ARRANGED BY REQUEST.

GOODS and FURNITURE CAREFULLY REMOVED.
MODERATE CHARGES.   PERSONALLY DRIVEN.

For Terms, apply—   'Phone—25 THATCHAM.
G. P. HOWLETT : Hawthorns : COLD ASH

Howlett's Garner 'Busvan' BL 8684 featured in this advert in the Newbury Weekly News.

Somewhat out of the blue, George announced that he was re-commencing the Cold Ash to Newbury service on Tuesdays, Thursdays and Saturdays, with effect from 22nd October 1922! This immediately put him in direct conflict with *Bert Austin*, who used the columns of the Newbury Weekly News to express his anger, reminding the public that he had purchased the same service from Howlett. He furthermore pointed out that 'Lest we forget, I gave up my career from 1914 to 1919 to do my bit for the cause of Right and Humanity, and you promised to make England a place fit for heroes to live in. Show that one district can do this by giving her ex-servicemen your full support, a travel by a disabled ex-serviceman's bus'. As it is evident that *George Howlett* had not seen military service, this was indeed a message that struck a cord with the many families who had suffered losses in the conflict.

Before we continue with the detailed development of Howlett's operations, along with the more pertinent events involving *Albert Austin,* it would be useful to take a more general look at the latter's operations.

The 1901 census shows 6-year old *Albert Austin* at Sellwoods Coppice, Bucklebury Alley, the son of a brickmaker, but of particular interest is that his 18 year old brother John was the carrier for Cold Ash and Ashmore Green! This was still the case at 1904 but, by 1906 his place had been taken by *William Hamblin*, who again had been replaced by Howlett by 1908. As *John Austin* perished in June 1918, whilst serving with the Wiltshire Regiment near Cologne, Bert no doubt had personal reasons for wanting to bring that service back into family hands.

Bert Austin had served in the Middle East and, as already noted, returned to become the carrier for the Cold Ash district, developing into a full bus service. He soon became a very familiar sight and knew everyone locally. Even his donkey, kept tethered in a field near his home, would hee-haw whenever his vehicle went by, though each year it was also used for distributing the cherries from his orchard around the village.

Apart from the bus service, Bert developed numerous local excursions catering for sports clubs etc. and, as a lifelong member of the Royal & Antediluvian Order of Buffaloes, he was also called upon to provide transport for visits to other lodges. Regular journeys took them to the Robin Hood pub in Newbury and to the Constitutional Club, Pangbourne to the lodges there. On another occasion he took a party of brethren to Southsea, plus an arranged stop for tea and cakes at the Gosport lodge. His dedication was duly acknowledged when the Cold Ash lodge was re-named Albert Austin Lodge in his honour.

On public excursions he had merely to place a card in the bus window, announcing 'Bournemouth Sunday', in order to attract sufficient patronage. Other local trips were also run, including a popular blossom-time evening tour of the cherry orchards in the Didcot area, followed by a stop for a drink in the pub at Blewbury.

With the coming of the 1930 Act, his bus operations were licensed, though his initial application for road service licenses for excursions and tours was refused! However, after submitting a much less ambitious list of destinations, approval was duly forthcoming.

The various events affecting the fortunes of *Austin's* services are combined with the foregoing account of *Howlett's* as the two are so interrelated.

However, although *Albert Austin* did consider selling his service a number of times, including to *N&D*, he continued on through the 1930's and the war years. To cover these operations he used the following vehicles:

MO 1750 – Ford T carriers van with 14 seats, painted green, new in June 1923 kept until September 1927;

RX 2843 – Morris-Commercial 30cwt 14-seater bus, brown and white, new August 1928 and used until September 1938, by which time was green and white;

MO 7043 – Morris-Commercial 25cwt 14-seater bus new in January 1926 to *Freddie Spanswick*, to Austin August 1932, repainted green with a mauve band, sold by the end of 1936;

RX 4374 – Dodge 14-seater bus new in April 1931 to *Reliance* of Maidenhead & Slough, passing to Austin circa February 1934;

MW 8759 – Morris-Commercial 'Viceroy' with Heaver 24-seater front-entrance bus body, new March 1931 to *Wilts & Dorset*, passing to Austin in 1940;

LJ 1414 – Morris-Commercial 'Viceroy' with 20-seater, new in April 1940 to *Easson's*, Southampton, passing to Austin in March 1941;

EKP 140 – Thornycroft 'Dainty' with Thurgood 20-seater front-entrance bus body, new in May 1937 to *West Kent*, passing to *Newbury & District*, then to Austin during 1944;

GS 4677 – Bedford WLB with 25-seater body, new to *Mitchell* of Callendar, coming to Austin via others in July 1948.

Two of Bert Austin's buses – above is shown Dodge RX 4374, with its owner doing some running repairs, the front bumper being tied up with string! Below is Morris-Commercial MW 8759 with Heaver bus body, which had previously served with Wilts & Dorset.

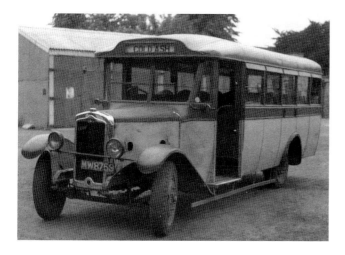

His service remained popular with his fellow villagers, though his buses are recalled as not the most reliable mechanically. This was partly because he was inclined to be tardy with the settling of his accounts with local garages, so several apparently declined to deal with him. For the same reason, he sometimes ran out of fuel, so the passengers either had to push or sit there until he returned with a can-full!

However, he had a kindly side too, and straightaway put his bus to the purpose of relocating the children and staff of the Cold Ash Children's Hospital after a fire, taking them the short way to their temporary billet in Lady Acland's home at Thirtover.

Bert had been in the habit of taking his breakfast at a café and cake shop in Cheap Street after driving the first journey in to Newbury, and there he met *Miriam (Midge) Smith*, who after a long friendship finally became his wife in 1942. They are recalled as a happy couple, who also offered a warm welcome to visitors, including lemonade or cakes to local children. During the Second World War they made presents for all the local children whose father's were serving in the Forces, also marking its end with a meal for all who had returned to the village after active service.

'Old Bert', as he was now generally known, became unwell in 1948, but had shown every sign of rallying, so his death on 21st August at the age of 54 was not anticipated. Indeed, his elderly mother had already lost another son earlier that same month. Midge took over running the service following Bert's death, but she decided to sell out to *Alan Hedges* (son of *George Hedges* of Brightwalton) in November 1948, and the Road Service Licenses were duly transferred to *Reliance Motor Services*.

It is worth noting that *Austin's* injuries were such that in the late '20's he employed boy to run errands for him in Newbury, at one point being Bill Eggleton, who in due course ended up with N&D, passed to *Thames Valley* and then went to *Reliance* in 1953. In the late 1930's schoolboy Reg Piper fulfilled the same role, helping Bert out with errands when not at school, having got to know each other as the lad travelled on his bus into Newbury daily.

However, returning to the chronological sequence of events, *George Howlett* continued nonetheless, with the service becoming daily from 19th November 1923. Despite the resumption of the Cold Ash route, some advertised excursions also featured from the 1923 season, with the usual coastal resorts, along with a circular tour of Bath, Cheddar, Wells and Glastonbury, Indeed, the carriage of passengers attained prominence over goods from now on, and after the departure of the CPT in 1927 there are no further mentions of household removals. Special occasions were also catered for, such as the extra journeys on Wednesday 31st January and Saturday 3rd February 1923 for those wishing to see the Newbury Amateur Operatic Company performance of Gilbert & Sullivan's 'The Gondoliers' with suitable timings.

From April 1924 *Bert Austin*, who lived just north of Cold Ash village at 'Fence Wood Cottage' (where his parents had been based since at least 1918), was taking in Ashmore Green on the Thursday journeys into Newbury, and from May he was also offering a Newbury to Reading carriers service on Fridays, which he ran via Bucklebury (Three Crowns), Douai Abbey and Upper Woolhampton. This left for Reading at 1pm, returning from the Dukes Head pub in Broad Street at 7pm.

In order to step up the competition on the Cold Ash bus service *Howlett* added a 20-seater Fiat 15TER-type bus at the end of September 1924, the route then being covered by 4 daily journeys on Mondays to Fridays and 5 on Saturdays. The 30-cwt chassis of this vehicle had originated in 1918, but it had been re-bodied with a front-entrance saloon bus body by the City Carriage Works. Registered as MO 3959, it was finished in a grey livery and offered the refinements of electric lighting, upholstered seats, removable windows and 'NAP' pneumatic tyres. Emblazoned along the sides was *The Kennet No.3*, and further research has confirmed that George had discounted the short-lived Wolseley-Siddeley in his fleet numbering, considering the CPT as the first vehicle and the Garner as the second.

The neat little Fiat bus MO 3959 on collection by George from the coachbuilders in Kentish Town.

With the arrival of the Fiat it was possible to further develop the Cold Ash service to include some Thursday journeys via Bucklebury (The Slade) which then ran through Thatcham to Newbury. The Reading journeys from Cold Ash, which were covered by the Garner, increased to run as Thursdays and Saturdays, with these journeys going via Bucklebury Common (The Slade). Indeed, Howlett became increasing interested in serving the Bucklebury area, re-locating to The Oak Tree Garage at Bucklebury Common (some 7.8 miles east of Newbury) by 1928.

Austin responded by altering his *Cold Ash & District Bus Service* from Thursday 8th October 1925 to start from the Hospital (just north of Cold Ash village), then by way of Ashmore Green, Thatcham (Park Lane) to Newbury (Market Place). Then, from July 1926, he also ran through Bucklebury to Newbury on Tuesdays, Thursdays and Saturdays. The timetable

was very complicated, as Bert intended to tap the wider area rather than just slog it out with *The Kennet* bus over a common route. His journeys were complex, but in essence were designed to cover: Bucklebury Village, The Slade, Three Crowns, Cold Ash and Newbury; Bucklebury Village, The Slade, Cold Ash; whilst others either ran by way of Harts Hill or were projected to start at The Bladebone. He also increased the frequency of his Cold Ash operation, adding a Sunday service from September 1926, with 3 return journeys. *Austin* also tried to obtain a license from Reading BC to allow him to run through to that town, but the Licensing Committee turned him down in September 1928. However, he did manage some diversification by adding some excursions from the 1928 season, and he was also aided by his younger sister Mina during the 1920's and '30's.

The pattern of *Howlett's* service then settled down though to 1930, with the Mondays to Saturday service between Cold Ash (Hospital) and Newbury, along with journeys between Bucklebury Common (Three Crowns) on Tuesdays (twice), Thursdays (four times) and Saturdays (three times), though the link to Reading had ceased by August 1929.

In view of the importance of private hire, *George Howlett* decided to invest in a pair of Star 'Flyer' VB4-types, upon which he had ordered coach bodies to a high standard. These were finished in a livery of citrol and deep russet brown and the seating was in brown antique leather. All 26 seats faced forward, but the pair opposite the driver could be detached to meet the Metropolitan Police restrictions when used in London. The bodies were built by Star (or perhaps in the associated Guy coachworks?), the first being of the all-weather pattern delivered in March 1930 (MY 3052) and the second had a saloon coach body and followed in April 1930 (MY 4213). The arrival of these resulted in both the Garner and Fiat being offered for sale with or without bodies in July 1930. These coaches were branded *The Spartan* by *Howlett*, though when used on the bus services they ran with roof-mounted route-boards proclaiming the *Kennet Bus Service*. One of his drivers at this time was Sid Coxhead, who later went onto N&D, finally ending up with *Reliance* of Brightwalton.

With the coming of the 1930 Road Traffic both *Austin* and *Howlett* applied for the Road Service License for the Cold Ash to Newbury road, and in a moment of poetic justice during the Hearing held during 1931, it was granted to *Bert Austin*! As a result of this George reinstated the Fridays-only service to Reading, starting from Cold Ash and running via Bucklebury Common, Bradfield and Theale. The Bucklebury – Newbury service was made up to a daily operation, though the timetable was relatively thin in respect of journeys on Mondays, Wednesdays and Fridays, the bulk of passenger still being those going shopping.

A GMC 20-seater bus was added during 1933, and there is good reason to identify this as SH 3380, a T30C-type with front-entrance Alexander body, which had been new in May 1929 to *Gardner* of Leitholm. That operator had sold out to *Scottish Motor Traction* in July 1932, the latter disposing of the vehicle as part exchange for new vehicles from Leyland Motors. The latter offloaded it to a dealer during 1933, and it is not recorded to whom it was sold. This vehicle is duly, and correctly, noted as being with *George Hedges,* though at that time he was part of *Newbury & District.* With incomplete motor tax records, it seems that the transfer to Berkshire of this vehicle, probably in the form of an inter-authority postcard, and the ownership by George *Hedges* on his resumption to independent operation, have been taken for the same. However, the author believes this to be after the vehicle had come into *N&D* with *Howlett.*

Thereafter the services remained at the same pattern through to acquisition by N&D on 1st March 1934, who also acquired the pair of Stars and the GMC, paying £1270 in total of which 1000 £1 shares were included. However, George was permitted to retain his parcels-carrying service between Bucklebury, Thatcham and Newbury, whilst N&D would abandon its similar service between those points. He was also paid a small retainer to be the local Booking Agent for N&D excursions and private hire. This acquisition substantially increased the Company's influence to the north-east of Newbury. *George Howlett* died in the Wokingham area in 1960 at the age of 85.

During March 1934 N&D applied to take over the E&T Licenses from the Bucklebury area , as well as adding more destinations and pick up points. Howlett had already held licenses to run excursions to Bournemouth, Ascot Races, Aldershot Tattoo, Tidworth Tattoo, and Southsea, whilst N&D sought to add Beacon Hill, California-in-England, Oxford Zoo, Marlborough, Swindon, Windsor, Burnham Beeches, Winchester, Whipsnade Zoo, Brighton, Bognor Regis, Weston-super-Mare, Weymouth and Southampton to the list. Additional pick up points were sought at Cold Ash Crossroads and Newbury Wharf, along with an increase from two to three coaches maximum on any day. All of these were approved at the Hearing in July, despite objections from *Bert Austin*, especially in respect of the Cold Ash pick up.

****

Further amendments to licenses were applied for during March 1934. Whilst applying for transfer of the licenses taken over from *Catherine Geary,* the opportunity was taken to add further destinations for excursions, these being Bognor Regis, Brighton, California-in-England, Epsom, Henley, Hungerford, Marlborough, Newbury, Oxford, Pangbourne,

Pewsey, Reading, Wantage, Weston-super-Mare and Windsor. The Company also requested additional pick-ups at Eastbury, East Garston, Lambourn and Welford. The Traffic Commissioner granted all these, which greatly extended the choice for residents in those areas, but the limit of one coach per day was still applied, although larger vehicles were now in use.

In respect of the bus routes, a new service was proposed between Newbury and Abingdon, to be worked on a daily basis, with three return journeys per day. However, *City of Oxford Motor Services* already operated between Rowstock and Abingdon, so at that point the *N&D* application was not granted. However, as we shall see in due course, contact between these two operators over that road would continue at local level until a compromise could be reached, though to give *N&D* full credit it did all the work!

The Hungerford – Shefford Woodlands route was put forward to run as Hungerford – Hungerford Newtown and on Wednesdays, Thursdays and Saturdays only. *N&D* also renewed the license for the Moulsford Special during March, being granted an additional pick up at Midgham in the process.

During March 1934 the Board considered the possible acquisition of two other local operators. The first was *Rodney Vincent* of Ashford Hill, some 8 miles south-east of Newbury, whose main activity centred on his bus service between his home village and Newbury via Kingsclere Woodlands – Plastow Green – Headley on Tuesdays, Thursdays, Fridays and Saturdays. He also undertook some limited private hire work whilst, at that point in time he was awaiting the outcome of an application to allow him to operate E&T's from those locations. The Board therefore made him a provisional offer of £150 in cash and £100 in shares for his bus and licenses, subject to him being granted the additional license. However, as the latter decision took some time, this takeover did not proceed, leading to a different sequence of events, as we shall see later.

On the other hand, the offer from *W.J. White & Son* of Hermitage was a more significant affair, as it added a sizeable area of the north-eastern flank to compliment that already brought in with recent purchase of the *Kennet Bus Service* of *George Howlett.*

W. J. White & Son

William James White of Hermitage, some 5.2 miles north-east from Newbury, had started a motorised carrier's service into that town by 1922. By May 1923 he had added another regular service into Reading, which ran by way of Hampstead Norris, Yattendon, Buckle Gate and Upper Basildon. The weekly pattern by that date was to travel to Newbury on Thursdays and Saturdays and to Reading (some 17 miles away) on Tuesdays, Fridays and Saturdays. On the latter day, the van actually worked through from Newbury for the transhipment of goods, whilst also providing a return run at 9pm for those wishing to spend some time in Reading that evening.

It is worthwhile noting the populations of the principle points served by *White's* services which, according to the 1921 census were Bucklebury 1063, Hermitage 502, Frilsham 233, and Hampstead Norris 1321.

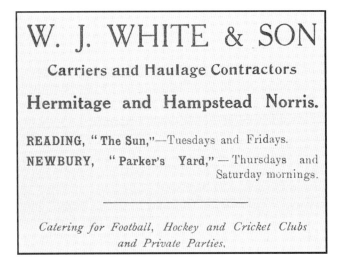

As regards the White family, William had been born at Bruton in Somerset in 1874, and in 1891 he was operating as a general dealer with a shop in that village. He married Mary Smith in 1894, who was in service there, though she originated from Hampstead Norris (and had a brother Richard who operated as a local carrier from that village). In 1896 their son *Edwin George* was born, and by 1901 William had joined the Police and was living at 9 Melbourne Road, St Lawrence, Bristol. By 1911 William was promoted to Detective Police Constable and living at 4 Hamilton Road in the St. Philip district, whilst Edwin was an apprentice engineer's pattern-maker.

No details are known of the original carrier's van used from 1922, though it was also used for haulage work at other times, possibly with an alternative body. Indeed, by 1924 he was also operating as the local coal merchant, collecting supplies from the Hermitage railway yard of the *Didcot, Newbury & Southampton Railway*. Taxi work was advertised by then, and the carrier's bus now also ran into Newbury on Tuesdays as well. A small number of advertised excursions also took place during the 1924 season, some to the usual South Coast resorts, with others to the very popular British Empire Exhibition at Wembley.

The success of these excursions convinced William that it was worthwhile purchasing a 14-seater charabanc body, painted in a livery of 'putty' (a shade of cream), which would become the standard for coaches, this was used on a Mason chassis (a rare type imported from America), registered in June 1925 as MO 5620, which featured pneumatic tyres and was christened *The Tony*. The latter became the trading

name for the bus and coach operations, though its origins have not been recorded, and at that time the base was the White's home at 'Blenheim House'. At other times the Mason carried a 14-seater varnished wood bus body, lasting until September 1931.

In order to further develop the bus services, a 14-seater Chevrolet T-type was purchased in October 1925 and registered as MO 6416, and this was followed by a similar bus in March 1926 as MO 7182. These buses were in a varnished wood finish and were quite likely bodied and supplied by Vincents of Reading. A third Chevrolet, but an LP-type with a sunsaloon bus body for 14, was registered as RX 3330 in December 1928. This was finished in the putty livery and was also used for private hire and excursion work. As with other local concerns, it was felt best to invest in vehicles that could cover the service routes, whilst being comfortable enough for excursions and private hire. It was also with this vehicle that we first hear of the Fernbank Garage as the base, along with the involvement of son *Edwin George White*, and this developed to provide the usual facilities of the country garage for the growing number of local motorists.

For November 1929 Dennis were favoured with the purchase of a 30-cwt, which was registered as RX 5493 and carried the putty livery, the body being of the all-weather type and seating 14 in a dual-entrance layout. The arrival of this vehicle saw the Mason relegated to solely haulage work in place of the old carrier's van, and it survived through to September 1931, with the coal business also continuing.

Dennis 30-cwt coach RX 5493 with Len Rouse as the driver, about to depart from the Fernbank Garage.

A further Dennis 30-cwt, with a 17-seater front-doorway body featuring fixed front and rear domes and a central sunshine roof section, was registered as RX 6401 in May 1930, and as a result of this arrival the original Chevrolet (MO 6416) was sold in July 1929 to the *Pococks* over at Cold Ash

The level of service on the Reading route had remained the same, though by 1930 the Saturday journeys had ceased, with a single return journey leaving Hermitage on Tuesdays and Fridays at

9.30am, returning from Reading at 3.30pm. Despite the reduction in frequency on this route, the points served had been further developed with timed stops at Hampstead Norris, Frilsham, Marlston, Bucklebury, Standford Dingley, Tutts Clump, Bradfield and Theale, with a 50-minute journey time. Even though a Hackney Carriage License had been obtained from Reading Borough Council, the private yard of The Sun pub in Castle Street was used as the terminus in the town. Indeed, in Newbury, *White's* still favoured the use of The Dolphin yard at 113 Bartholomew Street over the parking ground at The Wharf.

The 'Hermitage to Newbury' service had steadily developed throughout the late 1920's, so much so that it was no longer simply just that! The core journeys between Hermitage and Newbury ran by way of Long Lane, Grange Farm and Shaw, and had a 20-minute journey time. On various days journeys were back-projected to start at Frilsham or Marlston (Tuesdays, Thursdays and Saturdays), Yattendon (Thursdays), Ashampstead, Aldworh and Wyld Court (Thursdays and Saturdays), Compton (daily other than Sundays), whereas Bothampstead only saw a bus on Saturday evenings. All of these journeys also served Hermitage village or Hermitage church, whilst some flexibility was available if passengers on homeward runs requested drivers to go onto outlying points beyond the core timetable, and no doubt there were some 'regulars' who were known to drivers. There was also a schooldays-only journey leaving Marlston at 8.25 to arrive at Hermitage for 8.40am, whilst during school terms quite a lot of contract journeys were undertaken to transfer children to swimming lessons and cookery classes in Newbury.

Another view of Dennis RX 5493 out on the open road, once again with Len Rouse at the wheel and his lady alongside him in the popular front seat.

Hire cars were also available at the garage, though no details of the actual vehicles have come to light. It is also interesting to note that the *Whites* favoured types of vehicles not as common in Newbury, and this may be explained by the frequent opportunities to visit the showrooms of William Vincents in Reading, whose headquarters in the earlier years was just up Castle Street from the layover point at The Sun Inn, which had long been favoured by the carriers coming from the south and west and had a large yard for their vans.

A larger secondhand vehicle was acquired in 1931 in the shape of MW 6161, an AJS 'Pilot' with Eaton 26-seater front-entrance bus body, This had been new to *King* of Nomansland, Wiltshire in December 1929, who had sold out to Wilts & Dorset in January 1931. This was a useful bus, especially on busy days when duplicate 14-seaters would have been required, whilst also being a good size for larger excursions.

Secondhand Dennis 30-cwt 14-seater bus TP 7118.

The last arrival for the fleet was another secondhand purchase, being a Dennis 30-cwt 14-seater bus with a front-entrance body also built by Dennis, and was on offer by Vincent's of Reading. This was registered TP 7118 and had been new in December 1928 to *Percy Lambert* of East Meon, Hampshire, passing to *White's* in October 1933, and replaced Chevrolet RX 3330, which was sold that same month. Two months later Chevrolet MO 7182 was also disposed of. These later buses were painted in a livery of cream and black.

It should of course be appreciated that *Whites* were not the only operator to provide a link between Hermitage and Newbury or Yattendon and Reading, so a review of the relevant operations now follows.

W.J. & C.H. Silvey

The *Silvey Brothers*, *William John* and *Charles Henry*, were both born locally in 1885 and 1899 respectively, and Bill was a domestic gardener at 1901. His brother Charlie trained as a marine engineer, but with the outbreak of the Great War he duly joined the army in April 1917, though he did not go abroad until at least one year later, when he re-assigned to the 13th Kings Royal Rifle Company for service in France. After the war ended he transferred to the occupying force on the Rhine in Germany from July 1919, returning home in March 1920.

The return of Charlie evidently brought about the motorisation of the carriers service which Bill had evidently started sometime over the war years. Towards the end of May 1920 the brothers purchased a Ford 1-ton van with a wagonette body and seating for 8, registered as BL 7345 and finished in a stained and varnished livery. It is worth noting that the service was advertised from the outset as a bus service with carrying, commencing on 10th June, with journeys on Thursdays and Saturdays only, suggesting that the brothers had other business to occupy the rest of the week. The bus ran from Hermitage at 10.45am and 2pm, returning from The Olde Waggon & Horses, Newbury at 1pm and 4.15pm, whilst on Saturdays an additional journey left Hermitage at 7pm and returned from Newbury at 10pm, which gave the brothers an evening out as well. This vehicle was re-declared in 1921 as a van with 14-seats, so it would seem that the body had been either altered or replaced.

Sadly, Charlie was involved in a motorcycle accident on the evening of Saturday 17th September 1924, and that also had a bizarre twist to it. He had been out for the evening, visiting a couple of pubs and riding a loaned 3.5hp Phelan & Moore machine, as his own was in Maynard's Garage at Thatcham under repair. As he rounded the bend approaching Hermitage post office from the Newbury direction at 10.15pm, he ran into two men talking in the road, the weather being a bit foggy that evening. However, it was only when those men, which included Bill Silvey, went back to see how the motorcyclist was that it transpired that was in fact his brother! It would also appear that the rider's trousers had been caught in the gears, which had been left exposed after a noisy casing had been removed. Charles was freed with some difficulty from the machine and taken to the hospital, but he died of his injuries on 4th October at the age of 25.

Bill, who lived at Little Hungerford on the north side of the village, continued with the enterprise, and in July 1926 he met former *Prothero* driver Charlie Bishop in a pub at Hermitage as the latter cycled back from the Royal Agricultural Show at Caversham. The two men were talking when Charlie mentioned that he was working on an estate but had previously been a bus driver, to which *Bill Silvey* offered him a job! His offer of 35shillings per week (less 5shillings bed and board) was accepted and Charlie went to drive for him for some 3 years. During that time he also met his future wife, who was cook for Captain Eric Tate, coming there after service with Lady Tate at Roehampton in Surrey.

Charlie recorded the events of those days, which give an interesting insight into the activities of such operators. He recalled that he would drive the Ford, whilst Bill would call at cottages (who had left a card or ribbon visible to attract his attention on the gate or hedge), as well as shops and pubs who made use of the service. Passengers would also join, though mostly on Thursdays and Saturdays.

On reaching Newbury the van would pull up outside the Waggon & Horses in the Market Place, where Mrs. Cook and her son Cecil always made the carriers welcome. Bill and Charlie would then go off to the various shops to collect the provision, also sometimes to deliver local produce to them, such as eggs and even ducks or chickens in baskets. The traders were of course appreciative of such business and paid a levy to the carrier, the best payer being the Co-op, where 1s 3d was paid in the £, so there was no cost as such to the recipient for the transport element, just the need to settle the bill.

Other items such as clothes, shoes and boots, garden and household implements, along with medicines, could also be obtained, and again the traders were happy for the business brought in and paid a dividend. Parcels, along with other larger items were also carried for a fee, either payable by the consigner or recipient as appropriate.

Those carriers who operated one return journey per day would then stay in Newbury and have a lunch in one of the pubs, catching up on the news of the local and wider world. However, as *Silvey* operated twice daily, the van set off about midday back to Hermitage, there also not usually being passengers returning on this journey, and along the route the provisions were dropped off at the cottages, followed by a break for lunch. In the afternoon the pair set off again to reach Newbury for the second departure from the Market Place. On this run there might be 10-12 passengers who had done their own shopping, paying 6pence for the return journey. A stop was also made at Hunts Bar in The Broadway, where small barrels of beer were collected to order, these being 4.5 gallon ones for home use and charged at 4shillings and 10.5pence, i.e. a shilling per gallon plus the deposit refundable on the empty barrel! Charlie also recalled that during deliveries to pubs along the route, Bill would often have a 'swift half', and Charlie also joined him, with the passengers sitting outside in the bus patiently!

Apart from driving, Charlie was also expected to maintain the vehicle, something which Bill's brother had previously done, and in the event of a breakdown this would have to be rectified overnight. There was also a steady amount of evening private hire, in particular for dart's clubs and other local groups. However, the initial Ford was still rather basic and, as *Bill Silvey* became more confident about the business,

Charlie Bishop persuaded him to invest in something with better passenger accommodation.

So, in late May 1927 another Ford T 'tonner' was registered as MO 8936, and this was fitted with a rather large bus body with seats for 14 passengers in greater comfort than the previous example. This body, which resembled the practice of certain small crabs that re-use the discarded shells of larger creatures, soon earned the bus the name *The Hermit*, and this was also advertised as available for excursions when not engaged on the service. The vehicle itself had been new in December 1926 to Pass & Co., the Ford agent, so the unusual body may not have actually been specified by *Silvey*, and he paid them £400.

The original Ford was still in use, though it covered the purely carriers role, leaving Newbury on Thursdays and Saturdays at 3.30pm. The Wharf had been adopted as the terminus by 1930, as the Market Place had become too crowded, and the bus service had been further developed to operate on Tuesdays, Thursdays and Saturdays, which in terms of days of operation would remain its maximum level. Buses left Newbury at 1pm and 4pm on Tuesdays, with the same on Thursdays plus an additional run at 6pm. Service level on Saturdays was enhanced with journeys from Newbury at 1pm, 4pm, 6pm, 8pm and 10pm. Certain journeys also proceeded north of Hermitage to serve the small settlement of Eling, which was most likely also in response to family connections with that area.

Charlie Bishop's stay with *Silvey* came to an end in 1928, when *John Prothero* met him in Newbury and tempted him back to help him oppose the threat of the *GWR* buses, after which he was his right-hand man.

In November 1931 *Bill Silvey* found it necessary to place a notice in the Newbury Weekly News stating that rumours of the sale of his business were not true and, that as the oldest Hermitage carrier and bus operator, he would be continuing to operate. Indeed, he was duly licensed under the 1930 Act, and by March 1932 he had enhanced the Thursday service to the same level as that on Saturdays, whilst the carrier's service also now ran on Tuesdays. His general parcels service would also accept items on the buses, though only up to the departure at 4pm. He was also the local agent for the Newbury Weekly News, which he took to various shops along his route each Thursday.

The original Ford (BL 7345) was used through to June 1931 and the bus (MO 8936) continued until October of that year, but the identity of his replacement has not come to light. The passenger service had ceased prior to 1935, but the goods carrying continued until 1940, and during that period he used the yard of the White Hart off Market Street, running once a day on Tuesdays, Thursdays and Saturdays at 4pm from Newbury. Bill died in 1945 at the age of 60.

****

The story of the Yattendon succession of carriers is quite complex, so we shall now examine how events unfolded over the years into the motorised age.

Ilsleys and Rumbles

Carrying from Yattendon had for many years been in the hands of these two families. Indeed, three generations of *Charles Ilsley* had provided the links to Reading and Newbury since at least 1861. The earlier generation was based at Ashampstead Common, though by 1881 they had relocated to adjacent to the Royal Oak, Yattendon, where they also had stables. The final generation was *Charles George Ilsley*, who was his father's van boy in 1891 and the carrier by 1901, his father now being the baker and breadmaker. However, he relocated in the earlier years of the 20th century to open a cycle shop at Twyford, Berkshire.

The *Rumble* family also starts to feature as carriers to both Reading and Newbury from 1900, and they were also jobmasters and postmasters in Yattendon, though they had originated in Goring-on-Thames. In 1891 *William Rumble* is found as a gardener at Eye-and-Dunsden Parish, in Oxfordshire, though sons *John* and *James* were employed as coachmen, presumably at some local large house, whilst the other brother *George* was working as a groom. By 1901 *William* and sons *James* and *George* are all listed a jobmasters at Yattendon. Available evidence shows that *William* was at the base, with the sons acting as the carriers, though listings are inconsistent between various local sources. Photographs also confirm that the vans were lettered *J. Rumble* and *Rumble Bros.* at various times, whilst one carried a board proclaiming 'established 1854', though this is believed to refer to the origins of the link pioneered by the *Ilsley* family.

James Rumble was still operating as the carrier at 1911, whilst 73-year old *William* was still jobmaster, aided by his son *George*. However, the 1914 directory only shows the family as jobmasters, with *James* now running the Royal Oak pub, and with *E. Jerman* in his place now as the Yattendon carrier.

Thomas & Richard Harris

A horse-drawn carriers service had been started by *Thomas Harris* who lived at 'The Nutshell' in Yattendon sometime in 1915, as successor to *E. Jerman*. This ran between Newbury and Pangbourne going by way of Hermitage – Frilsham – Yattendon – Ashampstead – Basildon, operating on Mondays and Thursdays only from the Olde Waggon & Horses in the Market Place. He also ran from Hermitage to

Reading on Tuesdays and Saturdays, so transhipment of goods between the main towns was also possible, and his Reading base was The Peacock at 51 Broad Street. From 1916 the local directories give *T. & R. Harris* indicating that Richard had now joined him.

In late September 1920 the service was motorised with a green-painted 14-seater carriers van registered as BL 7928. This was on an American-built Republic model 11X chassis, which was enjoying some success then in Britain. As was usually the case, the advent of the motor van led to more carrying of passengers, plus the use of the vehicle for a certain amount of private hire work. The Reading venue was changed in 1922 to the Dukes Head at 41 Broad Street, with a departure time of 4.30pm

D. A. Stewart

In September 1922 *Thomas Harris* sold his business to Mr. Stewart, who also took over the Republic van. He continued to use the Dukes Head in Reading, though he brought the time forward to 3.45pm. *Stewart* also continued to run to Newbury though, as he only ran on Thursdays, he must have had another main occupation. This continued through 1923, but by 1924 the service had yet another operator, this being *T.K. Cheeseman.* He decided to take in Pangbourne once again (as had the *Ilsleys* and *Rumbles)*, but no doubt found that *Reg Bragg's* buses (*Reading & District Motor Services)* an effective competitor. He also ran between Reading (Dukes Head) and Newbury on Mondays and Thursdays

Herbert Corp Galpin

Herbert Galpin had been born in 1892 at Headbourne Worthy, just north of Winchester in Hampshire. His early work followed in the footsteps of his father, as cowman and promotion to farm baliff, with positions at Alverstoke in 1891, Eling in 1901 and by 1911 at Spearywell (near Mottisfont), all in his home county.

However, in September 1925 Herbert licensed a Ford T with stained and varnished 14-seater bus body as MO 5902 from his new base at Yattendon. At first he ran between Yattendon and Reading on Tuesdays and Saturdays only. Yattendon was 12 miles from Reading and Newbury was 7 miles away, whilst the nearest rail station on the *Didcot, Newbury & Southampton* line was some 2.5 miles away.

From 1926 he was taking in Pangbourne as well, though no doubt only in the role of a carrier, as the buses of *Thames Valley* and *Reading & District* gave a good level of passenger service.

Sometime in 1928 *Galpin* acquired *Cheeseman's* carrier's services between Yattendon and Reading and Reading and Newbury. Also acquired was the

Republic (BL 7928), which was now fourth-hand. He also added Frilsham to the journeys from Newbury, whilst the service to Reading also continued, being developed to two return journeys on Tuesdays and Saturdays by 1931.

During 1929 *Galpin* acquired a Ford T all-weather coach, new in May 1926 to the operational side of *Pass & Co.* of Newbury, which wore a red livery and was registered MO 7520.

The former *Harris, Stewart & Cheeseman* Republic was used until March 1929, and the Ford T bus until December 1931. The Republic must have suitably impressed him, his replacement for the Ford was also of that make, being a June 1924 example (MO 3439), which he purchased towards the end of 1931 from the carrier *Arthur Wickens* of nearby Bradfield. This was a truck-bodied vehicle which remained in use by *Galpin* until to March 1937.

A new Ford AA-type all-weather coach was purchased in June 1930, the secondhand coach having successfully developed the private hire side of the business. Indeed, the latter was retained until September 1932, whilst he new coach (RX 6889) was also supplied by Pass & Co. and wore a red livery. The 14-seater dual-doorway body is thought to have been constructed by Andrews of Newbury. This was joined in August 1933 by a new Ford BB-type, which carried a maroon-liveried 20-seater coach body, and was registered JB 2596, though towards the end of its career it was re-designated as goods only. The final vehicle to be operated was a forward-control Dennis 'Ace' (OY 9190), fitted with a Harrington coach body seating 20, which had been new to *John Bennett* of Croydon in June 1934.

Ford AA-type all-weather coach RX 6889 at Southsea.

The service between Newbury and Yattendon was not expanded beyond the Mondays and Thursdays-only operation, when it is evident that journeys ran by way of Frilsham and Wellhouse, plus one via Marlston. However, any competition between this rather limited service and those of *Whites* or later with *Newbury & District* was of course minimal. The Yattendon – Reading service was licensed under the 1930 Act, although the passenger side seems to have declined as better services had been developed by others. Indeed, once *Reading & District* reached Yattendon in about April 1929 he started to notice the difference. With the full takeover of control of that service by *George Jarvis & Son* of Reading from November 1933, the service was stepped up, and in June 1934 *Herbert Galpin* disposed of his license for the passenger service to *Jarvis,* going goods-only in respect of the Reading link. *Reading & District* was in turn sold to *Thames Valley* in January 1936, and the service became its route 5b.

In the meantime there had been several changes of base at Reading, with the Boars Head in Friar Street listed for the 1933-6 period, before relocation to the side of the triangular car park in Lower Thorn Street, just under the view of the *Thames Valley* head office.

The Yattendon – Newbury service continued, though by February 1936 this ran only on Thursdays, with 2 journeys from Yattendon ay 10.30am and 3pm, returning from Newbury at 12noon and 4.15pm. When Newbury Fair was on this was given another journey from Yattendon at 6pm, returning from The Wharf at 10.30pm. The single fare was 1shilling, with a return fare of 1shilling 10pence.

Private hire was further developed and continued alongside the Newbury route and the goods service to Reading. However, *Herbert Galpin* died in 1946 at the age of 65. The service continued, with the licenses being acquired by *C. J. King & J. Donovan* in April 1949, with Ford BB (JB 2596) and Dennis 'Ace' (OY 9190) passing to them. A new partnership of *Donavan & Crane* took over in February 1950, though one year later it was *John Donovan* as sole proprietor, his business passing to *Reliance Motor Services* in May 1955.

****

As one might expect with a small local independent, the drivers who worked for *Whites* tended to do so for many years, with Len Rouse, L. Smith and Jim Lawrence all falling into that category. Indeed, Jim had started out as the parcel's boy on the original carrier's service, becoming a conductor on the bus service in 1927, then later as a driver after *N&D* took over. All of these transferred to N&D and continued to work from Hermitage at least to start with, such local men being regarded as part of the 'goodwill' that *N&D* had purchased.

In respect of their excursions, under the 1930 Road Traffic Act, *Whites* were granted licenses at the Hearing in April 1931 for Bognor Regis, Bournemouth, Brighton, Southsea and Weston-super-Mare, together with circular tours to Oxford and Stonehenge. However, by the time of sale to N&D, a number of alterations had been made, resulting in the following selection: Southsea, Bournemouth,

Aldershot and Tidworth Military Tattoos, Lockinge, Ascot Races, Savernake Forest, Hannington point-to-point races, Kidlington, Reading, Yattendon, Newbury, along with two circular tours, one via Andover and the other via Lambourn.

Also, by the time of the transfer to N&D on 18th May 1934 only *Edwin White* was involved, as his father had passed away by then. N&D paid £500 in cash for the Dennis coaches (RX 5493 and RX 6401), the AJS bus (MW 6161) and the little Dennis bus (TP 7118), together with £1000 in £1 shares. Also Edwin was given employment, both in supervising the Hermitage out-station, and working more generally from The Wharf Office. Indeed, it should be appreciated that 'Ed' had been the driving force in securing so much private hire work and excursions patronage in his local area, and his wide range of contacts was something he soon put to very effective use over the whole *N&D* network!

In applying for the E&T Licenses, N&D added further destinations to Bognor Regis, Brighton, Weston-super-Mare, Weymouth, Windsor and Whipsnade Zoo, some of which of course *Whites* had previously dropped.

The Fernbank Garage continued as the base for the trio of N&D buses working the former *Tony Coaches* routes, for which the new owners paid 2 shillings per week. They also preferred to view the complicated bus operations as 4 distinct routes rather than one, which certainly fitted into the timetable books better! They considered these operations to be as follows when they applied for transfer of the Road Service Licenses in June 1934: Newbury to Yattendon (which included the Curridge journeys); Newbury to Aldworth; Newbury to Compton; and the Hermitage to Reading service. No modifications were made to the latter service, though the Newbury base for the other routes was changed to The Wharf in place of The Dolphin as had been used by *Whites*.

The actual garage business, along with car hire, remained in the hands of the White family, as did the coal merchant business.

****

As was the usual practice with operators coming into the fold, *White's* also became the local booking agent, though they did retain the carrier's service, so any parcels for the Hermitage area were left to them, as had been the case with *Tom Holman* and even *George Howlett,* and this was clearly reflected in the timetable booklets. The Hermitage allocation was changed initially to a couple of Ford AA's, succeeded, by the two Leyland 'Leverets' in 1935, then a pair of GMC's, followed by a Thornycroft and Star together up to the 1939 War.

If the early months of 1934 had not been busy enough, there was now the need to consider how the Company might be affected by the 'Road & Rail Traffic Bill', particularly as it was considered that this favoured the railways as prime movers of goods. A meeting of the 'South Berks Bus Proprietors & Carriers Association' was held in March to discuss possible issues, and it is interesting to note that number of non-members who attended decided to take up membership as a result. At the meeting George Hedges was the Vice Chairman, whilst another *N&D* constituent John Prothero had only just relinquished the Chair in favour of Walter Chalk, the long-established carrier of Kingsclere. It was agreed to watch such developments and to employ professional advice if required, though in reality there was no detrimental effect on the haulage aspects of *N&D*.

As already noted, Theo Denham had training as an engineer and liked tinkering about with things. He had considered the issue of effectively illuminating vehicle registration plates and, along with Mr. C.J.A. Robinson (a former iron-founder with Plenty & Sons), had devised a possible solution. This consisted of a box-like structure housing a 6-volt car lamp bulb, whilst the outside face of the box had an aluminium plate with small holes drilled to trace the figures of the registration. At night this clearly showed the figures, and working models were sent to the Minister of Transport and the Conference of Chief Constables, as well as a provisional patent being taken out.

After the failure to gain the licenses it had sought from Hungerford *Newbury & District* decided to build on the purchase of the business of *Burt & Greenwood*. When applying for the transfer of licenses in April 1934, the Company requested the addition of a pick up point at Hungerford, along with 16 extra destinations (to the 15 already held), these being Ascot Races, Epsom Races, Henley, Highworth, Marlborough, Maidenhead, Oxford, Pewsey, Reading, Shefford, Southampton, Swindon, Wantage, Windsor, and two circular tours, one via Hurstbourne Tarrant and the other via Lambourn.

To aid this serious attempt to expand E&T's to the western flank, *N&D* also found suitable premises in order to set up a booking agency in the High Street in Hungerford at a weekly rent of 5 shillings. However, with such strong local opposition from *Lampard's* of Pewsey and the *Swindon Motor Charabanc Company* (later better known as *Rimes of Swindon*), the matter was not resolved until August, losing virtually all of the season. So, although the application did eventually go through in favour of the Company, the office was discontinued from September 1934 and such a facility there was never resumed

Indeed, the provision of local booking agents was an important part of developing the excursions and also gaining private hire. At June 1934 the Newbury agencies were at Northcroft Lane (Andrews), Market Street (Durnford), Bartholomew Street (Whitington), The Wharf (N&D Office), London Road (Chalk) and Salcombe Road (Cartwright), whilst outlying areas were at Kintbury (Greenwood and Funnell), Great Shefford (Geary), Woolhampton (Bason), Thatcham (Spanswick), Brightwalton (Hedges), Beedon (Rosier), Ecchinswell (Holman), Bucklebury (Howlett), Hermitage (White), East Woodhay (Mercer), along with Barnes of Aldbourne (who were not at that time involved with coach operation). Those enquiring from Cold Ash were advised to contact either Howlett or Spanswick.

However, whilst the above round of applications for licenses had been proceeding, a particularly important personnel decision had been made by the employment of James Davies from April as Inspector and Traffic Assistant.

James Davies.

James Augustine Davies was born at Coppaquin in County Waterford, Ireland on St. Valentine's Day 1895, the son of a Lancastrian father and an Irish mother. The family had relocated to 20 High Street in Leigh, Lancashire by 1901, and on the census of 1911 James was a shopkeeper's assistant.

However, his father was a foreman iron-moulder, and James took up an apprenticeship at the Albion Agricultural Machinery Works also in Leigh. With the outbreak of war he joined the Royal Engineers, serving throughout the conflict, despite a badly wounded left arm sustained at the Battle of The Somme on 30th July 1916.

After the war ended, like so many ex-servicemen, he became involved in road transport, initially as a bus conductor, then driver with *Leigh Corporation*. He was duly selected as an Inspector, and later his talents for organisation resulted in him being appointed as the Traffic Manager with that municipal bus operator, whilst he married Alice Chadwick in Leigh in 1927.

Leigh, like many other municipalities had replaced its trams with motor buses, and was amongst other such public operators in Lancashire operating inter-urban links as well as purely local services. It is also interesting to note that they favoured Leyland chassis, in view of subsequent *N&D* vehicle policy.

He had certainly acquired the necessary organisational skills required to steer *Newbury & District* in the right direction, especially in respect of its dealings with the Traffic Commissioners. In respect of the latter, the Company had sometimes not really helped itself in the way it had presented license applications.

'Jim' got on well with people and was popular with the crews for his hands-on approach and practical solutions. Accommodation for him was arranged in Mill Lane, at the town end, in one of a pair of semi-detached houses backing onto the Kennet & Avon Canal built for Charlie Durnford by his brother George. Jim and Alice lived at 'Sunnyside', with Bill Durnford to their left at 'Sunny View', whilst Len Durnford was the other neighbour in an older cottage at No.14 – all very handy for the garage and just a short walk from The Wharf. By 1938 the Davies's had relocated to 'Kirby' in Stuart Road at Wash Common, by which time Ernie Durnford had also gravitated to reside in Mill Lane at 'Brierfield'.

On the other hand, John Prothero gave notice in April that he wished to leave the Company, and he offered his shares for disposal. James Davies straightaway demonstrated his commitment to *Newbury & District* by purchasing 500 of those, whilst the remaining 150 went to Charlie Durnford. However, Prothero also sought an assurance from the Board that he could return as a Director if he so wished, though that could not be given. Instead, it was agreed that he should be paid 30 shillings per week for as long as he held the remaining 1350 shares. He was not satisfied with this arrangement, so he offered the remaining shares for sale and left the Company to relocate to Dursley in Gloucestershire. During June 50 of the above shares were purchased by Bert Adnams, a coach driver with the Company, one of a number of employees to take a small holding in *N&D*.

Whereas the initial timetable booklet issued by *N&D* in October 1933 had consisted of 32 pages and cost 1

pence, the edition of June 1934 was double that content but free. This was achieved by making arrangements with G.S. & H. Advertising of Chiswick to support the cost of printing through advertising. The Company did actually expand its own content, though most of the additional pages were given over to commercial adverts. Two specific improvements were an index of places served and a route map, the latter actually hand drawn by James Davies.

As noted in February, a Strachans-bodied Gilford 166OT-type coach had come in the fleet, and there is good reason to believe this may have been TM 5639. It is seen with Boss Denham as the driver to a rather well-dressed party of ladies.

A number of local refreshment establishments saw the value in advertising to passengers, as a bus trip out to local beauty spots was still commonplace with so few private cars about. Both the 'Bolton Arms', Kingsclere and 'Green Garden Café', Bucklebury took ads in 1934/5, whilst Mr. Cleeverley of the 'Robin Hood' in London Road also featured in 1935. It is worth noting that a number of distant venues also featured, either to elicit trade from trippers or to tempt private party organisers, these being 'California-in-England', the 'Cave Man Restaurant' at Cheddar, Oxford Zoo and the 'Esplanade Assembly Rooms' at Southsea. The latter was adjacent to the large coach park there, and had formed the back-drop to numerous photographs of charabanc and coach outings during the 1920's and '30's. More locally a number of bakers and other trades took adverts, including Whitington's (who were related to the Dehams through marriage).

The arrangement with the advertising company was later reviewed and a one penny charge for the booklet reinstated in October 1934, and advertising for both the booklet and on the buses passing to the specialist Darby's Advertising of Australia House, London W2 from the May 1936 issue.

On the subject of adverts on buses, it was fairly uncommon for independent fleets of single-deck buses to carry adverts on roof-mounted boards. However, in a fleet with quite frequent changes, that was a very suitable method, as if a particular bus was sold, the ad board could be fitted to another easily. A number of local concerns featured, though the bulk of these were for the Newbury Laundry, who also took the prime spot on the rear cover of the timetable booklet.

During June former *Durnford* Maudslay 'allweather' coach 28 (YE 8768) was retired, whilst its fleet no. was re-issued to Star coach GU 7545 following a repaint into cream and green. With recent additional operators brought into the fold it had been found that there was a surplus of coaches at that point, leading to some being regularly used on service routes through the whole week.

From October 1934 the Kingsbridge Road terminus of the cross-town route to Shaw was amended to Clifton Road, Kingsbridge Road now being the terminus for a new more direct route from Newbury (Broadway).

On the excursions side, a number of trips ran during the Summer of 1934 of interest to Newburians, with the Bath & West Show held at Oxford, the Royal Counties Show at Salisbury and the Grand Fete held in aid of the Royal Berkshire Hospital in the grounds of Highclere Castle, the latter being provided with a shuttle bus to deal with the large crowds attending.

Another popular local evening outing was the Newbury Commons tour, which left The Wharf at 6.15pm. This took in the delightful scenery of a number of commons south of Newbury, including Greenham, Crookham and Brimpton, though the actual route tended to vary with the driver. This gave it an element of the 'mystery tour', though sometimes it was where the driver fancied taking the customary pub stop en route!

By August 1934 *Newbury & District* was authorised to run the following numbers of coaches from various locations in respect of excursions: Cold Ash (2); East Ilsley (7); Bucklebury (3); Brightwalton (4); Great Shefford (1); Hermitage (2); Inkpen (4); Kintbury (5); Thatcham (2); Woolhampton (3) and Newbury (9).

The taxi work inherited in 1932 had continued through 1933-4, but as this mainly looked after by Boss Denham and Percy Andrews, it ceased after they were appointed Garage Foremen from October 1934, the growing fleet requiring their full attention.

With the further services added since route numbers had been allocated in 1933, it was found necessary to re-organised these from 1st October 1934, and it is noted that these were on a geographical basis:

Route 1   Newbury – Chieveley – Beedon - East Ilsley
Route 2   East Ilsley – Compton – Reading
Route 3   Newbury – Chieveley – Peasemore
Route 4   Newbury – Brightwalton Holt – Wantage
Route 5   Newbury – Leckhampstead – Brightwalton
Route 6   Newbury – Boxford – Eastbury – Lambourn
Route 7   Newbury – Great Shefford – North Fawley
Route 8   Newbury – Wickham – Shefford Woodlands
Route 9   Newbury – Hungerford (via Bath Road)
Route 10 Hungerford – Hungerford Newtown
Route 11 Newbury – Kintbury – Inkpen – Hungerford
Route 12 Newbury – Ball Hill – West Woodhay
Route 13 Newbury – Ball Hill – North End
Route 14 Newbury – Ball Hill – East Woodhay
Route 15 Newbury – Woolton Hill – Highclere
Route 16 Newbury – Ecchinswell – Sydmonton
Route 17 Newbury – Thatcham – Cold Ash – Westrop
Route 18 Newbury – Thatcham – Bucklebury
Route 19 Cold Ash – Bucklebury – Reading
Route 20 *Vacant number*
Route 21 Newbury – Hermitage/Hampstead Norris/
           Compton/Aldworth
Route 22 Newbury – Curridge/Hermitage/Yattendon
Route 23 Hermitage – Bucklebury – Reading
Route 24 *Vacant number*
Route 25 Newbury Town Service
Route 26 Newbury Town Service
Route 27 Newbury Town Service
Route 28 Newbury (Broadway) – Wash Common
Route 29 Newbury (Broadway) – Kingsbridge Road
Leaving only the Moulsford Special without a number

However, to return to the chronological sequence of events, *Albert Austin* had contacted *N&D* with a view to selling his business during August 1934. No doubt he was feeling some pressure from their expansion to the north-east of the area. He also suffered from unreliability on his vehicles quite frequently, not made easier when 'he had worn out his welcome with some of the local garages due to tardy settlement of bills', as one of them once put it when recalling his dealings with him. The Company certainly gave this some serious consideration, and it would appear that the vacant route number 20 was put aside in anticipation, but his asking price was considered far too high and the matter was therefore left.

The Summer of 1934 had been a very busy one for the coach fleet, with some 2000 passengers carried each month, whilst the service buses were carrying some 100,000 persons per month.

However, such busy times were not without the occasional mishap, and a number of accidents befell the fleet during the month of September. A coach on an excursion to Southsea on the morning of Sunday 9th was involved in a collision with a private car just south of Whitchurch, after the car's driver had been dazzled by oncoming lights. Despite a fair bit of damage to the coach, which included a bent chassis, neither Driver Cecil Clark or any of the passengers was injured, and a replacement coach soon arrived to complete the journey.

The very next day another collision occurred, when a car driver pulled out from Cory's Petrol Station in London Road, Newbury into the path of a bus being driven by Eric Harwood. Fortunately the latter had anticipated what was occurring and had reduced his speed before contact was made. Damage was therefore minimal and driver Harwood was praised for his action, whilst the car driver was summonsed for careless driving.

The third incident occurred on the 14th, but was not a collision but a fire, and was the most severe of all of them. On that Friday evening former *White's* Dennis 30-cwt coach 42 (RX 5493) was being started up for Bert Greenwood to take over to Kintbury for use on the following morning for an excursion starting from there, when fire broke out in the engine compartment. This rapidly spread, causing extensive damage to the wings, windscreen, dash, front part of the roof and some seats. The Newbury Volunteer Fire Brigade was soon on the scene (with a Dennis fire engine of course), whilst the garage employees pushed the vehicle out of the Mill Lane garage in order to prevent other vehicles being damaged. This incident was all the more unfortunate because this vehicle had just come out from an extensive body refurbishment, during which it had been re-upholstered throughout in leather, including being re-seated to 16 after removal of the rear door of the original dual-doorway layout. A new hood had also been fitted and the coach fully repainted into the fleet scheme. In view of the damage the coach did not re-enter service, but at least none of the trio of accidents had resulted in personal injury.

And, if all that was not enough, events in the Boardroom during September 1934 were far from smooth. At the Annual General Meeting held on 19th of that month, it fell to George Hedges to retire from the Board, and his place as Chairman was taken by Arthur Andrews. Hedges offered himself for re-election, whilst George Howlett, Edwin White and James Davies all put themselves forward for election. It was decided not to increase the number of Directors, leaving a competition for the one seat, but Howlett and White then withdrew from the running, leaving a straight contest between Hedges and the relative newcomer Davies. A poll was held and the latter was indeed given the Directorship!

George Hedges' reaction was both swift and direct – he wanted to leave *Newbury & District* and resume an independent operation! A Special Meeting held the following day discussed his request, and it was agreed that he could buy back his former business. However, although the solicitors representing the parties set to work, it would be some time before the matter could be resolved to everyone's satisfaction.

One addition to the haulage fleet in September was the purchase of the first of a number of Bedford 2.5-ton lorries to be owned. This was registered RD 5922, having been ordered through a Reading dealer, though the fleet number is not recorded. This type was sound mechanically and gave good service with a minimum of specialist maintenance. At the September Board Meeting it was decided not to continue the Hungerford booking office, but instead a second phone was installed at No.6 The Wharf with the number Newbury 744.

Also at that meeting it was decided to regularise certain understandings between George Howlett and the Company, whereby he was paid 5 shillings per week in respect of the use of The Oak Tree Garage at Bucklebury as an outstation, 5 shillings per week for coach bookings from the Cold Ash and Bucklebury areas, plus 10 shillings per week for handling parcels consigned to those areas on the *N&D* buses. On the other hand, Howlett also made some suggestions regarding the way the traffic operations were arranged, leading to the appointment of Bert Greenwood as Ticket Inspector, though the latter still drove when required, especially the coaches.

With the further expansion during the year, along with the departure of both Prothero and Hedges, it became clear that the arrangements for daily duties required some revision. From October the following posts were appointed (or re-confirmed): Theo Denham (Company Secretary); Charlie Durnford (Engineer, Coach and Haulage Manager); Arthur Andrews (Coachbuilder and Chairman); James Davies (now Traffic Manager); Freddie Spanswick (Rolling Stock Manager); Boss Denham (Service Foreman, responsible for buses and traffic purposes); Bill Durnford and Percy Andrews (Garage Foremen, on alternate shifts). As already noted Ed White looked after the private hire and coach bookings in a very efficient way, whilst Olive Durnford was the clerk at the Market Street premises. The other 3 Durnford sons were mainly occupied at Mill Lane garage as mechanics, but were also available for driving duties at peak times and especially for coach work. Indeed, it made great sense to send skilled fitters out on longer journeys, whilst on Thursdays and Saturdays it was normal practice for them to help with driving duties, whilst others like the sign-writer and electrician stood in as conductors.

The presence of GMC's in fleet had quite a boost during December 1934, when no fewer than 4 were bought from London dealer H. Lane and all with some common ancestry. These had originated with the numerous smaller bus operators acquired by *Crosville Motor Services* in the North Wales area during its chequebook spree after the involvement of the *LMS Railway* shareholding. One had originated with the *Tocia Motor Omnibus Co. Ltd.* of Aberdaron in March 1930, passing into the *Crosville* fleet in February 1934. This was of the more powerful T60-type, powered by a Buick-built petrol engine of 6 cylinders developing 89hp, on a chassis wheelbase of 16ft 8ins. Registered as CC 9415, this carried a dual-doorway 26-seater bus body built by Strachans and it became *N&D* No.31.

GMC No.31 (CC 9415) still in maroon livery and the Crosville oval fleetname outline re-used by N&D.

The other 3 all had a common origin, though they had actually been delivered as new to *Crosville,* having been ordered by an operator taken over by them. This trio had been ordered by *W. Edwards* of Denbigh for his *Red Dragon Motor Services* and were in course of bodying when he sold out in July 1930. The bodies were built by Denbigh coachbuilder J. Hughes of Vale Road, with 20-seater front-entrance bodies on the 13ft 8ins-wheelbase T30C-type chassis with an engine rating of 75hp. They were delivered to *Crosville* in December 1930 as Nos. 629-31 (FM 6486-8) and these became *N&D* Nos. 36, 37 and 35 (i.e. out of sequence to the registrations).

GMC No.36 (FM 6486) in use as Crosville No.629.

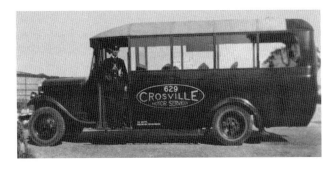

The quartet all carried the maroon and white livery used by *Crosville* at this time, which was of course in keeping with the scheme initially used at Newbury,

and these proved to be popular buses with crews and mechanics alike.

Outgoing in December was the last of a number of Lancia vehicles owned, this being YB 7442, which had come in from the *Durnford* fleet, and may have been the vehicle damaged in the accident on the road to Southsea in September?

The matter of the departure of George Hedges had still not been resolved by mid-November, as terms were haggled over by both parties, and during that month the Company spelt out its 'final offer'. There were two stumbling blocks, one being the cost of his re-purchase of the business, along with the vehicles to be transferred. Although he would regain his old Road Service Licenses, *N&D* sought assurance that should it wish to run between Newbury and Wantage in the future, that he would co-operate on fares, along with an undertaking not to poach coach work from them.

Whilst it had been concluded that George Hedges could re-purchase his business at the same amount he had sold it for, the issue of the vehicles to be taken was not as easily resolved. Obviously his pair of Ford AA-types (RX 4556 and RX 6888) were still active and would form half of that due to him, but *N&D* at first offered him the ex-Howlett GMC (SH 3380) and Thornycroft No.12 (TR 8198), though he turned down the latter. The matter was finally settled when another Ford AA in the shape of No.6 (RX 8261), the Andrews-bodied one with a sunshine roof, was offered and accepted by him. This quartet of vehicles then formed the new fleet of *Reliance Motor Services.*

George Hedges' decision to resume independent operation was of course borne out by the long and successful history of his *Reliance Motor Services,* as the bus operations continued through to the Summer of 1966, including the Cold Ash route acquired in due course from *Bert Austin,* whilst the coach fleet grew over the years to be the largest and best maintained in the area through to ceasing to trade in 1986.

No.31 (CC 9415) at The Wharf on the Inkpen route.

Chapter 8 – 1935

The year saw much less activity in respect of expansion, but it was a very busy time on other fronts, and in particular over changes to the fleet.

However, the year started with a small-scale takeover, when the sand and gravel haulage business of Walter Cleeveley was added to the goods portfolio.

Walter G. R. Cleeveley

Walter was the licensee of the Robin Hood, a large roadhouse-style pub built by Simonds Brewery of Reading and situated on the busy London Road in Newbury at No.104. Lunches and teas were also on offer, reflecting the large amount of passing trade in those days.

He also ran a business of supplying sand and gravel, along with some general haulage, which was in the daily care of his sons. Both enterprises first appear in the local directory for 1933, which ties in with his purchase of a pair of Bedford 2.5 ton open trucks (JB 1930 and JB 1984) in May of that year.

Charlie Durnford had of course had experience of the sand and gravel trade locally, and it was at his suggestion that Cleeveley was approached regarding the acquisition of his business. He was offered £200 for his lorries and goodwill of the business, and the transfer took place in January 1935, the pair of Bedfords being a preferred choice for the *N&D* haulage fleet.

Walter became the local booking agent for *Newbury & District* excursions and coach hire, whilst at 1937 he was still running the pub. This was also a popular venue for the Royal Antediluvian Order of Buffaloes Cromwell Lodge, whilst *Bert Austin* of Cold Ash, who was himself a RAOB brother, regularly arranged visits to there, along with visiting other lodges. On one such occasion he ran an outing to Southsea, stopping at the Gosport Lodge for tea and cakes on the way back.

****

There was another coach crash in the early hours of 21st January, though fortunately this time it was not an *N&D* vehicle that was involved. A 28-seater coach belonging to *Pearson's Motorways* of Liverpool had left the road and became imbedded in the wall of Lipscombe & Sons workshops in Oxford Road, Newbury. It was carrying part of the crew of the liner 'Empress of Britain', who were being transferred from Liverpool to Southampton, though it was fortunate that no injuries were sustained. A coach was laid on by *N&D* to cover the rest of the journey to the docks, whilst the Garage Fitters spent some two hours extricating the coach, after which it was fixed up in order that it could be driven back to Liverpool.

During February there was a small addition to the fleet, when Bert Greenwood received a Triumph motorcycle to use in his duties as Ticket Inspector. He already knew Jim Davies and the two worked well on Traffic duties. During the day the booking facility at his home in Newbury Street, Kintbury was covered by Mrs. Greenwood, who received a retainer from *N&D*.

During February a further attempt was made to obtain a license for an express coach operation between Newbury and Southsea. Pick-up points were requested at Woodhay, Highclere, Burghclere and Ecchinswell, and it was proposed that the service would operate once daily on Saturdays and Sundays during August. Once again, the application was turned down, no doubt in recognition of the *South Midland* service, but not really having addressed the needs of those living out in the villages, who *N&D* had of course factored into the equation

The events of 1934 leading to the departure of Hedges and Prothero had caused some concerns regarding the stability of the Company, so the Board resolved that in future those in the posts then occupied by Charlie Durnford, Theo Denham, Arthur Andrews, Freddie Spanswick and Jim Davies would all be subject to written contract, which would include the requirement to give 12 month's notice of withdrawal from the firm or a forfeit in salary.

Most of the shares made re-available through the departure of Hedges were bought by existing share-holders, but a new addition to the ranks was Mr. A.V. Culverhouse, an established haulage contractor based in Newington Causeway, London SE1, who took 100 shares. It is not known how he came to be aware of this opportunity, or if he had previous connections with the Company or any of its Directors.

The subject of premises for the expanding operations was raised once again in March, and it was resolved that the lease on Nos.6/7 at The Wharf would be renewed for three years. However, on the garage front there was some disquiet regarding reliance on *Thames Valley* for the provision of the main Mill Lane garage. In respect of the latter, *N&D* renewed the lease for one year, but set about finding an alternative solution. Initial enquiries led to an offer by the Company of £3500 for the former South Berks Brewery premises in Bartholomew Street, though that was unsuccessful.

Whilst mentioning The Wharf offices, it is worth noting the other occupants of the row, some of whom traded on the throughput of bus passengers: No.1 was occupied by Barrett (tobacconists); No.2 George Secker & Son (outfitters and also providers of the *N&D* uniforms); Nos.3/4 Dixon's (coffee bar); No.5

Milner's (wireless shop), whilst No.8 served both as the Police sub-station and the Royal Navy recruiting office.

Certain pre-season alterations to excursions were put forward during March, resulting in the successful addition of trips to California-in-England, Cheddar and Hannington (for the point-to-point races), as well as an increase in the maximum number of permitted vehicles to 14.

As a result of the incoming Bedfords from *Cleeveley,* Dennis G-type lorries OT 6861/2 were sold in March, whilst a bus on the same maker's 30-cwt chassis, Dennis-bodied 14-seater TP 7118, which had come from *W.J. White & Son,* was also sold that month.

In early March *City of Oxford* had put forward an application for a Saturdays-only extension of their Abingdon – Rowstock service onto Chilton for three journeys. The intention was to provide better shopping opportunities, as well as offering more recreational facilities for the large number of workmen involved in the construction of the RAF airfield near to there. The license was duly granted, leading to a further approach from *N&D* regarding co-operation between the two concerns. Jim Davies wrote to *City of Oxford* and pointed out that his Company would be willing to extend its East Ilsley route onto Rowstock to provide good connections, adding that he felt there would be mutual befits to both operators. The Oxford Company did not exactly show any particular keenness over the matter, though it did confirm that it would not raise an objection to the proposal, which we shall hear more of in due course. There was something of an historic decision made in March, when the Board agreed to Jim Davies's proposal to order a brand new Dennis 'Ace' coach, this being the first new PSV purchased since formation.

One of the incoming coaches for 1935 was No.50 (JK 1911), seen here decorated for the Newbury Carnival.

It should of course be appreciated that the nature of the local bus services did not really warrant the cost of new vehicles, whilst during the 1930's the dealer's yards were awash with sound second-hand vehicles, largely as a result of the territorial operators buying up independents. The good relations that already existed between Charlie Durnford and certain of the London dealers, like Harry Lane in SW10 and George Dawson in SW9 in particular, meant that on such visits it was possible to pick up good vehicles of the favoured types. Generally, these were inspected and brought back by Charlie and his sons, with older stock often going in part-exchange.

Incoming vehicles for April were both Gilfords, but one was actually purchased locally. This was VR 9822, a 32-seater bus on a 168OT-type chassis which had been new in July 1930 to *Thomas McLaw (Curtis Tours)* of Manchester. It had been with *Lovegrove's* of Silchester, who offered it to *N&D*, though the make of body and fleet number are not known.

The second Gilford was on the same chassis, but was a 28-seater coach with dual-entrance body by Duple of Hendon. This was new in July 1931 for *Southern Glideway* of Eastbourne, who had been bought out by *Southdown Motor Services* in March 1932, and sold it Lane (the dealer) in January 1935. This became No.50 (JK 1911), though in the course of preparation the rear door was removed and this raised the seating capacity to 31.

Maudslay FG 4427 on a private hire job.

Also acquired in April was a Maudslay ML4B-type with Buckingham front-entrance 29-seater bus body, which had been new in October 1928 to *Cormie Bros.* of Kirkcaldy in Fife. Registered FG 4427 this had duly passed to *General Motor Carrying* of Kirkcaldy, who in turn passed into the control of *Walter Alexander & Sons.* Latterly it had been with London dealer Dawson and came to *N&D* to take the vacant fleet No.6.

Leyland vehicles had featured in each of the original constituent fleets in a small way, and the pair of 'Lion' saloons was proving a sound purchase. In the Spring of 1935 the opportunity arose to purchase a pair of the smaller 'Leveret' PLA2-types, which were of normal-control layout and had 3.96 litre 4-cylinder petrol engines. Fitted with 20-seater front-entrance bus bodies also built by Leyland, there were RU 5796 and RU 5843, new to *Hants & Dorset* in July/August 1927, latterly being used on the Swanage town service. Their fleet numbers at Newbury are unknown, and both were in use by June. Being already painted green with a white roof they received only minimal attention, though the window surrounds were painted white and roof-mounted adverts boards were added. These were sent to the Hermitage outstation in place of the pair of Fords previously allocated, but they did not prove popular with the drivers, and despite their maker, were not regarded as reliable enough.

The little 'Leverets' had only a short career with N&D, and these two views show RU 5796 (above) at Fawley when still with Hants & Dorset, along with one of the batch (below) in a nearside view.

A major fire at The Jack Hotel, the old-established coaching inn at 22 Northbrook Street, Newbury had resulted in its closure, and it was chosen as the site for a new Marks & Spencer's store of the kind then being built throughout England. These followed a set pattern and the construction required large amounts of bricks, which were ordered from the London Brick Company and brought to Newbury by train. With experience in this type of haulage, *Newbury & District* was awarded the contract to transport the bricks from the railhead to the site, there being several large shipments per week. In order to provide a suitable vehicle for this task, the former *Durnford* Reo 'Major' was de-bodied and fitted with a flat-bed lorry body to allow easy handling of the bricks, which was undertaken entirely by hand, direct from the drop-side railway wagons onto the lorry. The identical of this vehicle is not known, but once this task was completed it was disposed of. This was not, however, No.26 (RX 6264) as previously thought, as that remained in use as a coach through to withdrawal in 1938.

The major national event of 1935 was the Silver Jubilee of King George V, which saw the *N&D* fleet very busy all Summer. The actual jubilee took place on 6th May, and the annual Newbury Carnival was re-scheduled to that date, with the Company providing an enhanced level of operation throughout the afternoon and the evening through to 1.15am in the following morning in order to cope with the crowds and the firework display held after dark.

Newbury & District entered into the spirit of the event, decorating two vehicles for the carnival parade, one being the newly-acquired Gilford coach No.50 (JK 1911), which bore the inscription 'progress – passenger transport', along with the Maudslay removals van L4 (CW 6802) representing 'progress – goods transport'. Many buses in the fleet were decorated, some extensively, whilst the coaches tended to carry a Union Jack or two. Several drivers excelled themselves with the amount of decoration, some of which probably fell foul of the Construction & Use Regulations, but the patriotism was self-evident for this popular monarch. George Amor painted the radiator of Tilling-Stevens No.5 (BU 5690) in red, white and blue, plus adding to the front end a number of rosettes and a portrait of the King and Queen framed in a large horseshoe design!

The decorated Tilling-Stevens bus No5 (BU 5690).

Another heavily-decorated bus was GMC No.31 (CC 9415) seen departing from The Wharf for Wickham.

Two further full-size Gilfords were acquired in June, though each had quite different bodies and origins. One was VM 3669, a 166OT-type new in August 1928 to an unknown Manchester operator and fitted with a 32-seater rear-entrance coach body by Spicer of Southport. No fleet number is recorded for this, and although it was painted in coach livery, it later received roof-mounted advert boards and a destination box and was also used on bus work.

Gilford VM 3669 working the Hungerford service.

The second was obtained through Major Allday, one of the London dealers, and this was a slightly longer 168OT-type new in June 1930 to *H.C. Motor Works* of Kingston-upon-Hull, who built the 32-seater rear-entrance body themselves and used it on services it ran until duly taken over by *East Yorkshire* in June 1932. The latter had used it until sometime in 1934 when it was replaced by standard types and sold. This was registered RH 2257 and became No.24, being the longest surviving of all the Gilfords owned, not going until April 1941, albeit latterly on a daily contract!

There were numerous events staged throughout the Summer in connection with the Sliver Jubilee, some being special versions of established events such as the Military Tattoos at Aldershot and Tidworth, whilst others were additional spectacles. The presence of the Royal Navy Fleet off Spithead for the Royal Review attracted a lot of interest and, between 13th and 17th July, *N&D* ran daily trips to Southsea which included a steamer cruise to view the ships at anchor. Similarly the annual Navy Week at Portsmouth that year drew record crowds, and again the Company obliged with a daily excursion from 3rd to 10th August, which was a very busy time for the coach fleet, with the Tidworth Tattoo in the evenings. Other regular events took on the jubilee theme, and the last one did not take place until the Air Display at Thatcham on 20th September. That month also saw special services travelling to St. Giles's Fair in Oxford, the Thame Show, and the local carnivals at Hungerford, Lambourn, Ramsbury and Pewsey.

The only known photo of No.24 (RH 2257) is this one taken when with in service with East Yorkshire M.S.

However, to return to the chronological sequence of events, the Board was rather annoyed to hear of some apparent poaching of business by *George Hedges* during July 1935. Apparently it had been the custom of the vicar at Stockcross to use *N&D* coaches for any outings he organised, but during 1935 he was using the *Reliance* coaches instead. Correspondence ensued between the Company and the reverend gentleman in which *N&D* pointed out that as providers of the bus service to Stockcross, they considered it their patch, and also that Hedges had undertaken not to seek work from established customers. What the response was is not recorded, but it would be interesting to know which operator was favoured with the next hiring!

History was made in July 1935, when the brand new Dennis 'Ace' coach was delivered. No.63 (JB 6834) carried a 20-seater front-entrance coach body built at Godalming by King & Taylor. Despite this significant purchase, no photos of this vehicle appeared in adverts, or have even so far come to light in its original condition! However, that the 'Ace' was a good buy is of course borne out by the large collection of that type assembled by *N&D*. Although the snout-nosed appearance was not to everyone's taste, the arrangement of setting the front axle a little further back, produced a vehicle with a very tight turning circle, ideal for negotiating narrow lanes and venues with restricted access.

Whilst considering width restrictions, it must be appreciated that in those days the only vehicular way of crossing the Kennet & Avon Canal in Newbury town centre was over the arched stone Newbury Bridge at the junction of Northbrook Street and Bridge Street. Apart from the restrictions this imposed on routing opportunities, it also frequently led to a traffic backlog at busy times. Indeed, the holiday exodus in August 1935 led to a continuous traffic jam for several hours, mainly caused by traffic from the midlands and north converging on the bottleneck, and this resulted in the Police putting in place a temporary one-way system around the Mansion House.

Newbury Bridge over the Kennet & Avon Canal.

The other coach to be acquired in July was a Bedford, though actually designated as a WLG-type (i.e. the goods model), having been built as a cattle-truck for Charles King of Little Coxwell, Faringdon in November 1931 and registered as RX 9463. This received fleet No.18, which placed it next to the former-*Pocock Bros.* bus of the similar WLB-type,

though it was fitted with a secondhand 20-seater 'all-weather' coach body, which quite likely was the one taken off the Reo 'Major' now in use as a brick-lorry.

Bedford No.18 (RX 9463) with the re-used bodywork.

At some time during the Summer of 1935, probably with the arrival of Bedford No.18, one of the older 'sunsaloon' coaches made its exit from the fleet, with the sale of the former-*Spanswick* Ford AA-type RX 6662, though it went for further service elsewhere.

Also received during July was JB 6909, a 3-ton Bedford lorry which was obtained as chassis only from Great Western Motors of Reading, and was fitted with a lorry body by *N&D*. That month saw the departure of the last of the G-type Dennis lorries with the sale of OT 7923.

Whilst referring to the popularity of various Dennis types at Newbury over the years, it is worth noting that the Newbury Volunteer Fire Brigade, some of whom were also *N&D* employees, had favoured that make since motor fire engines came into use. First there had been a May 1913 example, followed by an F-type (PG 3076) and that had been joined by an 'Ace' (JB 4752), with the latter pair continuing until after the Second World War.

Despite the Company having been established for over 3 years, 1935 actually saw an <u>increase</u> in the use of the original operator names! Whereas, *N&D* had responded to the return of the Durnfords to the fold by adding 'proprietors of C. Durnford & Sons' to adverts for removals and haulage, along with using 7 The Wharf as the contact address, the advert in the August 1935 timetable booklet urged customers to 'get Durnford's terms' and gave the Market Street address! In the same issue, those seeking bodywork, re-painting, hood repairs and 'Splintex' glass were told to contact Andrews at Northcroft Lane, though that ad did state 'a branch of Newbury & District'. These adverts continued to be displayed through to 1937, and others for haulage and removals also appeared under the Company title and The Wharf address.

Indeed, the value of the removals business alone can be gauged by the fact that during the relatively quiet months of January and February 1935 there were 64 such jobs undertaken, details of which appeared in the local paper in echo of *Durnford's* old practice!

A further full-size Gilford arrived in September as No.49 (MW 4028), being a 166OT-type new in March 1929 to *Sparrow & Vincent (Victory Motor Services)* of Salisbury. As built this had a dual-entrance coach body by the Gilford-associated Wycombe Motor Bodies. This had been altered when about 2 years old by Heaver, coachbuilders who were nearby at Durrington, when the rear doorway was removed and a sunshine roof added, and it passed into the *Wilts & Dorset* fleet when the Salisbury operator was acquired in December 1933. Various sources quote different seating capacities for this vehicle, but with *N&D* it was a 31-seater.

Also in September the small Morris-Commercial bus which had come from *George Brown* with his Wash Common service (RX 3553) was withdrawn from use, whilst the close of the excursion season saw the sale of Talbot 14-seater No.21 (BL 6490). This meant that no coaches under 20 seats were now available for the first time since the Company had been formed, whilst it also witnessed the passing of the final of a number of Talbot vehicles, all supplied by Percy Andrews.

Garage accommodation was further discussed during September 1935, and some land in Old Newtown Road was considered, but nothing further came of that. New arrangements were, however, put in place in respect of the buses out-stationed for the Cold Ash and Bucklebury operations, when the Company got a lease on a large shed owned by Mrs. Hattie Carter at 12 Bath Road in Thatcham. This had been used in connection with the family business of Rick Cloth Manufacturers from at least 1899, and *N&D* paid 22 shillings per week for keeping two buses there, plus in due course another transferred from Bucklebury.

Gilford coach No.49 (MW 4028) is seen at the coast with the sunshine roof rolled open, one of 4 coaches there on that occasion.

A further small takeover occurred in October 1935, when *Charles Ballard* of Bradfield South End sold his coaching interests.

Charles Henry Ballard

Charlie Ballard was born in Reading in 1878, the son of a draper at 124 Mount Pleasant, in St. Giles's parish. By 1901 the family had relocated to Spencers Wood, where he was assisting with the family business. His father died the following year, and by 1910 he had moved again to 17 Belsize Avenue in the Bowes Park area of Edmonton, north London, where he is listed as a gentleman's outfitter, also having married Florence Poulton in 1908.

However, by the time of his enlistment in July 1916 he was working as a motor driver, so he was sent to the Royal Army Service Corps in that same role, initially posted to Grove Park, the large mobilisation centre near Lewisham in South London. From there he joined the 766 Mechanical Transport Company and was shipped from Devonport in September 1916 to arrive at Salonika in Greece, remaining in that theatre of war throughout his service until returning to England in March 1919, contracting malaria during his time away. After being demobbed in April 1919 he established his South End Garage at Bradfield by 1924, some 9 miles west of Reading. Charlie and his wife Florence had lived at Hollywood, Bucklebury at the time of his call up, she originating from the Newbury area, so this no doubt had a bearing on the location of the venture.

In 1929 he added some coach work to his business, purchasing a new Chevrolet LQ-type, registered in June as RX 4706, which had a blue-liveried 14-seater body. It also had an alternative lorry body for when not in use for passenger work.

One of the incentives for his involvement with passenger transport may well have been the presence of the nearby Bradfield College, which added several 100 to the local population in term times, and required regular transport to and from the nearest rail stations at term ends for the boarders and their luggage.

The other bread-and-butter work was for local sports teams and other social outings, which also led to some advertised excursions. By the 1930 Act he was running the following on a regular basis: Aldershot (for Reading FC matches), Aldershot Tattoo, Bognor Regis, Bournemouth, Hayling Island, Newbury (every Thursday for shopping), Oxford and Swindon (for Reading FC matches).

Side view of one of the Dodson-bodied F-types.

These must have fared well, as he replaced the little Chevrolet with a larger Dennis F-type during early 1934. This was UL 7692, new in March 1929 and fitted with a rather luxurious 20-seater dual-doorway coach body built by Christopher Dodson of Willesden, London NW10. It had been constructed for use on the London to Liverpool express service of *Claremont Coaching Services* of London. The internal finish was to a high standard to reflect the long-distance work, and included heaters, diffused lighting and curtains. However, after only 3 months the Liverpool service was sold, so this coach and another similar one, passed to another London operator, *Westminster Coaching Services,* who worked it on express services from the capitol to East Anglian towns. They in turn were acquired by *Eastern Counties* of Norwich, but that operator sold the vehicles onto the neighbouring *Eastern National* based in Chelmsford, making it a 5th hand purchase!

Another view of one of the Dodson-bodied F-type coaches on test prior to registration.

The Dennis ran throughout the 1934 and 1935 seasons but Charles, now 57 years old, evidently then decided to concentrate on the garage business. He died aged 81 in 1959.

No record exists of what *N&D* paid for the coach and the licenses, though the latter was a further sound addition to strengthen the position on E&T's in the eastern area. As was often the case, Ballard then became the local booking agent, so his local contacts were put to good use. The coach was of course mechanically the same as the Dennis E-type saloon bus, No.41 (PR 9053), already in the fleet, and indeed both left *N&D* during 1937.

****

In October a further GMC 'Explorer' T30C-type of July 1929 vintage, fitted with an 'all-weather' 20-seat dual-doorway body by London Lorries and registered OU 2885 was purchased. This had been new to *E.R. & E.M. Whitren (Billie's Coaches)* of Pennington in Hampshire, whose business was acquired by *Hants & Dorset* in August 1935, and *N&D* numbered it as 58.

A London Lorries-bodied GMC of the design of No.58 (OU 2885) from a contemporary advert in the trade press.

Outgoing from the fleet by October was the other 30-cwt Dennis inherited from *W.J. White & Son*, No.43 (RX 6401), that type now being eliminated at *N&D*.

Ralph Revell with Gilford No.23 (TO 9554).

Also during October an application was submitted to the Traffic Commissioner for a new service between Newbury and Rowstock, which would run by way of Chieveley – Beedon – East Ilsley – Chilton, and was intended primarily to meet the needs of the increased workforce at the RAF base. The first journey departed Newbury ay 7am to reach Rowstock at 7.55am. Two return journeys were operated on weekdays, increased to three on Saturdays, the main return from Rowstock being at 5pm. This was in addition to the established services in that direction, and the license was granted in November on the conditions that no double-deckers were used, and that any journeys via Stanmore would be restricted to 20-seaters. The service commenced on 18th November, also allowing passengers the chance to transfer to *City of Oxford* buses onwards to reach Abingdon, Wantage, Oxford, Didcot, Steventon, Drayton and The Hendreds. An afternoon service was also operated on Sundays, but no route number was allocated as the service was regarded as part of Route 1 (Newbury – East Ilsley), though it was displayed separately in the timetable booklet.

As has already been noted, certain disagreements occurred between shareholders, who were former operators, over changes made to their old routes, and at the AGM in November it was agreed that they would in future be consulted before changes were made.

During November another of the Ford AA-types inherited from *Prothero* (RX 7772) was withdrawn,

leaving only his similar bus RX 9005 to represent that make in the fleet.

Eight vehicles were purchased in December from H. Lane in order to prepare them for service in 1936. In view of the popularity of the Bedford make in the haulage fleet, the passenger models were also sought out. Three of these had latterly been with *Crosville,* who had purchased their original owner's services. Two were WLB-types (UN 5227 and UN 5381) new in October 1931 and January 1932 respectively, to *J. Price* of New Broughton. Both had Willmott 20-seater front-entrance coach bodies, and these had passed to *Crosville* in 1935.

The third was also a WLB-type with a locally-built front-entrance bus body by Dobson (UX 9410), which had been new to *W.E. Jones* of Ifton Heath, Shropshire in December 1931. It passed to *Crosville Motor Services* in 1935 and thence to the dealer H. Lane. No fleet numbers are known for these three.

Bedford WLB coach No.61 (OY 2093) at Croydon, along with the rear layout of the bodywork.

Also of that chassis type was No.61 (OY 2093), which carried a 20-seater front-entrance coach body by Real of Ealing, and had been new in December 1931 to *Alex Dyer* of Croydon.

Two of the vehicles were once again GMC's, with one being registered RG 881 and new to *R. Raffan (Radio Bus Service)* of Aberdeen in December 1929 who sold out to *Alexanders* in July 1935. This was another T30C-type, but neither the details of the bodybuilder or the *N&D* fleet number are known. The other GMC was of the 14ft 7ins-wheelbase 'Crusader' T42-type which carried a Duple 24-seater front-entrance bus body and was new in October 1929 to *G.F. Eaton* of Heage in Derbyshire. Just over a year later it passed to *J.H. Booth* of Westhouses, who sold out to *Midland General* in July 1934. This became No.32 (RA 9830) and was very much regarded by *N&D* as a dual-purpose vehicle, painted in coach livery and often selected for private hires due to the power of its 6-cylinder engine. This vehicle would have cost £970 when new and was certainly a good buy.

The final pair of vehicles from Lane were both Gilfords, though of different models. One was of the normal-control AS6-type, which carried a dual-doorway 20-seater coach body by Petty of Hitchin and was new in November 1930 to *Western Star Motorways*. This had duly passed to *Chesham & District,* who were then absorbed by *Amersham & District,* which itself became a *London Transport* subsidiary before losing its separate identity in November 1933. This became No.53 (HX 1855) and was another good buy which saw widespread use.

Gilford No53 (HX 1855) is seen (above) when new to Western Star Motorways and (below) in Chesham High Street when with Chesham & District.

Photos of the coach fleet show the vehicles to be well kept, and Boss Denham pauses from cleaning Gilford No.22 (RD 1886) whilst laid over at the seaside. Note the style of sign-writing applied to the rear panels.

The second Gilford was a 32-seater service saloon with front-entrance body by Wycombe on a 168OT-type chassis. New in November 1929 to *James Penman & Co.* of Bannockburn, who sold out to *W. Alexander & Sons* of Falkirk, it duly passed to *Stanford Motors* of Stanford-le-Hope in Essex, who sold in turn sold out to *Eastern National* in 1935. Registered MS 9336 it became *N&D* No.48.

The histories of the above Gilfords illustrates how the industry was being reshaped through takeovers in the years after the 1930 Act, whilst the formation in 1933 of *London Transport* would provide a number of the vehicles entering the Newbury fleet during the next few years, all swept away prematurely in the interests of standardisation. In some cases, these processes also resulted in the very manufacturers of these vehicles types going out of business, particularly at the larger 'territorial' companies preferred more heavy-duty types of vehicles.

Also purchased in December, but from Arlington Motors of London SW1, was another Bedford WLB-type coach which became No.62 (OY 5807). This had been new in May 1933 to *H. Wright (Fram Coaches)* of Addiscombe, near Croydon and carried a front-entrance Duple body seating 20.

From the above it can be seen that the allocation of fleet numbers during 1935 was quite haphazard, with

a tendency to use more fresh ones, even though lots of vacant numbers were available.

Towards the end of 1935 there was another vehicle acquired, though in this instance it for use as spares only. This was the Thornycroft A1-type charabanc that *Edith Kent* had bought after it had demonstrated on behalf of the chassis maker, and latterly this had been stored unused. It was driven up to Mill Lane by Walter Corneby, who drove for *Mrs. Kent,* and in due course of time would join the ranks of *N&D.* There it stayed in the rear yard for at least two years before it was finally scrapped. This was one of a number of purchases for this purpose which can be seen in the fleet list, though there may be others unrecorded.

The only known photo of one of the Leyland 'Leverets' in service shows RU 5843 travelling coming in from Hermitage along Northbrook Street to The Wharf.

Most of the Gilford vehicles acquired were for coach work, but No.48 (MS 9336) had been constructed for bus duties and carried a 32-seater body built at the chassis manufacturer's associated coachworks set up at High Wycombe. Like many vehicles of that period, it had a number of changes in ownership before being purchased for use at Newbury, and remained in service until March 1939.

With this influx of vehicles, several were let go, with Star 'Flyer' bus 3 (TY 6174) departing in December, along with the first of the less than successful little 'Leverets' (RU 5843), which had gone by the end of the year. Due to repeated problems with these when at the Hermitage outstation, they had been replaced by a pair of the Hughes-bodied GMC's Nos.35-7 (FM 6488/6/7), which were more powerful and reliable.

Thames Valley had shown little interest in expansion westwards, though it had been very active in the areas to the south and north of Reading during the 1930's. However, in December 1935 it negotiated to purchase the *Reading & District* service between Reading and Yattendon from *G. Jarvis & Sons* of Christchurch Green, Reading. The service had originally been that of *Reg Bragg,* later aided by cash from Jarvis, who acquired it in due course.

The latter had a successful garage business, along with car hire and coaches, but wished to dispose of the bus operation. *Thames Valley* took over as Route 5b from the first day of 1936, which may have slightly concerned *Newbury & District.* However, they need not have been alarmed, as the real reason *TV* had been interested was in order to address calls to increase capacity between Reading and Pangbourne.

Chapter 9 – 1936

This was a year of virtually no expansion, and indeed consideration was given to selling the Company!

However, in January a number of modifications were proposed in respect of the bus services, some being to reverse earlier changes which had been unpopular with their former operators. These affected services from Newbury to Aldworth, Lambourn, Hungerford, Fawley, Frilsham and Yattendon, along with the link between Hungerford and Hungerford Newtown, as well as the Local Services between The Broadway and Kingsbridge Road or Wash Common.

Other proposed amendments concerned the Rowstock journeys, which had improved timings for those who wished to connect with *City of Oxford* buses or travel onto West Ilsley or Reading on *N&D's* services. The latter still found the response from the Oxford firm rather cool and indeed, after considering the revised arrangements, *City of Oxford* decided to withdraw its buses on the section to Chilton after 27th January!

As has been noted previously, both *Thames Valley* and the *Ledbury Transport Co. Ltd. (Thackray's Way)* operated between Newbury and Reading. Whereas the *Thames Valley* service consisted of a bus service from one town to the other, the purpose of the *Thackray's* service was to provide a link to its Reading – London express coach route. The competition between the two over the Reading – London road had been intensive for some years, but arrangements had been made for *Thames Valley* to acquire the *Ledbury* operations with effect from 2nd February 1936. However, for reasons of licensing, the journeys of the latter in respect of the Newbury route were shown within the *'Valley's* route 10. Whilst this had no immediate bearing on *N&D*, it certainly gave *Thames Valley* additional confidence over that road, perhaps also hastening the need for the Newbury company to seek its own garage site.

During February *N&D* applied for the addition of a Sunday service on the Rowstock route, which was duly granted. That same month it also objected to the proposal by *South Midland* to offer local fares over the Abingdon – Newbury of its express service to Southsea.

Indeed, *Newbury & District* once again attempted to provide a regular Southsea service. Bearing in mind that both the *South Midland* and *Midland Red* routes included pick ups at Newbury, this time it attempted to tap the potential by proposing a service starting at Inkpen. The application sought a license to run via Ball Hill, West Woodhay, The Derby Arms and Blind Man's Gate, operating on Saturdays and Sundays from 18th July to 20th September. However, when the application was dealt with in April, another refusal was forthcoming, which was a great disappointment!

Other applications heard in April were approved, one being the addition of a pick up at Whitway, and also an excursion to Ramsbury from Newbury on the day of the annual carnival.

It would seem that the *Thames Valley* management had taken a look at the area west of Reading following the takeover of the *Ledbury* operations, as during February it enquired how much the Newbury operator would seek for either just the Thatcham area routes or the whole undertaking! *Newbury & District* was at that time experiencing some financial issues, so the matter was certainly given some consideration. They informed the Reading-based company that £15,000 was the price for the Thatcham routes or £50,000 for the whole lot! This was rather high, and negotiations ended there, no doubt also partly due to other more pressing issues affecting *Thames Valley* that Summer.

The February Board Meeting also gave the Haulage Manager approval to seek a secondhand lorry, and Charlie Durnford obtained a 1934 Bedford 2.5-tonner from Great Western Motors of Reading. That same month the haulage operation of *Charlie Colliver* was purchased. It was about this time that the Reo 'Major' converted to a flat-bed lorry for brick-hauling was disposed of, so the Bedford may have been intended as its replacement.

Charles George Colliver

It will be noted that Charlie Durnford had acquired a number of local haulage operators, either in his own right or later on behalf of *Newbury & District*.

In the case of the business of *Charles Colliver*, the main purpose was to strengthen established areas of expertise. Charles was based at Wickham, some 7 miles west of Newbury, and his main source of work was on behalf of the Wickham Brick Kilns, and he first appears in the local directories in 1932. Brick-haulage was of course a long-established aspect of the *Durnford* business, and Charlie Durnford made the successful approach to buy the Wickham operator out, along with his lorry in March 1936.

The vehicle acquired was a rather elderly Dennis 4-tonner (HO 6306), which had started out as a service bus with *Aldershot & District* in March 1924. However, such vehicles were well-built machines and many went on to have further careers as lorries, also having been fitted with pneumatic tyres in due course.

It is interesting to note that adverts appeared under the *Durnford* name during the Summer of 1936 regarding the construction of roads and paths, along with sand and gravel haulage, these aspects no doubt boosted by the addition of the *Cleeveley* and Colliver operations.

****

One departure in March was the Wray-bodied Dennis GL-type coach No.53 (UV 6002), which had only a relatively short time at Newbury.

The slogan 'The Roads Are Yours' had been in use by N&D since the 1934 season on the coaching front, and from 1936 the public was also assured of 'First Class Travel at Halfpenny Per Mile', and both of these slogans refer to the intense competition between the railways and the increasingly luxurious coaches on offer, coming at a time when many railway lines were suffering from under-investment and ageing rolling stock.

The old *Durnford* practice of listing recent removals jobs continued, with March showing 35 such tasks, and 30 more undertaken during April.

On the bus front the Company was growing concerned over the poor receipts of the Hungerford Route 11 via Inkpen, and in April an application was put forward to delete the lightly-used Monday and Friday journeys, which was introduced from 9th May. Passengers who wished to travel between Newbury and Hungerford could still make use of the 'main road' Route 9 which ran on a daily basis.

It should be noted that whilst applications for changes to local bus services tended to go through quickly, any for excursions involved numerous objectors, with the railways and local authorities also weighing in. The latter were concerned with unfettered use of the roads under their care or the effects on town centres. Some were quite enlightened and even set up coach stations, or encouraged facilities along the number of by-passes then under construction, whilst others were successful in putting together standard conditions through bylaws, and these were often considered within the hearings of the Traffic Commissioners. This led to the reference to such conditions on approvals, the full version stating arrangements for drop-off/pick-up zones and in particular off-street coach parking arrangements. The larger operators could often avoid the latter by using the local garage of an associated company. In London the situation was more difficult, as the Metropolitan Police succeeded in getting buses and coaches banned from numerous streets, leading to the development of off-street coach stations such as those at Victoria and Kings Cross.

However, *Newbury & District* was not the only local operator seeking to expand on the coach front, as *Mrs. Kent* took over the activities of *Rodney Vincent* during April 1936. This added the bus service between Ashford Hill and Newbury, together with his E&T's license covering Ashford Hill, Kingsclere Woodlands and Headley, which N&D had previously considered purchasing. We shall hear much more of the development of *Edith Kent* of Baughurst and her *Kingsclere Coaches* in the following chapter.

The London dealer George Dawson was the recipient of many non-standard types taken over by *London Transport*, and a trip to his premises in May resulted in the acquisition of a further Gilford and a pair of 20-seater Thornycrofts. The Gilford was MY 346, which had been new to *Skylark Motor Coaches* of London W1, who had operated express routes out from the capitol, but were taken over by *Green Line Coaches,* which was part of *London Transport.* It was new in July 1929 and was a Duple-bodied 26-seater dual-doorway coach on a normal-control 166SD chassis. The fleet number at Newbury is not known.

Thornycroft No.20 (UR 7968) after passing to London General Country Services.

Both of the Thornycrofts had a common ancestry, being new to *Peoples Motor Services* of Ware. Each had a front-entrance body by Thurgood, who was also the owner of the bus company as well as being an established coachbuilder. One was an A2Long-type new in November 1930 which became No.20 (UR 7968), the other being an A12-type new in September 1931 and becoming No.21 (JH 492).

Thornycroft No.21 (JH 492) as new to Peoples M.S.

The other Leyland 'Leveret' (RU 5796) left the fleet at some point in the year, once the above had arrived, but the exact date is not known.

It seems that *Thames Valley* was not alone amongst *Newbury & District's* neighbouring operators having an eye on possible purchase of the Company. In May the *Wilts & Dorset* management reviewed figures sent by N&D regarding income from routes, and this was considered if worked by an expansion of the Salisbury operator. However, at the same time *Wilts & Dorset* approached *Thames Valley* regarding the prospect of a joint takeover, this being due to an understanding between those concerns that the roads east of Newbury and north of the A4 being the *'Valley's* territory. Although Raymond Longman travelled up from Salisbury to discuss this at Reading with Theodore Homer on 13th May, nothing further came of the proposal, as *Thames Valley* had rather a lot on its plate at the time.

The 'Leverets' did not really live up to the reliability experienced with the larger Leyland types and were replaced by further Thornycroft A-types, the latter becoming the preferred model for that capacity for a number of years.

Further changes were made to the timings on the Rowstock service from 15th May 1936, when the hours of work at the airfield were amended. The run back at 5pm was no longer relevant, so the 3.40pm ex-Newbury which formed the positioning journey was re-timed at 4.35pm, leaving Rowstock at 6.40pm. Jim Davies did, however, take the courtesy of writing to *City of Oxford* to point out that a connection was still possible at Rowstock to or from Abingdon or Oxford.

Various changes took place to the arrangements for booking agents from May 1936, when it was decided to remove the phone facility from both the Kintbury and Thatcham premises, whilst a request for a phone line by Howlett at Bucklebury was similarly refused. Mr. Bason ceased to be the agent at Woolhampton as he left the area and relocated to Waterlooville. The duties of Bert Greenwood were reviewed, and his post as part-time Ticket Inspector was rescinded, whilst he was also reminded of his obligations to maintain the booking facility at his home at 1 Newbury Street, Kintbury.

There was a certain amount of disquiet amongst the Directors during May, at the Extraordinary General Meeting held on 25th of that month. Charlie Durnford sought election as a Permanent Director and, on a show of hands, this would have gone through. However, Ed White held proxies for 4 others, so a vote based on shareholdings was taken, at which Durnford was defeated. However, a proposal to elect George Howlett as a Director did go through.

The process was repeated on 15th June at a further meeting called by Charlie Durnford, who this time brought sons Bill, Henry and Ernie, but intervention by Ed White ensured he again lost the poll.

Yet another neighbouring firm considered possibly buying *N&D*, though this time it was actually smaller in size. This was *Venture Ltd.*, the Basingstoke-based bus and coach operator set up by Thornycrofts. Their intention had actually been to obtaining a controlling interest in the Newbury company, which certainly had some logic about it from the geographical perspective. However, although the *Venture* Board discussed the matter on 5th June, the idea was deferred, whilst there are no references to this in the *N&D* minutes suggesting that they were not even aware of this.

The Venture fleet brought further variety to The Wharf with its dark red-painted buses. No.19 (OU 5659) was a forward-control BC-type with Challands Ross 32-seater bodywork and new in 1930. Like Newbury & District's fleet, this bus features roof-mounted advert boards, though it is the only such example known from photographs.

Meanwhile the growth of the coach fleet was brought to the attention of the travelling public, who were told that 'up to 600 persons' could be accommodated. On Saturday 27th June one party of 121 from the British Floorcloth Co., along with engineering staff from the Thatcham Board Mills at Thatcham, were taken to Bognor Regis for their annual outing. As the fleet was rather stretched on Thursdays, advertised excursions were limited on that day, though on the other hand there were a number of evening excursions and half-day tours on Wednesdays, which made use of vehicles on the quieter days.

The importance of annual local events in drawing big crowds may not be fully appreciated in this modern age of almost universal car ownership, but in the '30's all such dates were popular opportunities to get out to a day's entertainment, and *N&D* ensured that it provided special services to many of these. During June 1936 there was Yattendon Fair on Monday 1st June and the Police Sports Day at Benham Park on Wednesday 3rd June, whilst August saw buses to

Lambourn Flower Show on Saturday 22nd and Hungerford Carnival the following Saturday, and during September to Lambourn Carnival on Saturday 12th and the Newbury Agricultural Show on the following Saturday. The latter event was held at Elcot Park, half way between Newbury and Hungerford just north of the A4, so a special stop was set up on the main road for entrance into the site, with extra buses from Newbury, Hungerford and Kintbury. Also from Wednesday 2nd to Saturday 6th September events in aid of Newbury Hospital drew crowds to various events including a firework display, with extra journeys provided at 10.40pm on most routes to take the crowds home. The other routes locally were also treated in similar way with late journeys by *Bert Austin, Bill Kent, Edith Kent, Venture, Thames Valley* and *Wilts* & *Dorset.*

However, to return to the events of June 1936, there was a protracted strike by busmen at *Thames Valley,* which lasted from 14th June to 2nd July, resulting in *N&D* providing an 'emergency service' from Thursday 25th June. Extra buses were laid on between Newbury and Woolhampton, every 2 hours from 9.55am to 5.55pm (extended to 9.55pm from 27th on Saturdays). There were also some journeys extended onto Colthrop Mills, whilst those wishing to travel between Newbury and Reading could use the services via East Ilsley on Mondays to Saturdays. However, on Sunday a service was provided with departures from Newbury at 11.55am, 12.55pm, 1.55pm, 3.55pm, 5.55pm, 7.55pm, 8.55pm and 9.55pm, returning from Reading one hour later. These arrangements continued until the evening of Sunday 5th July.

Some amendments in respect of the Newbury - Bucklebury (Church) route were sought during July 1936, whereby all of the Thatcham short-workings would terminate at the Blue Coat School, but for some reason this was withdrawn before reaching a Hearing. Certain journeys did already proceed to that point at the appropriate times of day for the school pupils.

In August 1936 the Company found itself in the dock to answer a summons brought against it regarding two lorries it had used following Stop Notices being placed on them. The Examiner of the South Eastern Traffic Area had done this on 15th April, though in the defence of the Company it was stated that these were minor faults which were quickly rectified. Following such attention they were put back in use, though no one contacted the Examiner with this information, the latter taking the view that the prohibition remained in place unless rescinded. *N&D* was accused of 16 counts of using those vehicles during that period. The Examiner had also stated that he had served the notice on Charlie Durnford, whereas it was actually his son Len. As they all looked quite similar some small amusement was caused when the Examiner could not distinguish which one he had served the notice on, so

the case was dismissed! However, the judge did not grant costs for the attendance of all those appearing on behalf of the Company.

A number of vehicles left the fleet over the Summer, with Bedford WLB bus UX 9410 leaving in July after a rather short stay. This was followed in August by Garner coach 20 (YT 9565), which had come in with *Durnfords* and had proven a very good vehicle. From the old *Denhams* fleet, Tilling-Stevens B10A2 No.5 (BU 5690) departed in September, as did the last of a good number of Fords inherited form amalgamated concerns, this being ex-*Prothero* RX 9005.

A novel feature for the Autumn of 1936 was the offer of two excursions to view the Blackpool Illuminations leaving on a Friday and returning on the Sunday. This was certainly the farthest that any of the fleet had travelled to date, with the departures set for 25th September and 2nd October. Quite what support these had is not recorded, but the venture was not repeated.

During November the link between Hungerford and Hungerford Newtown was abandoned, whilst during December changes were made on two of the services to Reading. The route from Hermitage was re-routed via Hampstead Norris – Frilsham – Marlston – Cold Ash – Bradfield – Theale, though this still operated on Fridays only. The other alteration had actually been forced on the Company following the loss of the Palace Theatre Parking Ground to building, so the East Ilsley service now re-located its Reading terminus to a short distance away in Lower Thorn Street, alongside the Triangle Parking Ground and right opposite the headquarters of *Thames Valley!*

Also during December a revised timetable was put forward for the Newbury - West Ilsley service, whilst more journeys were sought for the Rowstock route, adding extra departures at 10.30am and 4.35pm from Newbury, though these ran on Thursdays and Saturdays only.

The possible sale of the Company was still a topic of discussion in the closing months of 1936, though there seemed to be some confusion between the Directors! However, at last some suitable land for the new garage was found in Mill Lane, east of the *Durnford* sheds and the *Thames Valley* dormy shed. This was purchased from Frank Cox for £380, and plans were submitted in December to Newbury Borough Council for the building to be erected there. *The locations of all of the premises used by the Company in Newbury will be found in Appendix 6.*

Gilford coach No.52 (TY 8886) as exhibited at the 1931 Commercial Vehicle Show.

In early December it was agreed to purchase two Gilford coaches on offer from Horne Products of Colnbrook, near Slough, though each of this had a twist in the tale. Firstly, there was TY 8886, one of the rare 168MOT-types which had been built to take the Meadows 44.6 hp 6-cylinder petrol engine. Due to the length of that engine, the radiator was set forward to sit between the Gruss air springs, whilst the grille was

much deeper in order to cool the larger unit. This had been bodied by Strachan with a 26-seater coach body and a sliding front entrance set in the second bay. It was ordered by *Orange Bros.* of Bedlington, who operated a thrice-daily 440-mile London – Edinburgh – Glasgow express service using a well-equipped fleet. Indeed, it had featured at the Commercial Motor Show when new in October 1931. However the Meadows engine had proved to be something of a disappointment, and when the operator sold out to *United Automobile Services* in May 1933 the vehicle was immediately sold.

By the time it was offered to *Newbury & District* the offending engine had been replaced by the standard 168OT unit, though the radiator position remained as originally built, making this an impressive looking vehicle. The seating capacity was increased by *N&D* to 31, as the original layout had been rather generous in reflection of the long distance, and this became *N&D* No.52.

The other Gilford was a 166OT-type new in January 1929 (MT 1842) and carried a Wilton 32-seater dual-doorway body. It had also started life on an express service, in the ownership of *Ralph Priest (Imperial Motor Services)* of London N1, who used it on his London – Hitchin – Bedford service. Whether this was a runner as purchased is not recorded, as both it and TY (above) had not run for a while.

However, the purchase of this was really to provide a replacement body for Gilford No.22 (RD 1886), as its original Vincent body was in poor shape. The Wilton body was transferred onto the chassis of 22, whilst the front hinged doorway was switched to the opposite offside bay to form an emergency exit, the resulting vehicle then being C32R in layout. As the side-lights on No.22 had been set on the front wings, these were retained along with the set attached to the Wilton body! The chassis of MT 1842 was then used as a source of spare parts until eventually cut up for scrap.

December also saw the disposal of another 20-seater Bedford, this time UN 5381, after only one year with the Company.

This was the result of the placing of the Wilton body off MT 1842 on to chassis of N&D No.22 (RD 1886), which resulted in the vehicle lasting until mid 1943!

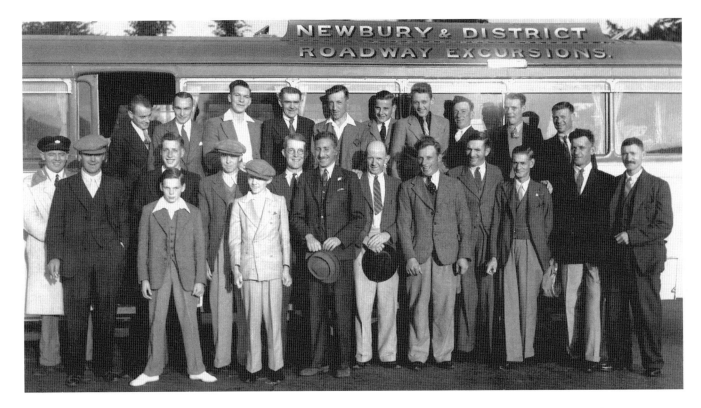

Gilford No.52 is seen on an outing to Hayling Island in September 1937 for the Shaw-based building contractor Edward Golde ('Goldie'), who is seen in the centre of the front row. Note the styles of dress of the men, and in particular the younger lads. Boss Denham was the driver on this excursion, whilst the use of the luggage carrier and roof panels for publicity is typical of the coach fleet at that time.

Development of bus services in the 'Tadley Triangle' (the area between Newbury, Reading and Basingstoke) took place throughout the 1920's and '30's, and we shall hear more about those involved in the following chapter.

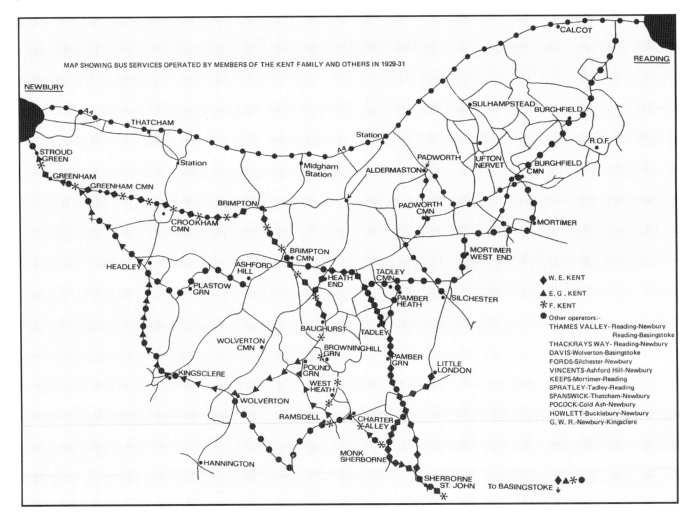

Chapter 10 – 1937

This year was another very busy one for the coach fleet, and it also saw many changes in the ranks of the shareholders.

During January further additional destinations were sought in respect of excursions from Newbury, these being Hayling Island and Lee-on-Solent, along with a circular tour out via Alton – Petersfield – Chichester – Bognor Regis – Worthing, returning through Arundel – Petworth – Petersfield – Alton.

From Cold Ash an additional pick-up point at South End Council Houses was requested, whilst on those from Thatcham, those travelling to Aldershot Tattoo, Ascot or California-in-England could also be joined at Theale, both of these points having been previously covered by *Ballard's* excursions. The addition of Cheddar to the excursions from Kintbury, Thatcham, Bucklebury and Hermitage was also requested, and all the above were granted during February.

It was also necessary to make some amendments to the Newbury Local Services, mainly in connection with the one-way traffic scheme being introduced around the Mansion House and Market Place area. The Clifton Road – Shaw section was deleted, though Shaw would still be served by other buses as we shall see. The service from The Broadway to Kingsbridge Road was altered to run via Northbrook Street - Mansion House Street – Cheap Street – Market Street – Bartholomew Street – Enborne Road, returning via Enborne Road – Bartholomew Street – Northbrook Street. The Broadway – Wash Common service was also routed out of Newbury via Northbrook Street – Mansion House Street – Cheap Street – Market Street – Bartholomew Street, returning via Bartholomew Street – Northbrook Street, whilst the Camp Close – Donnington service followed the same diversion in and out of the town.

At the same time permission was sought to alter the existing Hambridge Road – Speen service to run as Hambridge Road – Shaw Hill instead, with the revised route running via Boundary Road – York Road – Queens Road – Greenham Road – Cheap Street – Market Street – Bartholomew Street – Northbrook Street – London Road – Shaw Road - Kiln Road, and the return journeys followed the same route other than following the one-way around the Mansion House.

All of the above changes resulted in the quartet of routes being worked as two pairs, with one bus working the Shaw – Hambridge Road route and covering Camp Close – Donnington, whilst the other vehicle ran The Broadway to Wash Common and Kingsbridge Road services. The formal approval from the Traffic Commissioners for these changes came through in April, though in fact the Company had no

option but to start operating them in that form from the introduction of the one-way scheme on 7th March!

Thornycroft No.57 (TP 9164) with Southdown M.S.

The year also got off to a busy start with changes to the fleet, with no fewer than seven incoming 20-seater Thornycroft buses. Three of these had originated with *F. Tanner (Denmead Queen)* of Hambledon and had subsequently passed with that business to *Southdown Motor Services* in March 1935, with TP 9164 having worked for the latter on Hayling Island. These became No.31 (TP 7951), 43 (TP 8693) and 57 (TP 9164), all being A2-type chassis fitted with front-entrance bodies by Wadham of Waterlooville and new in June 1929, February 1930 and May 1930 respectively. The trio came from Lane, and in part-exchange he took the following vehicles – GMC No.31 (CC 9415), Dennis F-type No.43 (UL 7692) and Star MY 3052 (fleet no. not known).

Thornycroft No.14 (PG 2018) shown when new to Woking & District Bus Services.

The other quartet all had the same origins with *J.R. Fox & Sons (Woking & District Bus Services)* of Woking, who had been acquired jointly by *Aldershot & District* and *London General* in February 1931. As with many other oddities these had been replaced with standard buses in due course and sent to the dealer Dawson. All had front-entrance bus bodies by Challands Ross of Nottingham, though as with the Wadham examples above, they were to a standard Thornycroft design, and these became No.14 (PG 2018), 16 (PG 3236), 17 (PG 4226) and 46 (PG 1099). All were on A2Long-type chassis and were new in July 1929, September 1929, November 1929 and June 1929 respectively.

All 4 of the former Woking & District Thornycrofts had served with LGOC Country Services, during when they had received larger front destination boxes. It is also notable that LGOC did not favour the off-side spare wheel carrier. No.17 (PG 4226) is seen above on LGOC service 31 to Chelsfield, whilst No.46 (PG 1099) is seen below with N&D at The Wharf. These were amongst a number of service buses painted in reversed livery, usually applied to the coaches.

The first of the changes to shareholders this year occurred when Jack Burt sold his shares in February, whilst during that same month W.H. Cooper (an *N&D* driver from Wash Common) also disposed of his 100 shares. February saw the signing of the contract for the construction of the new garage in Mill Lane, which was awarded to Humphries Hollom Ltd. of Ashford, Middlesex for £1100.

This photo of the last of the quartet of Thornycrofts formerly with Woking & District and the LGOC shows No.16 (PG 3236), now with a reduced destination display, the spare wheel carrier panelled over, and the addition of the roof-mounted advert boards.

A particularly significant addition to operations came in April 1937 when *Edith Kent* decided it was time to retire.

Ellen Gertrude Kent

Ellen Allen (later known as 'Edith') had been born at Wootton St. Lawrence in north Hampshire in March 1867, and the family had relocated a little way south to Church Oakley by 1881. Her first job was at the Ramsdell Post Office in 1888, and the following June she married Frederick Kent. This initially led to a return to Wootton St. Lawrence, but sometime between 1891 and 1901 they took Bullers Farm, on the western outskirts of Baughurst. They had 4 sons, all of whom would see involvement with transport, though in their own right rather than as part of their mother's enterprise!

However, before we go on with Edith's story, a brief review of the activities of each of her sons follows.

William Ernest Kent

Bill Kent (born 1890) started out in 1911 as a horse-powered carrier based at Heath End, Baughurst and went motorised in March 1914 with a 30hp Daimler (BL 3536). This was laid up whilst he served in the Army during the Great War, but put back on the road, followed by a Ford 1-tonner (HO 5350) in February 1921. The latter was painted grey and white, which became the standard livery early on. Some passengers had been taken from the outset of the carrier's service, but the Ford had seats for 14 in an otherwise box-van body, and Bill used The Angel in Basingstoke as his lay-over point.

Bill Kent's Model T Ford bus MO 2520.

The first purpose-built bus was another Ford 1-ton Model T, with 14-seater body (MO 2520), obtained new form Pass & Co. of Newbury in February 1924. It later went onto his other activity, that of coal merchant, and lasted until September 1934 in that role. A secondhand charabanc of the same chassis type was also added about that time (DY 1801), being

registered in Hastings in 1921, and this was also used on the bus service at busy times. The fleet livery evolved from grey and white to grey and green, but some secondhand vehicles may have run in their existing schemes.

The bus services evolved steadily during the 1920's, very much in response to local preferences, and by April 1929 the following routes were established:
Baughurst – Tadley – Basingstoke, daily except Sundays;
Little London – Basingstoke, Wednesdays/Saturdays;
Basingstoke – Baughurst – Newbury, Thursdays

These services also developed in frequency and days of operation over this time, whilst other refinements, such as diverting buses via Park Prewett Asylum (later Hospital), as opposed to serving only the main gate, were also brought in, often as the result of suggestions from passengers, such was the understanding of local needs. From about May 1932 he took over the operation of his brother Fred's service, as will be further noted below, under his own heading.

Bill Kent used quite an array of passenger vehicles during the period 1924-1937, and these can be summarised as follows (in order of acquisition):

Reg. No.	Chassis	Seats	New	In	Out
MO 2520	Ford T 1-ton	B14F	1/24	New	9/34
DY 1801	Ford T 1-ton	Ch14	5/21	?/24	??
MO 3354	Reo Speedwagon	Ch14	6/24	New	12/30
DP 6725	Reo Speedwagon	B14F	7/25	New	c.6/32
DP 7662	Thornycroft A1	Ch20	?/26	New	6/34
TP 4650	Reo Sprinter	??	5/27	New	??
OT 5229	Reo Sprinter	C20D	6/27	New	b4/37
OT 8605	Reo Sprinter	B20F	5/28	New	??
OU 976	GMC	B20F	3/29	New	??
OU 1671	Chevrolet LQ	B14F	4/29	New	9/39
HB 3126	Thornycroft A2long	B20F	?/27	3/30	??
TM 4977	Reo Sprinter	B20F	5/30	1/31	?/35

Bill Kent built up an interesting and well maintained fleet, and this view taken outside his garage at Heath End, Baughurst shows him standing with one of his sons at the rear of Morris-Commercial 'Viceroy' CG 675, with Reos OT 8605 and OT 5229, along with Thornycrofts OU 9892 and HB 3126 beyond that.

GN 8035	Chevrolet U	B14F	3/31	New	10/37
OT 2960	Thornycroft A1	B20F	1/26	??	10/37
OU 9892	Thornycroft A12	B20F	11/31	New	10/37
CG 675	Morris-Com. Viceroy	B26F	3/32	New	10/37
TK 3312	Guy OND	B20F	8/29	?/32	??
TR 7581	Guy OND	B20F	9/29	?/32	9/37
TR 8594	Guy OND	C20D	5/30	?/32	10/37
LJ 2166	Chevrolet LQ	B14F	7/30	35-36	10/37
BOR 282	Bedford WTB	B26F	5/36	New	#
CCG 392	Bedford WTB	C26R	5/37	New	#

It should be noted that the apparent late disposals of some of the earlier vehicles reflects later use as goods vehicles.
These two vehicles were retained by Kents Coaches Ltd.

Route numbers were attached to the timetables for the services, though they were not displayed on the vehicles, these being:

Route 1 – Baughurst (New Inn) – Fox & Hounds – Tadley Hill – Pamber End (College Arms) – Sherborne St. John (Dixons Corner) – Park Prewett (Centre) – Park Prewett (Main Gate) – Basingstoke (The Barge);
Route 2 – Newbury (The Wharf) – Crookham Common (Volunteers) – Brimpton (Horse & Jockey) – Brimpton (Horse Shoes) – Baughurst (New Inn) – Fox & Hounds – Tadley Hill – Pamber End (College Arms) – Sherborne St. John (Dixons Corner) – Park Prewett – Basingstoke (The Barge);
Route 3 – Baughurst (Wellington Arms) – Browning Hill – West Heath – Ramsdell – Charter Alley – Monk Sherborne – Sherborne St. John (Dixons Corner) – Chineham Road – Soldiers Return – Basingstoke (The Barge).

Bill also built up a good trade on excursions and private hire, and Reo 'Speedwagon' MO 3354 is seen outside the original wooden shed at Heath End. The coaches also provided relief vehicles on busy days.

All his services, along with excursions and tours, were granted under the Road Traffic Act 1930, and the bus services further enhanced during the 1930's. However, Bill duly decided to accept an offer for his bus operations, which were sold to *Venture* of Basingstoke in October 1937. The coach side was retained as *Kent's Coaches Ltd.* and the business grew into the largest in the area, aided by his sons Arthur and John and daughters-in-law Joyce and Freda, until being sold in 1978 to *White's of Camberley.*

Frederick Kent

Fred Kent (born 1892) had served in the Army in France from 1914-7, when he was discharged with trench-foot. Initially he survived on his pension, but commuted that for a lump sum in 1924. By then he was living with his wife Lucy at Baughurst Road, Baughurst and he started his one-man bus service on 9th August 1924, using a 14-seater Ford 1-tonner (OR 5153) obtained from Pass & Co. on hire purchase.

The service ran to Basingstoke or Newbury on the following days and routes:

To Basingstoke on Mondays, Wednesdays, Fridays and Saturdays, departing at 9.45am–
Baughurst (School) – Browning Hill – West Heath (Vine Inn)– George & Dragon – Wolverton – Ramsdell X Roads – Charter Alley - Pamber (School) – Monk Sherborne (New Inn) – Sherborne St. John (Post Office) – Basingstoke (Barge Inn).
Extra journeys on Wednesdays and Saturdays –

Basingstoke 12noon	Baughurst 1.30pm
Basingstoke 3.15pm	Baughurst 4.15pm
Basingstoke 5.15pm	Baughurst 6.15pm*
Basingstoke 9pm*	*Saturdays only

He also ran to Newbury on Thursdays only, departing at 9.45am –
Baughurst (School) – Browning Hill – West Heath (Vine Inn) – Charter Alley – Ramsdell X Roads – George & Dragon – Wolverton – Kingsclere – Newbury.

Fred and Lucy relocated to Charter Alley in 1925, and he constructed a timber garage for the bus adjacent to their cottage. However, unlike the activities of his mother and his brother Bill, Fred's operations did not expand, mainly due to a series of events, some of which in hindsight, he might have been able to avoid.

He had indeed added to his business activities during 1926, when his mother sold him her milk-carrying business on the decision to enter passenger transport. Fred took over her Ford T milk lorry and the goodwill, taking a family loan, but a larger competitor soon came along and made it uneconomical.

On the bus front, he did suffer some competition when *Thames Valley* put on their new Tilling-Stevens single-deckers between Reading and Basingstoke routed through the Baughurst area in August 1926, these being based at the Tadley Dormy Shed. At first the service was certainly more frequent than Fred's, and the new saloons had front-facing seating in reasonable comfort, so no doubt some passengers found both factors more attractive. However, it was not long before *Thames Valley* cut the timetable back and, ultimately, it decided to serve Basingstoke using only the service south from Reading through Spencers Wood and Sherfield-on-Loddon, so the competition was only limited.

Of more concern was the attention of the *Great Western Railway,* whose services locally are detailed within this main section. They also caused some loss in earnings, which squeezed Fred's finances. This in turn caused him not to spend out on insurance for the Ford, which was unfortunately involved in a bad accident during August 1928. He then sold the milk lorry, which did not realise much, putting that with further loaned funds to buy a bus to cover the route. However, with his finances on difficult ground he could barely cover costs, resulting in it being impounded whilst in for repair!

A further cheap purchase in March 1931 then had a short career, after it was found not to comply with the new regulations under the 1930 Act, after which he bought yet another coach, this time with a loan from a cousin. However, this caught fire in December 1931, though this time it was insured and duly repaired, but subsequently he got behind with re-paying monies due for it. Just to top it all, the Winter of 1931/2 was the worst he could recall, resulting in a reduction in takings, together with a number of broken axles! It is also evident that his mother had tried to help him at one point by re-assigning the deeds of his cottage.

Realising that he could not extricate himself from this spiral of debt, he offered to sell out to *Venture* of

Basingstoke for the rather high price of £1000 in 1932. His debts were then some £700-£800, so once that plan had failed, he filed for bankruptcy, and the case was heard at Winchester on 13th May 1932.

Very little is known regarding Fred's ill-fated fleet, and his service was then absorbed by his brother Bill, who it is assumed paid off the outstanding liabilities.

Robert and Joseph Kent

The other two sons Robert Allen and Joseph Arthur (born 1895 and 1898), also set themselves up with mechanical transport, though not of the passenger variety, as they became steam haulage contractors and also hired their threshing equipment out to farmers. As they remained based at Bullers Farm until it was sold after their mother's retirement in 1937, they presumably also assisted on the farm. However, their business continued after that, with the agricultural contracting.

****

Unfortunately, their father Frederick Kent died in early 1914 at the age of 52, which was no doubt one of the reasons for *Edith Kent's* additional ventures.

Her first involvement with transport was to set up a milk round in order to collect from farms for transhipment at Basingstoke railway station to the London dairies. The exact date for this is not recorded, and for this a Ford Model T van was placed on the road in the early 1920's, though fuller details are lacking. However, the advent of this vehicle was the catalyst for repeated requests to take passengers into Newbury (8 miles) or Basingstoke (9 miles) for market day or other leisure pursuits, and it was such public interest that caused Edith to consider operating a bus service.

Edith Kent's Thornycroft charabanc when in use as a demonstrator.

Passenger carrying got underway properly in May 1926, when Edith decided to try her hand at a bus service and some charabanc outings, the latter type of vehicle also being considered as a suitable relief vehicle at peak times. For this she had acquired a former Thornycroft A1-type demonstration coach

(possibly registered as OT 816), which carried a red-painted 20-seater charabanc body of the 'Ariadne' design and built by Hall Lewis of Park Royal, north London sometime in 1925, and this passed to *Mrs. Kent* in March 1926. This chara carried an inscription 'The Ideal' across the rear, and both that and the red livery were retained. For the bus service she chose a Morris 25-cwt, which was fitted with a 14-seater front-entrance bus body, and this was registered as OT 1333 in May 1926, which may have also been used as a lorry at times.

Nearside view of the Thornycroft charabanc as new.

The charabanc proved popular from the outset, as the residents of Kingsclere were some way from the nearest rail stations, and early excursions ran to Southsea, along with the Royal Counties Show at Bournemouth and various race meetings, the Kingsclere area hosting a number of racing stables that have produced a remarkable number of Derby winners over the years.

In respect of a passenger service, she was not actually the first operator to cover the Kingsclere to Newbury road, there being a succession of country carrier's prior to that, plus other short-lived bus ventures, so it is appropriate that these are reviewed first.

Albert Wickens

Albert Wickens was born in 1855 a few miles north of Kingsclere at Brimpton, spending his earlier years as a general labourer. He married a Kingsclere girl in 1880, her father being blacksmith John Winterbourne, whose premises were adjacent to The Bolton Arms pub in Swan Street. He was still listed as a general labour in 1891, but by 1895, Albert had started running a carrier's service, going to Newbury on Mondays, Tuesdays, Thursdays, Fridays and Saturdays, as well as to Basingstoke on Wednesdays only. The lay-over point in Newbury was at the Catherine Wheel, opposite Black Bear Lane and very close to the Market Place, whilst the horse-drawn van was kept at the former premises of his father-in-law.

He was the first carrier from that particular location to offer motorised transport, placing a large Scout carrier's van (AA 62??) on the road in 1915. Bearing in mind that he was 60 years old when this occurred, he must have been the oldest of all the carriers to embrace the new-fangled motors! However, it is worth noting that the vehicle's sign-writing proclaimed *M.A. Wickens,* which strongly suggests that this was actually financed by his wife Mary Ann, who assisted him on the service, complete with a leather satchel for collecting fares and orders.

Albert Wickens and the Scout carrier's van.

The service was maintained as before, though obviously more passengers naturally followed the advent of the Scout. Indeed, when interviewed in 1918 by Motor Transport, Albert was found to be a most enthusiastic user of the Scout, which had an 18-20hp engine a 4-speed gearbox, both necessary for the hillier sections of the routes covered. The van was regularly doing over 100 miles per week, and he stated that it could do the 16-mile return trip to Newbury on under 2 gallons of petrol, whilst he had also successfully moved a 6-room house using it! However, either through the need to replace the van, or perhaps just his age, Albert ceased his service by 1920, though he stayed in Kingsclere and died in 1944 at the age of 89.

Hubert Hunt

Hubert Hunt was born in Kensington in September 1886 and joined the Army Service Corps by 1911, being then at Aldershot in 60MT Coy. He met Elsie Rolfe when at army camp near Kingsclere, and they married in 1915, living in George Street. On return from the war, he started a carrier's service in January 1920, initially using 1915 Daimler 28hp (BL 032) obtained from the Leckhampstead carrier *William Jacobs.* This proved unreliable, so a 'new' Dennis 16hp carrier's van came on the last day of August 1920, this being painted grey and registered as BL 0353, though it was probably ex-WD. The service left Kingsclere at 10am, returning from his layover point in Newbury at The Bear in Cheap Street at 4pm, which was also convenient for the market and other shopping areas. However, as Hubert was an Army Reservist, he was sent to northern India in order to support the Afghan Campaign, this occurring some time in late 1921, and did not resume the service.

Walter John Chalk

The gap was then filled by the another Kingsclere carrier *Walter Chalk,* who used a base in Swan Street which it is believed was that previously used by *Albert Wickens.* Walter had been born at the Richmond Barracks in Dublin in October 1881, and by 1901 he had moved to Chipstead in Surrey, where he was employed as a domestic groom. He evidently met Florence Cooper, who was working nearby as a domestic nurse, and she hailed from Kingsclere, and they married in April 1906. The couple were still in Surrey at 1911 at 'Heatherbrae', Court Road, Banstead, where Walter was employed as a coachman. They remained there until at least 1912, whilst exactly what he did during the war years has not been traced, though both persons of that name on record served in the Army Service Corps. However, in due course they moved to Kingsclere, probably on his demobilisation.

With his background as a coachman, it was a natural progression to take the opportunity to replace Hunt's service, though it is not known whether a purchase was involved, or whether he was originally intended only as a caretaker. Certainly he used the above-mentioned Dennis, which was joined by another vehicle bearing the Hampshire mark HO 7941 from 4th November 1921, but as motor tax records of that period are incomplete, the make is not known.

The Dennis was replaced in October 1922 by an ex-WD Crossley 14-seater carrier's bus from a Leeds area operator (NW 1185). He duly took a Ford 1-tonner with varnished 14-seater bus body from Ford agents Pass & Co. of Newbury in May 1924 (MO 3036), and the Crossley was last licensed in December 1925. Chalk ran between Kingsclere and Newbury twice-daily except Wednesdays, when he did a single day-long trip to Basingstoke instead.

Although he would duly decide to abandon carrying passengers, the business continued as *Walter Chalk & Son,* carriers, haulage contractors and coal merchants until at least the start of the Second World War, and Walter died at 22 Swan Street in November 1943 at the age of 62.

White Bros. & Bates

However, the first attempt to provide a daily bus service between Newbury and Basingstoke was by *White Bros. & Bates* in 1919. They first advertised their involvement with local transport by offering their '30 passenger handsome saloon motor bus (can be closed for cold or wet weather)' on excursions from Basingstoke to Bournemouth and the horse-racing at Gatwick, Newbury and Windsor, along with trips to Reading, Oxford and Southampton in the period between 20th September and 5th October.

The bus service then commenced on Tuesday 18th November, routed as Newbury – Greenham Common – Headley – Kingsclere – Wolverton – Baughurst – Tadley – Sherborne St. John – Park Prewett Asylum – Basingstoke, with positioning journeys between their base at Shernorne St. John, and 3 return trips per day. The Newbury terminus was the Town Hall and at Basingstoke it was the railway station. The bus used on this service was a Commer 32hp, which has also been described as a 27-seater, so it probably therefore had 3 tip-up gangway seats towards the rear of the saloon, something often found at that time, though not permitted by all local licensing authorities.

Although *White Bros. & Bates* persevered with the service over the Winter months, it ceased in early March 1920, as they decided to transfer the bus to a new service between Yeovil and Ilminster from a base at The Crown in South Petherton. As Somerset County Council insisted that the vehicle was re-registered locally, it became Y 8984 after this new venture passed to the *National Omnibus & Transport Co. Ltd.* in June 1920, though its previous registration is not recorded.

Kingsclere Transport Co. Ltd.

By early 1920 carriers *Harris & Oliver* were operating from Kingsclere to Newbury on a daily basis, and to Basingstoke on Wednesdays only. The Harris's were not local men, and *Douglas* and *Lloyd Harris* lodged at The Bolton Arms in Swan Street. Nothing is known of their backgrounds, whilst the other partner was either *Charles Oliver,* a carpenter of the same street, or perhaps more likely *John Oliver* nearby at 5 Sunnyside Cottages, noted earlier as a farm carter.

A newspaper announcement was made that the *Kingsclere Transport Co. Ltd.,* headed by the Kingsclere-based carrier *Mr. Harris*, would serve this road as part of its Newbury – Kingsclere – Basingstoke route from January 1923. He publicly announced that this 'long overdue link would be provided by an up-to-date comfortable bus with super cushion tyres, a 20-seater 22hp Vulcan saloon bus, with full-drop windows, painted dark blue with white trim, inside painted white with oak panelling, 4 electric lights, bucket-shaped leather seating, with one-man-operated, driver-controlled door, 6ft 10ins wide to cope with the narrow lanes traversed on parts of the route'. He went on to add that there would be 2 return journeys per day, with 4 on Saturdays, and the bus would call at both Newbury and Basingstoke railway stations. This bus was a VSD-type registered HO 6148 by the Company in December 1922.

The first bus left from Kingsclere at 9am to connect at Newbury with the 9.49am train to Reading and Paddington, then onto the Market Place to form the 9.35am departure to Basingstoke via Greenham

Common – Headley – Kingsclere – Wolverton - Baughurst - Tadley, reaching Basingstoke at 11.05am, before turning to reach Newbury at 12.40pm. On weekdays the last bus left Newbury at 4pm, arriving at Basingstoke at 5.30pm. From there it returned to Newbury, calling at Kingsclere at 6.25pm and arriving at Newbury at 7pm, from where it ran to reach its Kingsclere base at 7.35pm. On Saturdays the last Newbury – Basingstoke bus departed at 7pm and arrived at Basingstoke at 8.30pm, returning to Newbury to form the 10pm departure to Kingsclere. It should also be noted that, according to directory entries, the carrier's service also ran at its regular times in addition to the above.

The Harris's also undertook motor engineering at the base adjacent to the Bolton Arms, being only one of two such businesses then available in Kingsclere. It would seem, however, things evidentially did work out as planned, and no further publicity regarding the service was forthcoming after January 1923. Just the *Harris's* returned to carrying, travelling between Kingsclere and Newbury daily, other than on Wednesdays, when they ran to Basingstoke instead. What happened to the bus is not known, but it is likely as not they had to surrender it due to not being able to make the hire-purchase payments, as it was re-sold in Southampton in April 1925, by which date both *Douglas* and *Lloyd Harris* had gone from Kingsclere completely.

****

The arrival of *Mrs. Kent's* service also convinced *Chalk* to give up carrying passengers, so his Ford (MO 3036) was re-classified as a goods vehicle from 1927 and only the carrier's service was continued, going to Newbury daily except Wednesdays, when he travelled to Basingstoke instead. As he became the agent for her excursions, it certainly seems that there was some business arrangement resulting from these events, with her no longer competing in the role of carrier of parcels in return. He then placed a Ford AA goods vehicle on the road in April 1929 (OU 1830), which he retained until September 1936.

Although *Mrs. Kent* lived in Baughurst, her initial bus was out-stationed at Swan Street in Kingsclere, in a garage owned by Mr. Garrett, whilst her original driver Walter Corneby lived a short distance away at his parent's home in Mill Lane. The bus travelled to Newbury on Thursdays and Saturdays, whilst on Wednesdays it ran to Basingstoke instead for the market day there. It is worth noting that *Tom Garrett* had himself had a go at charabanc operation, when in June 1922 he placed a red-liveried 14-seater Ford Model T on the road as HO 9425, though the venture was fairly short-lived. The fact that it left-hand drive would indicate that it had originated during WW1 on military service.

Reo 'Sprinter' OT 3284 arriving at Southsea.

A Reo 'Sprinter' all-weather coach with 20-seat Wray bodywork was registered as OT 3284 in December 1926, also seeing use at busy times on the bus service. April 1927 saw the arrival of a Thornycroft A2long, fitted with a 20-seater front-entrance bus body by Wadham of Waterlooville, which was registered OT 4452. A Reo 20-seater bus followed in March 1928 as OT 7672, whilst a 14-seater front-entrance Chevrolet bus entered service in September 1928 as OT 9741.

With such expansion, the Kingsclere location could no longer hold the growing fleet, so a large wooden garage was constructed at Heath End, Baughurst, opposite the site used by her son *Bill Kent*, and this then formed her base, though the title *Kingsclere Coaches* was retained. Whether a standard livery featured in earlier days is not known, leaving aside the red charabanc which had been received thus painted, but a shade described as 'heather' became the chosen scheme. From this one would deduce that the vehicles were of either in a mauve or lavender colour, but certainly one of her 1930's Petty-bodied Commers is recorded as being maroon and black, though it could have come as such from that coachbuilder's stock.

The arrival of the Road Motors of the *Great Western Railway* in the area caused some concern for *Edith Kent,* and she certainly did her part in sending them away, though the conflict was a long one. On the one hand, her buses provided the journeys desired by the local people on the days they wanted them, largely in relation to local market days, whereas the *GWR* tried to establish daily operations, mainly to link railheads.

In respect of *Edith Kent's* area, the *GWR* arrived on 25th August 1927 with its 40 mile-long Calne – Marlborough – Hungerford – Newbury – Kingsclere route. This was re-organised from 24th May 1928, with the southern section as Newbury – Kingsclere – Basingstoke, which also competed with *Bill Kent*. The competition became more intense, with both Bill and his mother buying smaller faster types to out-run the *GWR* Thornrycroft A-types. In Edith's case these led to the choice of the Chevrolet OT 9741.

Due largely to these tactics, and having a great deal of local support, the Kent's forced the *GWR* to cut back as just Newbury – Kingsclere from 20th January 1929. With a final push, together with the general success of *Denham Bros.* on other routes, this section was abandoned by the railway buses on 7th July 1929, never to return!

During this period of competition she sold the milk-carrying business to her son Fred, as his passenger-carrying only occupied him part-time. And with the *GWR* out of the way, she expanded the frequency of the bus operations and increased the days of operation between Kingsclere and Basingstoke to Wednesdays and Fridays, her route running via Ramsdell. *Fred Kent's* blue-painted Ford took a slightly different route from Charter Alley, whilst the grey and green-liveried buses of *Bill Kent* ran more directly from his Heath End base in Baughurst, before joining his mother's heather-coloured vehicles in Basingstoke on those days – quite a colourful family group, so what a shame nobody took a photo of them together!

The Kingsclere to Newbury service had developed to meet the varied daily needs, with more journeys on Tuesdays, Thursdays and Saturdays, but less on Wednesdays (also early-closing in Newbury) and Friday daytimes, with additional evening journeys on Fridays and Saturdays, whilst Sundays were covered from the afternoon only (as was the common practice then).

AJS 'Pilot' OU 6047 in service with N&D as No.42 and on the main road route to Hungerford.

Further buses were added in the form of a new AJS 'Pilot', a forward-control type with 28-seater front – entrance bus body by Petty of Hitchin, which was registered OU 6047 in June 1930, and its arrival reduced the number of relief buses required on busier days. It was also a popular choice for larger party outings. Another bus arrived around October 1930, being a Guy OND with Guy 20-seater front-entrance bus bodywork, which was registered TK 2740 and had been new in May 1929 to *Poole & District*, who had sold out to *Hants & Dorset* in September 1930.

Most of the buses ran as one-manners, but on busier days conductors were carried, often dealing with the relief bus as well for the taking of fares, and in this role *Edith Kent* could be found sitting in the little tip-up seat provided at the front of the bus for the purpose. Another of the early drivers recalled is Walter 'Winkie' Wallis of Swan Street, whose bus she would often be on, and later on also Jack Lawrence.

The advent of the Road Traffic Act 1930 saw Edith's services almost at peak level, so she had no problem gaining the necessary Road Service Licenses for her established routes. Similarly, her quite extensive selection of authorised excursions passed through the Hearings, so she remained the main force serving the Kingsclere area. Indeed, *Mrs. Kent* was regarded as a 'good' operator, though she did get ticked off by Kingsclere & Whitchurch Rural District Council for allowing the washing of two of her buses in the river on one occasion on 13th November 1935!

Dates for disposals of most of the earlier vehicles are not known, though the original Ford had gone to son Fred in 1926. The Thornycroft chara was effectively replaced for the 1932 season, and such a vehicle would not have passed the new Construction & Use

Regulations anyway, so it was initially just laid up, also having only minimal re-sale value. Eventually in 1935 it was sold to *N&D*, who used the chassis as a source of spare parts for its other similar Thornycroft buses. Its old driver Walter Corneby took it for its final 'excursion' up to the field behind the Mill Lane garage, and found its remains still there some two years, when he also passed into *N&D* hands! Also in 1935 the Reo coach OT 3284 was disposed of.

The replacements for the Thornycroft chara and Reo coach were two Commers, both carrying 20-seater front-entrance coach bodies by Petty of Hitchin. The first was 'Centaur' CG 1724, which arrived in August 1932, followed by 'Invader' ACG 644 in April 1935, indicating that she was happy with their bodywork on the AJS 'Pilot' bought in 1930.

A Petty-bodied Commer 'Centaur' as depicted in a contemporary advert.

In order to increase bookings for coach excursions, a stop at The Harrow Inn at Headley was included, and bookings could be made at the pub from 1933. As already noted, it was common practice for the coaches to be used on the service runs at peak times, whilst regular hires were also undertaken for *Tibbles* of St. Mary Bourne and *Mongers* of Odiham. From the latter also came Bill Cripps in May 1935, who eventually became Depot Inspector for *Thames Valley* at Bracknell. However, it should be noted that the operations of *Mrs. Kent* and her son *Bill* rarely interacted in the business sense, though he did supervise her operations when she was ill at one time.

At this point we need to look at the operators who had served Ashford Hill and Headley, or as the wider area was known 'Kingsclere Woodlands', from earlier times before widespread clearances of the local trees.

Nelson Emmanuel Wooff

Nelson Wooff had been born at Kingsclere in 1900, and a year later his parents were residing at Headley. He married Ethel Robbins in 1922 and, by 1923, he had commenced a carrier's service covering Ashford Hill – Woodlands – Plastow Green – Headley and onto Newbury. They also had the Headley Stores & Post Office, where Ethel was postmistress.

The initial vehicle used is not recorded, and he used the yard of the White Hart in Newbury, just off the Market Place and Wharf Street, departing from there on Tuesdays and Fridays at 4pm. There were extra runs on Thursdays and Saturdays, when departures were at 1pm and 4pm. He replaced the original vehicle on the last day of 1924 with a new Chevrolet 1-ton carriers van, which had a grey-painted 14-seater body and was registered as MO 4343. Unfortunately the motor tax records are incomplete for this vehicle, so it has not proven possible to deduce how long the service was in operation, other than it was not listed from 1928. However, the couple continued to run the stores, and Nelson was still local at his death in 1982.

Rodney Vincent

Rodney Vincent, commenced his bus service from Ashford Hill into Newbury from about 1927, under the title *Vincent's Bus Service*, the service being so similar to that of *Wooff* that he must had succeeded him, though the Chevrolet evidently did not pass to him. Most likely this was rathermore a case of giving the public what they were used to, country folk in those days being creatures of habit, especially in terms of their shopping arrangements.

Rodney was not, however, a local man, being born at Skeffington Hall in Leicestershire in 1889, where his father held the post of coachman. Unsurprisingly, he also went into service and, by 1911, he was in Chelsea in London and employed as a motor chauffeur. With such a background, his enlistment in October 1914 saw he sent to the Army Service Corps at Grove Park in Lee, south London, after which he drove lorries on ammunition convoys on the Western Front.

Whilst on leave in August 1915 he married Charlotte White in Kensington, and after returning from the war, they relocated to Beenham Court, a short distance south of Headley on the Newbury Road, where he was also chauffeur. The couple were still at the cottages there in 1925, but by 1927 they had moved a short way south to Strattons Lodge on the same road.

This would appear to mark the commencement of the bus service, which he had no doubt heard had been curtailed by *Nelson Wooff*. The initial vehicle used was a Ford Model T, with a 14-seater bus body, the identity of which is not known. This was likely a used vehicle purchased from Pass & Co., and it was duly advertised for sale by Rodney in December 1929.

As noted, the service was basically the same as *Wooff* and also operated on Tuesdays, Thursdays, Fridays and Saturdays. On all those days the full route was covered through to Ashford Hill with the 4pm departure. However, the 1pm journey from Newbury on Thursdays and Saturdays ran only as far as

Woodlands. By 1934 an additional evening return journey had been added, leaving from Headley to arrive in town at 6.50pm, departing from The Wharf at 10.15pm, which catered for those wishing to visit the cinema, theatre or other entertainments.

This was an owner-driver situation, though he also did some excursions when the bus was not scheduled. As such, he did offer some competition, so *Edith Kent* accepted his offer to sell out, applying for his licenses in April 1936. At the time of the takeover, his service consisted of Newbury – Headley – Plastow Green – Ashford Hill – Kingsclere Woodlands (which she extended onto Kingsclere), together with a selection of excursions and tours starting from the Ashford Hill area. Latterly he used a 16-seater Chevrolet LR-type bus (UN 3196), which had originated with a North Wales operator in December 1929, apparently coming to him very soon afterwards. This vehicle also passed to *Edith Kent,* who kept it on the same route due to the very narrow lanes in places. *Rodney Vincent* passed away in 1962 at Epsom in Surrey.

****

Edith Kent's services were allocated route numbers, though these were not actually displayed on the vehicles. The timetables showed them as:
Service 1 - Kingsclere – Headley – Newbury;
Service 2 - Basingstoke – Ramsdell – Kingsclere – Headley – Newbury;
Service 3 - Basingstoke – Pound Green – Wolverton - Kingsclere;
Service 4 - Kingsclere – Ashford Hill - Plastow Green – Headley – Newbury.

As 1937 dawned *Mrs. Kent* was approaching 70 years of age, so she turned her thoughts to retirement. She contacted the Basingstoke-based bus operator *Venture Ltd.,* a company actually funded by the same Thornycroft family of vehicle manufacturing fame, also based in that Hampshire town, which had latterly also taken a renewed interest in running through to Newbury. The matter was put to the *Venture* Director's Meeting on 28th January of that year, and although the Company was indeed interested, their proposal was rejected by the Traffic Commissioners.

Following this disappointment, each party pursued slightly different options, with *Venture* offering to buy *Bill Kent's* bus services instead, which was indeed concluded in October 1937, leaving him with his coach business to carry on with. On the other hand, *Edith Kent* approached *N&D,* who were fairly interested in the prospect. The latter, however, had no particular desire to run through to Basingstoke, so the southernmost section of her route was not applied for, passing instead to *S. Huntley & Son* of Oakley (as she already knew Sid well). Later, in 1948 the Huntley business was offered to *N&D*, but *Red & White* decided it was best placed under *Venture* of Basingstoke instead, adding another twist in the tale!

N&D also had no desire to purchase her wooden garage, which as it happened also suited *Mrs. Kent*, as *Venture* expressed an interest in using the site to erect their Dormy Shed for covering the former *Bill Kent* operations as the various negotiations progressed. *N&D* took over from *Edith Kent* on 6th April 1937, taking all her current fleet of 6 vehicles, adding yet more variety to a fleet that had recently made steps towards a greater degree of standardisation! Those transferred were the Chevrolet bus UN 3196 (N&D No.5), Guy bus TK 2740 (N&D 8), Thornycroft bus OT 4452 (N&D 15), AJS bus OU 6047 (N&D 42) and Commer coaches CG 1724 and ACG 644 (N&D 38 and 39), along with all her drivers. The little Chevrolet, along with the Guy and the Thornycroft then formed the Kingsclere allocation, whilst the AJS and the two Commers were transferred to Newbury so they could be more widely used.

Newspaper cutting commemorating the retirement of Edith Kent, who is on the right with a rack of tickets.

After a busy and enterprising working life, *Edith Kent* moved to 44 Valley Road, Newbury, where she passed away in 1952 at the age of 85.

However, before we leave this area, there follows a brief review of the other operators within the 'Tadley triangle' who provided services to Newbury.

Albert Ernest Blake

Firstly we have the carrier *Albert Blake* of Baughurst, who had started about 1906 with a horse-powered van. The route ran to Newbury via Tadley – Brimpton – Crookham, going there on Mondays and Thursdays, and using The Catherine Wheel in Cheap Street as his lay-over point, and he departed for the return journey at 3pm. The service continued in similar fashion until at some point during the Great War, when he was evidently absent on military service. Albert returned to carrying by 1920, and during April of that year he offered his horse-drawn van for sale, though its

replacement vehicle is not known. However it must have been a motor vehicle, as he expanded by running to Newbury, Reading and Basingstoke on different days. On Mondays and Thursdays he went to Newbury via Aldermaston - Brimpton – Crookham, on Wednesdays he went to Basingstoke via Tadley, and on Tuesdays and Saturdays he went to Reading via Brimpton and Aldermaston, where he departed from the Boars Head in Friar Street at 4pm.

In February 1924 he purchased a Ford T 1-tonner, which carried a body with seats for 14 passengers and was registered as OR 3476. At some point before 1928 he had reduced the journeys to Newbury to Thursdays only, also revising his leaving time from there to 4pm, as the journey now took less time. By 1930 he had relocated to The Wharf, as many carriers did once they had no need for feed and stabling for a horse, which the inns had provided.

The operation never expanded beyond the above pattern and, under the 1930 Road traffic Act he was granted the Road service license for two routes as: Baughurst – Brimpton – Aldermaston – Reading (on Mondays, Tuesdays, Fridays and Saturdays); and Baughurst – Brimpton – Crookham – Newbury (on Thursdays only). At that point he ceased to travel to Basingstoke, which was well served by others.

Although licensed for carrying passengers, that side of the business was not developed, whilst there were a number of more convenient means of travel available, so the service was really only concerned with goods after that. Ford OR 3476 continued to be his sole vehicle until it was sold for scrap at the close of June 1937, making it one of the last Model T's is use locally, and its replacement was for goods only.

The next two operators to be considered both had some similarities, each starting out as cycle and motor repairers, Both added some passenger transport interests fairly early on, though each was to greatly expand that role with large contract fleets due to post-war local developments.

Albert Ford & Son

Albert Ford lived at 'Coombelands' in Silchester and was established as a cab proprietor by 1912, also undertaking cycle and motor repairs at The Garage in Pamber Road. A taxi service was offered until at least 1920.

He was joined by his 20 year-old son *Reginald Ford* by November 1922, when they purchased a secondhand Ford Model T (BL 8596), which had originally been registered by Pass & Co. as a goods vehicle in May 1921, though this was a 14-seater bus with Fords. For this they obtained a license from Reading Borough Council and ran it between

Silchester and Reading on Fridays for market day, and both Albert and Reg were licensed as hackney drivers. They also went to Basingstoke on Wednesdays and Saturdays, using the Railway Arms yard in Brook Street for the layover.

Little more is known of their activities on passenger work, nor of the vehicles used in the 1920's and 1930's, the above Ford bus being elsewhere before 1930. By that time they had changed the route over to going to Newbury on Thursdays only.

However, excursions and private hire was also evidently developed before the 1930 Act, which saw them applying and gaining licenses for a group of excursions and tours, along with the continuation of the Thursdays-only Newbury service, which ran from Slichester via Pamber Heath – Tadley – Brimpton. The local travel guide for March 1932 confirms the service as leaving Silchester at 10am, reaching the town at 10.45. Later it left at 1pm for a short-working to Brimpton, returning from there to arrive in Newbury at 2.15pm. The homeward journey to Silchester left Newbury at 3.45pm from The Wharf.

It is worth noting that *Venture* expanded its routes in the area following the acquisition of *Bill* Kent's bus services in 1937, running a Silchester – Newbury service from July 1938 to September 1939, when cuts were made due to wartime restrictions.

Wartime saw lots of activity locally, with shadow factories and military establishments, and *Fords* were allotted a Bedford OWB (EHO 142) in September 1942. However, post-war projects such as the AWRE at Aldermaston saw an increase in fleet size, along with a continuation of excursions and private hire. *Reg Ford* died in early 1957 and the business was sold to *Kent's Coaches* in December 1959, the two families having often worked together at times.

Lovegrove Bros.

Sidney George and *Herbert Lacey Lovegrove* had been born at Bramley in Hampshire in 1883 and 1886 respectively, their father being a thatcher and hurdle-maker. By age 15 Herbert was assisting his father, but at that time Sidney was a carrier and a labourer. In 1911 both were still at home at The Street, Herbert as a thatcher and Sidney now a motor car driver. A motor garage was established at nearby Silchester by 1916, where cycle repairs were also handled, Herbert joining his brother at that point.

In November 1921 they registered a 14-seater 21.7-hp Oldsmobile as HO 7958. It was painted grey and black and the body was described as a charabanc, but all the same it was duly licensed with Reading Borough Council in connection with a bus service despite the latter's concerns over traffic congestion!

The service ran from Reading to Tadley via Whitley - Three Mile Cross – Spencers Wood – Swallowfield – Riseley – Wellington Monument – Silchester, for which the Oldsmobile was first licensed with Reading BC on 19th September 1922, with Reading Garage in Cork Street at the town terminus.

A more suitable 20-seater bus was registered as DP 4919 in October 1923, this being a Fiat 15-TER-type, probably with bodywork by Vincents of Reading. At this time the service was operated on a daily basis, and in 1924 another 20-seater bus was added in the shape of Dennis 2.5-tonner DP 5628, again quite likely bearing a Vincent body. All references to the licensing of this service refer to Sidney, which suggests that his brother looked after the garage.

Lovegrove's Dennis bus DP 5628 with boards for the service to Reading.

However, these operations gained the attention of the *Thames Valley* management, so an offer was made to eliminate them from the Reading – Basingstoke road and as a competitor between Reading and Tadley, with *Lovegrove's* selling out in December 1926. The Fiat and Dennis were also acquired, but re-sold without use by the new owner, though the actual route was not operated, as the *'Valley* continued with its own routes to serve those points. Another factor in the decision to sell was no doubt the fact that when the license was renewed by Reading BC in March 1926 it was stipulated that the service should not run via Riseley, which is interesting in that RBC had no real juristriction over the route taken outside the Borough, though the intention was to reduce traffic out of the town on the Basingstoke Road.

It must be assumed that the Oldsmobile was retained and that some excursion and private hire work kept it busy. It is also likely that the market-day Wednesdays and Saturdays run to Basingstoke from Silchester continued to run, though there are no firm references after 1923, when they were using the Railway Arms yard as the Basingstoke layover point.

The brothers continued to provide coaches for hire, though few details are known of any passenger vehicles operated after 1926, apart from a Gilford 28-seater bus (VR 9822) sold to *Newbury & District* in

April 1935. The main business from then until the war years was the motor garage, with the brothers also acting as the local agents for procuring vehicles for other public transport operators in the area. It is also understood that a Thursdays-only run to Newbury ran for some years, but again firm evidence is lacking as such facilities were rarely advertised beyond word of mouth, being only of concern to local villagers.

With the vast increase in wartime activity locally, the brothers were soon providing transport for many involved in the war effort, even being allotted one of the famous Bedford OWB utilities (EHO 236) during October 1942. However, that and the subsequent enlargement of the fleet, utilising over 50 vehicles in all, is outside the remit of this study. Suffice to say that Herbert died in 1942, after which the business was known as *Lovegrove & Lovegrove*, with a new garage built at Tadley for the many contract vehicles, which included double-deckers used on the AWRE and ROF Burghfield contracts. The firm passed to *E.G. Martin & K.E. Hine (M&H Coaches)* in 1959, who continued under the *Lovegrove's* name. *Sidney Lovegrove* passed away in late 1971 aged 88.

> The last operator to be considered in this sub-area stemmed from another repeating theme, that of a shop owner or publican-turned carrier.

Wilfred J. Davis

Wilfred Davis was the landlord of the Hare & Hounds at Wolverton, so he would be aware of the need for a market-day service to the local towns. His service is first mentioned in the Hants & Berks Gazette on 26th August 1922, but no details of the vehicle have come to light. He went to Newbury on Thursdays and ran via Exmansford – Ashford Hill – Kingsclere – Headley, using the Free Library in Cheap Street as his layover point, though later he relocated to The Wharf. The single journey left Wolverton at 10am, returning at 3.30pm.

On Wednesdays and Saturdays he travelled to Basingstoke via Ewhurst Park – Ramsdell – Monk Sherborne – Sherborne St. John, all journeys on each route starting from the pub at Wolverton at 9am, whilst in Basingstoke he used the railway Arms yard and left there at 4pm. He licensed both routes under the 1930 Act, and the service remained the same until at least 1938.

****

However, only days after the acquisition of *Edith Kent's* business there was another crisis for the Board, when it learnt that Charlie Durnford wished to leave the Company! Given his wide-ranging responsibilities within the organisation, this was indeed an unexpected blow. However, he did offer to remain with them in a non-executive capacity until the end of September 1937 in order to oversee the building of the garage and handle coach and haulage bookings during that busy time. He also sought assurances that his sons could continue in employment with *N&D*, and that he could dispose of his shares to Arthur Andrews. The Board was agreeable to these points, and it was agreed that he would be paid a salary of £6 per week during that period. However, and no doubt still remembering the earlier episode of independent operation, the Board did insist that he signed an undertaking not to operate as a coach or haulage contractor within 10 miles of the Parish Church at Newbury for a period of 5 years from 23rd April 1937.

The vacancy on the Board was filled with a new and significant investor, who would influence a number of business decisions over the next few years, this being Angus Marshall, a solicitor and partner in the firm of Lucas & Marshall of No.5 Mansion House Street, Newbury. He purchased 1896 shares during April 1937 and, following the relinquishment of the Chair by Arthur Andrews later that month, he took that role. Theo Denham and Angus Marshall already knew each other and are recalled as being 'as thick as thieves'. The Company did, however, benefit from his business sense and this financial boost came at a good time. Also that month Mr. McNairmie sold his small interest in the Company.

Additions for the coach fleet were also forthcoming in the early months, two being full-size and the other pair 20-seaters. In February two 168OT-type Gilfords with Duple bodies from the *Banfield's Coaches* fleet in Peckham, south London arrived, and these featured the 'camel-back' style of coachwork with a luggage carrier built into a rear hump on the roof. They became Nos.54 (HX 7560) and 55 (JJ 8873), both with well-appointed front-entrance bodies seating 32, these coaches being new in March 1931 and March 1933 respectively. Both had been obtained from Arlington Motors, who had likely taken them in part-exchange against new vehicles, and *N&D* paid £370 for the 1931 example and £560 for the more recent one.

March saw a further two Dennis 'Aces' arriving, both probably through Lane, and they originated in the West Country. One was a front-entrance Duple sun-saloon bus, though *N&D* actually used it for coach duties mostly, and this became No.64 (FJ 9581). It had been new in February 1934 to *Milton Services* of Crediton in Devon. The other was a front-entrance coach with a body by Mumford of Plymouth and was new in December 1934 to *C.A. Gayton* of Ashburton, also in Devon, and this became No.65 (JY 4752). The body on this incorporated a sunshine roof, making it a very popular vehicle, as many passengers still had fond memories of the open-top coaches, at least on finer days!

A magnificent line up of N&D coaches (continued across the next page), showing from left to right Reo No.26 (RX 6264), Gilford No.55 (JJ 8873), Gilford No.50 (JK 1911), Gilford No.53 (HX 1855), Dennis 'Aces' Nos.64 (FJ 9581), 65 (JY 4752) and 63 (JB 6834), Gilford No.22 (RD 1886), GMC No.32 (RA 9830), Bedford No.62 (OY 5807), Gilford No.52 (TY 8886), Gilford No.54 (HX 7560), Star No.27 (HX 1059) and GMC No.58 (OU 2885), the occasion being the Coronation Day excursion to London, and the venue The Wharf.

During May a further 20-seater bus on Thornycroft chassis was purchased, though this came direct from another operator. This A2Long-type had been new in March 1929 to *J. Geddes (Burton Cars)* of Brixham in Devon and carried a front-entrance body by Wadham. UO 9841 passed to *G. Trice (Tillingbourne Valley)* of Chilworth in Surrey before becoming *N&D* No.8. It replaced the previous vehicle with that number, Guy 20-seater TK 2740 which had come in from *Mrs. Kent* the previous month.

Thornycroft No.8 (UO 9841) is seen prior to delivery to its original owner, who used it on a service between Brixham and Kingswear.

It is worth noting that these little Thornycrofts were the hardest worked of all the fleet, being in use daily and over significant mileages, including the busy town services. No.8 (UO 9841) is also known to have been sent to work from the Hermitage outstation soon after arriving.

The Wharf area had been used as a bus terminus and general parking area since the 1920's, but an unfortunate accident occurred during May, when a child was killed by a motor lorry. This was not an *N&D* vehicle, but it did prompt Newbury Borough Council to consider organising the layout better, and white lines were painted on the surface to regularise both the bus stands and those areas to be kept clear.

The front nearside view of Thornycroft No.8 (UO 9841) as new. It was later with Tillingbourne Valley for a while before coming to Newbury.

However, on a happier note, May 1937 will of course be remembered for the Coronation of King George VI, an event which occurred at Westminster Abbey on 10th of that month. In a fashion that was very much reminiscent of the Silver Jubilee just two years before,

Newbury & District soon found itself involved with transport to a wide range of special events. Also, as in 1935, many of the fleet were decorated, whilst on the day of the Coronation every vehicle that could be spared was pressed into service for the massive task of taking the crowds up to London, with 15 coaches going from Newbury alone!

Also as before, many annual events were given more of a royal theme, such as the Tattoos at Tidworth and Aldershot. There was a review of the Royal Navy fleet off Southsea, complete with illuminations, and *N&D* ran coaches to see that during May from Newbury, Inkpen, Thatcham and Hungerford, these leaving for Southsea at 1pm and returning at 11pm.

TIDWORTH TATTOO,
1937.

July 31st and August 2nd to 7th

Seating increased to 30,000

We are AGENTS FOR ALL ARENA SEATS.

Reserve Early for any Number.

Newbury & District Motor Services, Ltd.
7, The Wharf, NEWBURY.

May was also a significant month for the haulage fleet, with the arrival of a replacement for the former *Durnford* Maudslay removals van L4 (CW 6802) in the shape of a Bedford 2.5-tonner (AMO 455), which carried a 'mammoth' pantechnicon body, which cost £372, the money being loaned by Arthur Andrews.

A new slogan 'Roadway Excursions' made its way into the Company adverts during the early Summer of 1937, and also appeared on a number of the coaches along the roof sides or luggage-carriers. Indeed, after the acquisition of *Kingsclere Coaches* the Company quite rightly saw itself as the premier coach operator in the area. *A list of the destinations approved under Road Service Licenses for Excursions & Tours at May 1937 can be found in Appendix 4.*

Pride-of-the-fleet amongst the 20-seaters was Dennis 'Ace' No.65 (JY 4752) with its Mumford coachwork.

During May *Newbury & District* had the chance to further improve its hold on the local coach scene with the purchase of that aspect of the old-established Ford Agents *Pass & Co.*

Pass & Co.

As the Ford Main Agent for Newbury from 1915, Pass & Co. was an integral part of the local transport revolution following the end of the Great War. Although we have already seen how this shaped up in terms of the motorisation of carrier's services, bus operations, pleasure and haulage operations, it should also be appreciated that a parallel revolution took place on the land. This mechanisation was as much as a necessity as a desire, with so many men and the once ubiquitous working horses having lost their lives on the Continent and had left such a huge void on most farms.

Therefore, the products of the Ford Motor Company rapidly spread through the lanes, with Fordson tractors in the fields of the local area. As we have already noticed, the Model T was the basis of many business ventures, either in the extended variety or the subsequent 1-ton version. The English production had commenced in 1911 on a production-line basis at the Trafford Park Works in Manchester, at a time when other motor vehicles were being constructed in situ, bringing production times and costs down. A larger plant at Dagenham, Essex was opened in 1931 as a replacement for the Trafford Park Works, the author's maternal grandfather going to work there for a while.

The Model T or 'Tin Lizzie' as the original car was at times referred to, was introduced in 1908 and had been designed to cope with the extensive network of dirt-roads in America, which also made it perfect for the roads of rural West Berkshire! The controls were also simple but effective, in order to make the transition from horse to motor less complicated than many of its contemporaries, as speed was controlled by a throttle lever on the steering column, whilst there were only two forward gear positions. The three foot pedals operated the clutch, the brake and the reverse gear. The brake was activated by contracting bands on the transmission, which also kept the wheel arrangements so simple that changes of wheel were quick and easy, an important factor with the (then) high incidence of punctures. Of course, in common with all earlier petrol-engine types, starting was 'on the handle'!

One of Pass & Co.'s motor hearses on Ford Model T chassis, which could be bought complete for £440. The chassis is the 1-ton version which formed the basis of many a local bus, chara or carrier's van.

The later AA-type also found favour for bus, coach and haulage work with a number of local firms, and almost all these examples were obtained through Pass & Co.

However, the firm of *Pass & Co.* actually had its origins in the pre-motor age in *Henry Pass,* who had been born at Newport Pagnall, Buckinghamshire in 1849. He was apprenticed as a coachbuilder, duly residing in Aylesbury. In 1879 he had married Annie Laurie at Newbury, which explains why he would later return to that town. Between 1891 and 1895 he took over the established coachworks formerly operated by Robert Lovell at 60 Northbrook Street, the very same place that *Arthur Andrews* had received his apprenticeship, though now re-named as The Newbury Carriage Works.

There he produced a wide range of bodies for horse-drawn vehicles, also having his son Archibald as a coach bodybuilder. He was evidently joined in 1901 by George Salkeld, who had been born in Bermondsey, South London and noted in advertising that he was 'late of Barker & Co., London', when *Pass & Co.* was formed. Workshops were set up in West Street, whilst George also resided on the site at No.41a. This was the motor workshops, and apart from supplying Ford vehicles, they also hired them out, with vans, lorries and hearses being available.

Due to their status as agents, it can be difficult to ascertain from the surviving motor tax records which vehicles were used by them, as often they were sold on locally after a relatively short time. Similarly, although many bodies were constructed for local operators, no records survive. Also, in later years they would sometimes sub-contract coach-building to other firms, some orders going to Heaver of Durrington.

It is not known how long *Henry Pass* played an active role in the firm, though he continued to live in the area and died in 1925.

The regular operation of charabancs commenced with the 1923 season, but prior to that there had been several short-term passenger-carrying ventures recorded. The first involved the running of a motor brake from Newbury to Reading on Saturdays for the matches of Reading Football Club, which ran during the 1919 season. On Saturday 25th September 1920 there was an excursion to the large band contest held at the Crystal Palace at Sydenham in South London, leaving at 7am and returning at 7pm for a fare of 10 shillings.

Another venture saw a motor bus running 6 times daily between Wash Common and Newbury Post Office from 3rd April 1922. However, this is only known from the one advert in the local paper, and the Model T 14-seater carriers van used for it (BL 9713) was sold onto another user by December of that year, but with a lorry body. It is possible that this was just a stock vehicle put to work until a buyer could be found or as a result of a cancelled order, so the body may have been transferred to another vehicle?

Naturally enough the bulk of the vehicles employed were of Ford manufacture, though a notable exception was a 14-seater CPT (BL 5420), which was used from 1925 as a chara, but had been with them as a lorry or van since 1917. The other possible exception was the vehicle registered P 942, the origins and make of which are not known. This had perhaps started out as a large private car, but in April 1923 Pass & Co. re-declared it for hackney use, possibly as a charabanc. A list of the known charas from earlier days will be found in the Appendix of Operator's Known Fleets, but it is known that the maximum operation consisted of 4 vehicles, though more generally just 3. Known drivers were Ted Wale from Benham Hill, Ted Coxhead and Bill Eggleton, all of whom would transfer to N&D in due course.

Private hire and advertised excursions were operated, though little advertising seemed necessary in the local press compared with other local operators, but that is perhaps explained by the siting of the garage off a busy shopping street, whilst in later years there was also a booking facility at the musical instrument and gramophone dealers Alphonse Cary, whose premises were at 47/8 Northbrook Street.

For many years Ben Hambling, who lived at The Ridge, Cold Ash, was General Manager and the firm enjoyed a good reputation locally. In July 1931 Salkeld was approaching 60 and sold the business to Arthur J. Low, who actually lived adjacent to the garage at No.43 West Street and by 1933 was already involved in the business. This was most likely when the red livery so far used was changed to maroon though one coach wore a blue livery, which might indicate that it was originally intended for another operator and not taken up?

The Motor Transport Year Book entry for 1932/3 has the Company as holding E&T's licenses for coaches, of which there were 4 14-seaters on Ford T and AA chassis, and offering all types of vans and lorries for hire, with 16 in total from 10cwt to 2 tons capacity. The 1936/7 entry shows 3 Ford coaches with 20-seater bodies, whilst there were 15 vans and lorries between 10cwt and 2 ton capacity.

N&D were keen to eliminate the competition, particularly as Pass & Co. had E&T licenses to various popular destinations which duplicated theirs. Mr. Low accepted the offer of £1500 for the transfer of licenses, goodwill and the trio of Fords then in use at the end of May 1937. As a result N&D could now field up to 17 coaches on any one day on advertised excursions from Newbury.

The coaches in use at the time of the takeover were 1930 Ford AA-type RX 7150, 1932 AA-type JB 437 and a 1935 BB-type registered JB 5701. Whether the 1930 example saw use by N&D is uncertain, but the

1932 coach was used through to the end of the season, whilst the BB-type (which became N&D No.60) continued in use until 1941, making it the last Ford in the fleet.

Former Pass & Co. Ford AA-type RX 7150 after sale by N&D to Leather's Coaches of Maiden Bradley in Wiltshire.

****

Outgoing vehicles for this period were Leyland 'Lion' No.39 (VA 7942) that went about April, and the ex-*White's* AJS bus No.44 (MW 6161), which departed by June. Maudslays also became another make no longer represented in the fleet, with the sale of the old removals van and also bus No.6 (FG 4427) in June.

During June a further two full-size buses came into the fleet, with a pair of Tilling-Stevens from dealer H. Lane. These were TV 5363 and TV 6036 and had the same history, being new to *Dutton (Unity Services)* of Nottingham, who sold out to *Trent Motor Traction* in November 1935. TV 5363 was a B10A-type chassis and was new in December 1931, whilst TV 6036 was a B49A7 new in April 1932, and both carried front-entrance 32-seater bodies by Willowbrook, becoming Nos.44/5 respectively. Their arrival led to the Dennis E-type No.41 (PR 9053) being withdrawn late in the Summer, though it was still evident in the yard at July 1938 being cannibalised for spares. Apparently, this bus hadn't done much in recent times, being used only on a school run and peak days only.

One of Dutton's Tilling-Stevens buses similar to No.45 (TV 6036), seen when in service with Unity in Nottingham. This pair of buses were another sound purchase and saw a lot of service on the busier routes.

The practice of utilising garage and office staff at peak times continued for both the bus services and coach work. Indeed, the latter was regarded as both a regular source of overtime and a chance to get out the area for the day. All of the Durnford 'boys' carried on with such driving in addition to duties in the garage, though Ernie was often as not to be found driving the removals van. Boss Denham and Percy Andrews (both Garage Foremen) also did coach driving mainly, along with George Amor (coachbuilder), Tom Chadwick (fitter) and E. Vickers (electrician).

Although nothing further came of the *Thames Valley* offer for the Company, other parties evidently heard that it might be available. One was *Red & White* based in Chepstow, who had expanded throughout south-east Wales and were planning further expansion into England, along with extensive express coach interests. However, it was concluded by *Red & White* at that time that the possibility of acquiring a controlling interest for a good price was not practical in June 1937.

Although the new garage was going ahead, it was necessary to keep the old sheds in Mill Lane as well, so plans to improve these were approved by Newbury BC in mid-June.

On the services side, further alterations were made to the operations to The Ilsleys, effective from 5th July. The Reading – East Ilsley service was extended onto West Ilsley, whilst the Newbury – West Ilsley service was altered to go straight on from East Ilsley to reach Compton and Rowstock in place of what had been a separate route, those wishing to travel to West Ilsley from Newbury now having to change bus at East Ilsley instead. Also, from 27th July, some changes were made to the East Woodhay journeys and the Ashford Hill service, the latter in response to amended arrangements at the Kingsclere outstation.

The bus services between Kingsclere and Newbury, along with the service acquired from Vincent, were taken over by *N&D* with only minor changes, and an outstation for 3 buses was set up in the yard of the George & Horn pub in Newbury Road, though later this proved too small, so they were transferred to The Crown in Basingstoke Road instead. Whereas *Mrs. Kent* used a number of reliefs on Thursdays and Saturdays, the Newbury-based company used crew-operated 32/35 buses sent out from the main garage on those days in order to supplement the local allocation. The latter was duly reduced to just 2 buses once services were slightly adjusted.

However, it was not just the chance to expand bus services to the south that had attracted *N&D* to *Mrs. Kent's* operations, as the good trade in excursions and tours was also a significant boost, her licenses adding pick up points in Kingsclere, Headley, Wolverton,

Ashford Hill, and Plastow Green, the latter two places having been added through the acquisition of *Rodney Vincent's* business. The authorised excursions and tours were to Ascot Races, Aldershot Tattoo, Tidworth Tattoo, London, Brighton, Worthing, Littlehampton, Bognor Regis, Hayling Island, Southsea, Lee-on-Solent, Bournemouth, Weymouth, Southampton, Cheddar, Savernake Forest, Goodwood Races, Guildford, Epsom Races, Weston-super-Mare, Reading, Oxford, Windsor, Swindon, Marlborough and California-in-England (a popular 'inland resort' south of Wokingham). It will of course be recalled that *Mrs. Kent* had used *Walter Chalk* as her booking agent in Kingsclere, a role that he continued to fulfil on behalf of the new owners.

Newbury & District Motor Services Ltd.

ROADWAY
EXCURSIONS
TO ALL PLACES OF INTEREST

DAY, HALF-DAY and EVENING EXCURSIONS FROM NEWBURY.

(For Excursions from other places see our Agents throughout the District.)

SUNDAY, July 11th—	Start	Fare
Southsea	8.0 a.m.	5/6
Bournemouth	8.0 a.m.	6/6
Cheddar	8.0 a.m.	6/6
California	1.30 p.m.	2/6
Pangbourne	6.30 p.m.	2/6
Newbury Commons	6.30 p.m.	1/6
TUESDAY, July 13th—		
Southsea	8.0 a.m.	5/6
WEDNESDAY, July 14th—		
Southsea	8.0 a.m.	5/6
Bournemouth	8.0 a.m.	6/6
SUNDAY, July 18th—		
Southsea	8.0 a.m.	5/6
Bognor	8.0 a.m.	6/6
Bournemouth	8.0 a.m.	6/6
Swindon	2.30 p.m.	2 6

WEDNESDAY, July 21st : Special Excursion—
SOUTHAMPTON 1.15 p.m. 4/6
and other AFTERNOON and EVENING TOURS.

The first half of the extensive excursions advert which appeared in the NWN on 8th July 1937 – the other half is shown on the opposite page.

The Summer of 1937 was an exceptionally busy time for the coach fleet, but sadly a bad accident in July somewhat marred the season, though seemingly not the Company's reputation judging by contemporary reports.

but he then pulled out to overtake. As he did so, he saw the approaching lorry and decided to accelerate in order to drive off to his right and into a field entrance. However, he could not clear the lorry, and despite the efforts of both drivers, the two vehicles struck in a nearside-to-nearside collision.

The lorry came to rest in the road, with its cargo of strawberries strewn about, which 8-year old Jack Williams (who was a passenger on one of the other coaches) recalled made the scene look more horrific due to the blood-redness of the fruit scattered about along with the injured taken from the vehicles.

The coach came to a halt in the field and damage was quite extensive, with the front entrance area torn away and the nearside windows smashed. Unfortunately, one 29-year old man had been standing by the doorway at the time of the crash and subsequently died of his injuries, which were probably made worse because passengers were distracted by activity on the airfield. 16 others required hospital treatment, though it was accepted that the high-backed seats had probably saved many from worse injuries when flung forward during the crash.

The aftermath of the accident, with Dennis 'Ace' No.64 (FJ 9581) where it came to a halt in the field. Due to the extent of the damage it was not considered likely that the coach would see further use.

The incident occurred on the morning of Saturday 3rd July, when 3 *Newbury & District* coaches were travelling in convoy towards Winchester and onwards to the South Coast. Two 20-seaters were engaged on taking a party of mainly children from Headley Baptist Sunday School to Bournemouth, whilst the third coach was 24-seater GMC No.32 (RA 9830) with a party of mostly adults from Stanford Dingley for Southsea.

Although the pair of 20-seaters had started out in front, the rearmost one had fallen back on a hill and GMC 32 was now in the centre. George Amor was in front with GMC No.58 (OU 2885), followed by Gomer Davies with No.32, leaving Tom Chadwick at the rear with Dennis 'Ace' No.64 (FJ 9581).

Shortly after 8am the convoy passed the entrance to Worthy Down RAF base, when it came up behind a slow-moving horse and cart. George Amor, who had the best view, slowed down to keep in behind the cart, having seen a 2-ton Ford lorry approaching from the opposite direction. Driver Amor signalled by hand for Gomer Davies to slow down, and he in turn signalled Tom Chadwick. Whether the latter misunderstood why the coaches in front were slowing, or interpreted the signal as an invitation to overtake is not recorded,

Although some initial discussion centred around the braking ability of the coach, the Regional Examiner concluded that it was not at fault, and that the cause of the accident was human error. A lengthy hearing took place at the Coroner's Court at Winchester, held soon after the accident, but it would be the end of July before the three sittings were finally completed. This was of course also somewhat embarrassing for Jim Davies, as Tom Chadwick was his brother-in-law, though in his defence the Company pointed out that he had a good record to that point. It did, however, agree not to use him on coach driving duties again, whilst the court hearing over his driving resulted in a fine of £1 (which represented half his weekly wage) and a 2-year ban on driving. He continued as a Fitter with N&D, and in fact the Company was publicly praised for its sincere efforts for the injured and their families, which included taking people for hospital visits in Winchester and Newbury.

Once the Coroner had concluded his official business, the civil case against *N&D* on behalf of the injured parties got under way, but again it was to be a full year before this was to reach its conclusion. This in turn affected the insurer's view on whether the coach could be repaired, which at that point looked a not particularly likely prospect.

With such an exceptional season under way, its loss was soon felt, leading to a decision to buy an ageing Ford AA-type which *Pass & Co.* had for sale. This was RX 2907, which had operated for *Pass & Co.* as part of its own coach fleet, but was now with them as a dealer. It had been new in August 1928 and carried a 14-seater 'allweather' type body built by Vincent of Reading. It was pressed into use by the end of July, still wearing the maroon livery of its former owner, and it took over the fleet number 64 from the 'Ace'. Despite the instant decision to purchase this, it was destined to remain in use until late 1939, no doubt because of its small capacity, there being only this and the Chevrolet No.5 (UN 3196) with less than 20 seats after the end of 1937.

Ford AA-type No.64 (RX 2907) when with Pass & Co.

However, notwithstanding that unfortunate accident, July was a very busy month for excursions, as can be seen from the advertisement placed in the Newbury Weekly News for 8th July. Later that month the very popular British Legion Fete at Thatcham was provided with a frequent shuttle service of buses.

A new timetable booklet was issued from 25th July in order to take account of various recent changes, whilst the opportunity was taken to re-arrange the route numbering, which then became:

Route 1 N'bury – East Ilsley – Compton – Rowstock
Route 2 West Ilsley – East Ilsley – Reading
Route 3 Newbury – Chieveley – Peasemore
Route 4 Newbury – Headley – Kingsclere
Route 5 Newbury – Ashford Hill – Kingsclere
Route 6 Newbury – Boxford Eastbury – Lambourn
Route 7 Newbury – Great Shefford – North Fawley
Route 8 Newbury – Wickham – Shefford Woodlands
Route 9 Newbury – Hungerford (via Bath Road)
Route 10 Newbury – Kintbury – Inkpen – Hungerford
Route 11 Newbury – Woolton Hill – Highclere

Route 12 Newbury – Ball Hill – West Woodhay
Route 13 Newbury – Ball Hill – North End
Route 14 Newbury – Ball Hill – East Woodhay
Route 15 Newbury – Thatcham – Bucklebury
Route 16 Newbury – Thatcham – Cold Ash – Westrop
Route 17 Newbury – Thatcham – Colthrop Mills
Route 18 Newbury – Ecchinswell – Sydmonton
Route 19 Newbury – Hermitage – Yattendon
Route 20 Newbury – Hermitage – Frilsham
Route 21 Newbury – Hermitage – Aldworth
Route 22 Hermitage – Cold Ash – Theale – Reading
Route 23 Newbury (Broadway) – Wash Common
Route 24 Newbury (Broadway) – Kingsbridge Road
Route 25 Donnington – Newbury – Camp Close
Route 26 Hambridge Road – Newbury – Shaw

Once again the Moulsford Special was not numbered

During August 1937 *N&D* drew the attention of the travelling public to the connections afforded by its bus services for onward travel by other concerns. Those reaching Hungerford could connect with the buses of *Bristol Tramways* for Marlborough and Swindon, whilst at Rowstock there were still the connections with *City of Oxford* to Abingdon, Didcot, Wantage and Oxford. At Kingsclere passengers could change onto the former *Edith Kent* Basingstoke route now in the hands of *S. Huntley*, whilst of course at Reading there was the whole *Thames Valley* network and that of *Reading Corporation.*

Another of the original shareholders decided to dispose of much of his stake in August 1937, and this was Arthur Andrews. Once this had been arranged, he resigned as a Director in October, though he remained as Coach Repairer at the weekly salary of £4.

Both of the *Pocock Bros.* also decided to sell off their shares towards the end of the Summer, with Percy ceasing to be a shareholder on 25th August, followed by Norman on 6th September, after which they concentrated on their other business interests.

Charlie Durnford departed at the end of August, having purchased the motor garage business known as the Kennet Motor Works at 11 Charnwood Street, on the A4 in Hungerford from Mr. A.E. Ludford, which was established by 1931, having a Hillman car agency by 1939. In 1941 the garage was requisitioned by the Authorities for use as a War Factory, and Charlie became the driver of the ambulance at Newbury Hospital. The garage was subsequently returned after the war, and when Charlie passed away on 25th April 1953, there was a tribute to his pioneering transport days in the Newbury Weekly News.

During September the Board received a request from George Howlett in order to allow him to sell some of his shares to Charlie Durnford, but this met with a curt refusal!

Following Charlie Durnford's departure, *Newbury & District* placed an announcement in the NWN to inform the public of the change, making this the first time it had really advertised the haulage and removals side under its own name since the Company was formed over five years previously.

Each September brought its crop of special events, all of which required enhanced bus services, and notable items from the 1937 calendar were the carnival at Lambourn on Saturday 11th, and one week later there was the Newbury Agricultural Show, again held at Elcot Park, the latter having a 'continuous' service of buses from both Hungerford and Newbury.

During October the annual Newbury Fair was actually held on The Wharf rather than at Northcroft, so from Tuesday 12th to Friday 15th it was necessary to make alternative arrangements for bus departures. The buses for Thatcham, Cold Ash, Bucklebury, Peasemore, The Ilsleys, Hungerford, Lambourn and the group of routes out through Hermitage were re-located to the nearby New Car Park, whilst those serving Ashford Hill, Kingsclere, Ecchinswell, Highclere, East and West Woodhay and North End were operated from West Mills.

September saw the withdrawal of the Bedford WLG with secondhand coach body, No.18 (RX 9463), and it seems likely that the same month saw the demise of former *Pass & Co.* Ford AA-type RX 7150.

The resignation of Arthur Andrews left a vacancy on the Board of Directors, and this was filled from October by another new investor, Frank Frampton of

Burlington Garden, Close Lane, Wash Common, whilst the attempts by Boss Denham and George Howlett to gain election were both unsuccessful.

The Company approached the Traffic Commissioner for permission to carry for free any blind or disabled ex-servicemen on its bus services. However, before this application was heard it was withdrawn, no doubt because of the difficulties of identifying who would be eligible to such a concession, bearing in mind that many other people had obvious disabilities caused by accidents and even hereditary factors. However, such a proposal did reflect the feeling of the time.

Charlie Durnford had learnt in his early days the value of good publicity, and after he took over the Kennet Motor Works he placed a series of adverts to entice the public to use his facilities. Being so well-known locally, it is understandable that he wanted his reputation to transfer to the new enterprise. Note also the style of petrol pumps then in use.

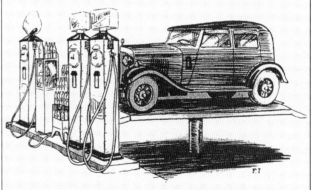

Several more old vehicles were withdrawn in December, leading to the sale of the ex-*Durnford Bros.* Ford AA lorry RX 4356, along with former *Pass & Co.* JB 437 of the same type but fitted with a 20-seater coach body, leaving only 60 (JB 5701) and 64 (RX 2907) to represent the Ford marque in the fleet. Also going then was No.30 (UU 7594) a 1929 GMC T42-type which had come into the fleet from *Durnfords* at formation in June 1932.

The policy on fleet replacements was discussed at Board level towards the close of 1937, when it was decided that Dennis types would be favoured for the 20-seater requirements and Leylands for the full-size vehicles, both for buses and coaches.

Despite the long association of Tilling-Stevens buses on Newbury area services, the pair purchased in 1937 would be the last. No.45 (TV 6036) is seen leaving The Wharf on the route to Highclere.

Arrangements for Christmas 1937 followed a similar pattern to previous years, with an enhanced service (to the Tuesday level) being provided on all those routes that were usually daily operations in respect of 21st - 23rd December. On Christmas Eve, all routes gained Saturday levels for last-minute shoppers and those getting away to relatives, but no services were operated on Christmas Day. On Boxing Day the service was as appropriate for the day of the week.

However, there was another fatal accident involving an *N&D* bus on Christmas Eve. Driver Bill Atkins of Chieveley was bringing his bus over the narrow bridge that crosses the River Lambourn at Welford when a 70-year old man appeared from the opposite way in his car. Bill stopped as soon as he could, but the fabric-bodied car was badly crushed against the bridge, resulting in the driver subsequently dying of his injuries, though it was accepted that no fault lay with the bus driver. Although speeds were relatively low in those days, car construction paid little heed to the protection of passengers, whilst seat belts were of course unknown then.

NEWBURY, STOCKCROSS, WICKHAM & SHEFFORD WOODLANDS.
ROUTE No. 8.

DAILY.

	NS a.m.	NS a.m.	p.m.	p.m.	p.m.	p.m.	S p.m.
Newbury ...	8 5	10 0	1 10	4 10	6 10	8 10	10 10
Speen ...		10 7	1 16	4 16	6 16	8 16	10 16
Stockcross P.O. ...		10 14	1 22	4 22	6 22	8 22	10 22
Wickham Heath ...		...	1 27	4 27	WS	8 27	10 27
Wickham ..	8 30		1 34	4 34	6 34	8 34	10 34

Wickham —	8 30	...	1 36	4 36	6 36	8 36	10 36
Wickham Heath	8 35	...	1 41	4 41	WS	8 41	10 41
Stockcross P.O.	8 43	10 15	1 47	4 47	6 47	8 47	10 47
Speen ...	8 47	10 22	1 51	4 51	6 51	8 51	10 51
Newbury ...	8 55	10 30	1 57	4 57	6 57	8 57	10 57

NS—Not Sundays

WS—Proceeds to Wickham on Sundays only.

EXTRA SERVICES ON THURSDAYS AND SATURDAYS.

	T A a.m.	p.m.	p.m.	S p.m.	A p.m.	p.m.	S p.m.	p.m.	T p.m.	S p.m.
Newbury ...	10 30	11 30	12 30	1 0	2 30	3 0	5 0	6 0	7 0	9 0	9 10
Speen ...	! 36	11 37	12 37	1 6	2 37	3 7	5 6	6 7	7 7	9 6	9 16
Stockcross ..	10 42	11 41	12 44	1 22	2 44	3 24	5 24	6 22	7 24	9 24	9 22
Wickham Heath	10 47	11 46	...	1 27	...	3 29	5 29	6 27	7 29	...	9 27
Wickham ...	10 54	...	...	1 34	...	...	5 34	6 34	...	...	9 34
Sheff. Woodlands	1059x	...	...	1 39	...	...	5 39	...	...	...	9 39

Sheff. Woodlands	11 0x	...	...	1 40	...	...	5 40	...	...	...	9 40
Wickham ...	11 5	...	...	1 45	...	...	5 45	6 36	...	...	9 45
Wickham Heath	11 17	12 11	56	1 51	...	3 40	5 52	6 41	7 30	...	9 52
Stockcross ...	11 17	12 0	12 50	1 57	2 45	3 45	5 57	6 47	7 35	9 24	9 57
Speen ...	11 21	12 8	12 57	2 1	2 52	3 52	6 3	6 51	7 42	9 30	10 1
Newbury ...	11 26	12 15	1 0	2 7	3 0	4 0	6 9	6 57	7 50	9 38	10 7

S—Saturdays only   **T—Thursdays only.**

A —To Hoe Benham on Thursdays.

X—Proceeds to Shefford Woodlands on Thursdays

Two examples of timetables from the booklet of July 1937, the Wickham and Stockcross route originating from Denham Bros, whilst the Yattendon route had come from W.J. White & Son of Hernitage. Note the variation of service levels on different days of the week, along with extended journeys, including those marked 'if required'.

NEWBURY—YATTENDON.
(Via Hermitage and Hampstead Norris).
ROUTE No. 19

	MONS. WEDS. & FRIS.				TUESDAYS.				SUNDAYS.		
	a.m.	a.m.	p.m.	p.m.	a.m.	a.m.	p.m.	p.m.	p.m.	p.m.	p.m.
Yattendon	8 0	...	...	4 45	8 0	...	1 25	4 45	...	...	...
Everington F'm	8 5	...	...	4 50	8 5	...	1 30	4 50	...	...	...
H'stead Norris	8 10	...	...	4 55	8 10	...	1 35	4 55	6 50	1 45	...
Four Elms	8 15	...	...	5 0	8 15	...	1 40	5 0	6 55	1 50	...
Hermitage	8 20	1020	1 45	5 5	8 20	1020	1 45	5 5	1 7	0 1	55 5	25 8 40
Long Lane	8 25	1025	1 50	5 10	8 25	1025	1 50	5 10	7 5	2 0	5 30 8 45
Grange Farm	8 30	1030	1 55	5 15	8 30	1030	1 55	5 15	7 10	2 5	5 35 8 50
Shaw ...	8 35	1035	2 0	5 20	8 35	1035	2 0	5 20	7 15	2 10	5 40 8 55
Newbury (W'f)	8 40	1040	2 5	5 25	8 40	1040	2 5	5 25	7 20	2 15	5 45 9 0

	a.m.	p.m.	p.m.	p.m.	a.m.	p.m.	p.m.	p.m.	p.m.	p.m.	p.m.	p.m.
Newbury (W'f)	9 0	1230	4 0	6 0	9 0	1230	4 0	6 0	0 8	1 5	2 30 5 45	9 15
Shaw...	9 5	1235	4 5	6 5	9 5	1235	4 5	6 5	8 20	1 2	35 5 50	9 20
Grange Farm	9 10	1240	4 10	6 10	9 10	1240	4 10	6 10	8 25	1 2	40 5 55	9 25
Long Lane	9 15	1245	4 15	6 15	9 15	1245	4 15	6 15	8 30	1 2	45 6 0	9 30
Hermitage	9 20	1250	4 20	6 20	9 20	1250	4 20	6 20	8 35	2 50	6 5	9 35
Four Elms	...	...	4 25	X	...	1255	4 25	25	X	X	X	X
H'stead Norris	...	...	4 30	6 30	...	1 0	4 30	6 30	8 45	3 0	6 15	9 45
Everington F'm	...	...	4 35	...	...	1 5	4 35	X	...	...	...	...
Yattendon	...	...	4 40	...	...	1 10	4 40	6 40	...	...	...	...

X—Proceeds only if required.

FARES.

Yattendon										
2	Everington Farm									
3	2	Hampstead Norris								
7	5	3	Four Elms							
8	1/-	6	9	4	7	2	Hermitage			
9		7		6	10	3	2	Long Lane		
10		8		7		5	4	3	Grange Farm	
11	1/4	9	1/2	8	1/-	6	10	6	2	Cemetery
1/-	1/6	10	1/4	9		7	1/-	6	4	3	2	Newbury
S	R	S	R	S	R	S	R	S	R	S	S

130

Chapter 11 – 1938

After all the activity of the Coronation year, this was a relatively quiet one, though it also included the last of those operators coming into the fold.

However, during February an offer of £38,000 was made for the purchase of the Company, through a firm of London solicitors who represented an undisclosed client. After a fair amount of discussion, the Board advised that an offer of at least £40,000 might be met with approval, but nothing further is heard after that.

During March a number of coaches were acquired for the forthcoming season, these comprising 3 Dennis 'Aces' and a pair of Bedfords. The latter were very recent models, being new in April 1936, and both had been new to *A. Young (Red Warrior)* and carried 25-seater front-entrance coach bodies with sunshine roof by Duple, and these became Nos.70/1 (BON 886/7).

The pair of Bedford coaches were in very good condition, so their original red and cream livery was retained. No.70 (BON 886) is seen at The Wharf.

The trio of 'Aces' were each quite different from each other. One became No.67 (AYA 102), and this was a June 1934 example fitted with a Harrington 20-seater rear-entrance coach body with sunshine roof. This had been new to *Harding (Scarlet Pimpernel)* based in Ilfracombe, north Devon. Also new the same month was No.68 (DG 9516), which carried a Duple 20-seater front-entrance coach body, and a sunshine roof was also fitted when ordered by *F.C. Cottrell* of Mitcheldean in Gloucestershire.

The third of the 'Aces' was No.69 (DYF 184), which was only new in May 1937 to *Glenton Tours* based in London SE14 and, as this operator continued for many years, its early sale seems unusual. This carried a 20-seater front-entrance coach body by Strachan and had a sunshine roof. As such, it was a high-quality addition to the fleet.

Dennis 'Ace' No.68 (DG 9516) is seen at Southsea with Bert Greenwood as the driver by the coach.

These incoming coaches led to the demise of older vehicles, with former *Edith Kent* Commer No.38 (CG 1724) being de-licensed at the end of February, whilst Bedford WLB's Nos.61/2 (OY 2093 and OY 5807) were withdrawn about March. The last of the former *Howlett* Star 'Flyer' coaches, No.4 (MY 4213) was withdrawn in March, whilst Gilford 166SD-type MY 346 also came out of use around then.

Sharped-eyed readers may well be wondering what No.66 was? Well, this was the fourth 'Ace' of the Spring intake, though it was not a new purchase, this being the former No.64 (FJ 9581) of the Worthy Down crash! After some delays to the insurance claim, it had finally been decided to have it repaired, and George Amor drove the damaged coach to Hendon, where Duple refurbished it before it came back to Northcroft Lane for re-painting. However, the fleet number 64 had been allocated to the Ford bought as an urgent replacement, so the 'Ace' took the next vacant number.

Whilst mentioning the Northcroft Road premises, it should be noted that No.5, which was formerly used by Percy Andrews, was now the confectionary depot for J.Lyons & Co. Ltd., cake manufacturers an the owners of a chain of restaurants. At The Wharf several changes took place during the year. Firstly, approval was given for Newbury Volunteer Fire Brigade to erect a drill tower in February, which often appears in the background of photos taken at that site and makes a useful source for dating, whilst Travis & Arnold re-located its wood-yard to Mill Lane in July, allowing more surface area for the use of buses.

There was another local takeover of a small coach operator during June, when *The Newburian* operated by garage owners *Murray & Whittaker* of St. John's Garage, Newtown Road, Newbury was taken over by *George Hedges (Reliance Motor Services)* of Brightwalton. He continued to run their 1934 Duple-bodied Bedford WLB coach (JB 4789) under its old name through to the war years, then later as part of the *Reliance* fleet. This acquisition right under the noses of *Newbury & District* no doubt irritated some of the Directors, as this now gave Hedges both booking and picking up facilities in the town!

The bodywork on the Dennis 'Aces' varied quite a lot, but No.69 (DYF 184) had the most differences, with its stepped waistrail, glazed quarter lights and extensive sunshine roof.

One route alteration introduced from June reinstated a link for the residents of Hungerford Newtown, though in a different format. Instead of providing the previous service to Hungerford, the new facility was formed by extending Route 8 (Newbury – Shefford Woodlands) onto Hungerford Newtown, a further 5 minutes on, this running on Thursdays and Saturdays only.

During the early part of July an offer was received from *Ernest Nobes* of Lambourn Woodlands, who was interested in combining with *Newbury & District.*

Ernest Edward Nobes

Ernest Nobes was born in 1894 in Bexleyheath, Kent, the son of Henry and Sarah. By 1915 his father took the position of Head Gardener on the Inholmes Estate of Henry Cubitt Gooch, south of Woodlands St. Mary in west Berkshire. Later still the family moved to Lambourn Woodlands, where they occupied Hurst Farm, some 12.3 miles north-west of Newbury.

During the First World War Ernie trained as an Engineer with Vickers-Armstrong Aircraft at Weybridge, lodging nearby in Addlestone. In such employment he was exempt from call-up for war service, and during those years he learnt much that was to stand him in good stead over the years to come. After the war was over, several moves saw him marrying Winifred Billingham in the Hungerford area

of Berkshire in 1919, with their son Derek following during 1921, and they then settled at The Square in Lambourn Woodlands. However the family tradition of growing and farming did not appeal to him, as he wished to make further use of the practical skills learnt over the war years.

Road transport was still emerging after the Great War and, with such engineering experience to hand, he decided that his new enterprise would be a motorised carrier's service. Although the area had been served in the pre-war era by several carriers, but *Albert Palmer* carried on, but as a farmer he was more concerned with the transport of livestock to Newbury market on Thursdays, though he did buy a Chevrolet van in order to modernise and continued after the 1930 Act.

Ernie understood that people wanted to travel now that the war was over, and he purchased a Ford Model T in July 1923, which was fitted with a carrier's van body with seats for 14 arranged longitudinally along the body sides, and the grey-painted vehicle had only small windows set high up. Registered MO 1846, the van was garaged at Hurst Farm, though his route actually started from the nearby Chalker's Arms. The Newbury standing point at first was the Queens Hotel, though this was duly switched to the yard of the Craven Cycle Works in Bartholomew Street.

The service ran to Newbury on Thursdays and Saturdays, starting from Lambourn Woodlands on Saturdays, but with an extension to Baydon on Thursdays. He also soon provided similar facilities to Swindon (13.6 miles away) on Mondays and Hungerford (6 miles away) on Wednesday, these being the market days in those towns. Tuesdays was reserved for maintenance and the building of wireless sets, a sideline of his which supplemented his income. The same applied to Fridays, though a certain amount of local haulage and private hire might also undertaken on those days.

The Swindon service left Woodlands St. Mary at 9.45am and called at Lambourn Woodlands and Baydon, returning from Swindon (Regents Circus) at 3pm, so when it was duly licensed under the 1930 Act is was classed as an 'express' service.

Behind Ernie's father and his chickens is the original Ford Model T carrier's van (MO 1846) at Hurst Farm. Note the small and high windows provided.

Maintenance was fairly straightforward on such basic engines and accessible axles, though a regular problem was that the wooden spokes of the rear wheels were prone to shrinkage in hot weather. Ernie soon found that driving the rear of the van into the pond at Hurst Farm worked a treat for a restorative soak! The early inflatable tyres were also quite easily punctured on the rough local roads, so even two spare wheels was not always enough. However, a nearby pond or cattle trough would also provide the solution to this ailment too, as the puncture could soon be located by the escape of air bubbles in the water!

On Saturdays he would travel into Newbury early and collect groceries etc., in order to return to Lambourn Woodland by midday. After lunch he would take the

local cricket or football team to a fixture, often as not playing himself, before returning home afterwards. He was indeed a keen local sportsman, playing cricket for Inholmes CC and football for Lambourn Woodlands FC and Baydon FC. The early evening saw him with a good load of passengers off to Newbury for the cinema, then a fish-and-chip supper before they set off home!

The venture was indeed a success, and in 1929 Ernest had the chance to buy a larger Ford 'Ton-bus', this being a 1925 model new to *Richard Pestell* of Wash Common for his *Wash Common Bus Service*. Registered MO 4614, it was named *The Doris* in honour of Mrs. Pestell, and the varnished wooden body had 14 seats in relative comfort. As Ernest had a sister-in-law of the same Christian name, he left the name on the sides. By that time he also had a Ford Model T car, and he undertook all of the maintenance, though the original Ford van (MO 1846) was sold in April 1930.

His son Derek had helped out during the school holidays, but in 1935 he became his full-time assistant, a carrier needing a lad to run the numerous errands. He would regularly go to the favoured grocer's shops in the towns visited, leaving a list to the cry of 'order for Nobes', and the completed orders would then be taken to the bus in time for the return journey by the grocer's boy. Other items were carried 'on approval', such as boots and shoes, the villagers then placing orders via Ernie for which the traders paid commission. All manner of goods, including medicines, were obtained by the carriers, whilst villagers could also send produce and small livestock to the towns. The latter was carried on the tailgate, though on one occasion some pigs managed to escape, leaving Ernie, Derek and the fitter passengers to round them up from a wood near Stockcross!

Ernie Nobes.

133

As if this was not a busy enough life, Ernie was also quite musical, playing the piano, mandolin and violin, and that tradition lived on with his son Derek and daughters Beryl and Mary all taking turns as the organist at Woodland St. Mary's Church. Derek even went a step further, forming his own dance band in due course.

That Ernie was a popular local man was certainly the case and, having one of the few motor vehicles locally, he was inevitably asked to do all sorts of tasks. On one occasion he did a favour for the family of an old gamekeeper friend of his from Baydon that was one he did not forget in a hurry. The old chap had died and, as the family was poor, and had offered to save them having to take the coffin by hand-cart the 4 miles for the burial. However, it was discovered that the narrow stairs of the cottage would not allow for the occupied coffin to be manoeuvred down, so he had no option but to carry the old chap down separately!

Despite being popular, it was still possible in a small community to fall-out with individuals. One lady decided that his fare of 2 shillings return to Newbury was excessive, thereafter walking the 4 miles each way to the nearest railway halt, where she paid 1 shilling and 6 pence, despite the bus offering a door-to-door service.

He also duly fell out with his relatives at Hurst Farm, thereafter keeping his bus at The Square and maintaining it by the roadside. With the better vehicle came some Sunday excursions to the coast, Southsea being the favourite destination. At one point near Wickham it was sometimes necessary for some of the fitter passengers to alight and walk up the hill, but generally the vehicle gave good service.

Chevrolet TM 5726 with its original owner.

In early 1936 the Ford was in need of replacement, so a secondhand Chevrolet LQ-type was purchased from a dealer on the Goldhawk Road in west London. This was TM 5726, which was new in September 1929 and carried a 16-seater front-entrance bus body by Economy of Lowestoft, and had been new to *F.A. Jenkins (Perseverance)* of Shillington. It retained the royal blue and cream livery of the former owner, though it nearly came to grief on the journey home from the dealers, as a runaway hay-cart careered towards it near Hungerford! The arrival of this led to the disposal of Ford bus MO 4614.

However, in June 1938 Derek joined the RAF as a Flight Engineer, though long-term the plan was to return to work in partnership with his father, as the two had planned to operate a petrol station, taxi and haulage business. On the bus front, Ernie decided to sell his routes to *N&D*, which they paid £50 cash for, employing him as the driver of what now became the Lambourn Woodlands outstation. The Chevrolet bus was also acquired, but it was not used, and it languished in the yard behind the Mill Lane garage for a while before disposal. With the outbreak of War again in September 1939 he was switched to a daily contract run to the Didcot Ordnance Depot from his home area and was then driving a Dennis 'Ace'.

Before we move on with the main story, there are two significant operators of the 'north-west frontier', just over the border in Wiltshire, which will be reviewed.

Edward John Claridge

Various members of the Claridge family of Ramsbury and Aldbourne, Wiltshire provided transport over a number of generations, the first being *James Claridge* (uncle of *Edward Claridge)* of Ramsbury, who operated two Wallis & Steevens traction engines by 1892 in partnership with the local iron-founder and agricultural equipment maker *Stephen Osmond*, undertaking haulage work, agricultural contracting, threasing, and even some local outings, towing wagons and hay-carts for the passengers!

Charles Claridge, who was Edward's father's cousin, also became involved with transport from around 1912-14, as driver of a Foden steam wagon for the Swindon-based removals firm Henly's, which was fitted with a large wooden box body for long-distance work.

John Claridge, father of Edward, had set himself up in early 1914 as a market gardener, and had a number of horses in connection with that business. This led him to operate some passenger work as a side-line, taking people in his 3-passenger 'trap' from Aldbourne to Hungerford station, some 7.5 miles away. This was interrupted by the Great War, as he enlisted in 1916 in the Devonshire Regiment.

The Ramsbury Primitive Methodist Sunday School Annual Outing 1892, at The Pond in Aldbourne, with James Claridge on footplate of the engine. The girls in white dresses are as far from the engine as possible!

Returning to peacetime in 1919, he re-commenced his trades as before, finding increased demand for his transport services, so he purchased a 5-seater 'buggy' and a 7-seater 'wagonette', both of these also being used for pleasure outings, though still limited to the scope of horse-power. Mechanisation came in 1924, when he purchased a 1907 Vulcan 20hp touring car (HR 1475), which had a canvas-roofed, blue-painted body large enough to accommodate an entire football team, as it did at times! With the British Empire Exhibition held at Wembley a popular destination that year, he also used it for a number of excursions there. At times he would also hire-in a larger charabanc if demand warranted, rather than turn trade away, and at least once it was a vehicle from the *Bristol Tramways* fleet that was used for a trip to Weymouth.

For 1926 he purchased a secondhand Ford Model T 14-seater charabanc from Reading operator *Charlie Cox*, which had a London area registration plate. This was a good vehicle and was quite capable of the longer runs to Bournemouth and Weymouth. At other times it could be used for some haulage or removals work, whilst the Vulcan car continued in use as a taxi. This chara later became a lorry in the Chiseldon area, whilst *John Claridge* is remembered for selling his produce by going round the village with an old pram.

Edward Claridge was born at Aldbourne in 1908, and his early jobs included being employed by the other Aldbourne carrier *Thomas Barnes,* who we shall hear more of shortly. In that capacity he took up his first transport task at the age of 13, when he took a single-horse 7-seater wagonette three times a day to meet the trains at Hungerford at 11.15am, 4.15pm and 7.15 pm on the occasion of the Aldbourne Fair in 1921. Even though *Ted Claridge* duly undertook carrying work from the same village, their services did not really compete. Ted and *Tommy Barnes* remained friends and often worked together, payment often being by cancelling out each other's bills!

In 1927 his father put him in charge of the transport operations, which were expanded under the title of *Ramsbury Motor Services* between 1927-9. The first regular service was started between Aldbourne and Swindon, running via Foxhill, and operated on Mondays (market day) and Fridays.

Next came a link to Hungerford via Ramsbury and Chilton Foliat on Wednesdays (market day), Fridays and Saturdays, followed by a Wednesdays-only route from Shefford Woodlands to Hungerford. Next came a service from Aldbourne – Marlborough, which ran via Ramsbury – Axford which operated on Tuesdays, Fridays and Saturdays, with an extension on Sundays onto Savernake Hospital and Savernake Forest, the forest being a popular local beauty spot, whilst also providing a useful link for hospital visitors.

Service 4.	Ald.	Bay	Lam.	Lic Frm	Ham New	Sheff Woodd	Wick	Wick Hth	Stock	New Bury
Aldbourne		4d	8d	10d	1/-	1/-	1/3	1/5	1/6	1/9
Baydon	4d		2d	5d	10d	10d	1/2	1/3	1/4	1/6
Lambourne (W).+Rds	8d	2d		2d	6d	6d	10d	1/-	1/2	1/4
Licwood Farm	10d	5d	2d		4d	4d	7d	10	1/-	1/2
Hungerford (New)	1/-	10d	6d	4d		2d	6d	8d	9d	1/-
Shefford (W).+Rds.	1/-	10d	6d	4d	2d		3d	5d	7d	10
Wickham	1/3	1/2	10d	7d	6d	3d		2d	4d	7
Wickham (Hth)	1/5	1/3	1/-	10d	8d	5d	2d		2d	6d
Stockcross	1/6	1/4	1/2	1/-	9d	7d	4d	2d		3d
Newbury	1/9	1/6	1/4	1/2	1/-	10d	7d	6d	3d	

Edward J. Claridge.

Fare-cards such as these were carried on the buses and were drafted out by Ted Claridge. They are shown at approximately one-third original size.

Service 3.	Ald	Fox	Lid	Swin
Aldbourne		5d	8d	1/-
Foxhill	5d		3d	8d
Liddington	8d	3d		4d
Swindon	1/-	8d	4d	

Edward J. Claridge

He duly turned his attention to Newbury, with a Thursdays-only run via Ramsbury – Hungerford – Wickham, plus another run via Baydon – Lambourn Woodlands – Wickham. All of the services took both passengers and goods, and when the Aldbourne to Swindon carrier *Charlie Wilkins* (who used a 14-seater Ford Model T bus) decided to give up, his service was absorbed.

The operation remained based at Aldbourne, but a branch office was set up in Oxford Street, Ramsbury through a relative there, helping to elicit bookings for excursions, private hire, removals and general haulage work. A livery of orange with black trim was adopted, though the Vulcan car remained blue, earning the vehicles the nickname *The Golden Arrows*. Full identities of the other vehicles owned are not recorded, though the following details of what they were, their use and origins were provided by Ted himself:

Ford T 1-ton covered lorry – This had a wood-and-canvas body and was used mainly for removals work. However, it could also be fitted with bench seats for 14 passengers, and it was particularly useful for more utilitarian jobs such as transporting the Aldbourne sheep-shearing gang or the Military Band from Chilton Foliat and the Silver Band of the Ramsbury Primitive Methodist's due to all their respective tools and instruments. This was later scrapped for spares.

Ford T 7-cwt van - This had originally been used by a baker and had a Berkshire registration. It was mainly used in the Swindon area for parcel deliveries, but it was fitted with 7 seats for occasional passenger duties. It ended its days as a tool shed at the market garden.

Ford T 1-ton 14-seater bus – This was Berkshire-registered and purchased secondhand from Pass & Co. The saloon bus body had forward-facing seats a central gangway and front entrance. It was one of the longest-serving vehicles in the fleet.

Ford T 1-ton 14-seater bus – Registered as XH 8592, this had started life as a van used on Post Office contracts by McNamara's in London, passing to *John Prothero*, who had a 14-seater bus body constructed. It stayed through to the end of operations by *Ramsbury Motor Services*, passing to a new owner at Hinton Parva, who converted it back to a closed van for parcels work in the Swindon area.

Ford T 1-ton open platform lorry – Purchased secondhand from a Swindon owner and used on general haulage work, including agricultural produce or sand and gravel. It was re-sold later to another firm in Swindon. A known photo suggests this might be HR 6311, but the motor tax records are incomplete.

Buick 'Majestic' 5-seater car – This was used for several years as a taxi and for small private hires until sold to a new owner in Swindon.

During the late 1920's the Road Motors of the *Great Western Railway* appeared on various roads with the area covered by *Ramsbury Motor Services*, though this made little difference to the loyal local clientele.

Regular excursions were operated from an early date, with those to the usual South Coast resorts between Brighton and Weymouth, along with more local trips to Savernake Forest, Oxford and Cheddar. In keeping with his father's principle of never turning a job down, young Ted did not worry if a hire exceeded his capacity, and he met an exceptional hire in connection with the Fairford Annual Carnival & Band Contest in 1930 by hiring a Ford 14-seater apiece from *Tommy*

Barnes and *Charlie Wilkins,* along with a pair of Reos from *Cosy Coaches* from Fairford.

The Ford bus XH 8592 seen at the Fairford Carnival with Ted Claridge leaning on a hired-in Reo coach of Cosy Coaches. Note the horse-shoe on the radiator!

However, the coming of the 1930 Act came hard to Ted and his little fleet, although he did get licenses to continue the bulk of his operations. When it came to the attentions of the Vehicle Inspectors, he soon found himself at loggerheads with the local man, who had already told him he had been with *Bristol Tramways* for many years. The latter was of course already nearby, following the transfer of the remaining *Great Western Railway* bus routes in exchange for a shareholding by the Railway, and *Ted Claridge* now came to the conclusion (as did so many others of his kind) that the Act unfairly favoured the territorial operators.

During early 1932 Ted's frustrations came to a head and the operations of *Ramsbury Motor Services* ceased, and all remaining vehicles were sold or reduced to spares. Ted now took up a job assisting *H.N. Pragnell* of West Tytherton, Hampshire, in expanding his established milk-collection service to the Newbury area. A trio of drop-side lorries was outstationned at Aldworth and Ted drove one of those.

Ted Claridge with Vulcan 4-tonner WV 3189, one of the lorries used on the milk collection operation.

136

After about two years on the milk-collection work Ted decided to leave and return to bus work, taking up the job of driver with *City of Oxford* and remaining with them for many more years, finally passing away in 2001 in his 93rd year.

However, the Claridge transport dynasty did not end there, as Ted's son *Michael Claridge* duly entered the industry on coaching work as partner on *Bennett's Coaches & Sliverline Holidays,* based at the Orchard Garage in Chieveley. There he met *Simon Weaver,* who in turn commenced his own bus and coach operations as *Weavaway Travel,* and Michael worked there until his own retirement in 2008, whilst it is also worth noting that latterly Simon's diverse operations have seen the revival of bus services running under the *Newbury & District* name!

Thomas Dixon Barnes

Tommy Barnes was born in the Wiltshire village of Aldbourne in February 1886, spending his early working days as a plough boy, agricultural labourer and also as a runner for the local carriers. The latter type of work appealed to him, resulting in him having the chance to succeed *Jimmy Martin* when he retired in 1920, having been running the service for him from 1916, after his son *Charlie* emigrated to Australia.

Tommy inherited the horse-drawn van, along with a 7-seater wagonette and an established coal merchant's business, taking on young *Ted Claridge* to help him out at busy times from 1921, and thereby being influential in his future involvement with transport. The carriers service ran daily on Mondays to Saturdays from Aldbourne through Preston – Whittonditch – Knighton – Chilton Foliat to Hungerford, and featured all the usual facilities of house-to-house collections and deliveries. Tommy also continued the previous owner's practice of collecting coal supplies from Hungerford station goods yard and carting them back to Aldbourne, before sweeping out the van for the afternoon return run from Hungerford. Parcels were also collected from the station for taking along the route, mail order shopping then being well-established for everything from clothing to seeds, and the van also conveyed newspapers delivered by train.

As noted previously, *Ted Claridge* duly set up as a carrier from the village, though he and Tommy were never rivals, as each offered different routes and later often worked together on larger private hires. Motorisation came with the purchase of a Ford Model T 1-tonner in 1924, which had removable seats for 9 passengers, these being designed by local carpenter Fred Jerram to slide into place through the rear doors, the vehicle being painted blue and black. It was new on the first day of 1924 from Pass & Co., supplied as an estate van at Benham Park, before re-sale to him.

The basic pattern of service was continued, though an extension onto Newbury was added on Thursdays at a return fare of 10 old pence. With the motor vehicle it was now possible to run into Hungerford earlier for the train to London for those wishing to travel there, whilst the practice of collecting the coal continued, with the seats removed. The same vehicle was then swept out after lunch and returned to passenger duties for the afternoon return journey. However, Tommy did not do the driving of the motor vehicle, employing others instead. In Newbury the lay-over point was The Bear, even as late as 1930, though that was relocated to The Wharf about 1932. The couple had sons *Robert Harris Barnes* (Bob) in April 1917 and *James Thomas Lionel Barnes* (Jim) in June 1922, who would join the business initially as carrier's runners on Saturdays and in school holidays.

The original business premises consisted of a house in The Square, with a café in the lean-to building next door. The former garden and orchard area became the parking area and coal yard, then later a garage was constructed. In 1957 the Bell Inn, on the opposite side of the entrance road into the garage, closed and was bought to form the office accommodation and to expand the yard area behind.

In January 1927 a second Ford T was added in the shape of MR 8557, which could also be used for both passengers and goods, and this was followed in January 1929 by a pair of 14-seater buses also on the extended Model T Ford chassis. These were registered as MW 3700/1, though one was painted blue whilst the other was in a stained brown finish, and their arrival saw the practice of using the passenger vehicles for coal work ceasing. However, the coal business was continued using one of the older vehicles, the 1924 Ford staying until the end of September 1934, whilst the trade was continued until 1983, when problems with industrial disputes led to its winding up.

Ford AA-type WV 1456 with rather basic carrier's bus body, is seen with sons Bob and Jim outside the Aldbourne premises.

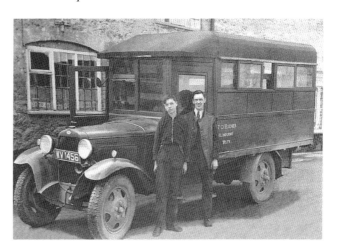

Two Ford AA-types followed in July 1931 (MW 9725) and June 1932 (WV 1456), both supplied by Pass & Co. with carriers van bodies with seats for 14, along with room for parcels and livestock. Also, from 1935, a regular contract for the carrying of eggs was obtained as another use for the goods vehicle.

The carriers service continued in similar fashion, with sons *Bob* and *Jim Barnes* becoming involved from about 1933, along with their sister *Ena* and her husband *Joe Hewlett*, whilst their mother continued with running a café and bed-and-breakfast, both of which had featured since the 1920's. Indeed, the family recalled that at leaner times, these businesses provided a useful additional income. Both *Tommy* and his wife *Ada* were prominent in local life, the former being secretary of the Aldbourne Band and a linesman with the Swindon District League of Football, whilst Mrs. Barnes was involved with the local Methodist chapel and other local causes, so naturally enough a lot of private hire work emanated from these widespread contacts.

The door-to-door carrying declined once villagers got cars, and it was finally abandoned in the early 1960's, though the parcels delivery service was continued. The older Ford T's were replaced by two Ford BB-type 14-seaters in December 1934 (WV 6826) and September 1935 (WV 8849), which again came from Pass & Co. The first was a bus, whilst the latter was described as a coach, reflecting the increasing importance of such work. These vehicles remained in use until June 1948 and June 1951 respectively, but dates for earlier disposals of vehicles are not known.

Both the sons were away on military service during WW2, with Bob serving in the 8th Army in Africa and Jim going into the RAF. Following their return, a re-assessment of the business saw the emphasis change to contract work and private hire, though the early post-war shortage of vehicles slowed the process. A good trade was developed on school runs, worker's contracts, including those to AERE Harwell, and as conditions improved the coach excursions were started. In due course they were also contracted to provide relief coaches for *Associated Motorways* of Cheltenham, taking the fleet to some new locations.

As already noted, both the carriers service and coal business continued after the war, and from the mid-1950's Jim's son *Lionel* was looking after the carrier's side using a brown Bedford van. Jim took charge of the coal business and Bob the coach side, the business being re-named as *T.D Barnes & Sons* in 1951.

Whereas the pre-war livery had been blue, a scheme of pale green was adopted post-war. *Tommy Barnes* passed away in early 1974 aged 87, preceded by wife Ada in 1967 aged 79, whilst Bob and Jim passed away in January and September 1990, and they were succeeded by Jim's son Lionel and his concert excursions and a travel bureau service. Subsequent developments are out of the scope of this study, though it is worth noting that further family members would come along and continue the firm's success through to the present day, and by the 75th anniversary in 1995 the fleet consisted of 23 coaches. At the time of writing the *Barnes Coaches* fleet can be seen widely, and some market-day contract operations still travel to Newbury as a link with the early days.

****

N&D took over the following pattern of operations from *Ernest Nobes:*
Thursdays and Saturdays-only Lambourn Woodlands – Newbury service, which ran by way of Woodlands St. Mary – Poughley – Shefford Woodlands – Wickham – Wickham Heath – Stockcross – Speen. There was also an extension from Baydon at 9.20am on Thursdays, with a return trip from Newbury at 3.45pm; and a Mondays-only 'express' between Woodlands St. Mary and Swindon, which perpetuated the original carrier's service on market day in Swindon, leaving at 9.45am and returning at 3.30pm.

These became Route 27 (Lambourn Woodlands or Baydon – Newbury) and 28 (Woodlands St.Mary – Swindon). The return fare from Baydon to Newbury was 2 shillings and 6 pence, or 1 shilling and 10 pence from Lambourn Woodlands, whilst the return fare to Swindon was 1 shilling and 3 pence from Woodlands St. Mary or Lambourn Woodlands. Ernest became the local booking agent and was also employed as the driver of his old routes, keeping the out-stationed bus outside his home in The Square.

Apart from the above there were remarkably few changes to the bus services during 1938, no doubt a reflection of the effort put into reviewing services during the previous couple of years. However, from early in August the Moulsford Special went over to operation on every Thursday rather than alternate ones only, and it also now started from The Wharf rather than Market Street.

Wycombe-bodied Gilford coach of the same batch as No.30 (JD 1220).

July saw the arrival three full-size vehicles, in the shape of a Gilford coach and a pair of Leyland saloon buses. The coach came from the dealer Dawson and was a 168OT-type carrying a 26-seater front-entrance body by Wycombe, new in April 1931 to the large fleet of that make operated by *Edward Hillman* from Romford, Essex. His operations were duly taken over by *London Transport* and re-organised under *Green Line*. This coach received vacant fleet No.30 (JD 1220), but when noted as such in the garage during September 1938, it had still not been repainted or put into use. Indeed, as it was sold by March 1939, this would seem to be a project that was not completed.

The Leyland saloons were both 'Lion' PLSC3-types chassis and carried Leyland 35-seater front-entrance bodies, and these became Nos.28 (RU 8058) and 29 (RU 7559). They came from one of the Southampton area dealers, Jeffries of Hedge End, but had been new to *Hants & Dorset Motor Services* in October and June 1928 respectively. As with previous examples from that fleet, the green paintwork was in good condition just a white waistband was added.

Leyland 'Lion' No.28 (RU 8058) at The Wharf on the service to Kingsclere in August 1939.

Star 'Flyer' coach No.28 (GU 7545) had evidently been withdrawn prior to July, though the date is not recorded. A number of other vehicles were also withdrawn by August, again with exact dates unknown, and these were Gilfords VM 3669, No.25 (VM 8638) and VR 9822, along with the Strachan-bodied 166OT-type (believed to be TM 5639). Former *Burt & Greenwood* Federal coach (GJ 9733?) had also gone by that date, along with the rear-entrance Thornycroft RA 1794.

During August the final sequel to the Worthy Down crash saw damages of £3,600 awarded against *N&D* on behalf of those injured.

September saw three further PLSC3-type 'Lions' coming from Jeffries and originating with *Hants & Dorset.* Two of these had Leyland 35-seater front-

entrance bodies and became Nos.40 (RU 5072) and 41 (RU 7560), being new in April 1927 and July 1928 respectively. The third example (RU 5394) carried a 32-seater Brush body, but this was not for operation and was used for spare parts for the other four. PLSC1 'Lion' No.40 (VA 7943) had evidently been taken out of service by then, and as it did not have a further owner, this may have also joined the spares pool?

Leyland 'Lion' No.40 (RU 5072) when new to Hants & Dorset. These PLSC3-types had 5.1 litre petrol engines with four cylinders and were fitted with bus bodies by Leyland's own coach-building shops.

Also departing in September was Reo 'Pullman' coach No.26 (RX 6264), which had been purchased new by *Durnford*, this being the last of that make in the fleet. That fleet number was re-issued in October to another incoming Thornycroft (RD 6270), though of a variety not yet represented at Newbury. This was an 'Ardent' of December 1934, which carried a Park Royal 26-seater front-entrance bus body. This had been new to *G. Jarvis & Son (Reading & Distrct)*, and had passed to *Thames Valley* with the Reading – Yattendon route on the first day of 1936. After that it saw a short spell of use until sold to *A. Ford & Son* of Silchester, from whom *N&D* acquired it.

Thornycroft 'Ardent' No.26 (RD 6270) seen on an outing from The Elephant pub, Reading when in use by Thames Valley. Could that really be Adolf Hitler in the front centre?

At the November Board Meeting the Directors sent their personal thanks to all employees for their efforts in keeping the services operating, and in particular for ensuring that good relations were maintained with the

Traffic Commissioner. Special praise was directed at Boss Denham and Percy Andrews in respect of the high standard of fleet maintenance and reliability.

The month of December saw one further vehicle withdrawn, this being Bedford WLB-type UN 5227, making it the last of that type in use by *N&D*.

Gilford VM 3669 is one of the vehicles for which the fleet number is not known, and despite this second photo having only just come to light, that remains the case, as here we see Ted Claridge standing in front of where the number was painted! Although Ted never mentioned driving for N&D, this photo suggests he may have undertaken some coach work for them.

The storm-clouds had been settling over Europe for several years, leading once again to the threat of war. As a result of this the Government had been pursuing various plans in preparation, one of which involved the building of 'shadow factories' in rural locations in order that essential production could be maintained away from the obvious targets of industry. All of this was undertaken 'on the quiet', using locations spread throughout the countryside, and for these projects the construction workers were taken to the site by buses. The pace of these activities speeded up as the latter-day optimism of 1938 gave way to the inevitability of further conflict.

Airfield construction, or the re-opening of those from the Great War, was also undertaken, and we shall hear more of this in the next chapter, though it had been taking place steadily since 1935. Once again, the area west of London was considered very suitable to receive further air bases, and again the local operators were contracted to get the workers to the sites.

However, another facet of the National mood was to enjoy the Summer of 1939, though no one quite realised how long it would be before a normal life would return. This final peacetime season would prove a bumper one for the coach fleet, most of which would soon be lost to the war effort, either as a direct result of requisitioning, or by spending those years on contract worker's services.

Over the Winter of 1938/9 several high-quality coaches were acquired and re-painted. One was this Leyland 'Tiger' TS1 of 1929, but by then with a 1935 Alexander 32-seater body, which became No.72 (MS 8438). It was turned out in superb fashion and became pride-of-the-fleet for its rather short stay. The driver is Boss Denham and the venue is Southsea. Note how the roof-line panels have been re-used by N&D.

Chapter 12 – 1939

During February *N&D* had acquired what was one of the finest coaches ever owned, when Harry Lane sold them Leyland 'Tiger' TS1-type MS 8438. Although new in April 1929 to *W. Alexander & Sons,* it was re-bodied in 1935 with a 'Bluebird' front-entrance 32-seater coach body built at their associated coachworks, and this was both stylish externally and well-appointed internally. This vehicle became No.72 and was turned out immaculately in time for Easter, very much pride of the fleet. Drivers recalled that this coach really sped along, powered by the Leyland 6.8 litre 6-cylinder petrol engine and, in normal circumstances this vehicle should have seen many more years of service at Newbury.

Also purchased during February were two secondhand Bedford lorries, which came from Marchant's Garage in Greenham Road, Newbury. One was new in March 1935 as JB 5917, when it was delivered to *James & Co.,* Great West Mills, Hungerford, whilst the other was ABL 459, new in October 1936 to an unrecorded (possibly also the same) owner. Both were 2.5-tonners, but their fleet numbers are not known.

However, on the coaching front, it was proving to be a very busy year, and in May another Leyland coach was acquired. This was of the less common LT5A variant of the 4-cylinder engined 'Lion' and had been new in May 1934 to *G. Burnham (The Grey Luxury Coaches)* of Clifton-on-Teme, near Worcester. It had another well-appointed and stylish rear-entrance 32-seater body, but this was by Burlingham of Blackpool, becoming No.73 (WP 6206).

By March two of the Gilfords, 168OT-types No.30 (JD 1220) and No.48 (MS 9336) departed, the former having not seen any use at Newbury. April saw a third vehicle of that make ousted, this being AS6-type No.53 (HX 1855).

As already noted, military planning was well underway since 1938, with the construction of air fields, 'shadow' factories and a number of storage depots with good rail access. In some instances where the distance was too far to make bringing the vehicle back during the day economical, contracts were covered by older types that would probably have departed by then, and these had part-time drivers who spent the day working as carpenters or bricklayers at the site. These additional contracts saw *N&D* vehicles out-stationed at Bucklebury, Hungerford, Lambourn, Stockcross and West Ilsley.

The building of airfields was particularly labour-intensive, though most were built in phases. Many never progressed beyond basic landing strips, whilst others were given heavy-duty runways, technical blocks and accommodation. Other existing airfields were re-activated or expanded for their wartime role. Harwell for instance, had a grass landing strip until construction of concrete runways between July and November 1941. Quite a few sites within striking distance of Newbury were surveyed, though as the war progressed, a number were handed over to the United States Air Force. The Company ran contracts to many of these over the period 1938-43, but no official records survive. For convenience those to which *Newbury & District* ran contracts (or are quite likely to have done so) are summarised below:

Airfield Name	Notes	Opened
Abingdon	RAF airfield already in use	1932
Aldermaston	Allocated to USAAF	1942
Andover*	RAF airfield already in use	WW1
Benson@	RAF airfield already in use	1939
Brize Norton@	RAF airfield already in use	1937
Chattis Hill*	Previously used by RAF	WW1
Chilbolton*	To assist RAF Middle Wallop	1940
Culham@	Royal Naval air station	1941
Frost Hill Fm.*	To assist RAF Odiham	1940
Greenham Cm.	Allocated to USAAF	1942
Great Shefford	Relief landing field (little used)	1940
Grove	RAF airfield north of Wantage	1942
Harwell	RAF airfield already in use	1937
Kingston Bagpuize@	USAAF base	1942
Larks Barrow*	To assist Worthy Dn./Andover	1943
Marlborough#	Private airfield used for training	1936
Membury	RAF, later used by USAAF	1941
Middle Wallop*	RAF airfield started 1938, ready	1940
Hampstead N.	RAF bomber training airfield	1940
Mount Farm@	Satelite field to RAF Benson	1940
Nuneham Pk.@	Camp only – no airfield	1940
Oakley@	RAF field north east of Oxford	1942
Overton Hth.#	Replaced Marlborough	1942
Ramsbury#	Allocated to USAAF	1942
Shellingford@	RAF airfield already in use	1931
Stanton Harcourt@	RAF airfield	1940
Thame@	RAF glider training field	1940
Theale	Public airfield taken by RAF	1940
Thruxton*	RAF airfield started 1940, ready	1942
Up. Heyford@	RAF airfield already in use	WW1
Wanborough#	RAF airfield south of Swindon	1940
Watchfield	RAF training/air traffic training	1939
Welford	RAF bomber base started 10/41	1943
Worthy Down*	RAF airfield already in use	WW1
Wroughton#	RAF base - built in phases from 1938	

*Those marked * were in Hampshire, those marked # in Wiltshire and those marked @ were in Oxfordshire, all others being in Berkshire at that time.*

N&D drivers also noted lengthy contract runs during the construction of Army Camps at Barton Stacey in Hampshire south of Whitchurch, and at Compton Bassett, just east of Calne in Wiltshire, as well as later camps around the Ogbournes north of Marlborough. Particularly significant were also the factories set up by Vickers Armstrong Aero at Eddington, just north of Hungerford and at Theale, which would see round-the-clock working in order to meet aircraft targets.

In respect of the bus services, there were no significant changes until 21st May, when the Newbury Local Services were once again revised as Routes A and B. In reality all the points previously served were still covered, but the re-arrangements made better use of the two buses employed. Route A ran between Shaw and Wash Common, travelling via The Broadway and Station Road, whilst Route B radiated out from The Broadway to various points in rotation. It started the day running out to Camp Close, returning to The Broadway, when it then went to Kingsbridge Road. On returning to The Broadway, it then left for Hambridge Road, then after that it was the turn of Donnington to be served, that pattern repeating throughout the day on weekdays and Saturdays. The Sunday service was somewhat sparser and only covered the afternoon and evening periods.

A couple of N&D drivers pose with Dennis 'Ace' No.65 (JY 4752), decorated with union jack flags on the radiator. Such carefree days would soon be over.

A sign of the building tension of those times was the last-minute cancellation of the Tidworth Tattoo, which should have run from late July into early August, this being due to military units being placed on stand-by. The Territorial Army companies were also mobilised and sent to training camps, and *Newbury & District* soon put in place a number of day excursions to allow relatives to visit those away at the camps on the designated 'visiting Sundays' during

July and August. These camps were at Corfe Castle (Dorset), Chiseldon (near Swindon, Wiltshire) and on Salisbury Plain, and coaches ran from Newbury, Hungerford, Thatcham, Headley, Chieveley and Kingsclere, with an additional run for the Sports Day held at Chiseldon on Monday 7th August.

One of the 'Yorkshire Lions' was No.56 (HD 4371), seen here on 15th June 1941 at Bucklebury. The driver was Bill Eggleton and the conductor Len Goodman.

Another significant purchase of Leyland vehicles occurred in July, when a quartet of identical LT2-type 'Lions' arrived. These had originated with *Yorkshire Woollen District* of Dewsbury in May 1931, and all carried 30-seater front-entrance Leyland-built bodies. These were allocated vacant fleet numbers 47/8 (HD 4369 and 4368) and 51/6 (HD 4370/1).

Vehicles disposed of at about this time were a mixed bunch, with No.42 (OU 6047), the last AJS in the fleet, along with Thornycroft No.15 (OT 4452), both having come from *Edith Kent* in 1937.

A further pair of Gilfords were also taken out of service by the time the 'Lions' arrived, these being No.51 (HJ 8718) and No.23 (TO 9554).

The only significant change in the ranks of the shareholders in 1939 occurred in August, when Percy Andrews sold his interest in the Company, though he continued in his employment as Garage Foreman with Boss Denham.

During August a further 20-seater Thornycroft bus was acquired, being an A2Long-type with a 20-seater, front-entrance body by Challands Ross. This had been new in July 1930 to *B. Mace* of Shouldham, near Kings Lynn in Norfolk, passing with his operations to *Johnson* of Kings Lynn. It became No.18 (VF 9339), and its arrival led to the sale of Thornycroft No.11 (KM 3028).

Also withdrawn in August was the last of the Stars, with No.27 (HX 1059), which was also the last of the vehicles brought in by Charlie Durnford. That month also saw the end of GMC bus No.37 (FM 6487).

The August Bank Holiday period proved another bumper time for the coach fleet, as people went out to take their minds off what was now becoming the inevitability of another Europe-wide war. As such, the coach fleet was at its zenith, though the active use of these as vehicles of luxury would soon be brought to an abrupt end.

GMC's had once been quite numerous at Newbury, and No.36 (FM 6486) was seen in service on the route to Aldworth on the August Bank Holiday 1939.

On Sunday 3rd September 1939 any hope of avoiding an all-out war was dispelled with the declaration of war by the British Government against Nazi Germany.

In view of the anticipated bombing and invasion threat, plans had been prepared to evacuate mothers and children from the towns most likely to be targets, and this process started on Friday 1st September. The Newbury area was regarded as a safe refuge, receiving scheduled evacuees from both Southampton and the London area. Those brought from London came by special *Great Western* trains to Newbury Racecourse station, being distributed in the town or surrounding villages by *N&D* buses. Of the 600 mothers and kids arriving on 1st September, 164 were taken to Thatcham, 150 to Cold Ash, 100 to Greenham and 86 to Brimpton, the remainder staying in the town. Some of those due had inadvertently got put off at Maidenhead, so these followed to Newbury the next day on *Thames Valley* buses.

During 1st and 2nd September some 500 mothers and children were brought up from Southampton to the station at Whitchurch on the Didcot, Newbury & Southampton line, being taken to their billets in Woodhay, Burghclere and Highclere by *N&D* buses, together with the rather lucky group of 30 treated to staying at Highclere Castle. Also on 1st and 2nd a further 800 evacuees were expected at Hungerford station, so about 30 *N&D* buses were sent there, but it transpired that they went further westwards.

Needless to say, these requirements led to the immediate cancellation of all tours and excursions due to run, and a public notice in the Newbury Weekly News outlined the Company's position. Private hire work was suspended in order to concentrate on contracts and other directed transport such as evacuees, whilst the haulage fleet was reserved for the transport of foodstuffs and other work of 'national importance'. Vehicles could still, however, be hired for the conveyance of Service Personnel, school children and workers involved in war-related tasks, the latter class of work soon involving many of the one-time coach fleet and some older saloons. Many of these locations were deliberately remote to avoid the chance of aerial bombing, which resulted in a number of vehicles being absent all day, only returning to Newbury infrequently, most spending the night parked at the driver's home.

As well as the various establishments set up locally to cope with war production and military centres, a number of large firms or government bodies were re-located outside the capitol, including The Law Society which took up residence at 142 Newtown Road in Newbury. In due course the *Great Western* moved some of its own departments to various properties in the Thatcham and Aldermaston area, though in that instance it was *Thames Valley* that provided the transport, basing 6 of its old Tilling-Stevens B9A's at Aldermaston station to undertake the daily transfers, with drivers either riding out on the Route 10 service buses or using one of the vehicles as they returned to Reading in rotation for maintenance and re-fuelling.

The 20-seater Thornycroft bought in August became No.18 (VF 9339) and is seen at Frilsham. Note the head-lamp masks, which made the lights virtually useless, along with the white-painted mudguards as an aid to other road users in black-out conditions. The removal of road signs meant that drivers had to rely on local knowledge, that having been done to confuse enemy paratroopers. However, the obliteration of 'Newbury' on the bus was just due to an accident!

Another view of Leyland 'Lion' No.56 (HD 4371) at The Bladebone Inn, Bucklebury Common in June 1941, as the bus was preparing to return to Newbury. This bus also has head-lamp masks and items painted white. The pub owes its name to the blade-bone of a mammoth unearthed in the area, a replica of which forms the inn sign over the front door of this Strange's Brewery house.

With the call-up of Reservists, the Company found itself with some temporary staffing difficulties, but as the Fitters and other Garage Staff held conductor's or driver's licenses, they helped out. 'Black-out' rulings applied to vehicles as well as buildings, with headlamps masked down to being virtually useless, so it was a good thing that the *N&D* drivers knew the local roads like the back of their hands, whilst the dim interiors made the work of the conductor difficult too! In order to make vehicles less conspicuous from the air, and therefore a tempting target for aircraft, white paintwork was replaced by grey, adding to the drab feel of the overall restrictions imposed by wartime conditions.

With so many vehicles committed to daily contracts, some reduction in the public service was inevitable, taking effect from the first week of September. These were kept to a minimum, and the only services that were completely withdrawn were the Fridays-only run from Hermitage to Reading, together with the Monday express service between Woodlands St. Mary and Swindon, plus the Baydon or Lambourn Woodlands to Newbury service, which only ran on Thursdays and Saturdays, Ernie Nobes was then switched to covering a daily contract run, of which we shall here more in due course. In order to partly compensate the residents of the Woodlands St. Mary area, arrangements were made for parcels to be dropped off using the contract bus - although that was for Thursdays and Saturdays

only, whilst an additional journey from nearby Shefford Woodlands was operated at 11.10am on Saturdays.

The separate Route 13 to North End was also deleted, as it shared the same roads out to Ball Hill with Route 12 to West Woodhay, which was modified to run via North End turn. All journeys timed to leave from The Wharf after 9.40pm were deleted, with the exception of those at 10.10pm and 10.40pm to Thatcham, which were garage-bound workings and provided a link to the eastern side of Newbury in place of the reduced Local Service.

A couple of weeks after the evacuees had arrived in Newbury, it was decided to transfer some 200 of the younger children to the Kintbury and Hungerford area as there was more suitable classroom accommodation there for them. In their place came 380 secondary school girls from the Godolphin & Latymer School in Hammersmith, London W6, who had previously been split between schools in Ascot, Sunningdale, Taplow, Burnham and Eton. Some of these transfers involved *N&D* vehicles, whilst the double-shift system then introduced to cope with classroom allocations meant that school buses had to be re-timed.

There were also general restrictions imposed by the Traffic Commissioner in order to conserve fuel, and these came into effect from the last week of September. A new 'Emergency Timetable' booklet was issued, with the prominent warning to 'keep this and mark any other changes notified via the local press'. The more significant of these restrictions saw the service to Rowstock cut back to East Ilsley except on Sundays, the late evening buses to Thatcham ended at 10.10pm, whilst the 9pm departure on Saturdays to West Woodhay was cut back to run as far as Ball Hill only. Other services affected were the East Woodhay

144

route, which lost its 5.45pm journey on Wednesdays, and the 12.30pm run to Yattendon, which was reduced to Tuesdays, Thursdays and Saturdays only. The buses to Ecchinswell and Sydmonton now only ran to the former, the road beyond there being very lightly used anyway, whilst the Moulsford Special reverted to running on the first and third Thursdays of the month once again.

The final style of pre-war advertising as used in the local trade directory of 1939.

It was also decided to ease the burden on crews in the black-out, and also create more passenger space, by not accepting parcels after 4pm departures from Newbury on most days, though these were permitted up to 5pm on Thursdays and 6pm on Saturdays.

Further changes were made from 5th October, partly in response to fuel restrictions, but also to take account of the amended pattern of school openings. The 2.45pm Thursdays journey on the Newbury – Inkpen – Hungerford route was cut back to Christ Church, and journeys from Newbury ay 7.40am and back from Hungerford at 12.30pm were inserted to cover the shift system at schools. On the service to Hampstead Norris and Hermitage, the 8.15pm bus on Tuesdays was deleted, whilst on the Bucklebury route the 9.40pm journey was curtailed at Thatcham, where the bus was garaged. The 11.30am journey to Stockcross was reduced to run on Thursdays and Saturdays, whilst Local Services A and B saw a general lower level of operation.

As already noted, the Authorities put many measures into place in order to deal with the expected warfare, especially that coming from the air, given the tactics seen under the 'blitzkrieg' (lightning war) already used against civilian targets as well as those of the military by the Germans. In view of what had been demonstrated on mainland Europe, it was considered that casualties from such attacks would be high. Apart from the evacuation already seen, other factors were considered, and these covered the handling of injured and dead civilians.

There is no record of any *Newbury & District* vehicles being converted for use as ambulances, as presumably the area was not a designated reception area for such casualties. However, air-raids were a possibility in any town, especially one on several strategic rail

routes, so in November 1939 the ARP & Emergency Committee of Newbury BC asked the Company to put aside a lorry ready to convey the dead if required. Also of local significance was the taking over of Greenham Common as a military base, and at that time it was stated that it would be returned to public use once the war had ended, a promise duly broken.

During November the last of the once numerous Ford AA-types was disposed of, this being coach No.64 (RX 2907) which had been purchased as a stop-gap in 1937, whilst December saw the end of the last Chevrolet in the fleet, No.5 (UN 3196), another of the vehicles from *Edith Kent,* making 20 seats now the smallest capacity in the fleet.

One other vehicle was purchased during November, in the shape of GMC T30-type bus UR 2932 of April 1929. This had been new to the *Albanian Bus Co.* of St. Albans, Hertfordshire, duly passing to *London Transport* and others, but it was acquired solely as a source of spares and did not run for *N&D.*

This GMC was identical to UR 2932 and helped keep the remaining examples going until 1941.

From November Boss Denham was made up to Senior Foreman in the garage, which gave him responsibility for keeping the wheels turning under the very difficult years yet to come. In order to achieve that various trawls of the dealer's yards was made to obtain whole vehicles for scrapping for spares, though full details are not recorded. Other existing vehicles ended their days 'out the back' of the Mill Lane garage until devoid of useful parts, when they joined the nation's plea for scrap metal.

Certainly, everything that Boss and Percy Andrews had learnt in rebuilding vehicles would now be needed to coax the fleet through the next 6 years, and it is indeed fortunate that a number of high-capacity buses had featured in recent purchases.

However, the war entered a period generally referred to as the 'phoney war', during which the anticipated air-raids on Britain had not materialised, though of course all the restrictions and black-out remained in place.

At the close of 1939 the passenger fleet of *Newbury & District* consisted of the following 51 vehicles, which are listed in order of chassis make then fleet number:

No.	Reg. No.	Chassis Type	Bodywork	Year
19	RX 9971	Bedford WLB	?? B20F	1932
70	BON 886	Bedford WTB	Duple C25F	1936
71	BON 887	Bedford WTB	Duple C25F	1936
38	CG 1724	Commer Cen.	Petty C20F	1932
39	ACG 644	Commer Inv.	Petty C20F	1935
63	JB 6834	Dennis Ace	K&T C20F	1935
65	JY 4751	Dennis Ace	Mumford C20F	1934
66	FJ 9581	Dennis Ace	Duple C20F	1934
67	AYA 102	Dennis Ace	H'ton C20R	1934
68	DG 9516	Dennis Ace	Duple C20F	1934
69	DYF 184	Dennis Ace	Strachan C20F	1937
60	JB 5701	Ford BB	?? C20-	1935
22	RD 1886	Gilford168OT	Wilton C32R	1932
24	RH 2257	Gilford 168OT	HCMW B32R	1930
49	MW 4028	Gilford 166OT	Wyc. C31F	1929
50	JK 1911	Gilford 168OT	Duple C31F	1931
52	TY 8886	Gilford 168MOT	Strachan C31F	1931
54	HX 7560	Gilford 168OT	Duple C32F	1931
55	JJ 8873	Gilford 168OT	Duple C32F	1933
32	RA 9830	GMC T42	Duple B26F	1929
35	FM 6488	GMC T30C	Hughes B20F	1930
36	FM 6486	GMC T30C	Hughes B20F	1930
58	OU2885	GMC T30C	Ldn. L. C20D	1929
28	RU 8058	Leyland PLSC3	Leyland B35F	1928
29	RU 7559	Leyland PLSC3	Leyland B35F	1928
40	RU 5072	Leyland PLSC3	Leyland B35F	1927
41	RU 7560	Leyland PLSC3	Leyland B35F	1928
47	HD 4369	Leyland LT2	Leyland B30F	1931
48	HD 4368	Leyland LT2	Leyland B30F	1931
51	HD 4370	Leyland LT2	Leyland B30F	1931
56	HD 4371	Leyland LT2	Leyland B30F	1931
72	MS 8438	Leyland TS1	Alex. C32F	1929
73	WP 6206	Leyland LT5A	B'ham C32R	1934
8	UO 9841	Thornycroft A2L	Wadham B20F	1929
9	MW 825	Thornycroft A2L	C. Ross B20F	1927
10	OU 3317	Thornycroft A2	Wadham B20F	1929
12	TR 8198	Thornycroft A2	Wadham B20F	1930
14	PG 2018	Thornycroft A2L	C. Ross B20F	1929
16	PG 3236	Thornycroft A2L	C. Ross B20F	1929
17	PG 4226	Thornycroft A2L	C. Ross B20F	1929
18	VF 9339	Thornycroft A2L	C. Ross B20F	1930
20	UR 7968	Thornycroft A2L	Thurgood B20F	1930
21	JH 492	Thornycroft A12	Thurgood B20F	1931
26	RD 6270	T'croft Ardent	Pk. Royal B26F	1934
31	TP 7951	Thornycroft A2	Wadham B20F	1929
43	TP 8693	Thornycroft A2	Wadham B20F	1930
46	PG 1099	Thornycroft A2L	C. Ross B20F	1929
57	TP 9164	Thornycroft A2	Wadham B20F	1930
7	VT 184	TSM B10A	S&B B32F	1927
44	TV 5363	TSM B10A	W'brook B32F	1931
45	TV 6036	TSM B49A7	W'brook B32F	1932

Fuller details of chassis types and model names can be found in the full N&D Fleet List in Appendix 1.

Representing two of the chassis types then numerous in the N&D fleet are:

Above – *Gilford No.50 (JK 1911), a fine Duple-bodied coach as new in 1931 to Southern Glideway of Eastbourne, complete with white-walled tyres. Unfortunately, this coach would soon be lost to the Requisitioning Officer, and its later fate is unknown.*

Below – *One of a number of very sound Thornycrofts that came to Newbury as a result of the various take-overs by London Transport is No.46 (PG 1099), seen when with London General Country Services on its route 454 to Tonbridge. The Challands Ross bodywork is typical of that built on Thornycroft buses of the period, the designs being drawn at Basingstoke and supplied to various favoured coachbuilders.*

Abbreviations used for bodybuilders on the fleet list:

Alex.	Alexanders	Falkirk
B'ham	Burlingham	Blackpool
C. Ross	Challand Ross	Nottingham
HCMW	H.C. Motor Works	Hull
H'ton	Harrington	Hove
K&T	King & Taylor	Godalming
Ldn. L.	London Lorries	London
Pk. Royal	Park Royal	London
S&B	Strachan & Brown	London
Wyc.	Wycombe	High Wycombe
??	Bodybuilder not known	

Chapter 13 – 1940

After the initial restrictions on coaching work, there was a slight relaxation for the Spring of 1940, and the Company was able to offer a limited programme of excursions during the Whit Bank Holiday weekend. On Sunday 12th May excursions left for Oxford, Swindon and Southsea, whilst on the following day there were trips to Oxford and Southsea again.

The situation was such that it was able to advertise a limited private hire capacity, though still within the parameters set out by the Traffic Commissioner to conserve fuel. Little could anyone then envisage how many long and weary years it would be before the *Newbury & District* coaches would once again be able to offer a full programme of excursions and private hire facilities!

Understandably, few changes were made to the bus operations at this time, as it was still very much a time of apprehension over the next move from Germany, with the constant threat of paratrooper landings and bombing raids.

However, with the local population already increased by the influx of evacuees, along with the construction workers preparing additional military camps, it soon became apparent that some routes would need larger vehicles than the 20-seaters traditionally used, whilst in other cases worn out vehicles needed replacement.

During June 7 vehicles were acquired with the above issues in mind. One pair were Leyland 'Lion' LT1's, which carried rear-entrance 31-seater bus bodies by the Ipswich firm of Ransomes, Sims & Jeffries. These had been new in July 1929 to *Maidstone Corporation* and became Nos.42 (KP 8372) and 49 (KP 8371).

One of the RS & J-bodied Leyland 'Lions' when new. Note the extra wide rear entrance on these buses.

The remaining vehicles were all smaller types, with a further pair of Dennis 'Aces' included. One became No.59 (YD 9912), which was a Dennis-bodied 20-seater, front-entrance bus new in June 1934 to *W.L.G. Waterman* of Broomfield, near Bridgwater, Somerset, but had latterly been operated by *C.J. Payne* of Buckingham. The other was No.61 (CKL 719), new to *West Kent Motor Services Ltd.,* based at Sundridge Aerodrome, near Sevenoaks. It was notable in having been fitted with a Perkins diesel engine when built in January 1936, though whilst at Newbury it ran with the standard Dennis petrol unit. The original owner had been acquired in October 1939 by the *LPTB,* but this vehicle had not been used by them, coming to its new operator through Harry Lane.

Two views of Dennis 'Ace' No.61 (CKL 719). Above it is seen before delivery, and below when in service. The Perkins badge can be seen across the radiator grille, and it is interesting to note how the different film types depict this vehicle much lighter or darker.

Another of the 20-seaters had also originated with *West Kent* and came to *N&D* by the same route, this being a Thornycroft 'Dainty' with a front-entrance body by Thurgood of Ware new in April 1938. This had been built to an enhanced standard and was evidently also used as a coach by the original owner, becoming No.74 (EKP 140).

Thornycroft 'Dainty' No.74 (EKP 140) is seen when in service with West Kent.

Dennis 'Dart No.23 (EV 5909) was originally with Romford & District and duly passed into London Transport ownership as DA44. The front destination box had been rebuilt to the same larger layout as DA35 (opposite) before it came to Newbury.

The final pair was both on the Dennis 'Dart' chassis and came via dealer Steel Breaking & Dismantling of Edgware after service with *London Transport*. One was a Metcalfe-bodied front-entrance 20-seater new in April 1932 to *Romford & District*, which passed into the *LPTB* net in July 1934 and saw service with them. This became No.23 (EV 5909) and proved to be a useful little bus. The other had actually been new to the *LGOC* in 1932, and carried a Chiswick-built 18-seater bus body with front entrance as their DA36 (GX 5327), but this did not run for *Newbury & District*, being sold again in October after being stripped of spares.

Also with the prospect of make-do-and-mend looming over the issue of vehicle maintenance, a further coach was obtained for spare parts for the remaining Gilford vehicles. This was Duple-bodied 1930 168SD-type GF 6677, which had originated with *Thackray's Way* of London and Reading, and had probably run at times on the Newbury route. As such it passed into *Thames Valley* hands, who then re-sold to *A. Ford & Son* of Silchester, from whom *N&D* acquired it on 15th July.

Two vehicles were disposed of in June as a result of the incoming stock, and these consisted of 20-seater Thornycroft No.9 (MW 825), and a Commer coach. The Thorny went as a mobile unit with the Air Raid Precaution Service at West Ham, London. The Commer withdrawn was No.39 (ACG 644), which saw further passenger use with *Baddeley Bros.,* of Holmfirth in Yorkshire, who favoured that make.

No sooner had the above changes taken place when, due to the number of vehicles that had been left in France after the miracle rescue of troops from the beaches of Dunkirk between 26th May and 4th June, the Military Requisitioning Officers came to call on bus operators to find suitable replacements during July 1940. No records exist of the vehicles taken from the *Newbury & District* fleet, but the following were certainly taken - Tilling-Stevens B10A-type No.7 (VT 184), Gilford 168OT No.50 (JK 1911) along with the pride-of-the-fleet Leyland 'Tiger' TS2 No.72 (MS 8438).

At the about same time, a trio of Gilford coaches also departed, though there is no evidence either way as to whether these were also requisitioned. These were 166OT-type Nos.49 (MW 4028) and 168OT-types 54 (HX 7560) and 55 (JJ 8873). However, the Military did tend to take older coaches, especially those with sliding roofs, as they could easily be fitted with a bren-gun position, so these were quite likely candidates.

There is also a curious situation regarding the bus which would later become the recipient of fleet number 45 (CK 4518). There are no records of this joining the fleet prior to this time, but in June 1942 the Company wrote to the Ministry of War Transport to seek its return (which then occurred), so it remains a possibility that this had been requisitioned, perhaps before it had even been placed in service?

From July 1940 further economies in services became necessary, as the fuel situation worsened. A number of journeys on Route 15 (Newbury – Bucklebury) were curtailed at Thatcham, and these were marked as 15T in the timetable, whilst the full journeys were noted as 15B. Also, to save fuel, the evening journeys on Route

19 (Newbury – Hermitage – Hampstead Norris – Yattendon) were designated as only proceeding beyond Hermitage if required by an onboard passenger, thereby allowing the bus to generally return direct to the Hermitage outstation. The Moulsford Special was reduced to run on only the first Thursday of the month also from July.

London Transport Dennis 'Dart' DA35 (GX 5331) was identical to DA36, which was acquired for parts.

In order to make best use of existing vehicles, and to counter profiteering, The Emergency Powers (Defence) Acquisition & Disposal of Motor Vehicles Order 1940 was enacted, which included the sales of buses. Also, the pre-war system of Road Service Licenses was suspended, the Traffic Commissioners now issuing Wartime Permits and also being responsible for fuel coupons for PSV operators.

During August former *Pocock Bros.* Bedford WLB No.19 (RX 9971) was sold locally to *T. &.J. Wood* of Basingstoke, where it saw further service with them. The following month Tilling-Stevens B49A7 bus No.45 (TV 6036) was sold, also seeing further use with *Bryn Melyn Motor Services* in Denbighshire.

Although some of the contracts could be covered by buses used on daily services, a number of those runs required dedicated vehicles, usually old coaches, which drivers took home in order to save fuel and outstationing costs. A pair of Gilford coaches, Nos. 54 (HX 7560) and 55 (JJ 8873) had been used on a contract between Lambourn and Devizes Camp, with drivers working the day on construction, but that had now ceased.

Ernie Nobes covered the Didcot Ordnance Factory contract from the Lambourn Woodlands area, being allocated a Dennis 'Ace' for that purpose, and spending the day working in the Depot Stores, with the bus staying outside his home in The Square overnight. George Amor took one of the surviving Gilfords, Nos.22 (RD 1886), 24 (RH 2257) or 52 (TY 8886), to his home at 'The Ferns', Speen, spending the rest of the day employed as a carpenter at the contract site. Incidentally, his brother Arthur, one time driver on *Norton Motor Services* was also still with *N&D* and lived in Lower Way, Thatcham by then.

Another vehicle was also outstationed at Kintbury for the run to Didcot, driven by Bert Greenwood, and this was usually Bedford 70 (BON 886). He also took with him on the run a teacher who worked in Didcot each Monday, bringing her back on Fridays, whilst another vehicle was based at Chilton Foliat for the same destination. Others were based at West Ilsley, Bucklebury, Stockcross and Hungerford at various times, mainly for Didcot runs, though *N&D* also covered contracts to the RAOC Depot at Thatcham, the RNVD Depot also at Thatcham, the RAF Depot, Milton, along with the Vickers-Armstrong works at Hungerford, Shaw and Theale. Charlie Morgan kept a bus at Lambourn for a run via Baydon, Aldbourne and Marlborough to various camps in the Ogbournes area.

Bert Greenwood stands in front of the bonnet of Bedford No.70 (BON 886) on an outing. Note the popularity of pipe-smoking then.

Further wartime-related manufacturing came into the area, necessitating contracts runs or relief buses on the local routes, with Opperman Gears at Hambridge Road and the setting up of a Vickers-Armstrong plant at Shaw for the construction of fuselages for Spitfires.

Newbury & District continued to use both the garages in Mill Lane, along with the Coachbuilding/Repair Depot at 7-9 Northcroft Lane. Since Dunkirk the need to keep vehicles running was greater than ever, whilst the prospect of any new vehicles was very limited. In some respects the Company was fortunate in that it had good supplies of spare parts for its preferred types, but things would get a lot worse yet!

Although no Company property was taken for war production, the *Thames Valley* dormy shed in Mill Lane was used for the construction of aircraft sections, that operator then outstationing the pair of buses at Newbury station for the duration.

One of the batch of Leyland 'Lion' LT5-types which included No.80 (HL 5228) seen in as new condition when delivered to West Riding Automobile Co. Ltd. It would continue to serve N&D through to July 1948.

During August 1940 Newbury Borough Council agreed to a proposal to park about 100 buses and other military vehicles on the roadway across Northcroft during the Winter months, this being in addition to the 8-10 lorries already stationed at The Wharf car park since late 1939. It is not known if the buses included any requisitioned from operators.

Despite the general cutbacks, Ecchinswell actually gained a Tuesday operation of two daily journeys from September 1940, only to lose it in the next round of restrictions due to fuel and rubber shortages in June 1941.

The remains of Dennis 'Dart' GX 5327 were disposed off for scrap during October, whilst that month saw two additions to the fleet. These were a further Dennis 'Ace' as No.75 (BPG 531) and Leyland 'Lion' LT5 which became No.80 (HL 5228). The former had been new in June 1934 to *Yellow Bus Service* of Guildford, Surrey and carried a Dennis 20-seater front-entrance bus body fitted with a sunshine roof section. The LT5 was one of a batch built for *West Riding Automobile Co. Ltd.* of Wakefield, Yorkshire in April 1932 and carried a 32-seater front-entrance bus body by Roe of Leeds. It had left their service in May 1939 and saw use by *A. Rowe* of Cudworth before reaching *N&D.*

The Dennis 'Ace' was very much an ideal vehicle for use in the narrow lanes of West Berkshire, as the set-back front axle provided a remarkable turning circle, whilst the same feature produced the snout-nosed appearance and the inevitable nickname of the 'flying pig'! Indeed, *N&D* would continue to acquire further examples of the type, as they continued to displace the 20-seater Thornycroft A-types.

A number of further Dennis 'Aces' were acquired over the war years, becoming the most numerous type in use by Newbury & District. No.75 (BPG 531) is seen when new to Yellow Bus Service of Guildford, where of course the Dennis works were situated.

The City of Southampton, dominated by its world-famous docks, was an obvious target for the Luftwaffe, and raids between 23rd November and 1st December 1940 resulted in some 45,000 buildings being damaged or destroyed. As a result of this *N&D* was contracted to run a busload of workers down to the city daily to undertake repairs to buildings.

November saw another Leyland 'Lion' acquired, but this time a much older PLSC3-type new in June 1928. This became No.45 (YV 5499) and had originated with *Birch Bros.* of Kentish Town, North London, who also built the 32-seater front-entrance coach body. However, it came to Newbury after some years operating on the Isle of Wight for *Taylor's Garage* of Ryde, and was assigned to a contract working.

Thornycroft No.17 (PG 4226) was taken out of service in November 1940, and this was followed in December by similar buses 8 (UO 9841), 12 (TR 8198), 20 (UR 7968) and 46 (PG 1099). It would seem that all these went to the same buyer, as they soon became ARP mobile units or ambulances with Local Authorities in and around the Capitol, with 8 and 20 going to Tottenham, 17 to Erith, 46 to Cheshunt, and 12 to an unrecorded location, their size being ideal for the new role.

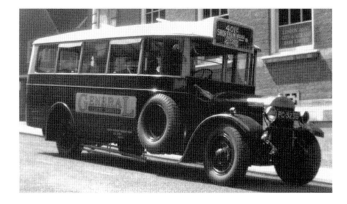

The little Thornycrofts were reduced in numbers by incoming Dennis 'Aces', but No.16 (PG 3236) would survive until February 1941. It is seen when with London General Country Services on route 401E to Shoreham village.

Also withdrawn in December was GMC No.58 (OU 2885), which may have become a source of spares for the remaining vehicles of that type, as it had no further user. In order to replace the above, no fewer than 6 'Aces' were placed in service in December. Although these were standard in chassis specification, the bodywork introduced further varieties into the growing fleet of little 'piggies'. In peacetime, the various features such as fleetname panels would have been sign-written with the Company name, whilst blinds would have been provided. Although some evidently gained blinds taken from older vehicles, many ran only with paper stickers for destinations.

Also from the Yellow Bus fleet was No.72 (CPA 828), caught by the camera in Guildford town centre.

The incoming vehicles were: Nos.72 (CPA 828) another Dennis-bodied bus from *Yellow Bus,* Guildford new in December 1934; 77 (ARA 370) with Willowbrook 20-seater bus body new to *A. Turner,* Brampton in June 1934; 79 (RV 6259) with Dennis 20-seater bus body new in January 1935 to *W.R. Parsons,* of Middle Winterslow, near Salisbury; 81

(AVO 977) another Willowbrook example but with more luxury seating and a sun roof, new in December 1934 to *Wright & Sons* of Newark, Nottinghamshire; 82 (KV 9903) new in June 1934 as a Willowbrook-bodied 20-seater coach to *Park & Bunty Motorways* of Coventry; and 83 (AUB 354) which carried a 20-seater bus body by an unknown coachbuilder, being new in December 1934 to *J. Marson & Sons,* Bentley.

The Dennis 'Ace' that became No.79 (RV 6259) seen as new to Parsons of Middle Winterslow. Note the large roof-mounted luggage-carrier, this operator using the vehicle on a service into Salisbury.

Also entering service that month was another Leyland 'Lion' LT2-type, No.50 (UR 9658) with a front-entrance 32-seater bus body by Birch, delivered to *St. Albans & District* in May 1931, but coming to *N&D* via *London Transport* and others.

As noted previously, light-coloured roofs on vehicles had been painted grey to make them less visible from the air. However, as time wore on, supplies of coloured paints were increasingly hard to come by, so repaints started to appear in grey relieved with a green band. It also seems probable that some of the vehicles obtained specifically for contract duties may not have even received repaints whilst the war was on.

Haulage work had been cut back severely, and had been mainly related to government-directed work. The Bedfords JB 5917 and RD 5922 remained on loan to the Newbury Volunteer Fire Brigade, following the call for assistance shortly after the war started. Some removals work had continued throughout 1940, so van AMO 455 had been kept occupied.

The staff of *Newbury & District* also supported the war effort in other ways, many of them serving in the Newbury South Unit of the Royal Berks Home Guard, with Jim Davies acting as Major and Boss Denham as his Sargeant. A store was set up on the edge of The Wharf site, where some equipment could be keep for ready accessibility, along with a static water tank for fire-fighting.

Newbury as a town was seemingly far from the main centres of air-raids, but being on several important railways lines it was potentially a target for planes returning from raids on the Midlands.

The arrangements for Christmas week services were broadly the same as in previous years, though all services ceased earlier in the evenings. Some extra buses were provided on local services on the peak shopping days in order to avoid excessive queuing, as even those who had cars were now finding fuel in very short supply. Essential war worker's services were provided throughout the Christmas period as required by the working arrangements of the factories and other sites served.

Looking rather care-worn is Dennis 'Ace' No.82 (KV 9903) had came to N&D via several other operators. It had latterly been with OK Motor Services of Bishop Auckland , but is seen here after sale by N&D.

Any earlier optimism that the conflict in Europe would quickly be resolved had soon faded during 1940, and Britain now stood alone against the imminent threat of invasion. Whereas there had been a trickle of bus chassis production, made possible by the 'un-freezing' of part-completed vehicles and some cancelled export orders, such production now ceased completely in order to meet the war effort.

A wartime line-up at The Wharf, including 3 buses purchased during 1940. On the left there is Leyland 'Lion' LT2-type No.56 (HD 4371) on the service to Highclere, then Dennis 'Aces' No.61 (CKL 719) for East Ilsley and No.81 (AVO 977). To their right is the Leyland 'Lion' LT5-type No.80 (HL 5228), whilst behind them is the drill tower of the fire brigade.

There was little comfort to be had regarding the end of the war, with increased U-boat activity, along with the apparent certainty of an invasion. But, of course, life had to go on, and people still needed to get about, and so the buses were busier than ever. Although no *N&D* buses were converted to perimeter seating, there are numerous stories of buses well over legal capacity!

Another rather worn 'Ace' was former N&D No.83 (AUB 354), which had several further owners through to 1960, when it was rescued for preservation, though unfortunately the project was not completed. The type weighed in at 3.5 tons un-laden, and this bus was lastly with Fuggles of Benenden in Kent.

Chapter 14 – 1941

Despite the lack of new buses, *Newbury & District* was well-placed with some many war-related contracts and local establishments to make the case for purchases, and it continued to buy Dennis 'Aces', along with Leyland 'Lions' and 'Tigers' in order to replace worn-out and non-standard types.

January saw the withdrawal of GMC T42-type No.32 (RA 9830), which carried a Duple 26-seater bus body but had often been used as a coach in earlier times due to its size and powerful engine. This found a new role with the Ministry of Public Works by March 1941.

Incoming in January was a Leyland 'Tiger' TS2-type which had originally carried a half-canopy coach body built by Leyland in March 1931 to resemble the Spicer bodied examples supplied to its first owners, *Scout Motor* Services of Preston. This vehicle, like many other former *Ribble* group vehicles, found its way to Scotland for further service with *Elgin & District Motor Bus Company,* before passing with that operator to *Alexanders.* It later ran for *Riley's Motor Tours* of Belper, and at some point was evidently re-fitted with a standard Leyland full-canopy saloon body seating 32. It became No.84 (CK 4573) and was destined to see some 7 year's service at Newbury.

February saw the demise of the Gilford 168MOT No.52 (TY 8886), used latterly on a daily contract run, along with Thornycroft A2Long-type No.16 (PG 3236). The Gilford initially went to Harry Lane and probably indicates where replacements were being sourced, though it went onto further service with *C.J. Towler* in Emneth, Norfolk for a further 5 years! The Thorny went to Eagle Star Insurance, perhaps as staff transport to relocated offices? It is most likely that the month also saw the withdrawal of the last GMC's in the fleet, these being former *Crosville M.S.* examples Nos.35/6 (FM 6488 and 6486).

Half a dozen replacement vehicles arrived during February and were soon placed in service. Two of these were further 'Tiger' TS2's, though each had a different provenance. One became No.86 (CK 3951) and was new in July 1928 as a 29-seater dual-purpose bus for use on the express services of *Ribble M.S.* of Preston. In due course it had been demoted to a 32-seater saloon, though still retaining the rear-entrance layout. The choice of the TS2 model meant that the rear overhang was relatively short, in order to comply with the varied regulations laid down by Licensing Authorities prior to the implementation of the 1930 Act. However, subsequent rebuilding when with *N&D* evidently extended this to the full legal maximum. In the meantime this vehicle had followed others with *Ribble* origins to Scotland for service with *Alexanders* from June 1937. A photograph of this vehicle after body overhaul will be found in the following chapter.

The other incoming TS2 was No.87 (DF 7841), new in May 1929 as a 26-seater coach to *Black & White Motorways* of Cheltenham. Its luxurious dual-door body was a Leyland standard shell, but fitted out to a higher standard by Abbotts of Wrecclesham in Surrey. However, *Black & White* had sold it in 1937, after which it had other owners. By the time it arrived at Newbury it had been re-bodied with an Alexander body as fitted to 1934 'Bluebird' coaches in that fleet, many of which were later re-bodied as double-deckers. Also, like many other older Leyland models still in use, this vehicle had received a replacement radiator of the longer 'CovRad' type manufactured by the Coventry Radiator Co. to fit a number of earlier models for which original units were not available.

Leyland 'Tiger' TS2 No.87 (DF 7841) at The Wharf.

The remaining quartet of vehicles entering the fleet during February 1941 was all on the Dennis 'Ace' chassis and seated 20. One became No.58 (MJ 4550) and had started out in June 1934 as a dual-purpose bus with bodywork by Grose of Northampton in the fleet of *Seamarks & Son* of Higham Ferrers. Another was No.76 (BBP 339), new in September 1935 with a Dennis bus body to *W.F. Alexander (Comfy Coaches)* of Horsham. There is a record that this ran at Newbury for a short time bearing the registration plates from No.63 (JB 6834), whilst the latter received attention, though strictly unofficially of course!

Dennis 'Ace' No.76 (BBP 339) seen when new.

The other 'Aces' had both been new as coaches, one becoming No.78 (BKE 720) and carrying a Duple body. This had been new in April 1934 to *Charles Bourne,* based in Tenterden, Kent. The other was

No.85 (JB 3354), and this hailed from elsewhere in Berkshire, being a Dennis-bodied example new in May 1934 to *A.&R. Try (Windsorian Coaches)*, though it first went to *Whippet Coaches* at Hilton in Cambridgeshire before returning to Berkshire.

'Ace' No.78 (BKE 720) seen after later sale by N&D.

Further Leylands, along with a single 'Ace' joined the fleet during March. The latter was No.89 (DNW 359), a June 1936 example carrying a 20-seater bus body by Fielding & Bottomley of Halifax, which had been new to *J. Marson & Sons* of Bentley, near Doncaster, Yorkshire.

The Leylands were quite a mixed bunch of 4-cylinder 'Lions' and 6-cylinder 'Tigers', as *Newbury & District* continued to cope with increased loading through the use of full-size single-deckers. Three of these were LT2-types, though each had a different origin. No.46 (WX 7898) was new in July 1931 with Roberts of Wakefield 32-seater front-entrance bus body to *Arthur Braim (St. Ledger Coaches),* based in Armthorpe, Yorkshire, who also had a green and cream livery. This vehicle was generally employed on one of the contract runs.

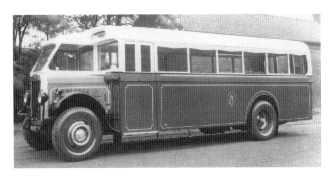

Leyland 'Lion' LT2-type No.46 (WX 7898) when new.

The second of the LT2's became No.52 (TF 4155), a Leyland-bodied 30-seater, front-entrance bus new in February 1931 to *Dallas Services Ltd.* of Earnshaw Bridge, Leyland, though it came to Newbury from *H. Wray* of Barnsley. This was notable in retaining its original radiator throughout *N&D* service, complete with the enamel Lion's-head badge on the header tank, at a time when CovRad units were increasingly replacing original units beyond patching up.

The third LT2 was from a much larger outfit than the previous two, this becoming No.53 (HE 5229), with Leyland front-entrance 30-seater bus body and new to *Yorkshire Traction* of Barnsley in May 1931. This and No.52 were in constant use throughout the war and amongst the last Leylands in use of the original fleet.

The other two Leylands were 'Tigers', one as No.88 (MS 8834), a TS1-type new in March 1929. This had been supplied to *Alexander's* of Falkirk, who built a coach body with sunshine roof section. However, it was re-bodied by them with a luxurious 32-seater body of their 'Bluebird' style in 1934 to modernise it. These bodies featured well-appointed interiors, whilst externally the bodywork incorporated a full-length luggage rack built into the roofline, all finished off with a striking blue and cream livery. However, it had known better times by the time it reached *N&D*, having already seen war service with *Ayer's* of Dover. In view of its sliding door and coach seating it tended to be used on contract work.

'Tiger' TS1 No.88 (MS 8834) outside Mill Lane depot.

The other was a TS2-type which became No.91 (CK 4312). This was another vehicle from the large *Ribble* fleet, being new in March 1930, initially for coaching duties. The standard Leyland body differed little in outward appearance between bus and coach examples, and this was later converted to serve as 30-seater bus. Although it departed that operator's fleet when sold to a Preston dealer in September 1938, no other users are recorded prior to arrival in Newbury.

No doubt as a result of the February/March intake, another make became extinct in the *N&D* fleet, with the sale of Ford BB-type coach No.60 (JB 5701), which was also the last of the vehicles acquired from *Pass & Co.* That went at towards the end of March, whilst Gilford 168OT bus No.24 (RH 2257) and Bedford lorry JB 6909 both departed in April. The Ford did not have any further owners, whereas the Gilford went to *A. & A.E. Blackbourn (Granville Tours)* of Grimsby for further service, and the Bedford is not recorded with subsequent owners, though it could have seen non-civilian use?

The only forward-control 'Mace' was No.92 (BUA 795), seen here with its original owner.

Also during April the remains of Gilford 166SD-type GF 6677 was sold, the only vehicle of that make still in use being No.22 (RD 1886). Despite 'GF' being short of a number of vital mechanical parts, it found another operator in Norfolk, who put it back to roadworthy condition and ran it for a further 5 years! No further vehicles were disposed of during 1941.

In the meantime, on Monday 10th March the German air raids on Portsmouth Naval Dockyard also brought tragedy to the Newbury area. Albert Miles, one-time *Denham Bros.* conductor and continuing *Newbury & District* employee, sadly lost his life whilst serving with the Newbury Volunteer Fire Brigade in response to the extensive fires at the dockyard. He, along with his colleagues Charlie Rawlings and Leslie Wyatt Ford, were killed that day, whilst four other local men were injured. The deceased were all married men, so their loss was keenly felt, and they received the full honours of a public funeral. The coffin of Chief Fireman Miles was borne by the NVFB Dennis F-type through the town, whilst those of Auxiliary Fire Service Officers Ford and Rawlings were carried on AFS tenders, the procession also including a large number of fellow fire-fighters from neighbouring towns and local busmen.

One further Dennis 'Ace' arrived during April, in the shape of No.90 (JU 4374), which had been new to *P. Whieldon* in June 1934 and carried a 20-seater front-entrance bus body by Willowbrook.

Two further Dennis vehicles came about May, though the exact dates are not known. One was 'Ace' No.55 (BPH 293), which carried a 20-seater front-entrance coach body by Weymann of Addlestone, notable for having no destination apparatus on its body. This was because it had been supplied in June 1934 to M.F. North Ltd., Cromwell Place, London SW7 for use at the Oaklands Hotel, Weybridge as a private coach, making it an all-Surrey vehicle. However, *N&D* used this on service routes, necessitating paper destination stickers in the front nearside window, as no display was built on, despite that being commonplace earlier.

Dennis 'Ace' No.55 (BPH 293) as new at Weymann's.

The other Dennis was rather different, being one of the scarce forward-control 'Mace' chassis, sometimes referred to as the 'Major Ace' in view of the higher seating capacity. This became No.92 (BUA 795), and it bore a centre-doorway 24-seater body by Brush of Loughborough. When new to *Hartshorn Brothers* of Doncaster in October 1935 it was as a dual-purpose vehicle with coach seating and a sliding door, neither of which made it ideally suited to rural bus work, but it was mechanically similar to the large fleet 'Aces'.

One of the batch-mates of Leyland LT2 No.53 (HE 5229) in service with Yorkshire Traction is seen above, whilst below is identical Dennis 'Ace' to No.85 (JB 3354) of Windsorian Coaches,

Out-stationing at Thatcham ceased by June, although the exact date is not recorded, this becoming necessary because of the larger buses now being used on that route, particularly onto the Thatcham Depot and the factories nearby. Indeed, buses working in on early worker's runs would then return to The Broadway in order to form the journeys to Cold Ash, Bucklebury and Newbury, which also saved fuel. In the afternoons, they resumed a more intensive service between Thatcham and Newbury.

During June 1941 the situation with fuel and rubber became more severe, so a number of service cuts were brought in. The Local Service routes A and B lost their Sunday workings, whilst Route 14 to East Woodhay ceased to run Wednesdays. The deviation via Marsh Benham between Newbury and Hungerford on Route 9 was restricted to Thursdays and Saturdays only. Also from that month Routes 4 (Newbury – Headley – Kingsclere) and 5 (Newbury – Headley – Ashford – Kingsclere) appeared under the heading of

Route 5. However, each continued to run as before, so it is not clear whether some rationalisation had been planned, or whether this was just to show all journeys possible between the common points?

An unfortunate accident occurred during the late evening of Saturday 13th September 1941, when the 32-seater being driven by Charlie Morgan of East Challow on a contract run was in collision with an Army Fordson 30-cwt lorry. The incident happened at the foot of Windmill Hill, about a mile from Lambourn, as the vehicles passed each other. Although this occurred at slow speed the lorry, which was carrying 27 soldiers of the Sherwood Forester's Regiment en route to a cinema in Swindon, overturned. This resulted in two fatalities, along with 9 requiring hospital attention and another 9 with minor injuries. Fortunately the bus was nearing the end of its regular contract run from camps west of Marlborough, with most passengers having alighted at Aldbourne and Baydon. Damage to the bus was not extensive, though 2 passengers were injured and Charlie Morgan was cut by flying glass. The Lambourn ambulance attended and ferried those requiring hospital attention to Wantage.

There were of course numerous military camps set up within the *N&D* area, some requiring transport during their construction. A number of prisoner of war camps also developed locally, along with those for displaced persons, in particular Polish refugees. In addition there were farm camps set up by the War Agriculture Committee of Berkshire at Chieveley and Kintbury, to which workers were transported.

One further vehicle was acquired during December 1941, this being another TS2-type 'Tiger', as No.93 (SY 4441). Although a type already represented at Newbury, this had yet another variety of bodywork, being a 28-seater dual-entrance coach body by Roberts of Wakefield. This vehicle had been new in June 1931 to *Bowen's Tours* of Musselburgh, who sold out to *Scottish Motor Traction* in May 1935. Not being particularly useful for bus duties, this was put to work on one of the out-stationed contracts and was rarely seen in Newbury.

TS2-type 'Tiger' No.93 (SY 4441) when with SMT.

Chapter 15 – 1942

This year saw a very marked downturn in changes within the fleet, as the supply of suitable vehicles all but dried up. A new phase of make-do-and-mend led to a strategy of refurbishment, in order to extend the working lives of existing stock.

Although it had been possible to continue with some limited haulage work throughout 1940/1, the situation with fuel now became so acute that this class of work had to be abandoned altogether in February 1942, but the A Licenses were retained for future use.

As already noted, two Bedford lorries were on loan to the Fire Service, whilst the ex-*Cleeveley* Bedfords JB 1930 and JB 1984 were sold in February. The old Dennis HO 6306 was either sold then, or had possibly departed at an earlier unrecorded date. This left only Bedford lorry ABL 759 and the pantechnicon AMO 455 in stock, but as the latter was a specialised vehicle it was placed in store in the hope of the possibility of resuming household removals in the future. The lorry then acted as the *N&D* service vehicle instead, assisting in the search for spare parts for the fleet at various locations.

The weather conditions over the Winter of 1941/2 provided some trying times for the fitters and the road crews, having to coax cold engines into life, whilst the drivers whose journeys ran over the more exposed areas risked not being able to complete their runs due to snow drifts. However, as the posters said, 'keep calm and carry on' was the watchword of the day!

As noted, the secondhand market in buses had been pretty well exhausted, leading to the decision by the Ministry of Supply to allow Vauxhall Motors to build a wartime version of the popular Bedford OB-type, which had started production just before war broke out. These started to be constructed from January 1942 and a total of 3398 were built through to September 1945. These were all fitted with the same 'utility' design of body, mostly with wooden slatted seats for 32 passengers. However, in order to obtain these, licences had to be sought from the Ministry, and *Newbury & District* soon presented its case, and they were allocated 5 such vehicles as and when they got to the top of the outstanding orders.

Understandably there were few other changes to the passenger fleet, though the Company was successful in its approach to the Ministry of War Transport in respect of the return of Leyland 'Lion' LT2-type bus CK 4518. Jim Davies wrote to the Ministry on 12th May, and on 24th June it was added to the insurance schedule and became yet another occupant of the fleet number 45. As previously discussed, it appears that it had been acquired earlier, but then taken away before seeing service with the Company.

No.45 had been new to *Ribble Motor Services* in March 1931, carrying a Leyland front-entrance bus body originally seating 30. *N&D* licensed it as a 32-seater, and it is possible that some of the other saloons originally built as 30/32-seaters my have acquired an additional pair of seats due to wartime loadings, this theory being borne out by the observations of various enthusiasts when noting vehicles from this fleet.

As it was, No.45 was destined to survive beyond its service at Newbury, with *Harry Luff* of Leatherhead, then latterly as a static caravan home at Chavey Down, just to the west of Bracknell in east Berkshire. The author discovered it there in the 1970's, and in due course it was abandoned and rescued by the well-known 'Leyland man' Mike Sutcliffe. Several changes of ownership have followed in order to ensure its eventual preservation!

'Lion' No.45 (CK 4518) as the author encountered it in the wood being lived in by a charming old couple, who had wall-papered the interior and re-painted the exterior in an appropriate shade of green. They also started it up every year in case they wanted to move!

The arrival of this additional 'Lion' allowed the disposal of Tilling-Stevens B10A-type bus No.44 (TV 5363), during June, though it did see further service with *Salopia* of Whitchurch in Shropshire. This meant that there were no vehicles of this make present in the fleet since formation, and in fact much earlier if the lineage back to *Denham Bros.* is also considered.

The general appearance of the fleet had certainly suffered from the increased usage of vehicles and some now had more grey paint than green as supplies ran out. A number of wartime photos show vehicles running on bald tyres, though the shortage of rubber made this unavoidable. Some of the coaches, often chosen for contract work and spending all their time outside, were also showing signs of deterioration in their wooden-framed bodies caused by a backlog of attention and lack of re-painting.

In order to arrest this decline, the Board agreed to make some funds available for the rebuilding of some vehicles, whilst also deciding that where necessary such work would be placed outside, something which so far the Company had remained self-sufficient over.

The degree of work varied from just a thorough strip-down to, in a few cases, virtually new bodies. Those receiving the more drastic attention returned with bodies rebuilt to strict M-o-S restrictions similar to the elements used for the new utility bodies being built, which was done both to minimise on scarce materials an avoided skilled and time-consuming features such as panel-beaten curves.

Dennis 'Ace' No.63 (JB 6834) is seen after a rebuild that left it looking more like a utility product than the fine coach it once was. The livery is now grey with a green waistrail, along with white black-out markings.

No complete records exist of the vehicles dealt with during this programme, though the following are known to have received attention: Dennis 'Ace' No.58 (MJ 4550) during 1942; 'Aces' Nos.59 (YD 9912), 61 (CKL 719) 72 (CPA 828), 75 (BPG 531), 76 (BBP 339) and 79 (RV 6259) were dealt with during 1943, as was Leyland 'Tiger' TS2 No.87 (DF 7841), all largely unaltered. However, both 'Ace' No.63 (JB 6834), the only one actually new to the Company, and Leyland 'Tiger' TS2 No.86 (CK 3951) both received heavier rebuilds by unknown sources and at unrecorded dates. One driver recalled taking vehicles to the Salisbury area for such attention, and there is a possibility that Heaver of Durrington were involved?

In addition to the variety of vehicles fielded by *N&D*, further types could be seen at The Wharf as *Venture* of Basingstoke turned to others to hire buses or supply secondhand ones. As with the Newbury Company, they had also experienced a significant increase in bus loadings, resulting in the use of more double-deckers. These included an ex-*Chesterfield Corporation* TD1-type Leyland 'Titan', AEC 'Regents' from *City of*

Oxford, Nottingham Corporation and centre-doorway examples from the *Burnley, Colne & Nelson Joint Transport Board*. In addition there were hired 'Titan' TD1s from *East Kent* and later open-staircase Tilling-bodied AEC 'Regents' from *London Transport*.

Venture's ex-Chesterfield Leyland 'Titan' TD1-type (RB 4888) is seen laid over at The Wharf.

Also in connection with *Venture* was the plea received from the Parish Councils of Brimpton and Crookham, who were seeking a replacement for the withdrawn *Venture* service between Silchester and Newbury. No details are known of what exactly was discussed and the timing of a solution, but, by the end of the year, a limited service between Newbury and Crookham Common was being provided by *Newbury & District*. In the main this facility had existed to provide journeys for war workers at the large Supply Depot at Thatcham Station, and may have operated as a contract, but after the plea certain off-peak journeys were made available for public use.

Venture ex-Nottingham AEC 'Regent' No.65 (TV 4493), seen at The Wharf on Route 37 to Basingstoke, with the N&D canteen in the background.

Former Ribble Tiger TS2-type No.86 (CK 3951) is seen at The Wharf after it had been extensively rebuilt with square windows, longer flared-out side panels and an extension at the rear to the full permitted length of 27ft 6ins. The cab area, on the other hand, has remained largely original. Note also the rather small headlamps. All of this work ensured that it outlasted all the other Leylands and remained in service until September 1948.

Also affecting the Newbury area was the requisition of Newbury Racecourse by the Ministry of War during 1942. This duly became both a prisoner of war camp and a marshalling yard for United States troops in the lead up to the Normandy landings, with a visit by General Eisenhower just before D-day in June 1944.

Also in 1942 a large camp was set up at Burghfield in order to house Irish women workers recruited for the Royal Ordnance Factory there. Later, in 1946, this would become HMS Dauntless, the training camp for Wrens, and in both guises this inevitably meant more transport requirements locally, some of which were met by *Newbury & District*.

During November 1942 the first of the Bedford OWB buses was delivered, this becoming No.94 (CMO 523) and fitted with a 32-seater front-entrance body by Duple of Hendon. It arrived in all-over grey paint, to which *N&D* added a green waistrail. In line with recent changes to regulations, the officially permitted number of standing passengers was set at 12, which represented an increase in 4 over the peacetime limit, even though that had been regularly exceeded ever since the start of the war in preference to leaving any passengers stranded.

Also from 4th November the insurance company agree to accept the following Leyland vehicles as being permitted to carry 12 standing passengers: Nos. 28 (RU 8058), 29 (RU 7559), 40 (RU 5072), 41 (RU 7560), 42 (KP 8372), 45 (CK 4518), 46 (WX 7898), 47 (HD 4369), 48 (HD 4368), 49 (KP 8371), 51 (HD 4370), 52 (TF 4155), 53 (HE 5229), 56 (HD 4371), 73 (WP 6206), 80 (HL 5228), 84 (CK 4573), 86 (CK 3951), 87 (DF 7841), 88 (MS 8834), 91 (CK 4312) and 93 (SY 4441). As this would leave 'Lion' LT2 No.50 (UR 9658) as the only Leyland not altered to 12 standing, it must be assumed that it had merely been left off the list.

It was also about this time that the final Thornycroft was purchased to become No.30 (EX 2861), this being an A12-type new in June 1931 to *Sid Page (Bee Line)* of Gorleston, Norfolk. It carried an Economy 20-seat front-entrance coach body, and had passed with that operator's express services between Norfolk and London to *George Ewer (Grey Green)* in 1934. After withdrawal it passed to *Tom Tappin* of Wallingford, from where *N&D* had acquired it.

A similar Thornycroft to N&D's No.30 (EX 2861), also acquired by Grey Green from Sid Page.

The first of the ubiquitous Bedford OWB's allocated to N&D became No.94 (CMO 523), and it is seen parked over by the Kennet & Avon Canal building at The Wharf in a later livery of red and white. These had wooden-slatted seating for 32 in a space usually intended for 26-8 passengers.

Seating capacity of another kind was also discussed towards the end of the year, now that more passengers were waiting for departures at The Wharf. Indeed, *N&D* had already responded to pleas for more seats by placing 10 dining chairs outside its office, but these had gradually disappeared until only 2 remained! The matter was aired in the Newbury Weekly News, and Councillor C.W. Burns responded on behalf of the Borough Council by making arrangements for half-a-dozen park benches to be transferred from Victoria Park and placed under the shelter of the over-hanging gallery of The Old Granaries.

The Enquiry Office at The Wharf was the hub of the Newbury & District operations throughout the history of the Company, with a good view of the buses coming and going. Drivers used the official clock to check on departure times, whilst the office could handle coach bookings and parcels traffic. Note the bicycle stored in the upper gallery, reached by a wooden staircase in the centre of the line of shop fronts. The Traffic Office was also situated in the same building.

The Traffic Commissioner, Sir Henry Piggott, called a conference of operators at Reading during November 1942 in order to discuss further operational restrictions necessitated by the shortages of fuel and rubber. The general principles were that no journeys should start after 9pm, also that Sunday services should not commence before 1pm, and that no relief buses should be provided for cinema-goers or other pleasure activities (in which he included church services). He also called for operators to delete some of the quieter daytime journeys wherever possible. At the same time the Ministry ordered that express coach services should cease and, with few exceptions duly sanctioned as in the national interest, and that came into effect from 1st October 1942. Although the latter had little direct effect on *Newbury & District* at that time, it would play some part in the future of the Company in the long run.

To take account of the above restrictions a revised timetable booklet was issued during December, though all routes continued to operate.

Yet another variety of Venture double-decker were the former Thomas Tilling AEC 'Regents' loaned to the Company by London Transport. These had open-staircase bodies designed and built by Tillings themselves, and ST 939 (GK 1031) is seen at The Wharf surrounded by 'Aces'.

Although further licenses had been obtained for Bedford OWB's, production was shared over a long list of operators, many of which would never have considered operating normal-control Bedfords under peacetime conditions. Although the bodies were built to a standard pattern, such work was divided between a number of coachbuilders, with Duple and Mulliner the most common. Allocation was strictly based on a proven need in relation to essential services, and quite a few local operators were granted just one example.

Chapter 16 – 1943

From the early months of 1943 there was a notable reduction in the demand for contract buses to take workers on Government-directed construction work. This at last allowed some time for those vehicles with serious bodywork issues to be thoroughly overhauled.

Bedford OWB No.95 (CMO 624) at The Wharf.

Also received during January was the second of the Bedford OWB-type buses, as No.95 (CMO 624), and this carried the standard 'utility' pattern front-entrance bus body with wooden slatted seating for 32. This was built by Duple of Hendon, as were those on Nos.96-8 (CMO 657-9), which followed during February.

Not withstanding these new arrivals there were no withdrawals other than Gilford No.22 (RD 1886), which departed by July of that year. This was in fact the last of some 23 of that make owned by the Company. It will be recalled that this coach had originally carried a rather open style of body, with dual-doorway layout and an extensive canvas central section, which lacked much in the way of rigidity, resulting in the fairly rare re-occurrence of it being fitted with another body taken from another vehicle. However, it was also wartime contract work that had extended this vehicle's life.

Apart from the constant threat of bombing raids on strategic targets such as factories, there were also times when German planes might jettison unused bombs over any area with a rail network. It was on such an occasion on 10th February 1943 that Newbury suffered its worst bombing. These fell on the Council Schools, St. John's Church and Lower Raymond's Almshouses, killing 15 people in all. Fortunately, only 4 people were in the church at the time, whilst the school lessons were over, otherwise far more than the 3 children, 1 teacher and the caretaker would have died. Nonetheless, it was a severe local tragedy which also served as a reminder that the war was still far from won, along with the loss of some 26 houses. As a result of this, a temporary St. John's church was

duly constructed, whilst the Girl's School was relocated to the historic Shaw House, just north of Newbury.

Whilst there is no doubt that *Newbury & District* and its employees wholeheartedly put every effort into the important of role of road transport during this difficult period, equally there was an inevitably strain on both maintenance standards and finances. Indeed, it was acknowledged by the Board that the Company was not in a good position to achieve re-construction of the fleet in respect of the anticipated post-war demands for bus and coach services. Therefore it was decided to once again seek a purchaser for the firm, though not all the Directors were agreeable to that option.

During the Autumn of 1943 a prospectus was drawn up outlying the fleet of 67 vehicles, comprising of the following:

Passenger vehicles –
Bedford:
70 BON 886 71 BON 887 94 CMO 523 95 CMO 624
96 CMO 657 97 CMO 658 98 CMO 659
Dennis:
23 EV 5909 55 BPH 293 58 MJ 4550 59 YD 9912
61 CKL 719 63 JB 6834 65 JY 4752 66 FJ 9581
67 AYA 102 68 DG 9516 69 DYF 184 72 CPA 828
75 BPG 531 76 BBP 339 77 ARA 370 78 BKE 720
79 RV 6259 81 AVO 977 82 KV 9903 83 AUB 354
85 JB 3354 89 DNW359 90 JU 4374 92 BUA 795
Leyland;
28 RU 8058 29 RU 7559 40 RU 5072 41 RU 7560
42 KP 8372 45 CK 4518 46 WX 7898 47 HD 4369
48 HD 4368 49 KP 8371 50 UR 9658 51 HD 4370
52 TF 4155 53 HE 5229 56 HD 4371 73 WP 6206
80 HL 5228 84 CK 4573 86 CK 3951 87 DF 7841
88 MS 8834 91 CK 4312 93 SY 4441
Thornycroft:
10 OU 3317 14 PG 2018 18 VF 9339 21 JH 492
30 EX 2861 31 TP 7951 43 TP 8693 57 TP 9164
74 EKP 140
Goods vehicles –
Bedford:
RD 5922 and JB 5917 (on loan to the Fire Service)
ABL 459 was in use as a service vehicle
AMO 455 was currently in store
Plus a garage towing tractor
Note: The Company held 9 Goods A-licenses, which had been voluntarily suspended due to wartime conditions, but for which the Traffic Commissioner had indicated would be re-instated if circumstances improved.

These details were sent to a number of parties, which included Basil Williams, owner of *Hants & Sussex,* who was known to be considering expansion of his operating area. Indeed, it is interesting to note that he did indeed have quite a presence in the area post-war, as he ran a fleet of buses on contracts to the building

Bedford OWB No.96 (CMO 657) at The Wharf and about to leave for Bucklebury Church. Behind it is Leyland 'Lion' No.51 (HD 4370) on the East Woodhay route, with one of the Tilling-bodied AEC 'Regents' then on loan to Venture parked at the rear.

of the Atomic Energy Research Establishment up at Harwell. This saw all sorts of secondhand buses of *Hants & Sussex* running over the local roads, with some even operating from villages previously served by *N&D* wartime contracts, and even included the building of a temporary garage at Harwell!

Earlier in 1943 there had been some optimism that service levels might be improved, but by the Autumn that had somewhat dissipated, so the timetable issue of September was merely a reprint of the previous one.

The latter months of this year were notable for two major events in the history of *Newbury & District,* and the first was a rather unfortunate and tragic accident which occurred on Friday 1st October.

The accident involved a collision between an *N&D* bus and a goods train at the Didcot Ordnance Factory. The regular driver of this contract route, Ernie Nobes, was proceeding through the shunting area at the wheel of Dennis 'Ace' No.89 (DNW 359), with a load of war workers from the Lambourn Woodlands, Baydon and Childrey areas, just after 5pm. The bus was following a Morris 10hp car and had reached a series of un-gated level crossings. The car driver briefly paused at the halt sign, but believing the area to be clear, he continued over the tracks, accelerating when he suddenly realised that a goods train was on the move towards his car. That driver's view had been obscured by a line of stationary goods wagons.

According to the evidence presented at the subsequent inquest and court proceedings, the signalman who should have been supervising the movement of the train on the ground had sent the train, which had 15 heavily-laden box cars and was being shunted from the rear, forwards before realising there were vehicles approaching the crossing. Whilst he claimed to have tried to alert the car driver of the danger, it was noted that no such signal had been seen by that driver, who had himself a rather miraculous near miss.

However, Ernie and his passengers were not so fortunate, as the bus followed the car onto the level crossing just as the buffers of the first box car reached that point. Although Ernie did try to brake at the last moment, it was too late, resulting in a collision between the heavy train and the bus. The latter was turned right over and the bodywork severely damaged, the train driver only realising what had occurred when the screams of the passengers were heard. To make matters worse one of the box cars came to rest on top of the bus, and it took two railway cranes over an hour to remove all the wreckage.

Thornycroft 'Dainty' No.74 (EKP 140) seen again under wartime conditions at The Wharf.

The human toll was indeed devastating, with 7 people killed, including Ernie Nobes and 8 others injured. The survivors and first aid parties were commended on their swift action following the accident, whilst 3 of the passengers were subsequently taken to the Radcliffe Hospital at Oxford. Despite all the dangers of wartime, this tragedy was a shock to the local population, occurring as it did on a routine journey, and several of the dead came from the small village of Lambourn Woodlands.

Ernie left his wife Winnie and young daughters Mary and Beryl, whilst 22-year old son Derek was serving as Sergeant Flight Engineer on a flying-boat of 209th Squadron of Coastal Command at RAF Congella, near Durban in South Africa when the news reached him.

The subsequent legal wrangling was complicated by the fact that the land was in the ownership of the MoS but the safety issues centred on the actions of *Great Western Railway* employees. The general conclusion was that, notwithstanding claims that hand signals had been given to try to stop the car driver proceeding, the presence of the other wagons and crates had made it impossible to see that another train was moving on the adjacent track. A legal claim was put forward on behalf of Mrs. Nobes at Oxford Assizes, and as a result of that she was duly awarded damages of £1,619 against the railway company for neglect. The Government subsequently agreed to meet the claims in respect of the other persons killed or injures.

This was a sad end to the life of Ernie Nobes, who was a well known and popular local figure, as clearly demonstrated by the large turnout at his funeral at St. Mary's Church in Woodlands St. Mary.

The solitary Dennis 'Mace' No.92 (BUA 795) is seen in wartime paintwork at The Wharf. Note the horse-shoe on the radiator, found on a number of buses in the Newbury area on various fleets over the years.

Newbury & District also brought action against the *GWR* in respect of the bus, which had been reduced to a pile of scrap, and a replacement was obtained in the shape of another 'Ace' in order to cover the contract. This became No.60 (DL 9011), which carried a front-entrance 20-seater bus body by Harrington of Hove. It had been new in June 1934 to the Isle of Wight based *Southern Vectis*, though latterly with the Ministry of War Transport. This vehicle was unusual for an *'Ace'* bus in having a large roof-mounted luggage rack, as it was for many years that operator's policy to provide extra luggage space for those visiting the island.

Dennis 'Ace' No.60 (DL 9011), bought to replace the bus lost in the Didcot smash, seen after sale by N&D.

It will be recalled that some years before, the Board of *Red & White United Transport* had considered whether to purchase *N&D,* so it was perhaps not a total surprise that they should now take the opportunity to acquire the Company. *Newbury & District* had hoped for £75,000, though this had been reduced to £62,000, which again meant that some Directors were not too happy, including Theo Denham, though the sale was approved at the Board Meeting on 23rd December, and a takeover date by the Chepstow-based owner was set for 1st January 1944.

Shortly before that, on 15th December, Newbury witnessed another tragedy, when two B17 bombers from 306th Battle Group collided after returning from a mission to Greenham Common, one coming down near The Swan at Newtown.

The *Red & White* story had been a steady one of expansion throughout South Wales, and eastwards into the Cheltenham, Gloucester and Stroud areas, as well as building up a good network of express routes, again through acquisitions as far flung as Liverpool and London. However, with the new investment from *Red & White* now secured, the future for *Newbury & District* could now be assured, as the Company was noted for its high standards in both engineering and operations.

Those familiar with the area south of Newbury will no doubt know of the Sandham Memorial Chapel at Burghclere, which the Behrend and Sandham families had constructed to mark their loss of Henry Sandham

Leyland 'Lion' LT2-type No.53 (HE 5229) seen at The Wharf on the East Woodhay service. The areas of white paint applied to the edges of mudguards and on life-rails were intended to avoid unnecessary accidents in black-out conditions.

from injuries sustained in the Great War. Others will know of it for the series of paintings commissioned from an artist they knew – one Stanley Spencer of Cookham, who used his own wartime experiences for the imagery, the property now being in the care of the National Trust. Somewhat lesser known will be a poem penned by 'Henry Sandham' (actually George Behrend), who was in the throes of the Italian campaign after some years in the North African desert, when he heard that his local bus company had been sold. Even so, it clearly demonstrates that he knew both the local firms and the *Red & White* fleet, and he was duly to become a noted writer on historic travel.

'Red & White'

By Henry Sandham, 8th Army 1944

Where once The Hermit ran, to Hermitage
Now smelly Albions crawl, o'er Newbury Bridge.
Or ancient Thornycrofts were wont to rock
Now only hear the common or Gardner knock
Of diesel engines, pounding where you will –
To Kingsclere, Hungerford or Woolton Hill.
Where Dennises on Thursdays, small in size
Served Ecchinswell or Inkpen, wartime Guys
Disturb our lanes with hideous noise and loud.
It might be Newport, Hereford or Stroud
Instead of Newbury. Never more to see
Those individual crocks, called N&D!
We make our movements, independence gone,
By order of The Bulwark, Chepstow Mon.

With the takeover by *Red & White* on 1st January 1944, the new owners appointed their Directors, all very experienced transport men from within its own ranks. Initially these were Guy Bown, David Lloyd Jones (Company Secretary), John Watts and Ralph Williams, and they were joined at the first Board Meeting held at Chepstow by Howell Davies, Thomas Jones and Arthur Watts. As the Company Secretary was still serving in the forces, his place was taken by Mr. G. A. Major until he returned.

On 15th January 1944 the shares held by the shareholders were transferred to *R&W*, and the following ceased to be active in *Newbury & District* – Theo Denham, Olive Minchin (nee Durnford), F. E. Frampton, George Howlett and Angus Marshall. On the other hand, the following former shareholders continued to be employed in the same capacities- Boss Denham (Garage Foreman), Bill, Ernie, Len and 'Nin' Durnford (all as fitters), James Davies (Traffic Manager), Ed White (Booking Clerk), Bert Greenwood and Bert Adnams (Drivers).

Theo Denham invested his money in property, and he also set up a taxi business known as the *Mill Lane Hire Service*. His brother Boss would also join him in later on, and we shall hear more of those activities in due course.

Chapter 17 – 1944

However, in order to fully appreciate the significance of this change of ownership, both in terms of the operation of services and the future fleet developments, an outline of the activities of *Red & White* is required.

Red & White United Transport Ltd.
Watts (Factors) Ltd.

The story of the development of both *Red & White United Transport Ltd.* and Watts (Factors) Ltd., of Lydney is inextricably linked.

Brothers Arthur and John Watts grew up in Lydney, then still a thriving industrial port serving the Dean Forest coal pits and other trades, their father having established an ironmonger's and 'universal provider's store in that town. The brother's early ventures saw Arthur as a motorcycle dealer and John undertaking mail delivery contracts by motorcycle and later by Ford T van. In 1912 Arthur took a Ford dealership, though sales were quite light locally and was of course interrupted in 1914 with the outbreak of war.

During the Great War Arthur served with the Royal Naval Air Service and John in the Army Motor Transport Corps, so naturally they wanted to use the skills gained to embark on new ventures after the conflict ended. Arthur decided to acquire war-surplus lorries and recondition them for re-sale, which John also initially joined him in. Watts' Garage was built in Lydney, which also continued the Ford dealership, whilst numbers of lorries of AEC, Federal, Peerless, Pierce-Arrow, Vulcan and Leyland types passed through the shops and were sold to meet the demand by other ex-servicemen who started up bus, charabanc and haulage operations all over South Wales and in the Bristol area, with both brothers putting lots of energy into the selling process.

However, in 1921 John commenced bus operations in the Tredegar area (as *Valley's Motor Bus Services)*, adding other services from Lydney the following year. The latter actually used some of the 200 Albion 32hp lorries that Arthur had heard were abandoned in Salonika, Greece after the Serbian Government had failed to complete their purchase. In a bold move Arthur borrowed the money to buy them, and they were shipped back to Newport, Monmouthshire! The choice of chassis was to prove a good one indeed, and it also influenced the shape of future bus purchases by what would become *Red & White* in due course.

Expansion on the bus front continued through the 1920's, and it is worth noting that from the outset it was the policy of the expanding Company to take on the former manager's of acquired firms as their local supervisors, whilst a number of former owners became shareholders and remained actively involved. This is significant when considering how *Newbury & District* had come into being and was developed.

Arthur also remained involved with the bus side, as well as developing haulage interest, and again his work on the refurbishment of vehicles, along with the use of heavy-oil (diesel) engines in road vehicles, both had a very significant bearing on the future shape of the passenger fleet.

Some banding together of operations had already taken place but, on 1st January 1930, all the passenger interests were formed into *Red & White Services Ltd.*, which was partly in response to the passage of the 1930 Road Traffic Act, which again had also shaped the decision to form the Newbury company.

Apart from further developing bus services in south-east Wales and the Chepstow and Hereford areas, the Company also became involved in long-distance express coach services from 1929, an area it would greatly expand in during the next decade. The tentacles of the growing network spread out to cover services to London from Liverpool, Chester, Hereford, Gloucester, South Wales and Birmingham, together with a Cardiff – Blackpool service! From the outset *Red & White* sought to co-operate with others in respect of ticketing and connecting services, and when *Associated Motorways* was formed with other express operators in July 1934 it was an enthusiastic advocate of the inter-changeability that afforded.

There was also a very significant purchase of a London coach operator in 1937, *Blue Belle Coaching*, which had built up a good trade on sightseeing and private hire work, whilst also providing *Red & White* with a coach station in Clapham. The other side of the business much developed before the Second World War was coach touring, ranging from day trips to 9-day holidays in France, Belgium, Holland and Germany, making the Company one of the pioneers. Holidays nearer home included the Wye Valley tours, something which would also feature in future *South Midland* programmes and put that Company on a firmer post-war footing, whilst also keeping the Newbury maintenance staff busy.

On the engineering front the experiments with diesel engines saw *Red & White* at the forefront of fleet conversions, which in those days offered sufficient savings (due to tax on heavy oil being so low) that it warranted the discarding of petrol engines! During this time Arthur Watts worked closely with Tom Gardner, head of the famous engine-builders based in Manchester, something else that would ultimately have a bearing on the future Newbury fleet.

The Company became *Red & White United Transport Ltd.* in 1937, though some other areas were set up under *United Welsh Services Ltd,* still with *R&W* Directors. Further consolidation took place, including the purchase of *Cheltenham District Traction Co. Ltd.* in July 1939 and, but for the war years, no doubt other operations would have been added. As it was there was several other London coach operators now partly controlled, together with the buses of the *Guernsey Railway Co. Ltd.,* and taxi operations in Birmingham, Gloucester, Leicester and Oxford. The group also had a hand in setting up Lydney Industrial Estates, which was a response to the poor employment situation latterly in that area once the old industries had closed, and even this would have its relevance to the *Newbury & District* story in due course.

Although the war did temporarily end the progress of the Watts' empire, it would be the same expertise in seizing the potential from such a situation which would result in further significant gains of territory even in those adverse conditions. Added to that, their strong engineering base, particularly the new works at The Bulwark, Chepstow, Monmouthshire, would be a vital ingredient in the struggle for post-war fleet renewals.

****

Mr. D.J.H. Flooks.

The first major task for the new owners was to take stock of both the Newbury operations and the vehicles in use. The *Red & White* Engineer, Mr. D.J.H. Flooks, inspected the fleet in early January, earmarking those vehicles worthy of overhaul for a further 2-3 years use, whilst others were listed for disposal as soon as practical. The fleet was numerically the same as when the sales prospectus had been prepared, although of course 'Ace' No.90 (DL 9011) had replaced the loss of similar bus No.89 (DNW 359). Although a number of the Leylands were considered as sound, the new owners were not interested in retaining the Dennis and Thornycroft vehicles any longer than was required.

However, the war was still on and materials even more scarce, so the timescale of such replacements would depend on a number of factors. Indeed, it would take all the skills of the Engineer (as Group Engineer from 1946) and his Central Works team to conjure up sufficient replacements!

In the meantime the Company was successful in having the outstanding *Newbury & District* permits from the Ministry of Supply for a pair of Bedford OWB's changed to Guy 'Arab' double-deckers, whilst during February permits for a further 4 of that type were sought. During April another application sought 4 more permits and, after these were considered, the Company was granted permits for a total of 7 from the Guy production line.

In order to hasten the departure of ageing 20-seaters, 10 Bedford OWB buses were loaned from the *Red & White* and *United Welsh* fleets, these being transferred to the Newbury fleet in 1946. They ran with original fleet numbers whilst on loan, and these were *Red & White* Nos.447 (EAX 647) and 454/76/9/80/1 (EWO 454/76/9/80/1) and *United Welsh* Nos.659/61/4/5 (DWN 258/95/8/9), all being new in 1942-3 with 32-seater utility bodies by Duple or Mulliner.

The arrival of these Bedfords allowed the disposal during April of the following: Thornycroft A-series buses Nos.10 (OU 3317), 14 (PG 2018), 18 (VF 9339), 30 (EX 2861), 31 (TP 7951), 43 (TP 8693) and 57 (TP 9614), along with Thornycroft 'Dainty' No.74 (EKP 140) and Dennis 'Dart' 23 (EV 5909). All of these, other than No.74, were sold to D. Penfold of Thatcham for scrap, though some saw further use as living vans for showmen. The 'Dainty', on the other hand, would continue to haunt The Wharf, as it was acquired by *Bert Austin* for his Cold Ash bus service! This clearout left only two Thornycrofts still in the fleet, these being A12-type No.21 (JH 492) and the 'Ardent' No.26 (RD 6270).

As already noted above, the new regime was intent on introducing double-deckers to the busier routes, which would also assist in reducing the fleet size at Newbury, as there had became an increased reliance on relief vehicles. However, the delivery of these was to be rather protracted, set as it was against the requirements of the war effort, so steps were taken to investigate whether any vehicles might be transferred from associated fleets, leading to additional variety.

Two of the Welsh Bedford OWB's seen together at The Wharf after official transfer to N&D, with former United Welsh 113 (DWN 295) and ex-Red & White 112 (EWO 454). These were initially in a grey livery, but are seen here after repainting to the new fleet livery of red and white in line with the R&W scheme.

It was also decided during February 1944 to rebuild and extend the Newbury garage, in order that this new outpost could be self-sufficient for its maintenance. It was also noted that the office accommodation was rather cramped, so an offer was made to Mr. Dennis (the tenant of No.5 The Wharf) to vacate in favour of the Company. The lease of No.8 (formerly used as a Police sub-station) was also added and permission forthcoming from the Borough Council (which owned the property) for internal alterations and also a renewal of the agreement for the use of the bus station area. The Wharf was the Head Office of the Company, whereas the Registered Office was now transferred to *Red & White's* headquarters at The Bulwark, Chepstow, Monmouthshire, where Board Meetings were also held.

Apart from those personnel changes already brought about by resignations from original shareholders, a further review took place early in 1944. It was decided that Freddie Spanswick would remain in post (as Rolling Stock Superintendent) to 31st December 1944, pending appointment of the new Works Foreman. Theo Denham would be retained in an advisory capacity for the same period, and each day he spent a couple of hours at The Wharf in the handover period to supervise transfer of records etc.

Other changes reviewed during the early months of 1944 were the introduction of new ticket machines to replace the old Bell Punch-type system in use since before *N&D* was formed, which would be done as soon as the equipment could be obtained, whilst new uniforms for the road crews were scheduled for September.

As previously noted, the search had been on to increase the number of double-deckers available for service at Newbury, and in April a one month old Guy 'Arab' Mk11 was able to be released from the *R&W*-controlled *Cheltenham District* fleet. This had become possible because the departure of a large number of American Forces from that area, and No.52 from the *Cheltenham* fleet became *N&D's* No.104 (FAD 253), the vehicle carrying a highbridge standard utility 56-seater body by Park Royal. This was therefore the first double-decker at Newbury, though it was not actually placed in service until the outstanding batch of 5 similar buses were received in due course.

The aim was of course to bring about a greater degree of standardisation of vehicle types. Whereas *R&W* had standardised heavily on Albion chassis, it also had significant numbers of AEC's and Leylands, along with the wartime Bedford OWB and Guy 'Arab'. The Gardner diesel engine had also been a standard type whenever practical, with many old types being fitted with such units.

In order to provide further replacement buses for use at Newbury, the Engineer searched other associated fleets for possible surplus vehicles, resulting in some arrivals later in the year, which will be reviewed in due course.

The future of haulage work was also considered, as in fact the *Red & White United Transport* did include some such subsidiaries. However, in respect of the Newbury area, it was decided to let the licenses go, providing that the Traffic Commissioner undertook not to oppose their reinstatement post-war. So the Bedford Pantechicon (AMO 455) was sold in July, but the Bedford lorry (JB 5917) continued in use as the Newbury service lorry, which now also included some journeys to Chepstow for spare parts.

During May the services were reviewed, along with the possibility of links to other *Red & White* areas or joint services with neighbouring concerns. Although some of these possibilities had be put back until there was an improvement in vehicle availability, services were amended where practical to reduce 'dead' mileage, and the more significant changes will be noted in due course.

The crimson and broken white livery of *Red & White* now started to feature at Newbury as vehicles returned from overhaul, whilst some of the Bedfords on loan from the other fleets already carried that scheme. The *Newbury & District* name was, however, retained on its vehicles, which now carried a fleetname in *R&W* style, with shaded serif letters in gold, with the first and last letter dropped and the remainder underlined.

By July the plans for the new garage were well advanced, and it was decided to try to acquire some additional land to the rear of the Mill Lane site, which at that time was being used by the Air Ministry for the production of aircraft parts.

Negotiations were also started with *George Hedges* regarding the purchase of his business, this being at the suggestion of Jim Davies, but nothing came of that. It is worth noting that Jim took well to the new regime, whilst there is little doubt that the Board soon recognised his talents for management. It was also at his suggestion that, in due course, the Board took the decision to expand yet further in the area, as we shall see at the appropriate time.

Whilst mentioning Reliance, it is worth noting that the fleet also contained a couple of Gilfords, and this 168SD -type (MY 3462) was set to become the last of that make to work into The Wharf, not being withdrawn until January 1948. It had been new to Skylark M.S. in 1930, working express routes into London and came to Brightwalton in 1938, when it was re-bodied with the body off a GMC (MW 2985).

Red & White also had a deserved reputation for taking care of the welfare of employees, whilst its active encouragement for staff to contribute to the National Savings Scheme saw the Company occupying the No.1 position in the industry for both 1944 and 1945. The scheme was extended to the Newbury staff who,

despite their relatively small number, achieved very good results. The inclusion of the *N&D* employees in the pension scheme was also considered as soon as it could be fully implemented, as of course all operators still had personnel away in the Forces.

Guy 'Arab' No.102 (CRX 282) at the Lower Thorn Street terminus in Reading, ready to return to East Ilsley with a full load of passengers.

In the meantime the first of the Guy double-deckers had gone to the bodybuilders during August, whilst some AEC 'Regal' saloons were being earmarked for transfer to Newbury. During September Guys 99-102 (CRX 279-82) were received, followed by No.103 (CRX 283) the following month. These were all on the 'Arab' Mk11 chassis and fitted with Gardner 5LW oil engines, though all needed to be painted before entering service. Their bodies were still to full utility standards, with few opening windows, wooden slatted seating, unglazed rear upper-deck emergency door and no internal panelling, all being constructed by Park Royal and of highbridge layout.

Nos.101 and 102 were the first licensed in October, whilst the others, along with No.104 (FAD 253), were in service by November. One was allocated to Kingsclere (invariably No.101 in the care of Driver Bill Cripps), and one to East Ilsley (No.99 at first, but variable, and in the care of Driver Charlie Bishop), whilst the others were based at Newbury. The outstation allocation at Kingsclere was reduced to just the one vehicle, with the Ashford Hill route now worked by Newbury garage.

Looking south from Newbury there was of course the territory of *Venture Ltd.,* whose buses already came to Newbury, whilst from the Oxford direction the coaches of *South Midland* had been a common pre-war sight. Both of those concerns had worked hard over the war years, particularly on contract work, and at the suggestion of Jim Davies *Red & White* explored the possibility of acquiring both operators. Indeed, as originally suggested, the aim was for them to be part of an enlarged single operator centred on Newbury.

Guy 'Arabs' Nos. 99-103 (CRX 279-3) at The Wharf.

However, in view of that proposal, it was decided to postpone the introduction of the pension scheme until the local situation was clearer. The new uniforms did, however, arrive and were issued during September.

On taking over the Newbury Company, *R&W* had inherited the unfinished business of the bus written off in the Didcot collision, so they issued a writ against the *Great Western Railway* in September.

Local builders were asked to quote for the work for the new garage, and in the meantime the existing garage was given a repaint by the Newbury maintenance staff when not busy, as this would be incorporated into the new enlargement scheme. The quotation of £13,980 from Cooke Bros. Ltd. of Northbrook Street, Newbury was accepted in November, and a start was made on clearing the site.

Although the maintenance staff at Newbury was no doubt skilful in the art of keeping the wheels turning, the new regime called for an expertise that they completely lacked, in the care of diesel engines. With that in mind, the *Red & White* Engineer, Mr. Flooks, held interviews for the post of Works Foreman.

The man he selected was Reg Hibbert, who had been born in Chester during 1908. At the age of 14 on 1st January 1923 he had started as an apprentice in the Central Works of *Crosville Motor Services* in Chester, arguably one of the best equipped bus works in the country. Such a works could tackle almost anything required to keep a bus fleet on the road, right through from fully-equipped machine shops to coachbuilders. During his 7-year training he worked through a number of areas, but from the mid-1930's he had been closely associated with the maintenance of the diesel engines then being introduced by that operator. In his work with these units Reg had attended training at CAV Bosch in Acton Vale, London W3 to learn all about fuel injection pumps.

Reg was engaged at the weekly rate of £7 5shillings, the appointment to commence at the start of January 1945. He stayed on through to his retirement in 1974, living at Roman Way, Thatcham in a house rented from Theo Denham and his successors, dying in May 1986. As he was a keen fan of horse-racing, it is amusing to note that he left Chester to work in Newbury for an employer that was based in Chepstow, all three towns having race tracks!

Reg Hibbert at the time of his retirement.

At the time of his appointment the maintenance staff at Newbury and main responsibilities were as follows: Boss Denham and Percy Andrews (Garage Foremen); Bill, Nin and Ernie Durnford (Fitters), Len Durnford (Fitter, but mostly concerned with tyres), George Amor (Coachbuilder) and a Vehicle Electrician and the Cleaners.

Also with the hoped for peace in the future, adverts started appearing in the Newbury Weekly News from September 1944, each highlighting the pleasures of a particular pre-war excursion destination, along with a evocative sketch, the series covering Cheddar Gorge, Brighton, Southsea, Wembley Stadium, Weymouth, Weston-super-Mare and Windsor, was intended to whet the appetite for the demand for post-war travel.

169

BRIGHTON

The Brighton advert used the following text –
'When the call of the sea can be answered, and heath and down, lake and mountainside are no longer considered 'unnecessary journeys', our omnibuses and coaches will be at your disposal to convert dreams of today into the realities of tomorrow'. That for Weymouth had 'in looking back you see the future: the present is an ugly phase that will pass. The happy days when you could enjoy the beauties of the countryside and the invigorating breezes from the sea, are on the way back, and our omnibuses and coaches will be there to bring it within your reach'. For Southsea the sentiment was 'the sacrifices you have made will help bring you a happier future. When the road is open again and the charm of the countryside no longer denied you, when the sea breeze comes within your reach once more, our omnibuses and coaches will be waiting to carry you to happy relaxation'.

The new ticket machines were available for a changeover from 1st October 1944, and this used the 'Bellgraphic' system. That utilised pre-printed ticket bases, with the company name, along with boxes for the class of ticket, fare paid and date of issue, all of which were written on by the conductor, which also created a carbon copy for retention within the ticket machine. The cancellation of return tickets was still undertaken by the use of the old 'nippers' which had previously formed the means of marking pre-printed tickets of different values. The new machines put the N&D crews on a par with their neighbours at *Thames Valley* and *City of Oxford*, along with other *Red & White* areas.

The first of the refurbished AEC 'Regal' saloons for use at Newbury were repainted during October 1944 and received there for service the following month, each of which had an interesting back history.

No.107 (TG 1568) had been new in May 1931 with *Bassett & Sons* of Gorseinon, and that operator was duly acquired by *United Welsh* in January 1939. It had a 32-seater rear-entrance bus body by Short, and was duly used by *Red & White* from November 1940 on internal transport at the Royal Ordnance Factory at Glascoed. It retained the original body, though this was probably rebuilt, and during the process it also gained a Gardner engine.

No.108 (TX 9498) had also originated in the same fleet in May 1930 and passed onto *United Welsh*. In 1942 it received a new utility style centre-entrance 35-seater bus body built by Duple, receiving its Gardner engine either at that time or when it passed into the *Red & White* fleet in July 1943.

The third vehicle was actually initially operated on hire from *Red & White*, so it ran for a time with their fleet No.89 (PJ 3827), which was of course vacant after the Didcot smash. According to motor tax files it was formally transferred to *Newbury & District* in May 1946 and it was re-numbered as No.109. It had started life as a very well-appointed coach with a rear-entrance 30-seater all-metal body by Arlington, the half-canopy cab being separated from the main saloon in a manner reminiscent of high-class cars of an earlier era. It ran for *South Wales Express* who, as the name implies, had pioneered an express service between Llanelly and London, which was acquired by *Red & White* in June 1933, and in December 1938 it was placed under the *Blue Belle* subsidiary in London. With the wartime curbs on coaching work it was hired to *Red & White* and in 1940 it was rebodied with a more workmanlike 35-seater centre-entrance bus body by Duple. When rebodied it still had an AEC petrol engine, though it is believed that a Gardner oil engine was duly fitted.

AEC 'Regal' No.109 (PJ 3827) after sale by N&D.

Now that these saloons and the Guy double-deckers were in service, another cull took place of the older stock, and this time it was the Dennis ranks that were selected, though finding buyers for these war-worn vehicles was not easy. The outgoing 'Aces' were No.55 (BPH 293), 65 (JY 4752), 66 (FJ 9581), 68 (DG 9516), 69 (DYF 184) and 76 (BBP 339) all in December 1944, along with the sole 'Mace' No.92 (BUA 795).

AEC 'Regal' No.108 (TX 9498) stands at The Wharf, with Venture AEC 'Regent' No.29 (BOU 699) on route 35 to Whitchurch, which looks a bit war-worn.

Having taken some time to fully examine the local operations, the parent company set about some re-organisation of services. Although there had been a noted decline in Government-related contracts, there remained a shortage of buses, so only a modest increase in service level was practical, with the following changes taking effect from 26th November 1944:

A service was reinstated over the Newbury – Wickham – Lambourn Woodlands route, which ran via Shefford Woodlands – Ploughley- Woodlands St. Mary on Thursdays and Saturdays only. This was Route 23, covering the route acquired from *Ernie Nobes*, though the new service was worked from the Newbury end and replaced the old Route 27.

In order to make better use of the vehicles outstationed at Lambourn, some minor timing changes were made to Route 6 (Newbury – Boxford – Eastbury – Lambourn), whereby the bus that had worked in from Lambourn for workers at the Shaw factory of Vickers-Armstrong continued through to Newbury Wharf. This bus then travelled back and forth between Newbury and Lambourn through the day before covering the worker's contract again in the afternoon, when a Newbury-based bus ran over the service route instead. At that point the timings for these contract journeys were not shown in the public timetable.

Most other existing Routes 1 to 21, with the exception of the suspended Route 13 (Newbury – North End on Thursdays and Saturdays only) were continued with only minor amendments. No further attempt was made to combine the Kingsclere Routes 4 and 5, as now the 5 ran only between Newbury and Ashford Hill, being

covered by Newbury garage, leaving the outstationed double-decker to cope with Route 4 to Kingsclere.

Route 16 was amended to run as far as Cold Ash Hospital crossroads, leaving *Bert Austin* to cover the section onto Downe House School and Westrop. The service was also now run as journeys to and from Newbury throughout, not starting with a short-working from Thatcham Broadway as was previously the case. However, the Bucklebury area services were still fed by buses coming off services to Thatcham Station, which then proceeded to The Broadway.

Interior view looking forward in the lower saloon of one of the Guy 'Arab' utilities, showing the wooden slatted seating. Note the eye-testing posting, with type size getting progressively smaller to make the point!

The previously un-numbered workings from Newbury to Crookham now became Route 17a, and ran as a full public service of 3 return journeys on Tuesdays, Thursdays and Saturdays.

The Moulsford Special continued as Route 33 and was reinstated to the pre-war level of operating on the 1st and 3rd Thursdays of each month.

The greatest revision, however, came with the Town Services in Newbury, which previously had been worked by 20-seater Thornycrofts, often necessitating the running of relief buses. A new set of 5 routes was set up as follows:

Route 24 Broadway – Post Office – Regal Cinema – Adam & Eve PH – York Road – Hambridge Road;
Route 25 Broadway – Post Office – Regal Cinema – Tydehams – The Gun PH – Battle Road;
Route 26 Camp Close – Chesterfield Road – St. Johns Road – Post Office – Regal Cinema – Broadway – The Greyhound PH – Shaw Bridge – Shaw Hill;
Route 27 The Wharf – Kimbers Corner – Grammar School – Kingsbridge Road;
Route 28 Post Office – Regal Cinema – Donnington Square – Donnington Village.

One of the newspaper announcements of the period.

The Post Office was in Cheap Street and the Regal Cinema in Bartholomew Street, and these services ran from Monday to Saturday only, whilst Route 26 incorporated some workings specifically convenient for workers at the Vickers-Armstrong factory at Shaw. Three buses were required to cover these duties, one working the 25, another covering the dove-tailed journeys on the 24, 26 and 28, whilst the third covered the sparser timetable of Route 27, together with other duties.

The above revisions also took in a number of journeys previously developed for wartime factory workers and made better use of the buses, eliminating quite a bit of dead mileage.

Discussions also got underway during November 1944 with *City of Oxford Motor Services Ltd.* over a joint operation between Newbury and Oxford, which will be further reviewed in due course. This link was a notable gap in local road communications, especially when considering the importance to each of the towns and the largely rural hinterland they served. Apart from the shopping and business opportunities such a service would provide, there were also the difficulties that people in the rural areas faced when requiring access to the hospitals in each town. Indeed, it is hard to see why the Oxford operator had not been more warmly disposed to earlier overtures by Jim Davies in his efforts to gain co-ordinated connections between the existing services at Rowstock. However, whatever the opinion of the *City of Oxford* management had been of the old *N&D*, it must surely have regarded the *Red & White* operations with due respect.

Guy No.101 (CRX 281) was for a number of years the Kingsclere allocation, in the care of Driver bill Cripps. The latter's careful handling ensured that the bus remained in good condition, requiring only the minimum of attention during its time outstationned. It is seen at The Wharf.

172

Chapter 18 – 1945

The prospect of obtaining sufficient replacements for all the aged buses at Newbury (and indeed other associated fleets) was much to the forefront of thought by the *Red & White* Engineer, and forays were made to various yards to see what might be found. On one such exploration a batch of 10 former *Scottish Motor Traction* AEC 'Regal' chassis of the 4-cylinder 0642-type were found in Broadhead's yard at Bollington in Cheshire. These had served for some time with the military and returned to *SMT* in poor shape. Their original Burlingham bus bodies were considered as beyond repair, but as AEC 'Regals' were already in use by *R&W* fleets it was decided to purchase these in February 1945. A start was made on refurbishing these, though at that point there were no bodies to be had for them, but they would indeed appear at *N&D* in due course.

A further Dennis 'Ace' departed in February, this being No.60 (DL 9011), which had been acquired to replace the smashed No.89 and had the shortest stay of all those of that type. Despite that it went on to have 5 further owners!

It will be recalled that Percy Andrews had a forte for refurbishing vehicles, and this evidently did not completely cease. Over the Winter of 1944/5 he overhauled a 1929 Ford AA (RX 4367), which had been new to *Charles Stout* of Shalbourne as a bus, but had latterly been a lorry with him. This was re-sold in February to yet another user in Salisbury.

The situation with double-deckers was a little better, though the pair currently outstanding had been sent to Massey Brothers due to other commitments by Park Royal, and their progress was rather slow. In view of vehicle requirements for the proposed Oxford service, permits were sought in February for a further pair of Guy 'Arab' chassis.

Indeed, agreement was reached between *City of Oxford* and *Newbury & District* on the joint service during March and, although neither concern was in a position to commence operation, it was decided to apply for the Road Service License in readiness. *N&D* had also been considering a Newbury – Swindon route, and in April they applied for a service to run on Mondays and Fridays only. This was granted and the service came into operation on Monday 3rd July as Route 29, with an 8.55am departure on those days from Newbury, and a return from Swindon at 3.55pm. The bus used for this also ran a short out to Lambourn and back, departing from Swindon at 12.55pm, which afforded a connection with Route 6 to or from Newbury.

By April over half the Newbury fleet had been repainted in the new livery, whilst negotiations were also underway with the Transport & General Worker's Union to bring the Newbury personnel in line with other *R&W* employees. These talks went on for some time, even resulting in the threat of a strike, though in the end the 52 drivers, 32 conductors and 34 other staff would benefit in the main from the new regime.

With the advent of VE Day on 8th May to celebrate the end of the war in Europe, as new wave of optimism swept the Country, and the Company found itself having to provide extra buses to cope with the crowds coming into Newbury. This also signalled hope that some excursions might resume soon, though once permission was forthcoming it was tempered by strict mileage restrictions.

The necessary Ministerial permission was also forthcoming in June for the construction of the new garage. The maintenance staff had worked wonders over the wartime years, but there was a lack of modern facilities, certainly by *Red & White* standards. The lack of proper inspection pits had led to some potentially dangerous practices whereby vehicles were driven up onto railway sleepers to provide access to the underside, whilst much of the fleet had to be kept outside. The new larger garage would address these issues, though with chronic shortages of all building materials, some delays would be incurred.

The better of the Leylands were overhauled and re-painted in the red and white scheme, such as No.48 (HD 4368) seen at The Wharf.

A few more redundant vehicles were weeded out, and Dennis 'Ace' No.59 (YD 9912) left in April, whereas the first of the Leylands, 'Lion' LT2-type No.51 (HD 4370) departed in May, followed in July by Dennis 'Ace' No.78 (BKE 720). However, very slow progress on the former *SMT* 'Regals' meant that there was still the need to retain older types a little longer.

July had brought some relaxation on restrictions for private hire work meant that garage-to-garage mileage of 70 miles was permitted for private hire, whereas only 50 miles was approved in respect of advertised excursions. The latter restriction, along with shortage of vehicles meant that only some local downland tours were operated on Wednesday and Sunday afternoons. Indeed, such was the situation with vehicles that wooden-slatted Bedford OWB's were used at times!

Bedford OWB No.96 (CMO 657) newly re-painted.

July saw commencement of the Newbury – Oxford Route 30, though the Company had hoped to have taken delivery of the pair of Massey-bodied 'Arabs' by then. The completion of these had been causing some concern, so Reg Hibbert had been up to Pemberton near Wigan to check on the progress. He returned to report that completion was not likely before the end of the Summer, whilst a further problem arose because *City of Oxford* was short of crews.

However, *N&D* was keen to see this underway, so it was resolved that two of the 99-104 batch of Guys (despite their wooden seats) would be allocated to the duty, one of which would cover the Oxford-based runs until the situation improved at *City of Oxford*. Driver Ernie Church and his wife Kathleen had been together as a crew throughout the war years, and they were sent to cover the Oxford workings.

The service commenced on Sunday 29th July, with departures from each end of the route at 2pm, 4pm, 6pm and 8pm. The full weekday service commenced the following day, with simultaneous departures at 9.30am, 11.30am, 3.30pm and 5.30pm, and initially the Newbury-based crew consisted of Driver Burden and Conductor Allen. The journey time stood at 1 hour and 40 minutes, had a route mileage of just under 30 and the adult return fare was 3 shillings 10 pence, the Oxford terminus being at the Gloucester Green Bus Station.

The Church's were not the only dedicated husband-and-wife pairing at *N&D,* as Charlie and Florence Penlington worked as driver and conductress.

From July a new style of cover graced the timetable booklets, featuring a sketch of a fictitious double-deck Albion on its way to Thatcham. As it was, there would be no buses of that type, though some single-deckers would make an appearance in due course.

The 2 Bedfords on loan to what had become the National Fire Service (RD 5922 and ABL 759) were returned by July and were sold without further service with *N&D*.

During August the last of the Thornycroft A-series buses was disposed of, this being No.21 (JH 492), whilst it is believed that 'Ardent' No.26 (RD 6270) also went at that time, bringing to a close an association with that make pre-dating the formation of *N&D*. Also out that month was another 'Ace' No.85 (JB 3354), and by that month Leyland 'Lion' PLSC3-type No.28 (RU 8058) had also gone.

174

It was also decided soon after the Newbury – Swindon service had started to put this on a daily basis, which commenced from Monday 17th September. This route had a mileage of 29.5 miles, a journey time of 1 hour and an adult return fare of 3 shillings 9 pence, using the Regent Circus terminus at Swindon.

Some discussions had been taking place regarding the contract for advertising on the buses, which in pre-war days had been with Darby's Advertising Agency. With a completely single-deck fleet, the adverts had consisted of those painted onto route boards or those carried inside the saloon. However, as part of the post-war repainting and the advent of double-deckers, new arrangements were made with Frank Mason & Co.

Rear view of Massey-bodied Guy 'Arab' No.105 (CRX 595), with a Thames Valley 'Titan' TD1 in the background. Note the adverts for local firms.

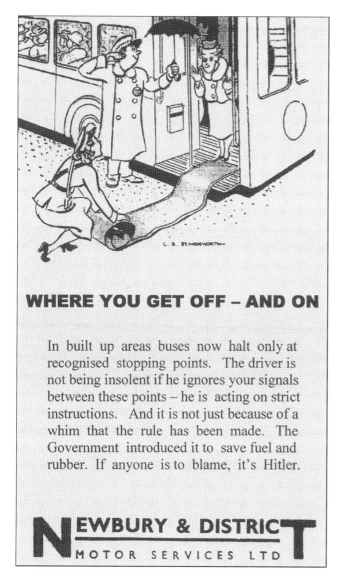

WHERE YOU GET OFF – AND ON

In built up areas buses now halt only at recognised stopping points. The driver is not being insolent if he ignores your signals between these points – he is acting on strict instructions. And it is not just because of a whim that the rule has been made. The Government introduced it to save fuel and rubber. If anyone is to blame, it's Hitler.

NEWBURY & DISTRICT
MOTOR SERVICES LTD

Above - The second in a series of public information notices placed in the Newbury Weekly News. Below – Guy 'Arab' No.100 (CRX 280) on the Oxford service.

The outstanding pair of Massey-bodied Guys arrived in September as Nos.105/6 (CRX 595/6). Their bodies were of highbridge layout and still owed much to the Ministry of Supply utility standards, even though other firms were supplying vehicles with upholstered seats by then. However, these still had wooden slatted seating and lacked interior panelling. They did have some relaxed features such as a sloping cab-line and more opening windows, though the amount of unseasoned timber used in their construction would soon prove problematical in terms of warping and leaking. Both were on the Mk11 'Arab' chassis and fitted with Gardner 5LW engines.

Indeed coach-building, in common with many other industries, had given way to the priorities of wartime, with most concerns working on aircraft production. As it was, several already had prior experience in such work, whilst other firms who started in that line would duly consider transferring the workforce to peacetime demands for bodywork or refurbishments. Some pre-war firms did not resume coach-building, whilst the decision not to re-open the famous *London Transport*

Leyland 'Lion' LT2-type No.53 (HE 5229) re-painted.

Chiswick bodyshops had a marked knock-on effect throughout the country on the availability of new buses. Added to this, was a shortage of sound wood for the construction of frames, resulting in many early post-war bodies having relatively short lives, and this made the refurbishment of existing bodies a viable alternative.

Work on the new garage proceeded well, with some delays awaiting materials, and by the end of October the steelwork was in the course of erection. Indeed, as *Red & White* had acquired *Venture* of Basingstoke in March, followed by *South Midland* in October, the new garage was destined to become the central works for all three fleets. Reg and his assistants would be kept busy over the next few years getting all the various vehicles into shape, so the facilities were an essential factor in the decision to make those additional acquisitions.

The latter months of 1945 saw only a few changes to services. In October agreement with *Wilts & Dorset* saw *N&D* running more buses along the Andover Road to Highclere and East Woodhay. As a result of new Route 30 (Newbury – Rowstock – Abingdon – Oxford), the Sunday terminus on Route 1 (Newbury – East Ilsley – Rowstock) was cut back to East Ilsley from November.

Indeed, it is an illustration of how busy the *Newbury & District* buses had been that in 1938 the annual mileage had been some 750,000. Whilst that had risen by one-third to the 1 million mark, the total number passengers had risen from 1,150,000 to over 3 million in 1945!

The connecting services of *Venture* were shown in the *Newbury & District* timetable booklet from October 1945 and some links, such as the ability to travel between Basingstoke and Oxford, by changing at Newbury, were highlighted. Unfortunately the route numbers of *N&D* and *Venture* services clashed, though that would be resolved later on.

The only other vehicle disposal that year came in December, with the departure of Leyland 'Lion' LT2-type No.93 (SY 4441) on the cessation of the contract it had been covering. This coach had been outstationed ever since it was acquired in December 1941, possibly at Hungerford, and was a very rare sight in Newbury.

Some alterations took place in the Directors during December, with the departure of R. Williams, T.J. Jones and H.M. Davies, with D. Lloyd Jones, F.W. Hodgkinson (as Managing Director) and G.A. Major (as Secretary) taking their place.

During December the parent company had gained permission from the Ministry to order a number of single-deck Albion chassis, though that manufacturer had then to report that it was not in a position to accept such an order! Although the order for 10 chassis was taken up by AEC of Southall soon after that, the delivery date of June 1946 would prove to be wildly optimistic. So, once again the search was on to find other vehicles that could be released from other associated fleets, along with further renovations of old stock. In connection with the latter, the search was on for some bodies suitable for the former *SMT* AEC 'Regals' now being refurbished and fitted with Gardner 5LW oil engines and earmarked for the Newbury fleet.

Chapter 19 – 1946

The prospects for new buses still seemed rather limited at the start of 1946, therefore it was decided that 7 of the Bedford OWB's currently on loan at Newbury would be officially be transferred from 1st January. These became *N&D* Nos.110-6 (EWO 480, EWO 479, EWO 454, DWN 295, DWN 258, DWN 298 and DWN 299).

These additions to the permanent allocation allowed a further trio of Dennis 'Ace' buses to come off their assigned contract runs, with No.72 (CPA 828) going in January, whereas No.61 (CKL 719) departed in March and No.67 (AYA 102) followed in May. As noted previously, new owners for these war-worn buses were not exactly queuing at the garage doors!

Bedford OWB No.118 (EWO 476) loads at The Wharf for Yattendon.

Work on the new garage was progressing well, and it was hoped to take occupation during March. Nearby was another building in use by the Air Ministry, but not within the area currently owned by the Company. However, once inspected, it was found to be too low to accommodate double-deckers, so the purchase of this was not pursued.

Further consideration was also given as to whether haulage operations should form part of the post-war *Newbury & District* set up. The Company had previously covered a total tonnage of 24.5 tons using some 9 lorries. Although the *Red & White* group did feature some haulage operations, it was decided that in the case of Newbury these would not be continued, and the A-licenses were therefore surrendered.

Regarding the bus services, some improvements were forthcoming during March, with an additional journey on Saturdays to West Woodhay from 23rd, whilst the Swindon service gained an additional Saturdays-only run that left Swindon at 8.15pm, together with some re-arrangements to the Sunday service, effective from Saturday 20th.

It was also found possible at last to increase the frequency of the Route 30 between Newbury and Oxford, which increased to 6 weekday journeys (in place of the original 4) from 1st April 1946.

Wilts & Dorset services operated to various points to the south and west of the *N&D* area, and during March they approached Jim Davies regarding their proposal to acquire the licenses of *Leonard Humphries* of Fosbury, a hamlet situated in Wiltshire and some 8 miles south of Hungerford. One of his operations was a Thursdays-only return journey to Newbury, though from the advent of the 1930 Act he had been precluded from taking passengers solely between the stops in Hungerford and Newbury, as protection for the *N&D* services. The latter confirmed that it had no objections to the Salisbury operator's proposal which, although it did go ahead, did not continue with that market-day link to Newbury.

As the *Thames Valley* Dormy Shed at Newbury was still held by the Ministry of Supply, arrangements were made to relocate the pair of double-deckers used on Route 10 (Newbury – Thatcham – Reading) to the enlarged *N&D* garage, the buses having been kept outside at Newbury Station overnight. They could now make use of the new bus-washing machine that had been installed, whilst the crews now had the benefit of improved facilities, these new arrangements taking effect from Saturday 18th May.

A further bus released from the *Cheltenham District* fleet arrived at Newbury in May as No.117 (HG 1221), though this was a rather unusual vehicle. It had originated with the Lancashire municipal operator *Burnley Corporation,* passing into the *Burnley, Colne & Nelson Joint* fleet. New in March 1932, this AEC 'Regent' had a petrol engine and carried a centre-entrance 51-seater double-deck body built by Brush. This was one of 3 such buses purchased by *Red & White,* the other pair going to *Venture* at Basingstoke. This type of bodywork was relatively common with northern municipalities where buses had replaced trams, and this body built to Roe design also featured twin staircases leading down to the centre doorway. Due to these features, this bus had proven very unpopular with the Cheltenham bus conductors, who had described the straight staircases as 'suicidal' in the local press! Being a one-off type at Newbury it was generally to be found on the relatively short but busy route between Newbury and Thatcham Station.

Whilst reviewing No.117, it is worth noting that it sported a 'Regal' radiator when at Newbury, indicative of the 'scrapyard trawl' that had taken place

when trying to keep these older types in service. Indeed, looking through the photos of the *SMT* AEC 'Regals', it is apparent that would become No.122 (FS 8560) carried a radiator from the normal-control 'Ranger' model, whilst No.130 (FS 8565) had a unit taken from a 6-wheeler 'Renown' chassis! Of course, all of these models used the same outline of radiator, though the exact finish changed over the years.

The same could also be said of the various Leyland types, as many of the early radiators would fit more than one model, so some exchanges did take place. Whereas many of the vehicles had originally carried radiators sporting specific model badges (e.g. Lion or Tiger heads), plainer replacements had later been fitted, or even replaced by longer Cov-Rad units.

The co-ordination of services with *Venture* was further discussed during March, resulting in some exchanges of coverage on certain roads. *N&D* Route 26 (Local Service between Camp and Shaw) was discontinued, being replaced by a pair of new jointly-operated routes, the 31 and 31a, which ran between Shaw (Factory) – Camp Close – Newtown – Newtown Common (31 only) or Burghclere (31a only) – Highclere Station – Whitway. Only a limited number of early-morning and late-afternoon journeys actually reached Whitway. *Venture* operated this out of its Whitchurch outstation, whilst also from the same 2nd June starting date, it solely operated a new Newbury – Whitchurch Route 35. It is worth noting that these service numbers fitted in perfectly with the *N&D* scheme at that time, with the *Venture* 35 being shown in the Newbury timetables with just the heading of *Venture Ltd.* to distinguish it, which gives even further

AEC 'Regent' No.117 (HG 1221) is shown working to Thatcham Station, flanked by former SMT 'Regal' No.125 (FS 8576) and ex-Yorkshire Woollen District Leyland 'Lion' LT2 No.56 (HD 4371).

credence to the claim by Jim Davies that at one point serious thoughts were given to fully combining the Basingstoke and Newbury operations as one unit.

A number of other changes came into effect from 26th June, the more significant being as follows:
Route 7 – (Newbury – Fawley) extended to Wantage on Wednesdays and Saturdays (with time changes);
Route 17a – (Newbury - Crookham) this link ceased in that form and was replaced by re-routing of the existing *Venture* Basingstoke – Tadley – Baughurst – Newbury service, which was re-numbered as Route 37 under the new co-ordination;
Route 26 – Having been replaced by the new Routes 31/31a, this number was allocated to a new Local Service (The Broadway – Western End);
Route 34 – A new link between Wantage and Lambourn, which ran on Wednesdays and Saturdays;
Route 36 – A new route between Lambourn and Hungerford, operating on Wednesdays only – that day being market day in both Hungerford and Wantage.

Those changes in respect of services to Wantage had already been discussed with *City of Oxford*, as it had a number of services there, though it was content to accept the proposal with the proviso that a protective fare would cover the local section into the town.

At the same time, what had for some time been the daily early-morning contract working from Lambourn to the Vickers-Armstrong factory at Eddington, just north of Hungerford, was now included in the table for Route 36. This also had a midday journey towards Lambourn on Saturdays only in reflection to half-day working on that day, though at one time the factory operated around-the-clock as part of the war effort.

It is interesting to speculate what might have taken place had events played out differently in respect of the further bringing together of *Newbury & District* and *Venture.* Certainly on the engineering side there was a lot of input between 1946 and 1950, which will be reviewed in greater detail in due course. As we have seen above, services were revised and some joint operations forthcoming, plus there were instances where the coaches from either fleet might be found helping out on exceptional hirings. At the time there were obviously other priorities and, in the longer term, other events would intervene, leaving each of the two concerns still continue as separate entities.

In the meantime completion of the new garage at Newbury had slipped to early May due to the shortages of materials. However, the new facility gave 4 fully-tiled inspection pits, along with a paintshop that could accommodate 2 buses. Indeed, there were now 2 full-time painters on the staff, making the garage self-sufficient in respect of repaints, which saved the long mileage to Chepstow for such work. All of the new garage area could take full-height double-deckers, whereas the older part of the garage, which fronted onto Mill Lane, could only take single-deck vehicles, this most commonly being used for the coaches (once they arrived).

Plan of the extended garage, with the old garage at the bottom, and the new part reached through the wash-down area, then the pits and paint shop.

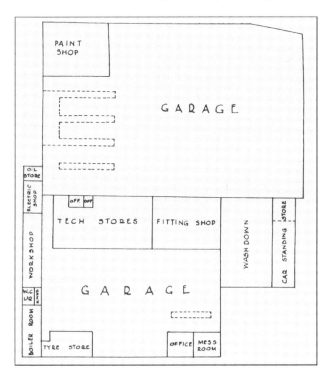

Indeed, on the latter point, although the mileage restrictions on private hire and excursions had now been lifted, the lack of a viable coach fleet was the cause for some anxiety, as none of the pre-war *N&D* fleet was considered worthy of retention! *Red & White* had placed large orders for chassis with Albion and Guy, though neither could promise delivery dates, whilst AEC had accepted a large order for 'Regal' chassis for bodying as both buses and coaches, though the proposed dates were invariably not met.

In order to get something moving locally, it was decided to run a very limited programme of excursions for Easter 1946, using coaches borrowed from the *South Midland* fleet. These ran to Southsea and Bournemouth, along with an evening tour via Pangbourne. Regular Sunday runs to Southsea were introduced from 12th May, and also every other Sunday there was an excursion to Bournemouth. In respect of Southsea, *South Midland* re-introduced its daily Summer express from Oxford from Easter, which of course already picked up at Newbury Wharf. Indeed, in due course it became very common for one coach to start from the town, hired to *South Midland,* as Southsea was a popular destination, either for a week's holiday or for those travelling on to stay on the Isle of Wight and using a period return ticket.

In view of the need to create a new coaching fleet at Newbury, it was decided that 4 of the Duple-bodied AEC 'Regals' originally intended for the *Venture* fleet would be diverted to Newbury instead. Even so, these would not materialise for over a year, which was indeed very frustrating.

Some bodies suitable for the former *Scottish Motor Traction* AEC 'Regals' had been acquired from the same yard at Broadhead's of Bollington, having been sent there by *North Western* as it prepared a batch of 1936 Bristol JO5G's for re-bodying. These bodies had been constructed during the period that the Lowestoft coach factory was changing from Eastern Counties to eastern Coach Works, but for the purpose of this history they will be referred to as ECOC bodies. They were originally built as 31-seaters and featured high-backed seats and some even had opening roofs, as they were used on some long inter-urban services.

Red & White acquired 22 of these bodies in May 1946 and set about refurbishing them for use on various chassis. As already noted, the ex-*SMT* 'Regals' had been earmarked for Newbury, so priority was given to completing these buses. In order to achieve this some of the bodies went to the *R&W*-associated Mumford's coachworks at Lydney.

This facility had been set up under the direction of Arthur and John Watts in order to provide employment locally, as the town in which they had grown up had in latter times become depressed in respcct of employment, whilst also increasing the capacity to produce new bodies for associated fleets. The original bodybuilding firm of Mumford's had been in Plymouth, whilst that family had also worked with John Watts on operating buses as *Southern General* for a time in the Plymouth area during the period 1930/1.

A few more excursions were operated in the Summer months, together with those to Royal Ascot Races on 18th/20th/21st June, again using borrowed coaches from Oxford, which left 1946 as a very disappointing year in respect of coaching work.

A further review of the single-deck fleet at Newbury led to the transfer circa June of the remaining trio of Bedford OWB's then on loan, and these became Nos.118-120 (EWO 476, EWO 481 and EAX 647).

During June the first of the 10 former *Scottish Motor Traction* AEC 'Regals' was completed and sent to *N&D* as No.121 (FS 8582), now seating 35 and fitted with a Gardner 5LW oil engine. These vehicles would continue to be received at the rate of one per month, with No.122 (FS 8560) in July, 123 (FS 8562) in August, 124 (FS 8567) in September, 125 (FS 8576) in October and 126 (FS 8572) in November, after which there was a gap before the final quartet were completed. As can be seen, the fleet numbers were allocated as they were ready, leaving the registrations in no particular sequence. All had been new in June and July 1934, being taken by the War Department in 1940 and returned to *SMT* in 1942/3 in poor shape.

AEC 'Regal' No.122 (FS 8560) at Mill Lane, with a 'Ranger' radiator.

With the some slight improvement in the vehicle situation, alongside reductions in dead mileage and contract commitments, it was possible to dispense with the services of a number of older saloons. No.70 (BON 886), the first of a pair of Bedford WTB's used on contract workings, went in June, along with Dennis 'Aces' Nos.77 (ARA 370) and 81 (AVO 977). Also departing that month were Leyland 'Lion' PLSC3-

type No.41 (RU 7560), and probably also identical bus No.40 (RU 5072), along with 'Lion' LT1-types Nos. 42 and 49 (KP 8372 and 8371). These were followed by two further Dennis 'Aces', with No. 82 (KV 9903) in July and No.90 (JU 4374) in August.

Nearside view of No.122 (FS 8560) at The Wharf. The distinctively shaped cab window came from the desire of North Western to have bodies similar to those it already had from Harringtons.

It is worth noting that the Lambourn outstation had grown over the years from 1939, when one Dennis 'Ace' was there, to requiring 3 such vehicles by the end of hostilities. These were replaced by a similar number of Bedford OWB's in 1946, being used for some journeys on Route 6 to Newbury, the Shaw factory workings and the Didcot contract. Sometimes one of the surviving Leylands might also make an appearance at Lambourn, whilst at the Kintbury outstation was the remaining Bedford WTB No.71 (BON 887) in the care of Bert Greenwood, and the other outstations at Chilton Foliat, Hermitage and West Ilsley were still covered by the surviving 'Aces' and Leylands, all of the latter working to the Didcot Ordnance Factory, which was now running down.

Indeed, it was not long before some of the former wartime sites became earmarked for redevelopment, each of these requiring at least as many contract buses as in wartime days. The former Chilton Airfield, just north of the Berkshire Downs and south of Harwell became the site for the Atomic Energy Research Establishment, whilst the Aldermaston site became the home of the Atomic Weapons Research Establishment. Although *N&D* did provide some buses to the latter, it fell mainly to *Thames Valley* and local independents to cover the contracts to that site.

On the other hand the AERE project required considerably more contract workings, in fact well beyond what *Newbury & District* could cover. In respect of that site, there was even a garage installed by *Hants & Sussex* to cater for its fleet based there, whilst *Banfield's Coaches* (of Peckham, South London) daily transported workers who were taken to

AEC 'Regal' No.124 (FS 8567) is seen on the route to Inkpen (Lower Green), with No.52 (TF 4155) going to Ashford Hill, and beyond that there is one of the ex-YWD Leyland 'Lion' LT2's. No.52 managed to remain the least altered of all the Leylands, retaining its original style radiator, with enamelled lion-head badge to the end.

the site from their lodgings in the old army camp at Kingston Bagpuize. *Reliance* of Brightwalton and *Tappin's* of Wallingford were also involved, along with *South Midland* from Oxford and Abingdon areas, whilst *N&D* provided runs from Aldbourne, Kintbury, Chilton Foliat, Hungerford, Lambourn and West Ilsley as well as contracts from Newbury via Hampstead Norris and Hermitage, all of which went on for many years.

Another contract job that *N&D* tendered for during May 1946 had been to transfer crews of British Overseas Airways between Bristol Airport and the airport at Hurn, near Bournemouth, though nothing further came of this.

The parcels service had been suspended during the war years, with very crowded buses and poor interior lighting making it unworkable, but this was fully reinstated after the return of peace. Although haulage work was no longer taken, the Company did now have an agency for Carter Patterson, the nationwide carriers, and The Wharf office was used in that respect.

During June further discussion took place regarding the position of the Newbury garage in relation to the fleets of *Venture* and *South Midland*, and it was decided that all major overhauls and repaints would be undertaken there. In view of this expansion of work it was also resolved to appoint a Garage Engineer, and in due course Sid Taylor was appointed. He had been

born in Newbury diring 1908, making him the same age as Reg Hibbert, though where he gained his training has not come to light. Also returning at that time was Eddie Whitington, a relative of Theo Denham by marriage, who was employed on general duties around the garage and had latterly been serving with the RAF. We shall hear more of both of these in due course.

Major overhauls commenced in September, and by the end of the year 4 *South Midland* vehicles and 1 from *Venture* had been dealt with, along with those from the Newbury fleet.

July 1946 saw two possible additions to the route network, with approaches from *Bert Austin* of Cold Ash and *S. Huntley & Son* of East Oakley, both of whom were desirous of selling out. *Bert Austin* wanted £4250 for his license and goodwill, though the Board only reckoned this to be worth some £2000 less, so nothing further came of that. In respect of the offer from *Huntley,* it was decided that this would be better dealt with under *Venture* instead.

A number of further alterations to services took place from Sunday 21st July:
Route 11 Was cut back from Highclere (Pheasant) to run only as far as Highclere (Red House);
Route 12 (Newbury - West Woodhay) was altered to run via North End, with journeys on Thursdays and Saturdays only (replacing a link lost in wartime);
Route 20 (Newbury – Frilsham) was amended to run via Hermitage Y-roads – Cold Ash – Slanting Hill and gained an 8.15pm bus from Newbury on Saturdays;
Route 21 (Newbury – Aldworth) gained a 9.15pm bus on Saturdays evenings from Newbury.

A new timetable booklet was issued dated 21st July in order to take into account the recent changes, some of which had only been announced by handbill and in the

local press. However, due to reductions in the working pattern at the Vickers-Armstrong factory at Shaw, there were further service amendments from 2nd September:

Route 6 (Newbury – Lambourn) the bus departed from Lambourn at 7.10am for Shaw Factory and onto Newbury Wharf, whilst the return run was amended to 5.35pm from Shaw. On Saturdays a 12.35pm journey ran from Shaw, the positioning journey providing an additional run in from Lambourn at 11am;

Route 8 (Newbury – Wickham – Hungerford Newtown) lost both its 7.15am and 7.30am journeys;

Route 9 (Newbury – Hungerford via Bath Road) in place of a previous contract working, this had a 6.40am departure towards the factory at Eddington, which then formed the existing 7.15am run back to Shaw Factory, making this an interesting example of a two-way worker's service primarily intended for the same employer, albeit in different towns. Homeward journeys were covered by suitably scheduled buses.

As will be appreciated, most of the above operations had their origins in dedicated contract routes, though with reduced numbers now employed at such sites, it was now practical to cater for workers using suitably timed service journeys, which reduced the need for vehicles to be retained solely for contract obligations.

However, within Newbury there were also other demands for services, both from the new Park House School, now opened as a replacement for the boy's school bombed in 1943, along with new housing estates being constructed around the town. Whereas, at one time a 20-seater single-decker might suffice for the service out to Wash Common, further extensive housing saw such services increasing to double-deckers in the early post-war years. Increasingly over the war years many more journeys to work had been undertaken by bus, and would continue to be the case.

The 10 rebuilt AEC 'Regals' of SMT and NWRCC origins saw a wide variety of use, and No.125 (FS 8576) was caught by Ken Rutterford as he cycled home from his RAF base. The location is The Round House at Halfway, a one-time toll-house on the Bath Road turnpike which, despite a campaign to save it, was demolished in 1966.

Throughout 1946 the *Red & White* Board had pressed both AEC and Duple for delivery of the outstanding vehicles, but without much success. Some Albion and Guy orders had now been accepted for chassis, but the most pressing issue was finding coachbuilders who could delivery. A number of projects were therefore direct to the Mumford works at Lydney, along with bodies ordered from other firms such as Pickering of Wishaw and Barnard of Norwich.

As Bedford production had continued on military lorries and the wartime OWB, that factory was in a better position than most, so it was decided to place an order for a number of Bedford OB-type coaches for delivery in 1947. At the outset a pair of these was earmarked to *Newbury & District*, but in due course these would be diverted to *South Midland* instead! Better news was, however, forthcoming in November 1946, when Duples advised that the 10 AEC 'Regal' buses would be ready about March 1947, which gave a further reprieve to the remaining Leylands, along with the 'Aces' and the sole Bedford WTB still in use.

Changes in the fleet had, therefore, been rather limited in the latter months of 1946, with the only additional disposal being of No.29 (RU 7559), which was the last of the former *Hants & Dorset* PLSC3-type Leyland 'Lions', and had departed by December. On the incoming front there was just one vehicle, an Austin 8hp car (FTX 109), which was for the use of the Depot Inspector.

Chapter 20 – 1947

This year saw the arrival of the first coaches for 8 years, whilst there were general improvements to services. As the provisions of the proposed nationalisation of road transport took shape, the *Red & White* Directors had to consider their future options.

However, as soon as the year got underway, there was a more immediate problem, caused by the 'big freeze of '47', when the country was gripped by severe and freezing conditions right through from Christmas to Easter!

Just between 1st and 15th January *N&D* lost 7,203 route miles of operations due to the road conditions, and the fleet suffered from cold-related defects, especially the Guys as they were prone to frozen radiators. At this time it was not unusual to see buses with cardboard stuffed into the radiators or rags and old coats draped over the radiators of standing buses. On several occasions buses had to be abandoned for weeks at a time after getting stuck in deep snow-drifts, as narrow lanes filled with snow and the wind blew it into drifts up to 10 feet high on exposed parts of the Berkshire Downs. Passengers caught in a bus at Gore Hill, on the summit of the A34 just north of East Ilsley, had to be rescued by the Police and Army and spent the night in temporary accommodation. Hardest hit were the crews at the open outstations, who, after digging a way clear for the bus, then had to coax it into life, before setting off across the snowbound landscape with no idea of whether they would get back home!

When the thaw finally came, there was widespread flooding over the Kennet, Lambourn and Thames valleys, and that at times also meant diversions to some services, whilst power cuts also experienced at that time disrupted maintenance.

A reduction in contract commitments did, however, mean that some further older vehicles could be sold, and during January Dennis 'Aces' Nos.58 (MJ 4550), 63 (JB 6834), 75 (BPG 531) and 79 (RV 6259) all went to the same dealer in Birmingham for re-use by UNRRA (the United Nations Refugee Rehabilitation Agency). That organisation shipped them to Czechoslovakia where they transport displaced persons from various camps, after which the buses were probably burnt. This left only one 'Ace' in evidence, as No.83 (AUB 354). That same month a pair of Leyland 'Lion' LT2's also departed, as Nos. 46 (WX 7898) and 53 (HE 5229).

In order to address the enhancement of the Newbury – Oxford (Route 30) service, it was decided during February that one double-decker would be diverted to *N&D* from those being prepared for associated fleets,

though in the outcome it would not actually materialise until the following Spring!

In the meantime delivery of the 10 new AEC 'Regal' buses had slipped to April, though the rebuilt former *SMT* examples continued to arrive, with Nos.127 (FS 8566) in February, 128 (FS 8574) in March, 129 (FS 8575) in April, and finally 130 (FS 8565) in May. The frontal treatment of these varied slightly, where it had been necessary to accommodate the different bonnet height of the AEC chassis, which may also indicate where the work was undertaken. However, there was some concern regarding the quality of those entrusted to the Lydney works, an issue that would indeed raise its head again in due course.

It is interesting to note that the half-canopy layout of the ECOC bodies necessitated the use of a single-line destination in one box only, whereas the other one was painted over and carried *Newbury & District,* this featured being added after they arrived at Newbury.

By now the Mill Lane garage was becoming rather crowded, so *Thames Valley* was asked to park its pair of Bristol K-type double-deckers on the forecourt at night with effect from Saturday 26th March.

However, delivery dates for new coaches were still not firm, which caused further frustration for *N&D*, so it was necessary to utilise some of the new 'Regal' buses as soon as they arrived in April! These were Nos.131-40 (DMO 320-9), all being essentially still the pre-war O662-type with oil engines. The bodies were 35-seater front-entrance saloons built by Duple Motor Bodies of Hendon, and these were to a high standard of finish, if somewhat plain internally, each costing £2,700 each.

The AEC 'Regal' buses were certainly fine vehicles, which would have a long working life at Newbury and elsewhere after sale. Before the new coaches came it was not unusual to see them on excursions, and No.134 (DMO 323) is seen soon after delivery at the Winchester Coach Station en route to the coast.

183

A more extensive programme of advertised excursions was started from Easter, though this was still quite moderate by pre-war standards. The usual coastal destinations of Bognor, Bournemouth, Southsea and Weymouth were covered, along with horse-racing at Ascot and Epsom, plus some more local half-day runs, and notable events such as the Thame Show. However, despite this optimism, the new coaches were not available, so other solutions were required.

Apart from being sometimes used on excursions, the AEC 'Regal' saloons could also be seen on hire to South Midland at busy times, and No.136 (DMO 325) is seen leaving Oxford on such duties. It must have been a warm day, as the door and cab windows are open.

In order to compensate for a number of the new saloons being sidetracked onto coaching duties, plus further assistance from the Oxford garage, it was decided to lend *Newbury & District* and *South Midland* some Albions, which could cover contract duties. These arrived in May and had come to *Red & White* when it had acquired *McShane's Motors* of Liverpool, who had used them on bus services in the Bootle area. Originally with rear-entrance 32-seater bus bodies by Roberts when new in July/August 1932, these 'Valkyrie' PW65-types had since been re-engined with Gardner 5LW's and re-bodied by Burlingham as 35-seaters during the war years. Those received retained their *R&W* fleet numbers as Nos.233, 240, 243, 244, 249 and 251 (EM 2723, 2730, 2735, 2736, 2741 and 2743). Nos.233 and 251 were sent to Oxford, whilst the others were for the Newbury area, though some at least were outstationed for contract workings. A reliable source also noted Nos.243/4 carrying *Newbury & District* fleetnames in August 1947, though they remained only on loan.

Their arrival led to a further phase of disposal, with the last of the pair of Bedford WTB's No.71 (BON 887), latterly at Kintbury outstation, going in May. The following month witnessed the departure of the final 'Ace' No.83 (AUB 354), though this did find

several more PSV owners, and almost managed to survive into preservation!

The other departures during June were all Leyland, with 'Lion' LT2's Nos.47/8 (HD 4369 and HD 4368), similar bus No.45 (CK 4518) and 'Tiger' No.91 (CK 4312). The last of the ex-*Yorkshire Woollen District* LT2-types, No.56 (HD 4371) also followed in July.

It is interesting to note that some of these later disposals, being of vehicles that had seen attention under the new regime's maintenance, realised up to 4 times their written down value when sold, finding new PSV operators at a time when new buses were still hard to obtain. Indeed, when even the '1934 van' was disposed of in April, it had realised a staggering £45, though it was only rated at £10!

In respect of the latter, it had been decided to buy a newer Bedford lorry to replace that vehicle, which came in the form of a 1943 OW-type 3-tonner (CMO 963), purchased secondhand and in use by September. However, no evidence for the '1934 van' has been found, and it seems possible this was an error for the 1936 2.5-ton Bedford lorry (JB 5917) latterly in use as a service vehicle? Certainly, during conversations with Reg Hibbert, no such additional vehicle was ever mentioned, though he clearly recalled several trips down to Chepstow in the older Bedford lorry.

In the meantime, improvements in the service to Oxford had been the subject of discussions with *City of Oxford*. During April, and despite *N&D's* shortage of double-deckers, alongside *COMS's* crew situation, it was decided to improve the level of service for the Summer. Due to the situation the Oxford operator had with intense competition from local factories offering better rates of pay, it even had to resort to bringing in men from other areas of the country and putting them up in redundant buses!

Jim Davies agreed that Newbury would provide 3 of the 4 scheduled vehicles and crews, though the outstationning at Oxford would cease. This meant that whereas a passenger from Newbury could leave at 8.30am and reach Oxford at 10.10am, a passenger from that town had to wait for the first bus at 9.30am in order to reach Newbury at 11.10am. After re-shuffling other double-deck duties, this was put into operation from 4th May. The Oxford Company had expressed some reservations about maintaining that level of service through the Winter, so it was agreed to review the operations for after 27th September, with 6 of the hourly departures noted in the timetable as running to that date only. This resulted in a Monday to Saturday level of 12 return journeys, though on Sundays 2 of these in the mornings were deleted. Each of the 4 buses operated an approximately 12-hour day, and in order to cover these duties, the Newbury crews now inter-worked with other duties.

A pair of the rebuilt 'Scottish Regals' are seen inside the Mill Lane garage as Nos. 129 (FS 8575) and 125 (FS 8576). Note the rather bashed-about appearance of the bonnet panels! There was also some variation in the treatment of the cab-line and the front dash panel, some work being undertaken at Lydney.

The two main reasons for the above increased level of coverage on the route were the build up of staff now at AERE Harwell, hence the earlier working from the Newbury end, along with a greater number of hospital referrals now coming from the Abingdon area to the Oxford and Newbury hospitals.

Another source of increased patronage on the buses was the large Polish Resettlement Camp at Hermitage, where a number of Poles displaced by the war and unable to return to their Russian-controlled homeland were housed in the old army huts temporarily.

It is also worth noting that a number of other activities that had been halted by the war, often due to the taking of venues by the authorities, or to discourage unnecessary travel, were now being fully resumed. One example was the greyhound racing at Reading Stadium, particularly popular with users of Route 2 from East Ilsley and the various villages en route. The East Ilsley crews worked that route, along with the Tuesday/Thursday/Saturday extensions to West Ilsley, as well as Route 1 (East Ilsley – Newbury), and they were renowned for their reliability. Apart from Toni Riccotti and Charlie Bishop, who we have already heard of, at various times there were also Harry Dore (conductor from Chilton), Bill Smith (conductor, later driver from Beedon), Harry Buckle (conductor from Beedon) and Bill Bradfield (conductor from one of the villages around Compton), along with driver Harry Eggleton (from Compton), whose brother Ron worked for the Company out of Newbury.

Consideration had also been given during the Spring to linking up the Newbury – Swindon service with the *Red & White* Stroud – Cirencester service, either by dove-tailing connections or by through-running, but nothing further came of this.

The parent company was indeed one for co-operating with connecting operators, though the tables were turned during June, when *George Hedges* suggested that his *Reliance* service should be better co-ordinated with the *N&D* services! However, it seems likely that the latter's increased presence in the Wantage area had caused him some concern, though nothing further came of this proposal.

In view of the situation with limited excursions, the Company publicly suggested that some good local excursions could be had by utilising the bus services, in particular the improved frequencies to Wantage, Oxford and Swindon, Abingdon also being a joining point for the Salter's Steamers for a round-trip by bus and boat to Oxford.

Since the new garage had opened, Newbury had become self-sufficient for its overhauls and a total of 12 of these, including some from *South Midland* and *Venture,* had been completed between January and April 1947.

Not too much heavy work had been necessary for the Oxford fleet, which had been prioritised with new coaches in order that the express service could be re-instated, along with the post-war touring programme, both of which were close to the hearts of the Board. Apart from overhauling the surviving Leyland coaches from that fleet, the other work had involved cannibalising vehicles for useful parts before the were consigned for scrap, some of these items being used to improve the features on the utility bodies.

An interior view of the pit area of Mill Lane garage, with the rear of ex-Ribble Leyland 'Tiger' No.91 (CK 4312), alongside one of South Midland's Harrington-bodied 'Tiger' TS7 No.36 (CWL 951) or 37 (CWL 953), in the process of being thoroughly refurbished. To the right in the paint-shop is one of the new AEC 'Regal' saloons, plus a Venture AEC 'Regent' in for a body overhaul.

On the other hand, the *Venture* fleet had seen a vast increase in mileage and many vehicles were certainly past their best. Apart from mechanical overhauls, a number of vehicles were in urgent need of thorough body strip-downs. Those known to have been dealt with at Newbury were (including some being sent to Basingstoke from the *Cheltenham District* fleet): AEC 'Regent' double-decker No.40 (JO 1632) sometime early in 1947; ex-*Cheltenham* AEC 'Regents' Nos.85 (BAD 30), 88 (DG 9820) and 89 (DG 9819) during October and November 1947; and AEC 'Regal' single-decker No.34 (COT 547) in December 1947. These were followed in March 1948 by AEC 'Regent' double-decker No.30 (BOU 699), then by identical buses Nos. 27 (BOU 697) and 28 (BOU 698) in April 1948 and November 1949 respectively, along with ex-*Nottingham CT* No.63 (TV 6753) in June 1948. However, it should be appreciated that records for the throughput at Newbury are incomplete, whilst it is also known that in order to address the back-log at *Venture*, some vehicles were also sent to other outside coachbuilders.

An increasing amount of time was being expended on the 'utility' bodies, due mainly to the amount of un-seasoned wood used in their construction. Platforms and window frames were found to be warping, whilst the lack of weather-stripping or louvres over windows only made the problem worse. A number of platforms had to be completely replaced, whilst leaking cabs were a frequent feature of the driver's defect sheets. In respect of the latter, Reg used the 'water test', usually sitting in the offending bus, whilst a garage-hand put the hose on the appropriate area!

However, not all was entirely well in the garage, as some of the old hands who had stayed on to see how things went under the new management, now decided it was time to leave. In fact 5 skilled fitters left that Summer, with Boss Denham and Percy Andrews (the Garage Foremen) going in June, followed by Ernie, Bill and Len Durnford in August, leaving only 'Nin' still working for the Company from the latter family, and he became Assistant Foreman. A further blow to the overhaul programme came sometime during that year, when George Amor also decided to leave, going to Lambourn Coachworks, where he worked on building horseboxes, specialist vehicles for the BBC Outdoor Broadcast Service and mobile clinics for the Blood Donor Service, as well as several rebuilds of coaches for *Reliance* and *Thames Valley*.

Another view inside the new garage shows the rear of AEC 'Regal' No.123 (FS 8562).

Percy Andrews and Bill Durnford then went into partnership as Andrew's Garage back at Percy's old premises in Northcroft Lane, whilst Ernie opened a petrol filling station at the junction of Kings Road and Winchcombe Road, and Len went over to taxi work.

The final trio of Leylands in service are seen parked behind the Mill Lane garage, along with AEC 'Regal' No.107 (TG 1568). From left to right they are No.80 (HL 5228), 86 (CK 3951) and 84 (CK 4573)

Of the Durnfords, Bill died in 1969, followed by Len in 1975, Nin in 1980, Ernie in 1999, whilst their sister Olive Minchin went in 2002, and Percy Andrews in 1972.

In respect of Boss Denham, he once again joined his brother Theo. After the war the latter had set up a taxi service, initially using a yard rented at West Mills from a Mr. Smith, though attempts to acquire the site failed. He then transferred to the old Mill Lane premises once used by *Durnfords* and situated between the *Thames Valley* dormy shed and the *N&D* garage in Mill Lane. The enterprise became the *Mill Lane Hire Service,* the other licensed drivers being Dickie Darling, Charlie Brown (ex-*N&D* Driver), Bill Hill and Mick Campbell.

The company built up 6 licenses, standardising on the Austin 'Ascot' 12hp 4-cylinder model, though one 6-cylinder model was purchased and was short-lived when it was discovered to have some serious mechanical issues, being broken up for spares in April 1947. Earlier a trio of 1934-6 Morris 16hp cars had been used, but sold between April and August 1947, whilst later the Standard 'Vanguard' became the preferred choice.

There was also a revival in the re-sale of vehicles during 1947, with an AJS 500cc and Matchless 250cc motorcycles in May 1947, along with a 1934 Bedford 12cwt van, and the term 'Mill Lane Garage' was used in one advert.

Theo died on 1st November 1950 after a long illness. He left behind many years of involvement in the local transport scene, though in reality what wealth he did acquire actually came from his investment in property,

as he owned some 20 houses locally at the time of his death. He had also continued his association with local solicitor and one-time *Newbury & District* Chairman Angus Marshall, both being Freemasons.

After that his widow did offer to transfer the 6 taxi licenses to Boss, but the latter did not relish the worries of running such a business, so these were sold to Sid Taylor (by then the former Engineer), who ran them from the Mill Lane premises alongside his *Enterprise Coaches* in partnership with Theo's cousin Eddie Whitington. After that Boss continued as a self-employed taxi driver, as he had a loyal customer base, using the rank outside the Queens Hotel and he continued to wear his old *N&D* driver's hat, which served as a reminder of the service he had given to Newburians over the years. His son Lionel also joined him for a while before undertaking National Service. Boss remained a well known and respected local personality, keeping in touch with his old associates, through to his death on 8th March 1985.

The arrival of the loaned Albions, along with further reductions in contracts, led to another cull over the Autumn months, this time making heavy inroads into the ranks of the Leyland types. September saw the end for Leyland 'Lion' LT2 No.52 (TF 4155) and 'Tiger' TS2 No.87 (DF 7841). These were followed by 'Lion' LT2 No.50 (UR 9658) and 'Tiger' TS1 No.88 (MS 8834) in October, and the 'Lion' LT5a-type coach No.73 (WP 6206) in November. The latter vehicle had been a fine vehicle when acquired, and was obviously still in fair shape, as it realised £1000!

This left only a trio of Leylands still in stock, these being 'Tiger' TS2-type Nos.84 (CK 4573) and 86 (CK 3951), along with the last 'Lion', the sole LT5-type No.80 (HL 5228).

As already noted above, the internal specification of the Guy double-deckers was improved as time went by, through the replacement of the wooden slatted seating with upholstered seats, along with the fitting of glazed rear upper-deck emergency doors and internal panelling. All of this was done as and when these buses came in for body overhauls.

Sometime during the Summer months the trio of OWB-type Bedfords based at Lambourn was replaced by the same number of ex-*SMT* AEC 'Regals' which, with their leather seating, brought a greater degree of comfort to the allocation. During the same period the number of vehicles based there rose to 5, due to increased activity at the AERE Harwell site. At that point there were four part-time drivers covering the contract routes, with Bill Allington and Peter Stagg doing the routes to Didcot, whilst Bill Harris and George Colburn drove the contracts to AERE Harwell. Both of the latter were employed at the site during the day, Bill's route travelling by way of Wantage, whereas George ran through Great Shefford, Farnborough and West Ilsley. Although these buses were generally regarded as reliable, they could be hard to start on cold mornings due to their 12-volt electrical systems, and Bill Allington recalled getting his wife to sit in the cab and hold down the starter whilst he coaxed the engine into life. It should also be noted that none of the Lambourn crews worked on Sundays, when the service (and indeed the later Saturday-evening journeys) was covered by Newbury crews.

At weekends and evenings the part-timers also covered private hires or worked as relief drivers, whilst the only full-time Lambourn crew consisted of the husband-and-wife team of Ernie and Kathleen Church, who worked route 106 (Newbury – Boxford – Lambourn). All of the part-time drivers duly became full-timers once the construction phase at Harwell gave way to contracts taking staff members instead.

Under the new regime the timetable booklet had been completely revised in order to present the information in as clear a fashion as practical, whilst other relevant details such as market and early-closing days in local towns were also included from the July 1947 edition as paper became a less scarce commodity once again.

Also during July, applications were put forward for licenses to operate 2 new express contract runs between The Wharf and RAF Milton, some 3 miles west of Didcot and just east of the A34. One ran by way of Chieveley - Langley Hall – Chaddleworth – Lilley – Farnborough – West Ilsley, whilst the other ran via Hampstead Norris – Compton – East Ilsley. The journey through Chaddleworth was timed to leave Newbury at 6.45am and took exactly an hour, whilst the other route had a journey time of 75 minutes, so it left at 6.30am. Both had a nominal return timing of 5pm, though the Company requested discretion to vary that if required by the working times at the RAF Supply Unit. Both were operated on the basis of a

contract charge to the Air Ministry, so no fares were collected and therefore no conductors were needed. Prior to that *N&D* buses had run to Milton under the Wartime Permit system.

Some four months later the above applications had not been determined, though *N&D* had already started to run in response to urgent requests by the Air Ministry. Various other local concerns were also involved in running contracts to that large site, including *Tappin's* of Wallingford, *Leonard Stevens* of Charney Bassett, along with *City of Oxford,* the latter having 6 separate runs from Kingston Lisle, Didcot, Wantage, Wootton, East Challow and Oxford itself.

Although there had to be a realistic acceptance by *N&D* that it was not in a position to undertake all such contracts emanating from its area, it nonetheless did object to *Tappin's* application to license a former contract working between Chilton and the Ordnance Depot at Didcot as a public service during October, but that application was still approved.

A later view of Charlie Bishop with AEC 'Regal' bus No.139 (DMO 328) taken shortly after it arrived in April 1947. By then Charlie had been on the buses since 1923, starting out with Prothero of Beedon.

AEC 'Regal' coach No.143 (DMO 332) is parked in the entrance to the newer part of Mill Lane garage. The same livery of red panels, white window surrounds and side flash, along with black lower panel and mudguards, was also carried by the coaches of South Midland and Venture, so any inter-fleet hirings attracted little attention from the public.

In the meantime, the first of the long-awaited coaches finally arrived in August! This was No.141 (DMO 330), an AEC 'Regal' 0662-type originally intended for the *Venture* fleet, which carried the classic Duple 35-seater front-entrance body with the characteristic side-flash. It was very much pride-of-the-fleet, and when not in use it could be seen during daytimes parked near The Wharf office for public inspection. Sadly, as we shall see in due course, the remaining coaches would still not arrive in time for the 1947 season. It is perhaps worth noting that this was not a situation unique to Newbury or even the *Red & White* companies, as the very same problems were besetting operators across the country!

When the enhanced operation of the Oxford route had started in the Summer, *City of Oxford* had stated that it did not propose to maintain that level over the Winter months, so when the service after September 27th was reviewed it opted to stick to that preference. However, *N&D* was keen to see the headway maintained, whilst there were soon representations from the AERE at Harwell, as the number of persons now employed was growing. Jim Davies pursued the matter with the Oxford Company, resulting in agreement during December that the route would return to the hourly frequency, though the date would

be 11th April the following year! Given the Newbury operator's willingness to bring this service into place, including even working more than half the schedule, the frustration Jim felt is evident from the continuing correspondence with his opposite number at Oxford.

Three of the outstanding AEC 'Regal' coaches arrived in October as Nos.142-4 (DMO 331-3), and all were to the same specification as the previous example. However, as it so late in the year it was decided to put them in store at Lydney Industrial Estate. They were joined there in November by identical coach No.145 (EBL 736), and plans were put in place for the first proper coaching season for 8 years to commence the following Easter.

'Regal' coach No.145 (EBL 736) was caught by the camera when parked outside the Bath Services depot for some reason, before being fitted with destination blinds. Presumably it stopped off there on its way out of storage at Lydney, either requiring attention or for the driver to grab a cheap lunch?

One of the Duple-bodied AEC 'Regal' Mk111 coaches finally received in early 1948 was No.148 (EJB 148), which is seen when in Leeds in 1951, with a Yorkshire-registered Bedford alongside.

Similar coach No.146 (EJB 146) is seen with the offside blind set to Newbury & District. Note also the semaphore indicator fitted just in front of the driver's door, which has not completely returned to its slot. These orange-coloured 'hands' also lit up and freed the driver from making the appropriate hand signals when turning left or right.

As already noted, the *Red & White* Board promoted the concept of working with other transport providers, and during December discussions took place regarding inter-availability of road and rail return tickets between *Newbury & District* buses and rail services operated by the *Great Western Railway* in the area. Such facilities already existed between the bus services of all the neighbouring 'territorial' concerns as a result of the railway shareholdings from the 1930's, and of course there were a number of points served by the Newbury routes and the local railways.

However, a far greater threat hung over the industry at that time, as the Labour Government proposed the nationalisation of transport in as wide a form as practical. The intention was to make better use of the available resources and bring co-ordination to these activities, the vital importance of which had been highlighted during the war years. This was, of course, a period of looking forward to a brave new future in a country still living in the daily grip of austerity. As it was the legislation moved fairly slowly, but the Board noted its concerns for the future.

Not long after the AEC 'Regal' buses were delivered, No.137 (DMO 326) was involved in a bad smash, and this photo by Reg Hibbert shows how it looked after being recovered. No doubt he had some choice words for the offending driver, whilst the work of returning it to service would have added to the already busy throughput of the workshops at that time. A telegraph pole is believed to have caused the damage.

Chapter 21 – 1948

The first event of the year was an unfortunate accident, involving a bus carrying players back from a whist-drive outing from the Agricultural Research Station at Compton on the evening of Wednesday 17th February. The party from East and West Ilsley and Chieveley consisted of a number of women and several boys. The bus was travelling near Mayfield Corner, on the East Ilsley side of Compton about 10.30pm, when it slid off a soft verge into a 4-foot ditch, spilling the passengers over to the nearside of the bus. The accident occurred at slow speed and there was no panic. Several ladies were treated for cuts and a number of passengers were bruised and battered, but fortunately only two required attendance at hospital. A nearby doctor from Chilton was soon on the scene and the local cottagers rendered immediate assistance. The more local passengers walked home after tea and rest at the cottages, whilst others were collected by a bus returning to the area from a visit to the pantomime at Oxford, and no action was taken against the driver.

On a brighter note, the stored coaches were brought back from Lydney during March in preparation for a season of work commencing at Easter. That same month they were joined by a further trio of Duple-bodied AEC 'Regal' 35-seater coaches with similar bodies. These were Nos.146-8 (EJB 146-8), though they were of the post-war improved Mk111 0682-type chassis, though still with the 7.7 litre oil engine. All seven of these were licensed during March, and along with No.141 (DMO 330) which had been in use all Winter, they were ready for a very busy year of coaching!

Indeed, a further pair of such coaches should have followed in May, but these were again delayed until later in the year, causing the parent company to review its ordering policy and widen the choice of suppliers.

Meanwhile, further discussions had taken place with *City of Oxford* regarding the return to hourly working of Route 30 (Newbury – Oxford), and initially it had been agreed to make that change from 7th March. This proved a little over-optimistic, as both operators found they had issues with finding enough suitable buses, as it had also been agreed that the Oxford Company would now do its full half-share of the schedules. They duly assigned either utility Guy 'Arabs' or AEC 'Regents' to the route, but at this time *N&D* had some difficulties with the double-deck contingent.

The problem had arisen due to the unexpectedly early demise of AEC 'Regent' No.117 (HG 1221), which had been laid up with some serious fault. No details are recorded of what the problem was, though of course it will be recalled that this bus was not popular with crews. However, whatever the issues (and

despite the well-equipped garage), it was decided that the fleet was definitely one 'decker down on requirements, so once again a diverted vehicle filled the gap!

The vehicle concerned was one of a batch of 3 buses almost completed for the *Venture* fleet, these being on AEC 'Regent' Mk111 0961-type chassis. The bodies had been part of a scheme to construct double-deckers at the Mumford works at Lydney by using framework supplied in kit form by Weymann's of Addlestone. As the Mumford operations became Lydney Coachworks in February 1948, it is debatable whether these should be referred to as Weymann/Mumford or completed as Lydney. They carried full-height 56-seater bodies, and the one diverted to Newbury became No.151 (EJB 521), the Nos.149/50 already being allocated to the outstanding coaches. With its 9.6 litre engine and pre-selective gearbox, it proved to be a very popular choice with drivers following its arrival in March.

AEC 'Regent' No.151 (EJB 521) seen after becoming Wilts & Dorset No.500.

Once the above 'Regent' was received, it was agreed that the return to hourly workings on the Oxford route would commence from 11th April, the Thatcham duty previously covered by failed No.117 now being re-assigned to one of the Guy 'Arabs' instead. 117 then hung around, pending a final decision on its future, before being sold for use as a static caravan, minus seats and other useful items in September 1948

Another transfer did take place between Newbury and Basingstoke back in January, when the Inspector's car (FTX 109) was transferred for further use by *Venture.*

Continuing discussions between *N&D* and the *GWR* had resulted in an agreement regarding the inter-availability of unused return tickets by either mode of transport from 1st March, though the railway was itself now the Western Region of the nationalised British Railways, the railways being State-owned from 1st

January. As a result of this a list of the points where the bus and rail services offered connections was included in the timetable booklet. This was a quite extensive list and comprised:

Route No.	Alighting Point	Station Name
2	Station Approach	Compton
2	George Hotel	Pangbourne
2	Western Elms Ave.	Reading West
2	Lower Thorn Street	Reading
4, 5 & 18	Railway Hotel	Newbury
6 & 7	Station Approach	Welford
9	High Street	Hungerford
10	Kintbury Square	Kintbury
10,11,12,14	Pound Street	Newbury
11, 12 & 14	Station Approach	Woodhay
17	Station Approach	Thatcham
19, 20 & 21	Station Approach	Hermitage
19 & 21	Station Approach	Hampstead Norris
24	Railway Hotel	Newbury
25 & 27	Pound Street	Newbury
6 & 29	The Square	Lambourn
29	Regents Street	Swindon
30	Railway Inn	Steventon
30	Market Place	Abingdon
30	Gloucester Green	Oxford
31 & 31a	Station Approach	Newbury
31 & 31a	Station Approach	Highclere
36	The Square	Lambourn
36	High Street	Hungerford

Note: For Newbury Station on Services 1, 3, 6, 7, 8, 9, 15, 16, 17, 19, 20, 21, 23, 29, 30 alight at The Wharf and board at The Wharf, Market Street or Regal Cinema. On other services alight or board as above.

However, despite the impressive list of possible connections, inter-availability was only agreed to the following places from Newbury: Great Shefford; Hungerford; Kintbury; Lambourn and Oxford, and even then a supplement would apply if the road passenger wished to return by rail. Clearly the main objective was better co-ordination of transport, but such restrictions imposed by one party can hardly be said to constitute entering into the true spirit with which the negotiations had started out with!

March saw the withdrawal of the Leyland 'Lion' LT5-type No.80 (HL 5228), leaving only 'Tiger' TS2-type Nos.84 (CK 4573) and 86 (CK 3951) still in active service. During July both of those were withdrawn, as well as AEC 'Regal' No.107 (TG 1568), the example still retaining its original 1931 bodywork. However, it was soon decided to re-license No.86 in favour of one of the Bedford OWB's that required urgent attention, thereby earning it a brief respite to final withdrawal in September. This was the first time that no Leylands had been present in the fleet since formation in 1932, though it would not actually be that long before the marque featured once again due to some exchanges of vehicles, as we shall see later.

Evidently, the disposal of such ageing buses was becoming an issue for the Group as a whole, so it was decided that vehicles could be stored at Lydney whilst their futures were resolved.

Also, on the Group theme, was the recovery by Reg Hibbert and his 'lads' of *Venture* utility-bodied AEC 'Regent' No.44 (ECG 645), which was overturned onto the grass verge whilst travelling along Picket Twenty, just east of Andover in June. The vehicle was righted and taken initially to Newbury, but pressure of work at that time resulted in the repairs being directed to Lydney instead. In fact it wasn't a good Summer for *Venture* double-deckers, as ex-*Nottingham CT* AEC 'Regent' No.66 (TV 4496) had a similar accident later on Overton Hill.

Venture No.44 (ECG 645) in course of recovery.

It is notable that from the May 1948 timetable booklet that the Newbury – Andover service of *Wilts & Dorset* was included, as well as notification that parcels could be accepted for its buses, along with the routes of *Thames Valley* and *City of Oxford*.

Also from May the last of the journeys operated as contracts to the Vickers-Armstrong factory at Shaw were fully absorbed into the public timetables, though passengers were warned that they might be re-timed at short-notice if requested by the employer to meet any changes in working patterns!

Throughout the Summer of 1948 the nice new coaches were indeed kept busy, and there was an expanded programme of excursions, covering full-day trips to Ascot Races, Bognor Regis, Bournemouth, Brighton, Cheddar Gorge, Hayling Island, Henley-on-Thames, Lee-on-Solent, Littlehampton, Salisbury, Stratford-upon-Avon, Weston-super-Mare, Whipsnade Zoo and Windsor, along with a number of local afternoon and evenings excursions or circular tours. In respect of the Hayling Island runs, the weight limit on the approaching causeway bridge precluded the use of the 'Regal' coaches, so *N&D* had to borrow one of the Bedford OB-type 29-seater coaches from the *South Midland* fleet as its Nos. 43/4 (LJO 756/7)

The pair of Bedford OB coaches would in fact come to Newbury & District a little later, and No.164 (LJO 756) is seen under that fleetname, though when hired back to South Midland! This pair of coaches would later carry the Thames Valley fleetname, though mainly used at Newbury and often helping out over at Oxford.

Private hire work was also once again promoted in 1948, whilst that year also saw Newbury's first involvement with the provision of coaches for relief duties on *Associated Motorways* express coach routes. *Red & White* had of course been one of the original partners in this extensive network of such services, in which individual operators worked on a mileage basis, there being a need at peak times to hire-in vehicles from other operators. An 'approved list' of operators was at the disposal of *Associated Motorways* staff, and such decisions often had to be made at short notice, as well as occasionally having to deputise for any failed coaches en route. *Newbury & District* was regularly called upon to provide coaches and drivers, either on the routes working through the town, or even further afield.

Old drivers recall how this work made a nice change from the usual haunts, and the depot held copies of the standard reference book compiled for drivers by *Associated Motorways,* which detailed the routes and contact numbers for coach stations, duty inspectors and operator depots where assistance could be found if required. There are numerous stories of drivers who set off for a journey to (say) Southampton, and was then re-directed by the Local Inspector onto somewhere like Exeter, where he would spend the night. The following day the coach would cover the journey up to (say) Cheltenham or Bristol, where it might be sent as a duplicate to Oxford or Reading, after which the pair returned back home! The drivers on reserve for these duties soon learnt to keep a case ready and packed. Such work also took the Newbury-based coaches to some unfamiliar places.

Having now got the three fleets back into shape, it was decided in July that all spares for *Newbury & District*, *South Midland* and *Venture* would be concentrated at the Newbury Works. Also, in order that Sid Taylor could carry out these responsibilities, it was agreed to provide him with a car, so in October a secondhand Hillman 'Minx' 8hp saloon (AMO 960) new in July 1937 was purchased for £380 locally.

September saw the arrival of the outstanding pair of AEC 'Regal' coaches, as Nos.149/50 (EJB 649/50), these being of the slightly modified 6821A-type and bearing the same Duple 35-seater front-entrance body as previous examples. As they arrived after the Summer peak was over, they were initially stored, though from 1st December they were in fact licensed due to the need for such vehicles.

That month also saw the departure of a familiar face from *N&D*, when Charlie Bishop left. In fact he had been offered a job as Inspector at Newbury, though he did not relish having to travel into the town, so with the new opportunities now available for drivers at the AERE at Harwell, and a growing family, he decided to make the move. After that he drove all manner of vehicles, even including a few stints as chauffeur, until his retirement in 1971.

Another significant change to the local bus scene also took place as a result of the unexpected death of *Albert Austin* in August 1948, after which his widow initially took over the service. However, word reached the ears of *N&D* during September that the Hedge's family were negotiating to take the licenses over. Although they decided to re-open talks with *Mrs. Austin*, it was too late, and the service passed into the care of *Alan Hedges*, son of *George Hedges* of *Reliance M.S.* of Brightwalton, remaining with them until finally being sold to *Thames Valley* in 1966.

Spring and Autumn were of course traditionally the times for operators to renew fleets, and a review in

October 1948 highlighted the need to replace certain vehicles at Newbury. These were Bedford OWB Nos.110/1/3/8 (EWO 480, EWO 479, DWN 295 and EWO 476), along with the other pair of older 'Regal' buses Nos.108 (TX 9498) and 109 (PJ 3827).

In order to make the above possible, the *Red & White* Group Engineer delved into the ranks of refurbished buses once again, coming up with another selection of AEC 'Regals', all with complex histories!

The first of these to arrive in October was No.152 (AGJ 929), which had originated as a petrol-engined coach in the *Blue Belle* fleet in April 1933. As part of a *R&W* subsidiary it was fitted with a Gardner 6LW oil engine in July 1938, though this had been replaced by a 5LW unit before it had reached Newbury. When new it carried a Beadle 35-seater, centre-entrance body, but that had been replaced in 1947 by one of the old ECOC rear-entrance bodies formerly on Bristol JO5G's of *North Western* and now seating 32.

'Regal' No.153 (AGX 455) at The Wharf.

No.153 (AGX 455) followed in November and had also originated with *Blue Belle* in April 1933, going on hire to *Red & White* from March 1941 due to lack of coaching work in London due to restrictions. It had received a new Burlingham 34-seater front-entrance bus body, built to utility standards, during January 1945, and by the time it arrived at Newbury was fitted with a Gardner 5LW oil engine.

Also received in November was another bus with a similar history of having been new to *Blue Belle* in April 1933, with subsequent hiring and transfer to *R&W.* This was No.155 (AGP 841), which had gained a Gardner 6LW engine in April 1938, though it is believed it carried a 5LW at Newbury. It too had been re-bodied like No.153 by Burlingham during 1944. A similar Burlingham body had also been used to re-body No.154 (TG 1819) in July 1944, which by that time featured a Gardner 5LW engine. Originating in the fleet of *Gough's Welsh Motorways* of Mountain Ash in June 1931, it had carried a 31-seater coach body by Metcalfe of Romford. That operator had passed into *Red & White* control in April 1936 and entered its fleet in due course.

AEC 'Regal' No.156 (AMD 47) with N&D.

No.156 (AMD 47) had also come to *R&W* from that same fleet, though it had been new as an AEC demonstration bus in March 1933, passing to *Gough's* in February 1935. It carried a 33-seater Park Royal bus body when new but, unlike the other 'Regals' in this collection, it was of the 642-type, originally with a 4-cylinder petrol engine, though it is believed to have had an oil engine when sold to *Gough's*. There is no record of the engine it had when sent to Newbury, which may have been a Gardner 5LW. It had also been re-bodied by Duple in 1942 with a 35-seater bus body with central-entrance, and which was still largely to peacetime standards externally.

Mystery 'Regal' No.157 (FAX 349) at The Wharf.

The sixth vehicle of the batch arrived in December and had no doubt followed a similar trail of events, though the exact origins of this vehicle remain unresolved. No.157 (FAX 349) was indeed such a rebuild that *Red & White* was granted a new registration for it, suggesting that all trace of its real origins had been obliterated, perhaps after service with the military? The chassis number quoted is already claimed by another vehicle, and it had been purchased un-registered from the Ministry of Supply at the end of the war, being fitted with a Gardner 5LW engine and re-bodied with a Burlingham 34-seater, front-entrance bus body to a 'relaxed utility' standard before re-registration in March 1946.

Another of the assorted AEC 'Regals' was No.155 (AGP 841), which is seen at The Wharf in 1950, after it had been joined by an even stranger hybrid, No.169 (LWL 995), a 1947 Leyland 'Tiger' PS1-type which had been paired with a 1936 ECOC body. The latter would be transferred to N&D from South Midland in the exchanges of 1950.

All of Nos.152-7 had seen service with *Red & White* where they had carried fleet numbers 734, 728, 284, 730, 290 and 795 respectively. At Newbury their main role was to cover contract workings or relief duties, meaning that several were rarely to be seen.

As already mentioned, Jim Davies got on well with the *Red & White* regime, being well-organised and welcoming the investment they had made at Newbury with the new garage, so it was a fitting tribute from the Board that he was made a Director once again from 12th October 1948, as well as over at *Venture*.

The outstanding orders for coaches were further reviewed towards the close of 1948, and it was decided that the Newbury fleet would be allocated one further AEC 'Regal' 6821A-type of the batch with Duple bodies, with the remainder of that batch going to *Venture* in place of those diverted to *N&D* earlier.

On the double-deck front, it was also resolved that a further double-decker would be transferred from the *Cheltenham District* fleet, and both this and the coach would arrive the following year.

On the services side, November saw Sunday services re-introduced on some of the Newbury Local Services, which was the last of the wartime reductions to be reversed. Local Services 25 (Broadway – Wash

Common) and 27 (The Broadway – Kingsbridge Road) gained a number of afternoon and evening runs, being worked by one bus on an alternating basis. No Sunday service was provided on the 26 (Broadway – Western End), as that was primarily used by weekday workers, whilst the road covered by Route 28 (Regal Cinema – Donnington) was served by other longer distance services.

The scope of road/rail inter-availability increased in November to include Boxford and Whitchurch, and *N&D* also started negotiations with *Thames Valley* over a similar arrangement on the common sections served by the buses of both operators.

However, whilst the Board was in favour of such co-operation, it was alarmed at recent developments on the progress on the plans to nationalise the industry. The newly-formed *British Transport Commission* had concluded negotiations with the *Tilling Group*, whereby some half of the largest bus operators in the country had passed into State control, along with the manufacturing facilities at Bristol and Lowestoft, both of which would no longer be supplying other operators.

On the other hand, the large *BET Group* was adamant that it did not want to sell out, whilst other smaller groups and individual operators also opposed the plan. At that point in time the full realisation of the proposal appeared almost inevitable, making it a worrying time for the parent Board. Added to that, Mr. Flooks resigned as Group Engineer in November, and his place was taken by Mr. G.A.H. Watts, presumably as it was felt best to keep it to family at that time of future uncertainty.

December saw a clearout of buses now released by the arrival of the 6 'Regals' Nos.152-7, with Bedford OWB Nos.110/1/3/8 (EWO 480, EWO 479, DWN 295 and EWO 476) and AEC 'Regals' Nos.108 (TX 9498) and 109 (PJ 3827) all going. At that time the situation with buses in London was in crisis due to the delays with deliveries of new vehicles, probably not helped by the decision to close the bodybuilding facilities at the Chiswick Works. Apart from direct approaches to other operators, including the temporary diversion of new Bristol K-types from former Tilling Group fleets, there were also a significant number of vehicles provided on a loaned basis by small operators which led to a new lease of life for No.108 on the streets of the Capitol!

Former N&D AEC 'Regal' No.108 (TX 9498) seen whilst covering London Transport route 27A for Twickenham. Note the LT badge hung on the radiator. Certainly, a single-decker with a sliding centre door was far from ideal from London service, though this photo suggests that the door was kept open for ease of operation.

The above is one of a series of photos taken to show off the AEC 'Regal' coaches, and appeared in adverts and other publicity. It shows No.158 (ERX 937) which would arrive in July 1949, in the pretty village of Eastbury. It is interesting to note that the negative has been doctored to remove the N&D fleetnames from both the side and the front destination box, as this coach would be transferred to the South Midland fleet in January 1950.

The Board also considered the plea from *London Transport* before releasing the above buses, but were put off by the need to provide maintenance facilities and crews, although it did have some discussions with Walter French of *United Services Ltd.* to see if they might provide such garaging, but that was not possible.

As already noted, a second AEC 'Regent' was in the process of transfer from the Cheltenham District fleet, and this would finally appear as No.159 (HAD 745) in March 1949, and it is seen later with Wilts & Dorset.

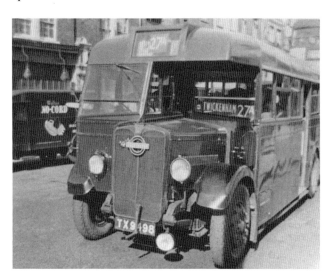

Chapter 22 – 1949

This year was a relatively quiet one at Newbury in terms of changes to the fleet, and it seems likely that the parent Board was being cautious in view of the pending threat of compulsory nationalisation. As it was, the sale of *Scottish Motor Traction* took place with effect from January.

However, that Spring also marked 30 years since the origins of *Red & White,* resulting in the compilation of a special volume recounting the developments and take-overs over those years. One of the facts contained in the section on *Newbury & District* stated that by then the route mileage was 328, with a total of 1,648,221 miles being run in the past 12 months and 4,525,000 passengers carried. A copy of this book was presented to all employees, and it is worth noting that the well-produced volume and its text went to much effort to point out how the success of that enterprise was the sum of all the hard work put in by everyone.

The Newbury fleet had now achieved a greater degree of standardisation, being mostly on chassis by AEC and Guy, with the Albions on hire and the surviving Bedfords being assigned mainly to contract work. Apart from the additional coach and double-decker in the process of arriving at Newbury, it was also decided that 3 AEC 'Regal' chassis would be allocated. However, although originally these were earmarked as coaches, the bodies they duly received would use part of a batch started for the associated *Ralph's* fleet, being some of a dozen for which the parent Board was having difficulties in getting commitments from bodybuilders. When they finally came they would occupy fleet nos.161-3, though it would be a full year before they materialised.

During March the double-decker being transferred from the *Cheltenham District* fleet arrived, in the shape of No.159 (HAD 745) and, like No.151 (EJB 521), this had originally been part of a batch intended for the *Venture* fleet! It was an AEC 'Regent' Mk111 0961-type, with a 9.6 litre oil engine and pre-selective gearbox. The body was similarly a Weymann-framed one built at Lydney, which was still Mumford's when it was completed in January 1948.

Fleet no.158 had of course already been assigned to the single coach being bodied at that time, which arrived in May and was registered as ERX 937. After the disappointments with coach deliveries in previous years, it is pleasing to note that this was actually received 2 months earlier than predicted, and needless to say it was soon out in use. The chassis was the same as the previous pair, being an AEC 'Regal' 6821A-type, fitted with a 7.7 litre oil engine and with a Duple 35-seater front-entrance body. It was actually one of a batch of 6 built at that time, the others going

to the *South Midland* fleet, where in due course it would also find itself.

It was announced in May that Jim Davies was leaving to take up another post. He was, of course, most certainly against the idea of the nationalisation of the bus industry, even though a more senior role was offered At the behest of the parent Board, he was appointed as the new Managing Director of the *Guernsey Railway Company* (by then a bus operator), along with a little later the associated *Guernsey Motors* and *Sarre Transport*, all of which were owned by *Red & White,* as part of its 'overseas' transport interests. The move was undoubtedly the latter's way of rewarding Jim for his loyal service and to allow him to avoid the impending nationalisation, and the new appointment took effect from 1st July. He also had the option of an East African post, but knew that the climate in Mombassa would not suit his health.

A farewell dinner was held for Jim Davies at the Chequers Hotel on the evening of Monday 25th July, and was a fitting tribute to a popular manager who had put much thought and energy into developing *N&D*. The dinner was attended by The Mayor, along with Gerald Nowell of South Midland, Jack Welling of Venture and Leslie Grimmett, and the proceedings were directed by none other than John Watts, Chairman of *Red & White*. Jim went onto to gain a similar respect on Guernsey, remaining in that post until after retirement age, not stepping down until July 1970, when he felt his health dictated it at the age of 75! When interviewed at the time, he said that although he still had 100% enthusiasm for the task, he could only now muster 65% of the energy required. He passed away on 26th September 1972, still active as a Director.

The man appointed to take over from Davies was Leslie Henry Grimmett, latterly the Area Manager for *Red & White* at Stroud, who came over to Newbury in mid-July. He had been born in Stroud in 1905 and was another example of promotion through the ranks under *R&W.*

1949 also saw the resumption of racing at Newbury, which was of course of high significance in an area with so many horse-training establishments, whilst also bringing a lot of trade to the area.

By June the trio of AEC 'Regal' chassis had reached Lydney, where the bodies were being constructed, and a delivery date of October was planned. However, as we shall see later, there were problems developing at the works there, which would cause further delays.

A new timetable booklet was issued from 5th June, but the only significant amendment was the extension of certain journeys on Route 1 (Newbury – East Ilsley) onto Rowstock on Thursdays and Saturdays, this being to alleviate a need for duplicates on Route 30 (Newbury – Oxford) over that section at such peak times.

It is also worth noting that the *Venture* garage at Basingstoke had seen a number of improvements during 1949, with five new inspection pits being added, after which it became self-sufficient for its maintenance, which took some pressure off Newbury. However, further co-operation on passenger facilities was forthcoming in respect of the inter-availability of return tickets by *N&D* and *Venture* between Newbury and Whitchurch from July.

Leslie Grimmett, who took over at Newbury.

A review of passenger loadings on Route 6 (Newbury – Lambourn) showed that it would be more efficient to operate that route with double-deckers. However, due to the low railway bridge where the Lamborn Branch crossed the road south of Boxford, the use of full-height 'deckers was out of the question. So, in August an application was put before the Traffic Commissioner to allow the route to be operated by double-deckers, whilst two of a large order for Duple-bodied Guy 'Arabs' were earmarked to receive low-bridge bodies for allocation to the Newbury fleet.

In connection with the above planning, Route 6 was extended onto Upper Lambourn on certain journeys, but otherwise there no other significant changes in the new timetable booklet issued on 2nd October.

Meanwhile, during September, a further double-decker had been transferred to Newbury as No.160 (EWO 484). This was one of a large number of wartime Guy 'Arab' Mk1 buses supplied to the *Red &*

White fleet, this example being fitted with a Gardner 5LW engine and carrying a Strachan 55-seater utility low-bridge body when new in June 1943. However, as with others of that type, it was re-bodied in 1949, when it received a high-bridge 56-seater body built by Lydney. The style of this body owed something to the Beadle bodies of the late pre-war period, though it did feature half-drop windows at the upper-deck front. It did various duties at *N&D*, though it spent quite a time outstationed at East Ilsley, and was therefore seen in Reading on a daily basis, whilst also making a more comfortable replacement for the wooden-seated utility Guy previously allocated.

There were also some 25 Guys on order at that time for use as single-deckers, some of which might have well come to the Newbury fleet, though they too would be the subject of yet another saga of delays!

The need for the remaining Bedford OWB's declined as a number of wartime-related contracts finally came to a close. In September No.114 (DWN 258) departed and was followed in October by Nos.112 (EWO 454), 115/6 (DWN 298/9), 119 (EWO 481) and 120 (EAX 647). This only left the 'native' examples Nos.94-8 (CMO 523, 624 and 657-9) still in service.

Lydney-bodied Guy 'Arab' No.160 (EWO 484) at Station Hill, Reading on the East Ilsley service.

Just before the Christmas break some discussions took place regarding the make up the fleets at Basingstoke, Oxford and Newbury, and as a result of that it was decided to make a number of transfers in the interest of standardisation. The recently-arrived AEC 'Regent' No.159 (HAD 745) was now finally sent onto *Venture* as its No.99, though the other similar 'Regent' No.151 (EJB 521) stayed on at Newbury – though it too would eventually take the trip south.

The other exchanges took place between the Newbury and Oxford fleets, resulting in *N&D* losing a trio of its 1948/9 AEC 'Regal' coaches Nos.149/50 (EJB

649/50) and 159 (ERX 937), which became *South Midland* Nos.68-70.

AEC 'Regal' Mk111 coach now as South Midland No.68 (EJB 649) seen on an excursion to Southsea.

In return for those, and in reflection of specific needs at Newbury, came a mixed bunch of vehicles. Firstly, the pair of 1947/8 Bedford OB's that had been *South Midland* Nos.43/4 (LJO 756/7) finally came over to Newbury as originally intended. Indeed, these had actually spent quite a bit of time working for Newbury that year, necessitating the loan to *South Midland* of a pair of similar coaches from another *R&W* associated fleet, these being *Liberty Motors* Nos.7/8 (HAX 657 and HAX 828).

Former South Midland Leyland 'Tiger' TS7, now as Newbury & District No.167 (BWL 349).

The remaining quartet of vehicles that emanated from Oxford were all Leylands, a type only recently eliminated from the *Newbury & District* fleet! Three were Harrington-bodied 'Tiger' TS7's new in 1935/6 as *South Midland* Nos. 35-7 (BWL 349, CWL 951/3), which became *N&D* Nos.167, 168 and 166. The last of the four was quite an oddity indeed, being a 1947 'Tiger' PS1/1-type, but which was carrying one of the 1936 ECOC bodies formerly used by *North Western*, the combination having been made necessary due to the original planned Duple body not being available when it was new! As *South Midland* No.38 (LWL

995) it saw use mainly on contracts, though it did also work on the express services, the old body being one of those fitted with a sliding roof, which was retained, along with higher backed seats for 31 passengers. This became *N&D* No.169, and would in due course see an amazing metamorphosis, and indeed a long career.

The ECOC-bodied 'Tiger' PS1 seen above as N&D No.169 (LWL 995), and below when working London express services at Oxford as South Midland No.38.

All of these changes were effective from 1st January 1950 though, of course, the livery of the three fleets was common, so only fleetnames and numbers required changing. As an interesting footnote, it will be recalled that 'Regal' No.158 (ERX 937) had been used for publicity photos, though the negatives were doctored to show no fleetname, possibly because of the above transfer, or just to give a generic look?

Another of the Harrington-bodied Leyland 'Tiger' TS7's became Newbury & District No.168 (CWL 951). Note the stepped waistrail used on this pair of coaches along with the raked front end.

Chapter 23 – 1950

The transfer of vehicles between *Newbury & District* and *South Midland* resulted in the latter fleet now consisting entirely of 30 Duple-bodied AEC 'Regal' coaches, so if a 29-seater Bedford OB was needed, it would be loaned from Newbury. The pair of Albions on loan from *Red & White* were now returned, whilst the 4 Leylands sent to Newbury displaced those of that make in use there on contract work.

In January there were also two older *South Midland* Leyland coaches sent to Newbury for disposal, these being 1931 'Tiger' TS3 No.28 (JO 1597), which had a 1936 Harrington body, along with No.34 (BFC 675) a 'Tiger' TS7 with Harrington body new in 1935.

The hiring of coaches for *Associated Motorways* duties had proven a useful source of additional income so it was agreed that 3 coaches would be kept available during the Summer months.

A review of the fleet highlighted the poor shape of the bodies on Guy 'Arab' double-deckers 103 (CRX 283) and 104 (FAD 253), which were suffering from issues relating to the use of unseasoned timber. It was also noted that the 1947 'Tiger' PS1/1 should be provided with new bodywork in order that it might realise its full potential as a frontline coach. However, it was subsequently decided that the bodies on the Guys would be refurbished, but as Newbury was rather busy at the time, these were sent to Heaver's at Durrington, near Salisbury for attention.

During January an approach was made by *George Hedges* regarding the possible sale of his business, though nothing further came of this due to the Board being pre-occupied over the nationalisation situation. Indeed, on 10th February the parent Board met at the Great Western Hotel in Paddington for a Special Board Meeting. At the meeting the historic decision was taken to sell the bus interests in England and Wales to the State. The logic was, apparently, that a voluntary sale would be beneficial, but subsequent events pose the question 'what if', as not all operators were in fact nationalised under those proposals.

The matter was ratified on 28th March at an Extraordinary Meeting at the British Transport Commission offices at 55 Broadway, London SW1, when the *R&W* Directors stepped down in favour of the new *Newbury & District* Board of S. Kennedy (Chairman), R.I.H. Longman, L.H. Balls and K.W.C. Grand.

Whilst this mementos decision was being taken, the outstanding trio of AEC 'Regal' buses were delivered, with Nos.161/2 (FBL 919/20) arriving in February and No.163 (FBL 921) following in March. These had 35-seater front-entrance saloon bodies very much of the *R&W* style built by Lydney. They were on the

6821A-type chassis with 7.7 litre engines and, despite being new, they were mainly to be found on contract runs to the AERE at Harwell.

Very few photos were taken of the Lydney-bodied AEC 'Regals' 161-3, and this offside view of No.162 (FBL 920) shows the unusual window arrangement in the cab area.

The arrival of these saloons allowed the disposal in February of Bedford OWB's Nos.97/8 (CMO 658/9), though they would actually be the only withdrawals of that year.

Also during March the pair of low-bridge Guy 'Arab' double-deckers was delivered as Nos.170/1 (FMO 515/6), these being on the Mk111 chassis and fitted with Gardner 6LW engines. Their bodywork was a stylish design by Duple, with seats for 53 and rear conductor-operated platform doors. At the time it was publicly stated that the latter feature was designed to keep out the winds experienced when working up to the Berkshire Downs, though in reality the feature also appeared on similar examples built for the *Red & White* fleet. These were intended for use on Route 6 (Newbury – Lambourn), and were indeed associated with that route for many years, though they saw initial use on the Oxford route until the tree-cutting on the Lambourn road was completed.

Lowbridge Guy 'Arab' No.171 (FMO 516) when new at Gloucester Green, Oxford on the Newbury service.

Guy 'Arab' No.170 (FMO 515) in original livery at The Wharf. It is working the Oxford service, but the blind has slipped to read Shefford – East Ilsley – Oxford!

A third Guy 'Arab' was also in course of preparation, and had been diverted from *Venture* as the replacement for AEC 'Regent' No.159 (HAD 745) transferred there in January. It was delivered in May as No.172 (FMO 517), but unlike the previous pair its Duple body was of high-bridge layout and seated 57. The chassis was of the Mk111-type with a Gardner 6LW engine, and the other members of this batch did get delivered to *Venture* as its Nos.103-6 (HOT 391-4) – though these would also gravitate to Newbury in due course!

One aspect of co-ordination not mentioned so far, concerns the repeated attempts by *Venture's* General Manager Mr. Welling to encourage the Chisnell family who owned *King Alfred Motor Services* to work together to offer a Newbury – Winchester link. The latter were reluctant to participate in a full joint operation, knowing as they did that they already covered the more profitable part of the route. However, eventually they did agree to modify some timings, which meant that passengers could change at Whitchurch for Winchester, and this took effect from 13th March 1950.

On the vehicle front, problems were again besetting planned orders, and the batch of Guys on order for various operators in the *R&W* group were so delayed that the Board sought to cancel the order for the front-engined 'Arabs' outstanding. However, Guy Motors resisted that move, and instead they sought to supply its new underfloor-engined model instead. This was agreed to and the original order of 25 was to be bodied at Lydney using the style of body as used by Leyland Motors on its 'Royal Tiger' chassis. During May it was decided that 2 of these would go to *South Midland* and another pair to *Newbury & District*.

However, control from Chepstow soon passed, as the British Transport Commission decided that the operations based at Basingstoke, Newbury and Oxford

should be managed more locally. In order to do this the *Newbury & District* and *South Midland* operations were placed under the control of *Thames Valley*, whilst the *Venture* operations went to *Wilts & Dorset*, as it was considered that the Reading-based operator had quite enough on its plate.

Control officially passed over from 1st May and, in the case of *Thames Valley* it found its fleet of 335 vehicles suddenly increased by nearly 100 more! The increase in area also gave much extra work for the *TV* staff, and it was agreed that those staff affected would receive an increase in salary for the extra duties these additions brought with them.

Thames Valley now found itself with two garages in Mill Lane, though a short way from each other, one being the *N&D* garage and the other its original dormy shed for Route 10 (Reading – Newbury). The spare capacity at the latter had also been used for the Winter storage of coaches, along with Leyland 'Titan' TD1's for disposal. Shortly after they took control there was a re-organisation at Newbury, whereby the previously outstationned buses were kept at the main garage, whilst the dormy shed became the body and paint shop, with storage at the rear for the increasing number of redundant vehicles passing through in the 1950-2 period.

The highbridge version of the Duple-bodied 'Arab' Mk111 was initially respresented just by No.172 (FMO 517), seen when new on the Oxford service. These elegant vehicles, with the mid-decks polished strips, in the crimson red and white livery, looked very smart indeed and were a tribute to Red & White.

In order to assist at Newbury, *Thames Valley* sent a number of buses from its fleet, these being 1930 Leyland 'Lion' LT2 No.50 (RX 6246), 1932 'Tiger' TS4 Nos.246 and 255 (RX 9700/9), along with 1935 'Tiger' TS7 coaches 262/4 (JB 5841/3), all loaned from 1st April. On the same date the pair of Bedford OB coaches Nos.164/5 (LJO 756/7) was transferred to *Thames Valley* ownership, though still kept at Newbury and as often as not hired back to *South Midland!* On 12th April these were joined by 1929-vintage Leyland 'Titan' TD1 Nos.179/81 (RX 4341/3). Also, although not noted so officially, it is known that 1929 'Titan' TD1 No.184 (RX 4346) and 1932 'Tiger' TS4 Nos.247/52 (RX 9701/6) were in use at times over the Summer, perhaps deputising for others requiring attention? All retained their *TV* fleet numbers, as there was no clash between the fleets.

As a result of these transfers, the remaining utility Bedfords and a few other older *N&D* vehicles had been parked up at the newly-extended Southern Railway yard at Reading Stations. Whilst there a number were stoned by some boys, though they were apprehended and prosecuted by the Police.

Mr. Grimmett had held the post of General Manager at *N&D* from July 1949, and since the resignation of Gerald Nowell (who had gone to the independent *Hants & Sussex* in late 1949), he had also looked after the Oxford operations. Under *Thames Valley* he was the Traffic Superintendent based at Oxford, whilst Newbury was controlled from the Head Office at Reading. It is understood that this did not exactly suit him, so he moved on in December 1952 to become the General Manager at *Black & White* of Cheltenham, a company he already knew well from his dealings with *Associated Motorways.*

Reg Hibbert was certainly not impressed by the vehicles initially sent out to Newbury, which coloured his view that the garage was sent 'old rubbish'. Even in the late 1960's the author can recall him cursing the secondhand buses sent there! Whilst mentioning Reg, the author recalls that in later years he had one of the Guy Red Indian-head radiator mascots on his desk, all painted up, the Guy motto being 'feathers in our cap'.

However, in August 1950 the Reading management did redeem itself a bit with the allocation of a pair of brand new Bristol LL6B-types with rear-entrance 36-seater bus bodies as Nos.558/9 (FMO 940/1), and they were joined by similar bus 557 (FMO 939) a month later. These were Newbury's first 30-footers, whereas their 7ft 6ins width was ideal for the local lanes. They proved themselves to be useful and reliable buses, even later being rebuilt to forward-entrance for one-man-operation through to the mid-1960's!

It will be noted that these new arrivals were in the main *Thames Valley* fleet numbering, and indeed they carried full *TV* livery of red and cream. The original *Newbury & District* vehicles remained in their own series of numbers, and no re-numbering (in the ordinary sense) took place, though later it was found advisable to re-number the remaining high-bridge double-deckers into a separate 'H' series. Nos. 170/1 would therefore be the final buses from that fleet to remain in service with original numbers. Despite this, the following year would see further additions to the *N&D* series as we shall see later.

In respect of livery, repaints were duly undertaken into the standard *Thames Valley* scheme, though the *Newbury & District* fleetnames continued to appear until supplies ran out in 1952/3. The surviving vehicles carried legal lettering showing their ownership as *Newbury & District,* but followed by the full *Thames Valley* Head Office address, to where the Newbury Company had been relocated, the brass plate fitting neatly into the screw holes at No.83 Lower Thorn Street left by the winding up of the *Ledbury Transport Company* at much the same time!

During September 1950 another two of the garage staff had departed, though in this instance it was to set up their own coach business! The Garage Engineer Sid Taylor and Garage Hand Ed Whitington formed *Enterprise Coaches*, and soon acquired some half-a-dozen secondhand coaches for their venture. Mostly they covered contracts and private hire work, offering a cheaper alternative to the somewhat superior coaches of *N&D.* Indeed, it would seem that they had started on this idea when they had purchased former *South Midland* Leyland 'Tiger' TS7 No.34 (BFC 675) just a short time beforehand 'for scrap'.

However, several passengers recall that their fleet was generally past its best, so a hirer tended to get what they paid for. The partnership with Ed only lasted for a year or so, though Sid carried on for some years more, also acquiring the taxi business previously operated by Theo Denham in 1950. The coaches were kept at the old *Durnford* sheds in Mill Lane, along with the taxis. The business was sold to *Reliance M.S.* in 1958, that base becoming the Newbury outstation until the Boundary Road garage was opened in 1963.

With the departure of Sid Taylor, the post of Engineer was given to Reg Hibbert, who had of course already proved himself a very capable and skilled engineer. Reg was then responsible for the high standard of fleet presentation at Newbury and Oxford. In respect of the Oxford fleet the Foreman there, Mr. Bessell, was now under the direction of Reg.

With regards to the Newbury area services, *Thames Valley* was initially content to leave the operations as they were, the transfer having come at short notice, though some re-organisation would follow in due course.

On the vehicle side, an inspection by the *TV* Chief Engineer Basil Sutton soon after the transfer had led to the withdrawals of the remaining wartime Bedfords and a couple of the Guy 'Arabs' with poor bodywork, though all the latter would return to use in due course.

However, the vehicle that stood out for attention was the 1947 Leyland 'Tiger', which Sutton saw as the basis for a useful coach. This became a Winter project for the Reading Works, after Sutton had been to the Kingston Works of Leyland Motors to see the kit available for extending such 'Tigers' to the new maximum length of 30 foot. However, although the regulations had been amended to an 8 foot width, the chassis was not widened or provided with wider axles, as happened on some interim models at that time.

Before this work got underway, the chassis was driven to Darby Green, where the body was dropped off for £10 scrap value. Indeed, an attempt had been made to sell the body to staff for £30, making this the last example of a body being sold separately by *Thames Valley,* a common practice during the 1920's and '30's. A new body, with full-front and similar to those on order for Bristol LWL6B chassis was scheduled at Eastern Coach Works for 1951 delivery.

It is interesting to note that the intention was to have this vehicle re-registered as 'new', and Leyland Motors were even willing to issue a new chassis plate if required. However, when Berkshire CC Licensing was contacted, it refused to accept it as a new vehicle!

1950 saw several significant events in the Newbury area affecting bus operations. Firstly, the A339 was diverted from its original course to Greenham Common to run via The Swan at Newtown as part of the extension of the airfield to take USAAF B47 and B52 bombers from 1951 under the 'Cold War' use of their UK Bases, which effectively employed Britain as an aircraft-carrier, providing the capability to attack Eastern Europe and monitor Soviet military movements.

The second event, though linked to the peaceful use of atomic power, was the opening of the AERE Harwell establishment, which marked the change from the construction phase to full occupation by the staff, many of whom still travelled there by bus.

As an aside it is worth noting that the Kennet & Avon Canal closed to through traffic that year, following a lock collapse, and would not re-open until 1990 after a long campaign by volunteers!

In very late 1950 it was agreed to make some further exchanges between the *Venture* and *Newbury & District* fleets in the interest of standardisation. The AEC 'Regent' 0961-type double-decker No.151 (EJB 521) was at last sent to Basingstoke, where it had originally been intended way back in 1948! It was of course the only bus in the fleet now with a pre-select gearbox.

On the other hand, the need for double-deckers on intensive services serving factories that had been busy on war production had tailed off to such an extent the Basingstoke operator now had a surplus of such buses. It therefore took the opportunity to rid itself of all the Guy 'Arabs' in stock, with 6 such buses coming to Newbury to join others of that type, not to mention the examples already owned by *Thames Valley* that would understandably gravitate to Newbury in due course.

These consisted of a pair of former *Red & White* 1943 examples on Mk11 chassis with Gardner 5LW engines, though by then carrying 56-seater high-bridge bodies built by Park Royal in early 1950, just before being sent to Basingstoke as Nos.100/1 (EWO 490/2), becoming *N&D* Nos.173/4. The other four were, however, the batch-mates of *N&D's* No.172, all being Mk111 chassis with Gardner 6LW engines and 57-seater high-bridge bodies by Duple, and were *Venture* Nos.103-6 (HOT 391-4) delivered in May and June 1950, and these became Nos.175-8. Incidentally, the number 102 had been put aside by *Venture* for receipt of the above AEC, though as this occurred later than originally anticipated, it got a new one under the re-numbering by *Wilts & Dorset* instead of taking up that number.

Duple-bodied Guy 'Arab' No.178 (HOT 394) seen in service with Venture as its No.106, destined soon to transfer to the Newbury fleet.

The latter Guys looked very much at home at Newbury, and retained the painted Simonds Beer adverts, being equally appropriate in their new location. In due course these would be the last high-bridge buses in the *Thames Valley* fleet and, along with low-bridge examples Nos.170/1 (FMO 515/6), would be the last vehicles still legally the property of *Newbury & District,* remaining in service until March or April 1968. Seeing these buses the first time at The Wharf still stands out in the Author's mind as the time when more had to be known about the old *N&D!*

Chapter 24 – 1951

Work on the chassis extension of 'Tiger' PS1/1-type No.169 (LWL 995) was completed for it to be sent to Lowestoft on 27th February, with the idea of the new coach returning prior to the busy Festival of Britain scheduled to commence in early May.

During the early months of the year a start was made on ousting older stock at Newbury, whilst *TV* looked for short-term replacements from within its own fleet.

The double-deck situation was not a problem, after the recent transfers from *Venture,* but Basil Sutton soon identified the former *Scottish Motor Traction/North Western* rebuilt AEC 'Regal' 4's as a priority for sale. It is of course an interesting point to consider that the 0642-type was known the 'Regal' 4, though as these now had 5-cylinder engines, perhaps 'Regal' 5 might have been a better designation?

One of the other double-deckers transferred from the Venture fleet was Guy 'Arab' No.173 (EWO 490) on the busy Local Service 38 to Bartlemy Close.

In order to achieve that a number of Leyland 'Tigers' from *Thames Valley* were sold for a nominal £1 each to *Newbury & District,* officially from 1st May, though the physical dates of arrival varied, and these were also joined by a Guy 'Arab' from September. They received fleet numbers in the old Newbury series, and would be the last buses to do so:

N&D	TV	Reg.No.	Type/Body	New
179	342	AJB 814	Tiger TS8/Brush B35R	1937
180	344	AJB 816	Tiger TS8/Brush B35R	1937
181	372	BBL 558	Tiger TS8/ECW B35R	1938
182	346	AJB 818	Tiger TS8/Brush B35R	1937
183	379	BBL 565	Tiger TS8/ECW B35R	1938
184	333	ABL 763	Tiger TS7/ECW B35R	1937
185	343	AJB 815	Tiger TS8/Brush B35R	1937
186	368	ARX 990	TigerTS8/ECWB35R	1938
187	420	CJB 139	Guy Arab/Strachan L55R	1943

Although these fleetnumbers, along with fleetnames as *Newbury & District* were applied, and indeed these buses served at Newbury, in due course they would revert to their old *Thames Valley* fleetnumbers and, in common with other Newbury allocations, would receive *Thames Valley* fleetnames.

The arrival of the above allowed a wholesale cull of the hybrid 'Regals', with 123 (FS 8562) withdrawn in February, followed in March by 122/4-30 (FS 8560, 8567, 8576, 8572, 8566, 8574, 8575 and 8565), which left only No.121 (FS 8582) of that type still active. Also disposed of by then was AEC 'Regal' No.156 (AMD 47), which was in a withdrawn, and apparently immobile, state at the takeover and therefore did not operate under *TV,* the latter obviously not considering it worth rectifying.

Also disposed of were the former *South Midland* Leyland 'Tiger' TS7 coaches No.166-8 (CWL 953, BWL 349 and CWL 951), though they had actually spent quite a bit of time working for their old owner over the previous year anyway!

The 'Tigers' transferred from *Thames Valley* largely covered contracts, though some of those also worked relief duties during busier days, and *TV* No.373 (BBL 559), another 1938 ECW-bodied 'Tiger'TS8 was also on loan to Newbury during July 1951. The Duple-bodied 'Tiger' TS7 coaches Nos.262/4 (JB 5841/3), remained at Newbury, having been part of a batch of 3 built in 1935, all of which had been requisitioned by the War Office. Only 262/4 returned, though not at the same time, and in very poor shape. The amount of effort put into their refurbishment is testament to how difficult it was to obtain new coaches, though they repaid the investment by running until 1954, and spent most of that time at Newbury or on loan to *South Midland.*

As already noted, the Festival of Britain generated a lot of extra coaching work, both for excursions to London and in relation to more local events or those annual excursions with an enhanced significance that year. The festival had been conceived in order to cheer up the public, who were still very much subject to daily austerity, even though the war had ended 6 years ago. Indeed, the last vestiges of rationing did not cease until 1954!

The main theatre for this was a bombed out former brewery site on London's South Bank, which was, in an echo of the 1851 Great Exhibition of two centuries before, a showpiece for all the enterprise and modernity that the Country to offer, with the emphasis on the better days soon to come! The area was between Waterloo Station and the River Thames, and the Festival Hall was its centrepiece and lasting legacy. The rest of the site had all sorts of displays of modern equipment and artwork with the theme of 'the

The ugly duckling becomes a white swan, suitably photographed by the River Thames at Reading. Note the Festival of Britain logo on No.169 (LWL 995).

future', even including future space exploration, at a time when many homes still featured outside toilets and were not on electricity!

Other features in London included the Festival Pleasure Gardens (later known as Battersea Fun Fair), a large theme park just upstream from the main site, which also had its own pier for steamers. Elsewhere, the theme was rolled out to such events as the Royal Navy Fleet Review at Portsmouth, along with numerous more localised celebrations.

The Festival opened on 3rd May 1951, and *Newbury & District* was granted a license to run excursions from various points on a weekly basis from 6th May until 30th September, such restrictions being necessary in order to control traffic congestion in the Capitol. It was also a condition of the license that coaches were parked away from the site, so *N&D* used coach parks in the Battersea area. The authorised excursions were operated from Newbury, Thatcham, Cold Ash, Great Shefford, Bucklebury, Inkpen, Kingsclere and Hermitage, though there were also some private hire parties for the same purpose.

Unfortunately, the work on the ECW-bodied Leyland 'Tiger' PS1/1-type too a little longer to complete, probably because it required some adjustments to the frontal appearance of the body, and it was collected from Lowestoft on 6th June, meaning that it missed the first month of that very busy period. It soon became a regular sight in the Capitol, as well as further afield.

The bodywork was the same 'Queen Mary' style as used on the Bristol LWL6B-type coaches then being delivered to *Thames Valley,* except that No.169 still had the exposed radiator. However, despite being an oddity, the Newbury staff took it as their pride-and-joy, and it was always kept in very good condition. It was of course the last vehicle to be delivered with the *Newbury & District* fleetname, and the Newbury team made sure it retained that so as long as possible. It did duly get *Thames Valley* fleetnames, but later it was selected for the Irish Tour (being a Leyland, and a type used by the Irish operator looking after it whilst outstationned), at which point it reverted to carrying the *South Midland* name! It would also have the distinction of being the last Leyland in use in 1960.

In the meantime *Thames Valley* had been studying the Newbury area services, leading to a number of items going to the Traffic Commissioner in March. These were duly approved and led to the following changes:

Route 1 – (Newbury – East Ilsley) – the extension on Thursdays and Saturdays to Rowstock was now not necessary due to improvements on the Oxford service, though a couple of journeys were extended on Mondays to Fridays to the AERE Guardroom on the Chilton side of the large site;

Route 2 – (West Ilsley – East Ilsley – Reading) – the Reading terminus amended from Lower Thorn Street to Station Hill;

Route 7 - (Newbury – Wantage) – some journeys were extended on Wednesdays, Saturdays and Sundays to Childrey Ridgeway (also see Route 34);

Route 8 – (Newbury – Hungerford Newtown) – on Thursdays and Saturdays was extended onto Poughley

– Woodlands St. Mary – Lambourn Woodlands – Baydon, also now worked by double-deck buses;
<u>Route 34</u> – (Lambourn – Wantage) – service was withdrawn, with Route 7 modified to provide cover.

However, by the time these changes were approved, it had also been decided to re-number the Newbury area services in order to avoid a clash with the main *TV* series, achieved by using the 100 series of numbers, which resulted in the following:

Route 101 Newbury – East Ilsley or Chilton (AERE)
Route 101a Newbury – Peasemore - Stanmore
Route 102 West Ilsley – East Ilsley – Reading
Route 103 Newbury – Greenham - Ecchinswell
Route 104 Newbury – Headley – Kingsclere
Route 104a Newbury – Headley – Ashford Hill
Route 105 Newbury – Shefford – Wantage
Route 106 Newbury – Shefford – Upper Lambourn
Route 106a Lambourn – Shefford – Hungerford
Route 107 N'bury – Lambourn W'lands –Swindon
Route 108 Newbury – Wickham – Hungerford
Newtown or Newbury – Lambourn W'lands - Baydon
Route 109 Newbury – Thatcham – Cold Ash
Route 110 N'bury – Thatcham – Thatcham Station
Route 111 Newbury – Thatcham – Bucklebury
Route 112 Newbury – Abingdon – Oxford
Route 113 Newbury – Inkpen – Hungerford
Route 114 Newbury – Ball Hill – East Woodhay
Route 114a Newbury – Ball Hill – West Woodhay
Route 115 Newbury – Woolton Hill – Highclere
Route 116 Newbury – Hungerford (via Bath Road)
Route 119 Newbury – Hermitage – Yattendon
Route 119a Newbury – Aldworth – Ashampstead
Route 120 Newbury – Hermitage – Frilsham
Route 121 Shaw – Newbury – Whitway
Route 127 Newbury (Broadway) – Wash Common
Route 128 Bartlemy Close – Maple Crescent
Route 129 N'bury (Broadway) – Hambridge Road

These changes came into effect from the Summer timetable issued on Saturday 16th June, and as a result of that the booklet went up from 168 to 188 pages.

Thames Valley had also been studying the loadings on various services, particularly in order to reduce the need for relief workings, though some reflected the increased carriage of school children on services. This resulted in the use of double-deckers on various routes, after the necessary clearance by the tree-cutting crew in their old Leyland 'Titan' TD1 No.29 (RX 1758) converted to the Route Servicing Vehicle. Those working arrangements altered were as below:

Route No.	Route	Date Altered
107	Newbury – Swindon	September 1951
114	Newbury – East Woodhay	June 1951
115	Newbury – Highclere	July 1951
119	Newbury – Yattendon	September 1951

On 10th September the Newbury area conductors were issued with new Setright ticket machines, which issued tickets on a pre-printed roll, using a system of dials set to print the date, class of ticket and fare. This was a considerable step forward in the speed of ticket issue, whilst from the accounting point of view it was regarded as 'fiddle-proof'. However, there are tales of those who learnt how to dismantle the machines and turn the recording dials back, though not specifically from that area.

Also from 23rd September it was decided to end the Sunday workings on Route 105 (Newbury – Wantage – Childrey Ridgeway) due to lack of patronage.

During October a further cull of older types took place, resulting in the demise of the last Bedford OWB's Nos.94-6 (CMO 523, 624 and 657), along with the final ex-*Scottish Motor Traction* AEC 'Regal' No.121 (FS 8582). A further trio of the later 'Regal' rebuilds, Nos.153 (AGX 455), 154 (TG 1819) and 155 (AGP 841) also departed that month, leaving only No.157 (FAX 349) of that type still in service.

It will be recalled that a pair of the outstanding Guy coaches of the underfloor-engined UF-type were due for *Newbury & District,* these being fitted with the horizontal version of the Gardner 6LW engine and bodies by Lydney. However, this was to be the most protracted of all the sagas of delayed deliveries, and by the time these coaches eventually entered service in April/May <u>1953</u>, they had been re-assigned to the *South Midland* fleet. Indeed, such were the problems at Lydney that the works was closed in March 1952, so those coaches had to be completed by the State-owned Brislington Body Works at Bristol.

Although the Newbury fleet and operations still retained a character of their own, developments were inevitably much more integrated with the new parent Company as time went by.

The full story of all developments in the Newbury area, along with the main Thames Valley history will be found in 'A History of the Thames Valley Traction Co. Ltd., 1946 – 1960' – see page 4 for more details.

Thames Valley 'Tiger' TS8 No.379 (BBL 565) as N&D 183 and with the Newbury & District fleetname.

A Newbury & District Gallery

Illustrating the earlier life of some of the AEC 'Regal' vehicles later at N&D is Blue Belle AGX 455, with an observation-style coach body at Clapham.

Above – Guy 'Arab' 177 (HOT 393) had gained a TV fleetname, though the blind still shows the old service number when seen passing 'The Harrow' at Headley. Below – AEC 'Regent' 151 (EJB 521) passed to the Venture fleet just as Wilts & Dorset took control.

Above – Former Thames Valley 'Tiger' TS7 (ABL 760) in service with Reliance. Below – Lydney-bodied AEC 'Regal' 161 (FBL 919) outside Mill Lane depot.

Leyland 'Tiger' 169 (LWL 995) seen in later years.

What might have been! – underfloor-engined Guy coach which became South Midland 89 (SFC 504).

Fleet No.	Reg. No.	Chassis/Model	Bodywork	Seats	New	Acq.	Sold
21	BL 6490	Talbot 25/50hp	Andrews	C14D	Apr-20	Jun-32	Sep-35
	DP XXXX	Lancia Tetraiota	Vincent	C20D	?/25	Jun-32	by 12/33
	VA 3156	Lancia Tetraiota	??	B20	Dec-24	Jun-32	by 12/32
	??	Guy J	Andrews	C20D	c.1925	Jun-32	Jun-33
25	VM 8638	Gilford 166SD	Lewis & Crabtree	C26	Apr-29	Jun-32	Aug-38
22	RD 1886	Gilford 168OT	Vincent	C30D	Jun-30	Jun-32	by 7/43
6	RX 8261	Ford AA	Andrews	B20F	Mar-31	Jun-32	Dec-34
	??	Thornycroft J	??	Lorry	Ex-WD	Jun-32	by 4/33
Note:	*The above vehicles were the contribution of A.Andrews & Son, Newbury at formation of N&D*						
	KE 3196	Talbot 25/50hp	Andrews	B14F	Feb-21	c.1927	?/33
	TR 1231	Leyland E	Southampton CT	B26F	Nov-25	Jun-32	?/33
7	VT 184	Tilling Stevens B10A	Strachan & Brown	B32F	Jul-27	Jun-32	Jul-40
	WU 9870	Minerva	Metcalfe	B20	Feb-27	Jun-32	Oct-32
9	MW 825	Thornycroft A2long	Challands Ross	B20F	Nov-27	Jun-32	Jun-40
5	BU 5690	Tilling Stevens B10A2	Northern Counties	B32F	Nov-28	Jun-32	Sep-36
23	TO 9554	Gilford 166OT	Strachan & Brown	B32F	Mar-29	Jun-32	?/39
	??	Gilford	??	B28	??	Jun-32	Jun-33
12	TR 8198	Thornycroft A2	Wadham	B20F	Feb-30	Jun-32	Jun-40
	TB 2522	Daimler CK	??	Lorry	Ex-WD	Jun-32	by 4/33
Note:	*The above vehicles were the contribution of Denham Bros., Newbury at formation of N&D*						
	YB 7442	Lancia Pentaiota	Wray	C20F	Sep-26	Jun-32	Jun-34
29	YT 9565	Garner 55hp	Buckingham	C26D	Sep-27	Jun-32	Aug-36
	??	Reo Major	??	C20F	c.1927	Jun-32	by 4/36
	VX 43	Gilford CP6	Thurgood	C20D	May-29	Jun-32	Jun-33
Not run	UV 9116	Gilford CP6	Wycombe	C20F	Jul-29	Jun-32	Jul-32
30	UU 7594	GMC T42	Wilton	C26	Jun-29	Jun-32	Dec-37
26	RX 6264	Reo Pullman	Wray	C25D	Mar-30	Jun-32	Sep-38
27	HX 1059	Star Flyer VB4	Strachan	C24D	Mar-30	Jun-32	Aug-39
28	YE 8768	Maudslay ML4	London Lorries	C26D	Mar-27	Jun-32	Jun-34
L4	CW 6802	Maudslay ML2	Andrews - Removals	Van	Jun-26	Jun-32	Jul-33
	??	Guy	Lorry or van	Goods	??	Jun-32	by 4/33
	??	Star 50cwt	Lorry or van ex-PSV	Goods	c.1923	Jun-32	by 4/33
	??	GMC K41	Lorry or van ex-PSV	Goods	c.1925	Jun-32	by 4/33
Note:	*The above vehicles were the contribution of Durnford & Sons, Newbury at formation of N&D*						
	PE 2077	Dennis 2.5 ton	Strachan & Brown	B20F	Apr-25	Jun-32	Jun-33
	??	??	??	Lorry	??	Sep-32	??
	??	Talbot 25/50hp	Andrews	C14	??	Sep-32	??
	RX 4556	Ford AA	??	C14D	May-29	Sep-32	Dec-34
	RX 6888	Ford AA	Duple	C14D	Jun-30	Sep-32	Dec-34
Note:	*The above 4 vehicles came from George Hedges, Brightwalton on joining N&D*						
	RX 4272	Ford AA	Andrews	B14F	Apr-29	Sep-32	Jan-34
	RX 7256	Ford AA	Andrews	B14F	Jul-30	Sep-32	?/34
	RX 7772	Ford AA	Andrews ?	B20F	Dec-30	Sep-32	Nov-35
	RX 9005	Ford AA	Andrews ?	B20F	Jul-31	Sep-32	Sep-36
	??	Gilford f/c	??	C32	??	Sep-32	??
Note:	*The above vehicles came from John Prothero, Beedon on joining N&D*						
	OT 6861	Dennis G	Lorry	Goods	Dec-27	Sep-32	Mar-35
	OT 6862	Dennis G	Lorry	Goods	Dec-27	Sep-32	Mar-35
	OT 7923	Dennis G	Lorry	Goods	Mar-28	Sep-32	by 7/35
	??	Chevrolet	??	C14	??	Oct-32	Jun-33
Not run	MO 8231	Chevrolet X	??	B14F	Jul-26	Oct-32	Oct-32
19	RX 9971	Bedford WLB	??	B20F	Mar-32	Oct-32	Aug-40
		The above 3 vehicles came from Pocock Bros., Cold Ash on joining N&D						
	MO 6744	Ford T 1-ton	Andrews	B14F	Jan-26	Jan-33	Jun-33
	RX 6662	Ford AA	Andrews	B20F	Apr-30	Jan-33	?/35
Note:	*The above vehicles came from Freddie Spanswick, Thatcham on joining N&D*						
53	UV 6002	Dennis GL	Wray	C20	Jul-29	Jul-33	Mar-36
10	OU 3317	Thornycroft A2	Wadham	B20F	Aug-29	Jul-33	Apr-44

	RA 1794	Thornycroft A2long	Challands Ross	B20R	Feb-27	Sep-33	by 8/38
3	TY 6174	Star Flyer VB4	Robson	B20	Jun-29	?/33	Dec-35
39	VA 7942	Leyland Lion PLSC1	Leyland	B31F	Jul-28	c.9/33	by 4/37
40	VA 7943	Leyland Lion PLSC1	Leyland	B31F	Aug-28	c.9/33	Sep-38
41	PR 9053	Dennis E	Strachan & Brown	B32D	Apr-27	Nov-33	Sep-37
Not run	RX 5432	Ford AA	??	C14	Oct-29	Jan-34	Jan-34
Note:	The above vehicle was taken over from Catherine Geary, Great Shefford but re-sold						
	GJ 9733	Federal	??	C	Jul-30	Jan-34	by 8/38
Note:	The above vehicle came from John Burt & Bert Greenwood, Inkpen on joining N&D						
	RX 3553	Morris 25cwt	Morris	B14F	Jan-29	Jan-34	Sep-35
Note:	The above vehicle came from George Brown, Wash Common on joining N&D						
28	GU 7545	Star Flyer VB4	Thurgood	C26	Apr-29	Jan-34	by 7/38
51	HJ 8718	Gilford 166SD	??	C26	Mar-29	Jan-34	Sep-39
	RX 4356	Ford AA	Lorry	Goods	Apr-29	Jan-34	Dec-37
Note:	The above 3 vehicles came from Durnford Bros., Newbury on joining N&D						
L4	CW 6802	Maudslay ML2	Andrews - Removals	Van	Jun-26	Jan-34	Jun-37
Note:	This Maudslay re-entered the fleet after service with Bill Durnford						
11	KM 3028	Thornycroft A2	Strachan & Brown	B20F	Feb-29	c.2/34	c.8/39
	(TM 5639)	Gilford 166OT	Strachan	C32F	Sep-29	c.2/34	by 8/38
	(SH 3380)	GMC T30C	Alexander	B20F	May-29	Feb-34	Dec-34
	MY 3052	Star Flyer VB4	Star	C26D	Mar-30	Feb-34	Jan-37
4	MY 4213	Star Flyer VB4	Star	C26D	Apr-30	Feb-34	Mar-38
Note:	The above 3 vehicles came from George Howlett, Bucklebury on joining N&D						
	TP 7118	Dennis 30cwt	Dennis	B14F	Dec-28	Mar-34	Mar-35
42	RX 5493	Dennis 30cwt	??	C14D	Nov-29	Mar-34	Sep-34
43	RX 6401	Dennis 30cwt	??	C17	May-30	Mar-34	by10/35
44	MW 6161	AJS Pilot	Eaton	B26F	Dec-29	Mar-34	by 6/37
Note:	The above 4 vehicles came from W. J. White & Son, Hermitage on joining N&D						
	RD 5922	Bedford 2.5 ton	Lorry	Goods	Sep-34	New	Jul-45
35	FM 6488	GMC T30C	Hughes	B20F	Dec-30	Dec-34	?/41
36	FM 6486	GMC T30C	Hughes	B20F	Dec-30	Dec-34	?/41
37	FM 6487	GMC T30C	Hughes	B20F	Dec-30	Dec-34	Aug-39
31	CC 9415	GMC T60	Strachan	B26D	Mar-30	Dec-34	Jan-37
	JB 1930	Bedford 2.5 ton	Lorry	Goods	May-33	Jan-35	Feb-42
	JB 1984	Bedford 2.5 ton	Lorry	Goods	May-33	Jan-35	Feb-42
Note:	The above 2 vehicles came from W. R. Cleeveley, Newbury who sold out to N&D						
50	JK 1911	Gilford 168OT	Duple	C31F	Jul-31	Apr-35	Jul-40
	VR 9822	Gilford 168OT	??	B32	Jul-30	Apr-35	by 8/38
6	FG 4427	Maudslay ML4B	Buckingham	B29F	Oct-28	Apr-35	Jun-37
	VM 3669	Gilford 166OT	Spicer	C32R	Aug-28	Jun-35	by 8/38
24	RH 2257	Gilford 168OT	HC Motor Works	B32R	Jun-30	Jun-35	Apr-41
	RU 5796	Leyland Leveret PLA2	Leyland	B20F	Jul-27	by 6/35	?/36
	RU 5843	Leyland Leveret PLA2	Leyland	B20F	Aug-27	by 6/35	?/35
	JB 6909	Bedford 3-ton	Lorry	Goods	Jul-35	New	Apr-41
63	JB 6834	Dennis Ace	King & Taylor	C20F	Jul-35	New	Jan-47
18	RX 9463	Bedford WLG	Body ex-Reo Major?	C20	Nov-31	Jul-35	Sep-37
49	MW 4028	Gilford 166OT	Wycombe	C31F	Mar-29	Sep-35	by 6/40
43	UL 7692	Dennis F	Dodson	C20D	Mar-29	Oct-35	Jan-37
Note:	The above vehicle came from Charlie Ballard, South End, Bradfield who sold out to N&D						
58	OU 2885	GMC T30C	London Lorries	C20D	Jul-29	Oct-35	Dec-40
	UX 9410	Bedford WLB	Dobson	B20F	Nov-31	Dec-35	Jul-36
	RG 881	GMC T30C	??	?20?	Dec-29	Dec-35	?/38
	UN 5227	Bedford WLB	Wilmott	C20F	Oct-31	Dec-35	Dec-38
	UN 5381	Bedford WLB	Wilmott	C20F	Jan-32	Dec-35	Dec-36
32	RA 9830	GMC T42	Duple	B26F	Oct-29	Dec-35	Jan-41
48	MS 9336	Gilford 168OT	Wycombe	B32F	Nov-29	Dec-35	by 3/39
53	HX 1855	Gilford AS6	Petty	C20D	Nov-30	Dec-35	Apr-39
61	OY 2093	Bedford WLB	Real	C20F	Dec-31	Dec-35	c.3/38
62	OY 5807	Bedford WLB	Duple	C20F	May-33	Dec-35	c.3/38
Not run	OT 816?	Thornycroft A1	Hall Lewis	Ch20	Mar-26	??/35	Spares

Note:	*The above vehicle was acquired from Edith Kent for spares and had been a demonstrator*						
	HO 6306	Dennis 4-ton	Lorry	Goods	May-24	Mar-36	by 2/42
Note:	*The above vehicle came from C. G. Colliver, Wickham who sold out to N&D*						
	MY 346	Gilford 166SD	Duple	C26D	Jul-29	May-36	c.3/38
20	UR 7968	Thornycroft A2long	Thurgood	B20F	Nov-30	May-36	Jun-40
21	JH 492	Thornycroft A12	Thurgood	B20F	Sep-31	May-36	Aug-45
Not run	MT 1842	Gilford 166OT	Wilton	C32D	Jan-29	Dec-36	Spares
52	TY 8886	Gilford 168MOT	Strachan	C31F	Oct-31	Dec-36	Feb-41
14	PG 2018	Thornycroft A2long	Challands Ross	B20F	Jul-29	Jan-37	Apr-44
16	PG 3236	Thornycroft A2long	Challands Ross	B20F	Sep-29	Jan-37	Feb-41
17	PG 4226	Thornycroft A2long	Challands Ross	B20F	Nov-29	Jan-37	Nov-40
31	TP 7951	Thornycroft A2	Wadham	B20F	Jun-29	Jan-37	Apr-44
43	TP 8693	Thornycroft A2	Wadham	B20F	Feb-30	Jan-37	Apr-44
46	PG 1099	Thornycroft A2long	Challands Ross	B20F	Jun-29	Jan-37	Dec-40
57	TP 9164	Thornycroft A2	Wadham	B20F	May-30	Jan-37	Apr-44
54	HX 7560	Gilford 168OT	Duple	C32F	Mar-31	Feb-37	?/40
55	JJ 8873	Gilford 168OT	Duple	C32F	Mar-33	Feb-37	c.6/40
64 (66)	FJ 9581	Dennis Ace	Duple	B20F	Mar-34	Mar-37	Dec-44
65	JY 4752	Dennis Ace	Mumford	C20F	Dec-34	Mar-37	Dec-44
5	UN 3196	Chevrolet LR	??	B16F	Dec-29	Apr-37	Dec-39
8	TK 2740	Guy OND	Guy	B20F	May-29	Apr-37	May-37
15	OT 4452	Thornycroft A2long	Wadham	B20F	Apr-27	Apr-37	c.7/39
38	CG 1724	Commer Centaur	Petty	C20F	Aug-32	Apr-37	Feb-38
39	ACG 644	Commer Invader	Petty	C20F	Apr-35	Apr-37	Jun-40
42	OU 6047	AJS Pilot	Petty	B28F	Jun-30	Apr-37	c.7/39
Note:	*The above 6 vehicles were acquired from Mrs. E. G. Kent, Kingsclere who sold out to N&D*						
8	UO 9841	Thornycroft A2long	Wadham	B20F	Mar-29	May-37	Dec-40
	AMO 455	Bedford 2.5 ton	Pantechnicon	Goods	May-37	New	Jul-44
	RX 7150	Ford AA	??	C14F	Jul-30	May-37	?/37
	JB 437	Ford AA	??	C20	Jun-32	May-37	Dec-37
60	JB 5701	Ford BB	??	C20	Feb-35	May-37	Mar-41
Note:	*The above 3 vehicles were acquired from Pass & Co., Newbury who sold out to N&D*						
44	TV 5363	Tilling Stevens B10A	Willowbrook	B32F	Dec-31	Jun-37	by 6/42
45	TV 6036	Tilling Stevens B49A7	Willowbrook	B32F	Apr-32	Jun-37	Sep-40
64	RX 2907	Ford AA	Vincent	C14D	Aug-28	Jul-37	Nov-39
67	AYA 102	Dennis Ace	Harrington	C20R	Jun-34	Mar-38	May-46
68	DG 9516	Dennis Ace	Duple	C20F	Jun-34	Mar-38	Dec-44
69	DYF 184	Dennis Ace	Strachan	C20F	May-37	Mar-38	Dec-44
70	BON 886	Bedford WTB	Duple	C25F	Apr-36	Mar-38	Jun-46
71	BON 887	Bedford WTB	Duple	C25F	Apr-36	Mar-38	May-47
30	JD 1220	Gilford 168OT	Wycombe	C26F	Apr-31	Jul-38	by 3/39
Not run	TM 5726	Chevrolet LQ	Economy	B16F	Sep-29	Jul-38	Jul-38
Note:	*The above vehicle came from Ernest Nobes, Lambourn Woodlands on joining N&D*						
28	RU 8058	Leyland Lion PLSC3	Leyland	B35F	Oct-28	Jul-38	by 8/45
29	RU 7559	Leyland Lion PLSC3	Leyland	B35F	Jun-28	Jul-38	by 12/46
Not run	RU5394	Leyland Lion PLSC3	Brush	B32F	May-27	Sep-38	Spares
40	RU 5072	Leyland Lion PLSC3	Leyland	B35F	Apr-27	Sep-38	?/46
41	RU 7560	Leyland Lion PLSC3	Leyland	B35F	Jul-28	Sep-38	by 6/46
26	RD 6270	Thornycroft Ardent	Park Royal	B26F	Dec-34	Oct-38	by ?/45
	JB 5917	Bedford 2.5 ton	Lorry	Goods	Mar-35	Feb-39	Apr-47
	ABL 459	Bedford 2.5 ton	Lorry	Goods	Oct-36	Feb-39	Jul-45
72	MS 8438	Leyland Tiger TS1	Alexander (1935)	C32F	Apr-29	Feb-39	Jul-40
73	WP 6206	Leyland Lion LT5A	Burlingham	C32R	May-34	May-39	Nov-47
47	HD 4369	Leyland Lion LT2	Leyland	B30F	May-31	Jul-39	Jun-47
48	HD 4368	Leyland Lion LT2	Leyland	B30F	May-31	Jul-39	Jun-47
51	HD 4370	Leyland Lion LT2	Leyland	B30F	May-31	Jul-39	May-45
56	HD 4371	Leyland Lion LT2	Leyland	B30F	May-31	Jul-39	Jul-47
18	VF 9339	Thornycroft A2long	Challands Ross	B20F	Jul-30	Aug-39	Apr-44
Not run	UR 2932	GMC T30	Strachan	B20F	Apr-29	Nov-39	Spares
42	KP 8372	Leyland Lion LT1	Ransomes	B31R	Jul-29	Jun-40	Jun-46

49	KP 8371	Leyland Lion LT1	Ransomes	B31R	Jul-29	Jun-40	Jun-46
59	YD 9912	Dennis Ace	Dennis	B20F	Jun-34	Jun-40	Apr-45
61	CKL 719	Dennis Ace	Dennis	B20F	Jan-36	Jun-40	Mar-46
74	EKP 140	Thornycroft Dainty CF	Thurgood	B20F	Apr-38	Jun-40	?/44
23	EV 5909	Dennis Dart	Metcalfe	B20F	Apr-32	Jun-40	Apr-44
Not run	GX 5327	Dennis Dart	LGOC	B18F	Dec-32	Jul-40	Oct-40
Not run	GF 6676	Gilford 168SD	Duple	C26F	Apr-30	Jul-40	Apr-41
75	BPG 531	Dennis Ace	Dennis	B20F	Jun-34	Oct-40	Jan-47
80	HL 5228	Leyland Lion LT5	Roe	B32F	Apr-32	Oct-40	Mar-48
45	YV 5499	Leyland Lion PLSC3	Birch	C32F	Jun-28	Nov-40	by 6/42
50	UR 9658	Leyland Lion LT2	Birch	B32F	May-31	Dec-40	Oct-47
72	CPA 828	Dennis Ace	Dennis	B20F	Dec-34	Dec-40	Jan-46
77	ARA 370	Dennis Ace	Willowbrook	B20F	Jun-34	Dec-40	Jun-46
79	RV 6259	Dennis Ace	Dennis	B20F	Jan-35	Dec-40	Jan-47
81	AVO 977	Dennis Ace	Willowbrook	DP20F	Dec-34	Dec-40	Jun-46
82	KV 9903	Dennis Ace	Willowbrook	C20F	Jun-34	Dec-40	Jul-46
83	AUB 354	Dennis Ace	??	B20F	Dec-34	Dec-40	Jun-47
84	CK 4573	Leyland Tiger TS2	Leyland	B32F	Mar-31	Jan-41	Jul-48
58	MJ 4550	Dennis Ace	Grose	DP20F	Jun-34	Feb-41	Jan-47
76	BBP 339	Dennis Ace	Dennis	B20F	Sep-35	Feb-41	Dec-44
78	BKE 720	Dennis Ace	Duple	C20F	Apr-34	Feb-41	Jul-45
85	JB 3354	Dennis Ace	Dennis	C20F	May-34	Feb-41	Aug-45
86	CK 3951	Leyland Tiger TS2	Leyland	B32R	Jul-28	Feb-41	Sep-48
87	DF 7841	Leyland Tiger TS2	Alexander (1934)	C32F	May-29	Feb-41	Sep-47
46	WX 7898	Leyland Lion LT2	Roberts	B32F	Jul-31	Mar-41	Jan-47
52	TF 4155	Leyland Lion LT2	Leyland	B30F	Feb-31	Mar-41	Sep-47
53	HE 5229	Leyland Lion LT2	Leyland	B30F	May-31	Mar-41	Jan-47
88	MS 8834	Leyland Tiger TS1	Alexander	C32F	Mar-29	Mar-41	Oct-47
89	DNW 359	Dennis Ace	Fielding & Bottomley	B20F	Jun-36	Mar-41	Oct-43
91	CK 4312	Leyland Tiger TS2	Leyland	B30F	Mar-30	Mar-41	Jun-47
90	JU 4374	Dennis Ace	Willowbrook	B20F	Jun-34	May-41	Aug-46
55	BPH 293	Dennis Ace	Weymann	C20F	Jun-34	?/41	Dec-44
92	BUA 795	Dennis Mace	Brush	DP24C	Oct-35	?/41	Dec-44
93	SY 4441	Leyland Lion LT2	Roberts	C28D	Jun-31	Dec-41	Dec-45
30	EX 2861	Thornycroft A12	Economy	C20F	Jun-31	??/42	Apr-44
45	CK 4518	Leyland Lion LT2	Leyland	B32F	Mar-31	Jun-42	Jun-47
60	DL 9011	Dennis Ace	Harrington	B20F	Jun-34	Oct-43	Feb-45
94	CMO 523	Bedford OWB	Duple	UB32F	Nov-42	New	Oct-51
95	CMO 624	Bedford OWB	Duple	UB32F	Jan-43	New	Oct-51
96	CMO 657	Bedford OWB	Duple	UB32F	Feb-43	New	Oct-51
97	CMO 658	Bedford OWB	Duple	UB32F	Feb-43	New	Feb-50
98	CMO 659	Bedford OWB	Duple	UB32F	Feb-43	New	Feb-50
104/H6	FAD 253	Guy Arab II 5LW	Park Royal	UH56R	Mar-44	Apr-44	Jun-56
		No. 104 had been delivered new to Cheltenham District as No.52, then transferred to N&D					
99/H1	CRX 279	Guy Arab II 5LW	Park Royal	UH56R	Nov-44	New	Jul-56
100/H2	CRX 280	Guy Arab II 5LW	Park Royal	UH56R	Nov-44	New	Jun-56
101/H3	CRX 281	Guy Arab II 5LW	Park Royal	UH56R	Oct-44	New	Jun-55
102/H4	CRX 282	Guy Arab II 5LW	Park Royal	UH56R	Nov-44	New	May-56
103/H5	CRX 283	Guy Arab II 5LW	Park Royal	UH56R	Nov-44	New	May-56
107	TG 1568	AEC Regal 662 5LW	Short	B32R	May-31	Nov-44	Jul-48
108	TX 9498	AEC Regal 662 5LW	Duple (1942)	UB35C	May-30	Nov-44	Dec-48
89/109	PJ 3827	AEC Regal 662 5LW	Duple (1940)	B35C	Mar-32	Nov-44	Dec-48
		Nos 107-9 were transferred from Red & White Nos.570, 568 and 89. 107 ran as 89 at first.					
105/H7	CRX 595	Guy Arab II 5LW	Massey	UH56R	Sep-45	New	Jun-56
106/H8	CRX 596	Guy Arab II 5LW	Massey	UH56R	Sep-45	New	Jun-57
110	EWO 480	Bedford OWB	Duple	UB32F	Apr-43	Jan-46	Dec-48
111	EWO 479	Bedford OWB	Duple	UB32F	Apr-43	Jan-46	Dec-48
112	EWO 454	Bedford OWB	Mulliner	UB32F	Oct-42	Jan-46	by 10/49
		Nos 110-2 were initially loaned, the transferred from Red & White Nos.480, 479 and 454					
113	DWN 295	Bedford OWB	Duple	UB32F	Nov-42	Jan-46	Dec-48

114	DWN 258	Bedford OWB	Mulliner	UB32F	Nov-42	Jan-46	Sep-49
115	DWN 298	Bedford OWB	Duple	UB32F	Nov-42	Jan-46	by 10/49
116	DWN 299	Bedford OWB	Mulliner	UB32F	Nov-42	Jan-46	by 10/49
	Nos.113-6 were intially loaned, then transferred from United Welsh Nos. 661, 659, 664/5						
117	HG 1221	AEC Regent 661	Brush	H51C	Mar-32	May-46	Sep-48
	No.117 was transferred from Cheltenham District No.61						
118	EWO 476	Bedford OWB	Mulliner	UB32F	Jan-43	c.6/46	Dec-48
119	EWO 481	Bedford OWB	Duple	UB32F	Apr-43	c.6/46	by 10/49
120	EAX 647	Bedford OWB	Duple	UB32F	Aug-42	c.6/46	by 10/49
	Nos.118-20 were initially loaned, then transferred from Red & White Nos. 476, 481 and 447						
121	FS 8582	AEC Regal O642 5LW	ECOC (1936)	B35R	Jul-34	Jun-46	Oct-51
122	FS 8560	AEC Regal O642 5LW	ECOC (1936)	B35R	Jun-34	Jul-46	Mar-51
123	FS 8562	AEC Regal O642 5LW	ECOC (1936)	B35R	Jul-34	Aug-46	Feb-51
124	FS 8567	AEC Regal O642 5LW	ECOC (1936)	B35R	Jun-34	Sep-46	Mar-51
125	FS 8576	AEC Regal O642 5LW	ECOC (1936)	B35R	Jul-34	Oct-46	Mar-51
126	FS 8572	AEC Regal O642 5LW	ECOC (1936)	B35R	Jul-34	Nov-46	Mar-51
127	FS 8566	AEC Regal O642 5LW	ECOC (1936)	B35R	Jun-34	Feb-47	Mar-51
128	FS 8574	AEC Regal O642 5LW	ECOC (1936)	B35R	Jul-34	Mar-47	Mar-51
129	FS 8575	AEC Regal O642 5LW	ECOC (1936)	B35R	Jul-34	Apr-47	Mar-51
130	FS 8565	AEC Regal O642 5LW	ECOC (1936)	B35R	Jun-34	May-47	Mar-51
131	DMO 320	AEC Regal O662	Duple	B35F	Apr-47	New	Dec-60
132	DMO 321	AEC Regal O662	Duple	B35F	Apr-47	New	Dec-60
133	DMO 322	AEC Regal O662	Duple	B35F	Apr-47	New	Sep-60
134	DMO 323	AEC Regal O662	Duple	B35F	Apr-47	New	Dec-60
135	DMO 324	AEC Regal O662	Duple	B35F	Apr-47	New	Jul-58
136	DMO 325	AEC Regal O662	Duple	B35F	Apr-47	New	Jul-58
137	DMO 326	AEC Regal O662	Duple	B35F	Apr-47	New	Dec-60
138	DMO 327	AEC Regal O662	Duple	B35F	Apr-47	New	Jul-58
139	DMO 328	AEC Regal O662	Duple	B35F	Apr-47	New	Aug-60
140	DMO 329	AEC Regal O662	Duple	B35F	Apr-47	New	Jul-58
240	EM 2730	Albion Valkyrie PW65	Burlingham	UB35F	Aug-32	May-47	by1/50
243	EM 2735	Albion Valkyrie PW65	Burlingham	UB35F	Aug-32	May-47	by1/50
244	EM 2736	Albion Valkyrie PW65	Burlingham	UB35F	Aug-32	May-47	by1/50
249	EM 2741	Albion Valkyrie PW65	Burlingham	UB35F	Aug-32	May-47	by1/50
	The Albions were on extended loan from Red & White and retained their own fleet numbers.						
	They had been rebodied during the war years and fitted with Gardner 5LW engines.						
141	DMO 330	AEC Regal O662	Duple	C35F	Aug-47	New	Dec-58
142	DMO 331	AEC Regal O662	Duple	C35F	Oct-47	New	Oct-57
143	DMO 332	AEC Regal O662	Duple	C35F	Oct-47	New	Jan-59
144	DMO 333	AEC Regal O662	Duple	C35F	Oct-47	New	Dec-58
145	EBL 736	AEC Regal O662	Duple	C35F	Nov-47	New	Jan-59
146	EJB 146	AEC Regal O682	Duple	C35F	Mar-48	New	Jan-59
147	EJB 147	AEC Regal O682	Duple	C35F	Mar-48	New	Jan-59
148	EJB 148	AEC Regal O682	Duple	C35F	Mar-48	New	Jan-59
151	EJB 521	AEC Regent O961	Weymann/Lydney	H56R	Mar-48	New	Jan-51
149	EJB 649	AEC Regal 6821A	Duple	C35F	Sep-48	New	Jan-50
150	EJB 650	AEC Regal 6821A	Duple	C35F	Sep-48	New	Jan-50
152	AGJ 929	AEC Regal 662 5LW	ECOC (1936)	B32R	Apr-33	Oct-48	Jan-52
153	AGX 455	AEC Regal 662 5LW	Burlingham (1945)	UB34F	Apr-33	Nov-48	Oct-51
154	TG 1819	AEC Regal 662 5LW	Burlingham (1945)	UB34F	Jun-31	Nov-48	Oct-51
155	AGP 841	AEC Regal 662 5LW	Burlingham (1944)	UB34F	Apr-33	Nov-48	Oct-51
156	AMD 47	AEC Regal 662 5LW?	Duple (1942)	UB35C	Mar-33	Nov-48	by 3/51
157	FAX 349	AEC Regal 662 5LW	Burlingham (1946)	UB34F	c.1930	Dec-48	Oct-53
	Nos.152-7 were transferred from Red & White Nos.734, 728, 284, 730, 290 and 795						
159	HAD 745	AEC Regent O961	Weymann/Mumford	H56R	Jan-48	Mar-49	Jan-50
	No.159 was transferred from Cheltenham District No.65						
158	ERX 937	AEC Regal 6821A	Duple	C35F	Jul-49	New	Jan-50
160/H9	EWO 484	Guy Arab I 5LW	Lydney (1949)	H56R	Jun-43	Sep-49	Jun-57
	No.160 was transferred from Red & White No.484						
164	LJO 756	Bedford OB	Duple	C29F	Jul-47	Jan-50	Dec-56

165	LJO 757	Bedford OB	Duple	C29F	Mar-48	Jan-50	Dec-56
166	CWL 953	Leyland Tiger TS7	Harrington	C32F	Apr-36	Jan-50	c.3/51
167	BWL 349	Leyland Tiger TS7	Harrington	C32F	May-35	Jan-50	c.3/51
168	CWL 951	Leyland Tiger TS7	Harrington	C32F	Apr-36	Jan-50	c.3/51
169	LWL 995	Leyland Tiger PS1/1	ECOC (1936)	DP31R	Feb-47	Jan-50	Jul-60
	Nos.164-9 were transferred from South Midland Nos.43, 44, 37, 35, 36 and 38						
161	FBL 919	AEC Regal 6821A	Lydney	B35F	Feb-50	New	Nov-59
162	FBL 920	AEC Regal 6821A	Lydney	B35F	Feb-50	New	Nov-59
163	FBL 921	AEC Regal 6821A	Lydney	B35F	Mar-50	New	Nov-59
170	FMO 515	Guy Arab III 6LW	Duple	L53RD	Feb-50	New	Apr-68
171	FMO 516	Guy Arab III 6LW	Duple	L53RD	Feb-50	New	Apr-68
172/H10	FMO 517	Guy Arab III 6LW	Duple	H57R	May-50	New	Mar-68
173/H11	EWO 490	Guy Arab II 5LW	Park Royal (1959)	H56R	Jul-43	Jan-51	Oct-55
174/H12	EWO 492	Guy Arab II 5LW	Park Royal (1959)	H56R	Jul-43	Jan-51	Oct-55
	Nos.173/4 were transferred from Venture Nos.100/1, but were new as Red & White Nos.490/2						
175/H13	HOT 391	Guy Arab III 6LW	Duple	H57R	Jun-50	Jan-51	Mar-68
176/H14	HOT 392	Guy Arab III 6LW	Duple	H57R	Jun-50	Jan-51	Apr-68
177/H15	HOT 393	Guy Arab III 6LW	Duplc	H57R	May-50	Jan-51	Mar-68
178/H16	HOT 394	Guy Arab III 6LW	Duple	H57R	Jun-50	Jan-51	Mar-68
	Nos.175-8 were transferred from Venture Nos.103-6						
179	AJB 814	Leyland Tiger TS8	Brush	B35R	May-37	May-51	Apr-53
180	AJB 816	Leyland Tiger TS8	Brush	B35R	May-37	May-51	Nov-53
181	BBL 558	Leyland Tiger TS8	ECW	B35R	Jun-38	May-51	Mar-54
182	AJB 818	Leyland Tiger TS8	Brush	B35R	May-37	May-51	Apr-53
183	BBL 565	Leyland Tiger TS8	ECW	B35R	Jun-38	Jun-51	Dec-53
184	ABL 763	Leyland Tiger TS7	ECW	B35R	Mar-37	Jun-51	Nov-52
185	AJB 815	Leyland Tiger TS8	Brush	B35R	May-37	May-51	Jul-53
186	ARX 990	Leyland Tiger TS8	ECW	B35R	Mar-38	Jun-51	Dec-53
187	CJB 139	Guy Arab I 5LW	Strachan	UL55R	Jan-43	Sep-51	Aug-55
	The above Leylands and Guy were transferred from Thames Valley Nos. 342, 344, 372, 346,						
	379, 333, 343, 368 and 420, and all reverted to those numbers within a year						
	All other vehicles after this were numbered in the main Thames Valley series						

STANDARD BODY CODES

Before the seating capacity:

B - Single-deck service bus
C - Single-deck coach
L - Lowbridge double-deck bus
H - Highbridge double-deck bus
U - Body of utility construction

Following the seating capacity:

C - Centre entrance body
F - Front entrance body
D - Dual doorway body
R - Rear entrance body
RD - Double-decker with rear doors

Examples:

UB35C   Single-deck bus with utility-type 35-seater, centre-entrance body
L53RD   Lowbridge double-deck bus with 53-seater body fiitted with rear doors

Please note:

Many of the earlier vehicles such as carrier's vans were of basic construction and had the entrance in the centre rear of the body. Where entrance positions are not known they are omitted, e.g. C31.

Appendix 2 - Known fleets of operators absorbed by Newbury & District M. S. Ltd.

A. ANDREWS & SON, NEWBURY - June 1932 — Favourite Coaches

Reg. No.	Chassis/Model	Bodybuilder	Layout	New	Acq.	Sold	Notes
MO 218	Ford T	Andrews	Van14	Jul-22	New	Jan-25	
MO 1714	FIAT 15TER	Andrews	Ch14	??	Jun-23	By 1930	Ex-WD
BL 6490	Talbot 25/50hp	Andrews	C14D	Apr-20	Oct-25	To N&D	
XK 7225	Dennis 3-ton	??	Ch28	Apr-22	May-25	Aug-26	Ex-WD
??	Lancia Z	Andrews	Ch14	??	by 1927	By 1930	
??	Lancia Tetraiota	Andrews	Ch18	c.1927	c.1927	by 6/32	
??	Guy J	Andrews	C20D	c.1925	c.1927	To N&D	
??	Lancia Pentaiota	??	B26-	??/28	by 1931	Jan-32	Unconfirmed*
??	Reo	??	C26		c.1929	by 6/32	
RX 8261	Ford AA	Andrews	B20F	Mar-31	New	To N&D	
VA 3156	Lancia Tetraiota	??	B20	Dec-24	c.3/31	To N&D	
DP ????	Lancia Tetraiota	Vincent	C20D	??/25	May-31	To N&D	
VM 8638	Gilford 166SD	Lewis & Crabtree	C26	Apr-29	May-31	To N&D	
RD 1886	Gilford 168OT	Vincent	C30D	Jun-30	May-31	To N&D	
??	Studebaker	Landaulette body	Taxi	??	??	Oct-25	
??	Daimler		Taxi	??	By ??/26	To N&D	
*This Lancia was offered for sale in January 1932 but has not been confirmed as Andrews							
??	Leyland	??	Lorry	??	??	??	Ex-WD?
??	Thornycroft J	??	Lorry	??	??	To N&D	Ex-WD

DENHAM BROS., NEWBURY - June 1932

Reg. No.	Chassis/Model	Bodybuilder	Layout	New	Acq.	Sold	Notes
AF 1344	Star 20-25hp	??	B12F	Jun-14	byApr-22	??	
??	Buick 25-cwt (lhd)	(WD ambulance)	W10R	c.1916	byApr-22	Jan-27	Later used as van
BL 9861	Delauney-Belleville	Andrews?	Ch14	??/18	Apr-22	Jul-23	28-32hp ex-car
??	GMC K16	??	Ch14	??	c.5/23	??/27	
MO 1797	Ford T	Pass?	B14	Jul-23	New	Jan-27	Also as a lorry
MD 8213	Talbot 25/50hp	Andrews	?12?	Jul-21	??/23	Mar-32	
MO 2406	FIAT 15TER	??	B20R	Dec-23	New	By ??/30	
OR 4295	Chevrolet B	??	B14F	Jul-24	New	Jun-30	
MO 3875	Tilling-Stevens TTA1	Tilling	O32ROS	May-13	Sep-24	Dec-26	
This was formerly LF 9044, the d/d body was soon cut down to B20R, then rebodied as BT&CC B26R ex-AE 3792 5/25							
MO 4984	Tilling-Stevens TTA1	Tilling	B20R	1912-13	Mar-25	May-27	
This was a former (unidentified) Thomas Tilling bus, the d/d body being cut down to B20R before use							
BL 7936	Daimler CC	??	As a bus	Dec-12	c.1925	Dec-28	Ex-Durnford
TB 2522	Daimler CK	??	Ch28	Ex-WD?	c.1925	To N&D	Also as a lorry
PM 581	Talbot 25/50hp	Andrews	B10F	??/22	By 5/26	by 6/32	R/b Andrews B14F
Later rebodied by Andrews with a larger B14F body							
KE 3196	Talbot 25/50hp	Andrews	B14F	Feb-21	c.1927	To N&D	
MO 1714	FIAT 15TER	Andrews	Ch14	Jun-23	c.1927	Jun-30	Originally WD
BL 8006	Ford T	??	Ch14	Oct-20	Aug-29	??	Not run
HX 1059	Star Flyer VB4	Strachan	C26D	Jul-30	??/30	To N&D	
TR 8198	Thornycroft A2	Wadham	B20F	Feb-30	??/30	To N&D	
MW 825	Thornycroft A2	Challands Ross	B20F	Nov-27	Apr-31	To N&D	
TR 1231	Leyland E	Southampton CT	B26F	Nov-25	??/31	To N&D	
VT 184	Tilling-Stevens B10A	Strachan & Brown	B32F	Jul-27	May-31	To N&D	
BU 5690	Tilling-Stevens B10A2	Northern Counties	B32F	Nov-28	??/31	To N&D	
TO 9554	Gilford 166OT	Strachan & Brown	B32F	Mar-29	??/31	To N&D	
WU 9870	Minerva	Metcalfe	B20	Feb-27	Jan-32	To N&D	
??	Gilford	??	B28	??	??	To N&D	From Denhams?
??	??		Taxi	??	??	To N&D	
Goods Vehicles (also see those converted from PSV use)							
AE 3792	Bristol C50	Bus body off	Lorry	Jul-14	??/24	??	Body to MO 3875
BL 8474	Palladium YE 3-4 ton	??	Lorry	Mar-20	Apr-27	??	Ex-BL 0301

J. C. DURNFORD & SONS, NEWBURY - June 1932

Reg. No.	Chassis/Model	Bodybuilder	Layout	New	Acq.	Sold	Notes
BL 0336	Commer WP3	??	Lorry	Jun-20	New	??	Also as a lorry

J. C. Durnford & Sons, Newbury continued

Reg. No.	Chassis/Model	Bodybuilder	Layout	New	Acq.	Sold	Notes
BL 7936	Daimler CC	??	Ch25	1912	Dec-20	Apr-22	Also as a lorry
BL 8804	Daimler B	??	Ch28	1914	Jul-21	??	Also as a lorry
CR 4021	Hallford EA	??	Ch30	1912	May-22	??	Also as a lorry
MO 53	Dennis 3-ton	??	Ch20	1915	May-22	Dec-26	Also as a lorry
??	Maudslay A	??	Ch30	c.1915	Oct-22	??	Also as a lorry
MO 1763	Dennis 3-ton	??	Ch25	1915	Jun-23	Sep-26	Also as a lorry
MC 3937	Dennis 30-cwt	??	Ch14	1915	Aug-22	Sep-25	
EL 3769	Dennis 3-ton	??	Ch30	Jun-19	??/23	Sep-29	Also as a lorry
??	Leyland	??	Ch28	??	May-24	??	Also as a lorry
MO 3343	Dennis 3-ton	??	Ch25	1915	Jun-24	Mar-31	Also as a lorry
??	Star 50cwt	??	Ch14	c.1923	by Jul-24	To N&D	Also as a lorry
??	Thornycroft J	??	Ch28	Ex-WD	by 6/25	??	
MO 7924	Talbot 25-50hp	Andrews	C14-	1918	May-26	??/29	
CC 5083	Lancia Z	Spicer	C20F	Dec-24	Jun-26	Jun-29	
RX 1992	Dennis G	??	C18-	Mar-28	New	Feb-31	
DL 2122	Dennis 2-ton	Margham	C20-	??/21	by May-28	??	
??	GMC K41	??	C20-	c.1925	by May-28	To N&D	As a lorry or van
YB 7442	Lancia Pentaiota	Wray	C20F	Sep-26	Feb-29	To N&D	
??	Lancia Pentaiota	London Lorries	C25F	??	??	To N&D	
??	Reo Major	??	C20F	c.1927	??	To N&D	Later as a lorry
??	Guy	??	??	??	??	To N&D	As a lorry or van
YE 8768	Maudslay ML4A	London Lorries	C26D	1927	Nov-29	To N&D	
CW 6802	Maudslay ML2	??	C28F	Jun-26	Jan-30	To N&D	As pantechnicon
YT 9565	Garner 55hp	Buckingham	C26D	Sep-27	Feb-30	To N&D	
RX 6264	Reo Pullman	Wray	C25D	Mar-30	New	To N&D	
VX 43	Gilford CP6	Thurgood	C20D	May-29	??	To N&D	
UV 9116	Gilford CP6	Wycombe	C20F	Jul-29	Dec-30	To N&D	
RX 8210	Diamond T	Newns	C20-	Mar-31	New	Apr-32	
UU 7594	GMC T42	Wilton	C26-	Jun-29	Jan-32	To N&D	

G. E. HEDGES - September 1932   Reliance Motor Service

Reg. No.	Chassis/Model	Bodybuilder	Layout	New	Acq.	Sold	Notes
BL 9886	Ford T	Andrews?	Van 14	Jun-22	New	Dec-29	Carrier's van
MO 3514	Ford T 1-ton	Andrews?	B14-	Aug-24	New	Oct-30	
??	??	??	Lorry	??	??	To N&D	
??	Talbot 25/50hp	Andrews	C14-	??	??	To N&D	Also used as van
RX 4556	Ford AA	??	C14D	May-29	New	To N&D	
RX 6888	Ford AA	Duple	C14D	Jun-30	New	To N&D	

J. PROTHERO - September 1932   XLCR Motor Service

Reg. No.	Chassis/Model	Bodybuilder	Layout	New	Acq.	Sold	Notes
BL 8278	Ford T	Pass?	Van 12	Jan-21	New	Dec-21	Carrier's van
BL 9316	Ford T	Pass?	Van 14	Dec-21	New	Sep-25	Carrier's van
??	Austin 20hp	Prothero	B14F	??	c.1923	??	
XH 8592	Ford T 1-ton	Prothero	B14F	Dec-21	May-25	c.1929	
??	Talbot 25/50hp	Andrews	Ch14	??	Apr-26	by 9/32	
??	Chevrolet	??	B14F	??	??	by 9/32	
??	Ford ?	??	Lorry	??	by 1928	by 9/32	
RX 4272	Ford AA	Andrews	B14F	Apr-29	New	To N&D	
RX 7256	Ford AA	Andrews	B14F	Jul-30	New	To N&D	
RX 7772	Ford AA	Andrews?	B20F	Dec-30	New	To N&D	
RX 9005	Ford AA	Andrews?	B20F	Jul-31	New	To N&D	
??	Gilford f/c	??	C32	??	c.1931	To N&D	

T. HOLMAN - October 1932   (Carrier to Ecchinswell)

Reg. No.	Chassis/Model	Bodybuilder	Layout	New	Acq.	Sold	Notes
??	??	??	??	??	??	??	Carrier's van
OR 2576	Ford T	??	Van 14	Sep-23	New	Jun-29	Carrier's van
??	??	??	??	??	Jun-29	??	Kept by Holman

POCOCK BROS. - October 1932 — *Taxis were also operated but details of these are not known*

Reg. No.	Chassis/Model	Bodybuilder	Layout	New	Acq.	Sold	Notes
MO 1573	Ford T	Pass?	Van 14	Jun-23	New	Sep-32	Carrier's van
??	?? FIAT	??	Ch14	by Jul-26	New??	??	'The Scout'
MO 8231	Chevrolet X	??	B14F	Jul-26	New	To N&D	Back as a lorry
MO 6416	Chevrolet T	??	B14F	Oct-25	Jul-29	Dec-30	
RX 9971	Bedford WLB	??	B20F	Mar-32	New	To N&D	
??	Chevrolet	??	C14-	??	??	To N&D	

F. SPANSWICK - January 1933 — Spanswick's Bus Service

Reg. No.	Chassis/Model	Bodybuilder	Layout	New	Acq.	Sold	Notes
BL 946	Argyll 45LS	Carrier's van with seats		Aug-06	Jul-12	Apr-22	Later as goods
??	??	Carrier's van with seats		??	??-15	??	Ex- Fred Maslin
BL 884	Ford T	Carrier's van with seats		??/19	New	Apr-30	Later as goods
MO 6744	Ford T 1-ton	Andrews	B14F	Jan-26	New	To N&D	
MO 7043	Morris 25cwt	Andrews	B14F	Jan-26	New	Aug-32	
RX 6662	Ford AA	Andrews	B20F	Apr-30	New	To N&D	

DURNFORD BROS. - January 1934 — The Scarlet Runners

Reg. No.	Chassis/Model	Bodybuilder	Layout	New	Acq.	Sold	Notes
CW 6802	Maudslay ML2	Andrews	Luton	Jun-26	Jan-30	To N&D	Pantechnicon
HJ 8718	Gilford 166SD	??	C26-	Mar-29	Jun-33	To N&D	
GU 7545	Star Flyer VB4	Thurgood	C26-	Apr-29	Jun-33	To N&D	
RX 4356	Ford AA	??	Lorry	Apr-29	Jun-33	To N&D	

C. GEARY - January 1934 — Joy Coaches

Reg. No.	Chassis/Model	Bodybuilder	Layout	New	Acq.	Sold	Notes
RX 3981	Ford AA	(detachable seats)	B14-	Mar-29	New	Jan-37	Later as a lorry
RX 5432	Ford AA	??	C14-	Oct-29	New	To N&D	but not used

J. F. BURT & A. V. GREENWOOD - January 1934

Reg. No.	Chassis/Model	Bodybuilder	Layout	New	Acq.	Sold	Notes
MO 7517	Ford T 1-ton	Pass?	B14-	Apr-26	??/30	Dec-33	
MO 2059	Ford T	Pass?	Van	Aug-23	??/30	Dec-30	For coal delivery
GJ 9733*	Federal AB6	??	C28	7/30??	1933?	To N&D	*query on reg. no.
RX 4272	Ford AA	Used as a truck		Apr-29	Jan-34	Dec-36	From N&D

G. BROWN - January 1934 — Wash Common Bus Service

Reg. No.	Chassis/Model	Bodybuilder	Layout	New	Acq.	Sold	Notes
RX 3553	Morris 25cwt	Morris	B14F	Jan-29	Oct-33	To N&D	Ex-R.A. Pestell

G. P. HOWLETT - February 1934 — Kennet Bus Service

Reg. No.	Chassis/Model	Bodybuilder	Layout	New	Acq.	Sold	Notes
BL 3415	Wolseley-Siddeley	Carrier's van with seats		Jan-14	New	Mar-14	18-24hp
BL 3850	CPT 18-20hp	Carrier's van with seats		Mar-14	New	Jun-27	Originally BL 027
BL 8684	Garner 15 Busvan	Carrier's van with 20 seats		Jun-21	New	Jul-30	
MO 3959	Fiat 15TER	City Carriage	B20F	Sep-24	New	Jul-30	
MY 3052	Star Flyer VB4	Star	C26D	Mar-30	New	To N&D	
MY 4213	Star Flyer VB4	Star	C26D	Apr-30	New	To N&D	
SH 3380	GMC T30C	Alexander	B20F	May-29	??/33	To N&D	Not confirmed

W. J. WHITE & SON - March 1934 — Tony Coaches

Reg. No.	Chassis/Model	Bodybuilder	Layout	New	Acq.	Sold	Notes
??	??	Carrier's van with seats		c.1922	??	Nov-29?	Later as a lorry?
MO 5620	Mason	??	B14F	Jun-25	New	Sep-31	Also as Ch14
MO 6416	Chevrolet T	??	B14F	Oct-25	New	Jul-29	
MO 7182	Chevrolet T	??	B14F	Mar-26	New	Dec-33	
RX 3330	Chevrolet LP	??	B14F	Dec-28	New	Oct-33	Also as a lorry
RX 5493	Dennis 30cwt	??	C14D	Nov-29	New	To N&D	
RX 6401	Dennis 30cwt	??	C17-	May-30	New	To N&D	
MW 6161	AJS Pilot	Eaton	B26F	Dec-29	??/31	To N&D	
TP 7118	Dennis 30cwt	Dennis	B14F	Dec-28	Oct-33	To N&D	

W. J. CLEEVELEY - January 1935

Reg. No.	Chassis/Model	Bodybuilder	Layout	New	Acq.	Sold	Notes
JB 1930	Bedford 2.5-ton	??	Lorry	May-33	New	To N&D	
JB 1984	Bedford 2.5-ton	??	Lorry	May-33	New	To N&D	

C. BALLARD - October 1935

RX 4706	Chevrolet LQ	??	C14-	Jun-29	New	Jul-34	Also as a lorry
UL 7692	Dennis F	Dodson	C20D	Mar-29	Jul-34	To N&D	

C. G. COLLIVER - March 1936

HO 6306	Dennis 4-ton	??	Lorry	May-24	??	To N&D	

E. G. KENT - April 1937   Kingsclere Coaches

??	Ford T		Van	1921/2	New	c.1926	Used for milk run
OT 816 ?	Thornycroft A1	Hall Lewis	Ch20	??/25	Mar-26	??/35	Ex-demonstrator
OT 1333	Morris 25cwt	??	B14F	May-26	New	by 4/37	Also as a lorry
OT 3284	Reo Sprinter	Wray	C20D	Dec-26	New	??/35	
OT 4452	Thornycroft A2long	Wadham	B20F	Apr-27	New	To N&D	
OT 7672	Reo	??	B20F	Mar-28	New	by 4/37	
OT 9741	Chevrolet	??	B14F	Sep-28	New	by 4/37	
OU 6047	AJS Pilot	Petty	B28F	Jun-30	New	To N&D	
TK 2740	Guy OND	Guy	B20F	May-29	c.Oct-30	To N&D	
CG 1724	Commer Centaur	Petty	C20F	Aug-32	New	To N&D	
ACG 644	Commer Invader	Petty	C20F	Apr-35	New	To N&D	
UN 3196	Chevrolet LR	??	B16F	Dec-29	Apr-36	To N&D	

PASS & CO. - May 1937

P 942	??	??	??	??	by 4/23	??	Used as chara?
BL 5420	CPT	??	Ch14	Jun-17	New	??	Lorry until 1/25
BL 9713	Ford T	??	Van 14	Mar-22	New	Dec-22	Van with 14 seats
MO 659	Ford T	??	Ch14	Nov-22	New	by 9/29	Sold before then
MO 2059	Ford T	??	Ch14	Aug-23	New	Apr-25	
MO 5313	Ford T	??	Ch14	May-25	New	by 7/32	Sold before then
MO 5899	Ford T	??	Ch14	Jul-25	New	Sep-28	Scrapped
MO 7520	Ford 1-ton	??	Ch14	May-26	New	by 9/32	Sold before then
RX 2907	Ford AA	Vincent	C14D	Aug-28	New	Jul-37	Sold to N&D
RX 4109	Ford T rebuild	?? (re-used body)	Ch14	Mar-29	New	Nov-37	Sold before then
RX 6887	Ford AA	??	C14-	Jun-30	New	Mar-41	Later as a hearse
RX 7150	Ford AA	??	C14F	Jul-30	New	To N&D	
JB 437	Ford AA	??	C20-	Jun-32	New	To N&D	
JB 5701	Ford BB	??	C20-	Feb-35	New	To N&D	
	It is likely that the earlier charabancs were bodied by Pass & Co.						

E. E. NOBES - July 1938

MO 1846	Ford T	Pass?	Van14	Jul-23	New	Apr-30	Carrier's van
MO 4614	Ford T 1-ton	Pass?	B14F	Feb-25	??-29	Aug-36	
TM 5726	Chevrolet LQ	Economy	B16F	Sep-29	by Aug-36	To N&D	but not run

Throughout this volume we have repeatedly seen how the Army Service Corps was ultimately responsible for shaping many a post-war transport venture. Here we see one-time Kingsclere carrier Hubert Hunt (right) and another re-assembling an engine somewhere on the North-west Frontier in 1923, complete with his inevitable pipe, which was inserted though not always full or even alight.

Appendix 3
List of scheduled departures from Newbury Wharf on Thursdays in June 1934

A.M.	Destination	Single Fare	Return Fare	Journey Time
07.25	Highclere	8d	1s 3d	32 mins
07.45	Colthrop Mills	5d	6d	25 mins
08.30	Stockcross	4d	7d	14 mins
08.50	Wash Common	3d	5d	8 mins
09.00	Highclere	8d	1s 3d	32 mins
09.00	Inkpen (Craven Arms)	4d	7d	50 mins
09.00	Yattendon	1s	1s 10d	60 mins
09.00	Sydmonton	8d	1s 3d	35 mins
09.00	East Ilsley	1s	1s 6d	35 mins
09.15	Brightwalton	1s 3d	2s	45 mins
09.17	Lambourn	1s 2d	1s 9d	45 mins
09.30	Wash Common	3d	5d	8 mins
09.30	West Woodhay	8d	1s 2d	30 mins
09.30	Hungerford (via A4)	11d	1s 6d	40 mins
09.35	Thatcham	4d	6d	15 mins
09.45	East End	8d	1s 2d	30 mins
10.00	Stockcross	4d	7d	14 mins
10.10	Wash Common	3d	5d	8 mins
10.15	Highclere	8d	1s 3d	32 mins
10.20	Peasemore	10d	1s 4d	30 mins
10.30	Shefford Woodlands	10d	1s 6d	28 mins
10.30	Thatcham	4d	6d	15 mins
10.40	Inkpen (Lower Grn.)	8d	1s 2d	46 mins
11.10	Cold Ash	6d	11d	20 mins
11.15	North End	7d	1s	25 mins
11.30	Wash Common	3d	5d	8 mins
11.30	Bucklebury (Slade)	8d	1s 2d	20 mins
11.30	Hoe Benham	7d	1s	18 mins
11.30	Hermitage	6d	9d	20 mins
11.30	Highclere	8d	1s 3d	32 mins
11.49	Thatcham	4d	6d	15 mins

P.M.	Destination	Single Fare	Return Fare	Journey Time
12.00	Wantage	2s	3s	75 mins
12.00	Inkpen (Craven Arms)	4d	7d	50 mins
12.00	Brightwalton	1s 3d	2s	45 mins
12.10	East Ilsley	1s	1s 6d	35 mins
12.10	Sydmonton	8d	1s 3d	35 mins
12.10	Westrop	8d	1s	40 mins
12.15	East End	8d	1s 2d	30 mins
12.20	Thatcham	4d	6d	15 mins
12.30	Stockcross	4d	7d	14 mins
12.30	Bucklebury (Peach's)	7d	1s	25 mins
12.30	Wash Common	3d	5d	8 mins
12.30	Hungerford (via A4)	11d	1s 6d	40 mins
12.45	Hampstead Norris	8d	1s	35 mins
12.45	Highclere	8d	1s 3d	32 mins
12.45	Bucklebury (Church)	1s 1d	1s 6d	40 mins
01.00	Lambourn	1s 2d	1s 9d	45 mins
01.05	Wash Common	3d	5d	8 mins
01.10	Wickham	7d	1s	23 mins
01.10	West Woodhay	8d	1s 2d	30 mins
01.20	Curridge	6d	9d	25 mins
01.30	Peasemore	10d	1s 4d	30 mins
01.40	Inkpen (Lower Grn.)	8d	1s 2d	50 mins
02 05	Highclere	8d	1s 3d	32 mins
02.05	Thatcham	4d	6d	15 mins
02.15	East Ilsley	1s	6d	35 mins
02.30	Bucklebury (Slade)	8d	1s 2d	20 mins
02.30	Hungerford (via A4)	11d	1s 6d	40 mins
02.30	Brightwalton	1s 3d	2s	45 mins
02.30	Stockcross	4d	7d	14 mins

P.M.	Destination	Single Fare	Return Fare	Journey Time
02.35	Wash Common	3d	5d	8 mins
03.05	Thatcham	4d	6d	15 mins
03.10	Cold Ash	6d	11d	20 mins
03.10	Hoe Benham	7d	1s	18 mins
03.15	North End	7d	1s	25 mins
03.20	Wash Common	3d	5d	8 mins
03.25	H'ford (via Inkpen)	1s	1s 6d	65 mins
03.25	West Woodhay	8d	1s 2d	30 mins
03.30	Winterbourne	6d	10d	15 mins
03.30	Yattendon	1s	1s 10d	50 mins
03.30	Wash Common	3d	5d	8 mins
03.45	Sydmonton	8d	1s 3d	35 mins
03.45	Highclere	8d	1s 3d	32 mins
04.00	Bucklebury (Church)	1s 1d	1s 6d	40 mins
04.00	Aldworth	1s	1s 9d	55 mins
04.00	Lambourn	1s 2d	1s 9d	45 mins
04.00	Brightwalton	1s 3d	2s	45 mins
04.00	Wantage	2s	3s	75 mins
04.05	Thatcham	4d	6d	15 mins
04.10	East Ilsley	1s	1s 6d	35 mins
04.10	Westrop	8d	1s	40 mins
04.10	Wickham	7d	1s	23 mins
04.10	Wash Common	3d	5d	8 mins
04.15	East End	8d	1s 2d	30 mins
04.30	Hermitage	6d	9d	20 mins
04.45	Inkpen (Lower Grn.)	8d	1s 2d	50 mins
04.45	Highclere	8d	1s 3d	32 mins
05.00	Hungerford (via A4)	11d	1s 6d	40 mins
05.05	Thatcham	4d	6d	15 mins
05.10	Wash Common	3d	5d	8 mins
05.10	Peasemore	10d	1s 4d	30 mins
05.10	Shefford Woodlands	10d	1s 6d	28 mins
05.30	Hampstead Norris	8s	1s	35 mins
05.45	East End	8d	1s 2d	30 mins
05.50	Bucklebury (Church)	1s 1d	1s 6d	40 mins
06.05	Thatcham	4d	6d	15 mins
06.10	Wickham	7d	1s	24 mins
06.10	Cold Ash	6d	11d	20 mins
06.15	H'ford (via Inkpen)	1s	1s 6d	65 mins
06.20	Colthrop Mills	5d	6d	25 mins
06.25	Highclere	8d	1s 3d	32 mins
06.30	Brightwalton	1s 3d	2s	45 mins
06.30	Wash Common	3d	5d	8 mins
07.00	Ecchinswell	8d	1s 2d	25 mins
07.00	East Ilsley	1s	1s 6d	35 mins
07.05	Thatcham	4d	6d	15 mins
07.05	Wash Common	3d	5d	8 mins
07.10	Wickham Heath	5d	9d	19 mins
07.30	Hungerford (via A4)	11d	1s 6d	40 mins
07.45	Christ Church	7d	1s	35 mins
08.05	Thatcham	4d	6d	15 mins
08.10	Wash Common	3d	5d	8 mins
08.10	Wickham	7d	1s	23 mins
08.10	Highclere	8d	1s 3d	32 mins
08.10	Westrop	8d	1s	40 mins
08.15	Lambourn	1s 2d	1s 9d	45 mins
08.15	Marlston	6d	9d	30 mins
08.15	East End	8d	1s 2d	30 mins
08.30	Brightwalton	1s 3d	2s	45 mins
08.40	East Ilsley	1s	1s 6d	45 mins
09.05	Thatcham	4d	6d	15 mins
09.10	Stockcross	4d	7d	14 mins
09.18	Highclere	8d	1s 3d	32 mins
10.05	Thatcham	4d	6d	15 mins
10.35	Highclere	8d	1s 3d	32 mins

Appendix 4
Excursions & Tours
Licenses held by
N&D at May 1937

From Bradfield

Aldershot Tattoo
Bognor Regis
Bournemouth
Hayling Island
Newbury
Oxford
Reading Football
Southsea
Swindon/Aldershot for
Reading FC matches

From Bucklebury
Three Crowns
Blade Bone
Oaktree Garage
Standford Dingley

Aldershot Tattoo
Ascot Races
Beacon Hill
Bognor Regis
Bournemouth
Brighton
Burnham Beeches
California-in-England
Cheddar
Hungerford
Marlborough
Newbury
Oxford
Reading
Southampton
Southsea
Swindon
Tidworth Tattoo
Weston-super-Mare
Weymouth
Whipsnade Zoo
Winchester
Windsor

From Cold Ash
Post Office
Council Houses

Aldershot Tattoo
Ascot Races
Bognor Regis
Bournemouth
Brighton
Henley
Oxford
Pewsey

Reading
Salisbury
Savernake Forest
Southampston
Southsea
Tidworth Tattoo
Wallingford
Weston-super-Mare
Weymouth
Whipsnade Zoo
Winchester
Windsor

From East Ilsley
Chieveley, Beedon,
Compton, West Ilsley

Aldershot Tattoo
Ascot Races
Abingdon
Andover
Basingstoke
Bognor Regis
Bournemouth
Brighton
Cold Ash
Compton
Curridge
Didcot
Hampstead Norris
Henley
Hermitage
Highclere
Kingsclere
Marlborough
Marlston
Newbury
Oxford
Pangbourne
Reading
Southsea
Streatley
Swindon
Thame
Thatcham
Tidworth Tattoo
Wallingford
Wantage
Weston-super-Mare
Weymouth
Whipsnade Zoo
Winchester
Windsor
Winterbourne

From Great Shefford
East Garston,
Eastbury,
Lambourn, Welford

Aldershot Tattoo

Ascot Races
Bognor Regis
Bournemouth
Brighton
California-in-England
Epsom Races
Henley
Hungerford
Marlborough
Newbury
Oxford
Pangbourne
Pewsey
Reading
Southsea
Swindon
Tidworth Tattoo
Wantage
Weston-super-Mare
Weymouth
Windsor

From Hermitage
Hampstead Norris,
Shaw, Frilsham,
Marlston, Eling,
Bothampstead,
Curridge, Long Lane,
Wellhouse, Aldworth,
Burnt Hill, Yattendon

Aldershot Tattoo
Andover Circular
Ascot Races
Bognor Regis
Bournemouth
Brighton
Cheddar
Hannington
Kidlington
Lambourn Circular
Lockinge
Newbury
Reading
Savernake Forest
Southsea
Tidworth Tattoo
Weston-super-Mare
Weymouth
Whipsnade Zoo
Windsor
Yattendon

From Inkpen
Lower Green, Inkpen
Common, Hungerford

Aldershot Tattoo
Ascot Races
Bognor Regis
Bournemouth

Brighton
Burnham Beeches
California-in-England
Eastbourne
Epsom Races
Hayling Island
Henley
Highcliffe
Highworth
Hungerford
Hurstbourne Circular
Lambourn Circular
Littlehampton
London
Marlborough
Oxford
Pangbourne
Pewsey
Reading
Savernake Forest
Shefford
Southampton
Southsea
Stonehenge
Swindon
Tidworth Tattoo
Virginia Water
Wantage
Weston-super-Mare
Weymouth
Whipsnade Zoo
Windsor
Worthing

From Kingsclere
Headley, Plastow
Green, Wolverton
Ashmore Hill,

Aldershot Tattoo
Ascot Races
Bognor Regis
Bournemouth
Brighton
California-in-England
Cheddar
Epsom Races
Goodwood Races
Guildford
Hayling Island
Lee-on-Solent
Littlehampton
London
Marlborough
Oxford
Reading
Savernake Forest
Southampton
Southsea
Swindon
Tidworth Tattoo

Weston-super-Mare
Weymouth
Windsor
Worthing

From Kintbury
Hamstead Marshall, Speen, Stockcross, Wickham

Aldershot Tattoo
Ascot Races
Blewbury Circular
Bognor Regis
Bournemouth
Brighton
Burnham Beeches
California-in-England
Cheddar
Eastbourne
Epsom Races
Hayling Island
Henley
Highworth
Hungerford
Littlehampton
London
Marlborough Circular
Newbury Commons
Oxford
Pangbourne
Pewsey
Reading
Savernake Forest
Southampton
Southsea
Stonehenge
Swindon
Tidworth Tattoo
Virginia Water
Wantage Circular
Weston-super-Mare
Weymouth
Windsor
Worthing

From Newbury
Highclere, Burghclere, Woodhay, Whitway, Ecchinswell

Abingdon
Aldershot Tattoo
Andover
Ascot Races
Basingstoke
Bognor Regis
Bournemouth
Brighton
Burnham Beeches
California-in-England
Cheddar

Cold Ash
Compton
Didcot
Eastbourne
East Woodhay
Epsom Races
Hannington
Hants & Sussex Tour
Hayling Island
Henley
Highclere
Hungerford
Kingsclere
Lambourn
Lambourn Downs Tour
Lee-on-Solent
Marlborough
Newbury Commons
Oxford
Pangbourne
Pewsey
Ramsbury
Salisbury
Savernake Forest
Southampton
Southsea
Stratford-upon-Avon
Streatley
Swindon
Thame
Tidworth Tattoo
Wallingford
Weston-super-Mare
Weston via Cheddar
Weymouth
Whipsnade Zoo
Winchester Tour
Windsor
Worthing
Wye Valley

From Thatcham
Midgham, Crookham, Theale, Woolhampton

Aldershot Tattoo
Ascot Races
Beacon Hill
Bognor Regis
Bournemouth
Brighton
Burnham Beeches
California-in-England
Cheddar
Cold Ash
Henley
Hungerford
Lambourn
Marlborough
Newbury Commons
Oxford

Pangbourne
Salisbury
Savernake Forest
Southampton
Southsea
Stockcross
Swindon
Thame
Tidworth Tattoo
Wallingford
Weston-super-Mare
Weymouth
Whipsnade Zoo
Winchester

Examples of fares for some day, afternoon and evening excursions

Fares are shown as shillings and old pence

Destination	Depart	Type of trip	Fare
Bognor Regis	8am	Day excursion	6s6d
Bournemouth	8am	Day excursion	6s6d
Brighton	7.30am	Day excursion	8s0d
California	1.30pm	Afternoon exc.	2s6d
Cheddar	8am	Day excursion	6s6d
Chichester	8am	Circular tour	8s0d
Hayling Island	8am	Day excursion	5s6d
Lambourn D'ns	6.30pm	Evening tour	2s6d
Lee-on-Solent	8am	Day excursion	5s0d
London Zoo	8am	Day excursion	7s0d
Newbury Com.	6.30pm	Evening tour	1s6d
Oxford Zoo	2.30pm	Afternoon exc.	2s6d
Pangbourne	6.30pm	Evening tour	2s6d
Southampton	1.15pm	Tour of Liners	4s6d
Southsea	8am	Day excursion	5s6d
Swindon	2.30pm	Afternoon tour	2s6d
Tidworth Tat.	6.45pm	Coach seat only	3s6d
Weston-s-Mare	8.0am	Day excursion	7s6d
Weymouth	7.30am	Day excursion	8s0d
Whipsnade Zoo	8.0am	Day excursion	6s0d
Windsor	1.30pm	Afternoon exc.	4s0d
Wye Valley	7.0am	All day tour	10s6d

Local Booking Agents

Greenwood	Newbury St., Kintbury
Burt	Ambleside, Inkpen
Ballard	South End, Bradfield
Spanswick	Broadway, Thatcham
Cleeveley	Robin Hood, N'bury
Durnford's	Market St., N'bury
Whitington's	Bartholomew Street
Andrews	Northcroft Lane
Cartwright	Salcombe Rd, N'bury
Barnes	The Square, Aldbourne
Rosier	The Stores, Beedon
Holman	Ecchinswell
Howlett	Bucklebury
White	Fernbank, Hermitage
Mrs. Denham	Howard Rd., N'bury
Chalk	Kingsclere

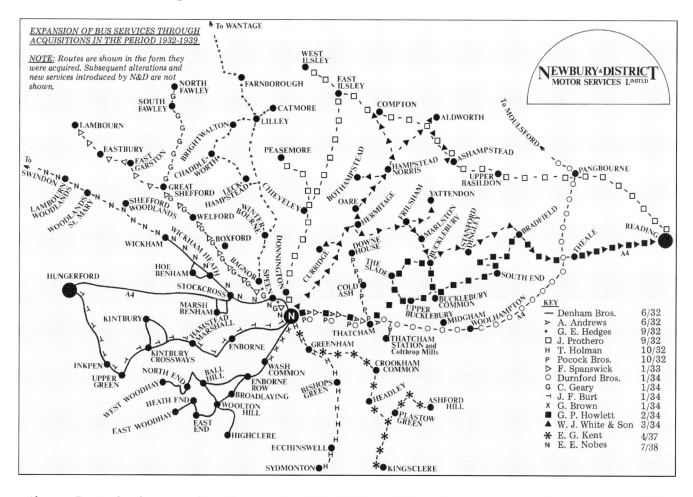

Above – Route developments through expansion 1932-1939, and below the route system and connections at 1948.

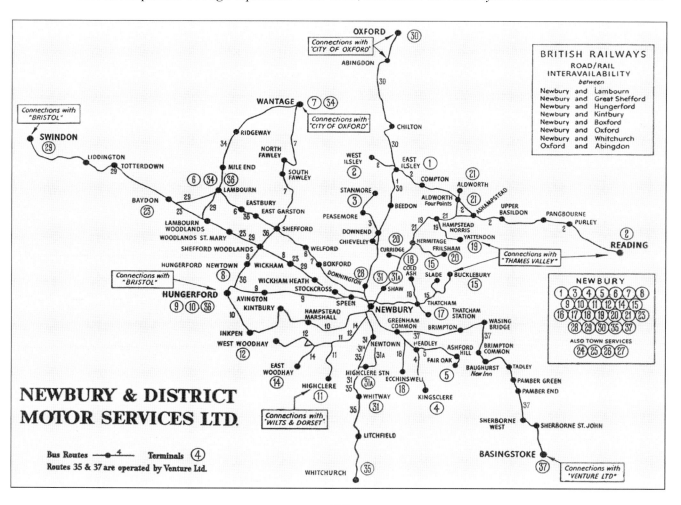

Appendix 6 -
Newbury & District Outstations 1932 - 1939

Town/village	Location	1932	1933	1934	1935	1936	1937	1938	1939
Brightwalton	Hedge's Garage	2	2	2	0	0	0	0	0
Bucklebury	Howlett's Garage	0	0	1	0	0	0	0	0
Chieveley	Prothero's Garage	3	0	0	0	0	0	0	0
Cold Ash	Pocock's Garage	1	1	0	0	0	0	0	0
East Ilsley	Swan Inn	0	2	2	2	2	2	2	2
Hermitage	White's Garage	0	0	3	3	3	3	3	3
Kingsclere	George & Horn PH	0	0	0	0	0	3	0	0
Kingsclere	Crown PH	0	0	0	0	0	0	2	2
Kintbury	Parked by driver	0	0	1	0	0	0	0	0
Lambourn Woodlands	Parked by driver	0	0	0	0	0	0	1	1
Thatcham	Spanswick's yard	1	1	2	0	0	0	0	0
Thatcham	Bath Road shed	0	0	0	3	3	3	3	3
Totals		7	6	11	8	8	11	11	11

Notes:

The above chart only shows buses outstationed for service routes, and other locations for contract vehicles from 1938 on are not included. References to these will be found in the main text for the wartime period.

CHIEVELEY - The use of Prothero's Garage ran through to December 1933, when the allocation was reduced and the buses transferred to a large rented shed at The Swan Inn, East Ilsley.

COLD ASH - This allocation was transferred in 1934 to Spanswick's yard off The Broadway in Thatcham, and again to the rented shed in Bath Road, Thatcham from September 1935.

BRIGHTWALTON - The departure of George Hedges saw his resumption of the workings from that location, which then became his main base through to the building of the Boundary Road, Newbury garage in 1963.

BUCKLEBURY - The use of Howlett's Garage ceased when the vehicle was transferred to the rented shed in Bath Road, Thatcham in September 1935.

KINGSCLERE - When Mrs. Kent's services were acquired in April 1937 the allocation was placed in the yard of The George & Horn, but this was switched to The Crown in at some time in 1938.

KINTBURY - This was continued after the acquisition of Burt & Greenwood's service in January 1934, but it ceased in June 1934, when the route was altered to be operated from Newbury instead.

GARAGE ADDRESSES:	
Hedge's Garage	Ash Close, Brightwalton
Howlett's Garage	Oak Tree Garage, Bucklebury Common
Prothero's Garage	Langley Garage, Oxford Road, Chieveley
Pocock's Garage	Cold Ash Hill, Cold Ash
White's Garage	Fernbank Garage, Hermitage
Spanswick's yard	The Broadway, Thatcham
Lambourn Woodlands	The Square, Lambourn Woodlands
Thatcham	12 Bath Road, Thatcham
East Ilsley	The Swan Inn, High Street, East Ilsley
Kingsclere	The George & Horn, Newbury Road, Kingsclere
Kingsclere	The Crown, Basingstoke Road, Kingsclere
Kintbury	Newbury Street, Kintbury - parked by driver

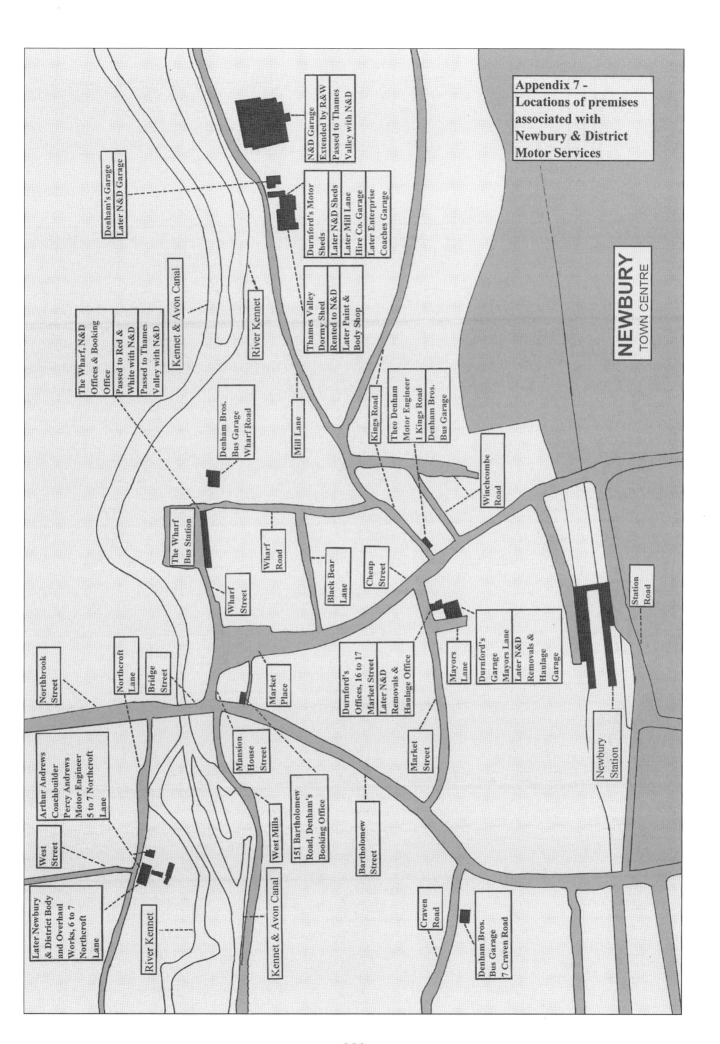

Appendix 7 -
Locations of premises
associated with
Newbury & District
Motor Services

NEWBURY
TOWN CENTRE

N&D Garage
Extended by R&W
Passed to Thames
Valley with N&D

Durnford's Motor
Sheds
Rented to N&D
Later N&D Sheds
Later Mill Lane
Hire Co. Garage
Later Enterprise
Coaches Garage

Thames Valley
Dormy Shed
Rented to N&D
Later Paint &
Body Shop

Denham's Garage
Later N&D Garage

The Wharf, N&D
Offices & Booking
Office
Passed to Red &
White with N&D
Passed to Thames
Valley with N&D

Kennet & Avon Canal

River Kennet

Mill Lane

Kings Road

Theo Denham
Motor Engineer
1 Kings Road
Denham Bros.
Bus Garage

Winchcombe
Road

Denham Bros.
Bus Garage
Wharf Road

The Wharf
Bus Station

Wharf
Road

Wharf
Street

Black Bear
Lane

Cheap
Street

Station
Road

Northbrook
Street

Northcroft
Lane

Bridge
Street

Market
Place

Mansion
House
Street

West Mills

Arthur Andrews
Coachbuilder
Percy Andrews
Motor Engineer
5 to 7 Northcroft
Lane

West
Street

Later Newbury
& District Body
and Overhaul
Works, 6 to 7
Northcroft
Lane

River Kennet

Kennet & Avon Canal

151 Bartholomew
Road, Denham's
Booking Office

Bartholomew
Street

Durnford's
Offices, 16 to 17
Market Street
Later N&D
Removals &
Haulage Office

Market
Street

Mayors
Lane

Durnford's
Garage
Mayors Lane
Later N&D
Removals &
Haulage
Garage

Newbury
Station

Craven
Road

Denham Bros.
Bus Garage
7 Craven Road

Index to other local operators included in the main text